Acting for Love & Money

Connecting the craft to the industry

Paul G. Gleason & Gavin Levy

MERIWETHER PUBLISHING LTD.
Colorado Springs, Colorado

Meriwether Publishing Ltd., Publisher
PO Box 7710
Colorado Springs, CO 80933-7710

www.meriwether.com

Editor: Theodore O. Zapel
Assistant editor: Amy Hammelev

Library of Congress Cataloging-in-Publication Data

Gleason, Paul G.
  Acting for love & money : connecting the craft to the industry / by Paul
G. Gleason and Gavin Levy. -- 1st ed.
      p. cm.
  Includes bibliographical references.
  ISBN 978-1-56608-167-2
  1. Acting--Vocational guidance. 2. Acting. I. Levy, Gavin. II. Title.
III. Title: Acting for love and money.
  PN2055.G54 2010
  792.02'8023--dc22

                                            2009050728

1 2 3   10 11 12

This is the most relevant and practical book on acting for today's actor. It guides the aspiring actor and the working actor to look at acting as a vocation in which to practice the art of acting. It helps them to understand the training they are getting in regards to a career and helps them to recognize the good training they must seek. It is a must for all actors who want to learn and remember their craft.

— Jack Wiant, former CFO Los Angeles Music Center

Plenty of great information to read again and again, helpfully reminding a true actor that you always have more mountains to climb as you grow. It is important to keep your nose up to avoid scraping your chin and this book illustrates the visual in many ways!

— Romie Szal: Owner-Director of the K Hall Agency

This book is a continuation of a master's class on a much higher level. The book has exercises and much, much more. For an actor this book is indispensable. It gives such a great insight into the craft and the business. This book is wonderful and so easy to read!

— Linda Weitzler, mentor program coordinator for Women In Film

It's a very appealing book to actors serious about their craft. The organization in short sections makes it an easy-to-read, honest, no-nonsense approach to the entire acting world from classroom, to rehearsal, to performance, to managing your career. Acting for Love & Money tells it like it is.

— Ginny Kopf: Author of *The Dialect Handbook*

This refreshing book advances commonsense diagnoses and solutions to the artistic and professional problems of the modern actor. A reader can dip into the book, picking up specific information needed for a specific problem or situation, or work his or her way from beginning to end. Either way, the reader comes away with a greater appreciation for the complexity and the commitment necessary for success as an actor in today's entertainment world.

— John Hanners, editor of the *Texas Theatre Journal*

This book is an absolute must for working and training actors alike. The authors speak with wisdom and clarity and have created a gem of a handbook that is really easy to use. Good actors need to be able to balance their skill and talent with instinct and common sense. This book helps you to find these qualities. As a teacher of acting who works with well-known professionals and emerging stars, I will be using this book as a teaching aid and as one of my recommended texts.

— Amanda Fawsett, senior acting coach at Guildford School of Acting

This is a fairly simple and straightforward book for a sometimes quite complicated craft. It has an amazing overview of many aspects of acting. One of the greatest things is that it pulls from many perspectives, be it acting coaches, directors, other artists ... giving you many things to try and think about and ultimately helping you to develop your own process.

— Dante Basco, Hollywood actor

This is not a book to read like an instruction manual, but it is dense with experience, guidance, philosophy, challenges, practical magic, and support. The authors ask of the actor this: Do you want to accept this as your field, your life's work? Open it anywhere and begin. By the way, once you start this work, this "calling," if you are called, you're never finished.

— Joanna Gleason, Tony-winning stage actress

As a director, I have worked with actors for years. Since reading Paul Gleason and Gavin Levy's new book, Acting for Love & Money: Connecting the craft to the industry, I have actually gained real insight into working with actors and getting the most from their skill and artistry. This is a must-read book not only for actors interested in honing their skills, but for any film or theatre professionals who deal with talent.

— Richard Delighter, director of Real Productions, Inc.

This book is a must for every actor's library. There is an answer for every problem ... no matter how difficult it may seem. It is a true reference guide and so easy to understand. You can open it anywhere ... and learn something. God bless you Gavin and Paul for caring so much about the people who love the performing arts, as I do — with all my heart.

— Dorothy Barret, director of American National Academy of Performing Arts

Every actor needs to buy this book and not give it away for love or money! It is an essential guide to connecting to the professional world of performance. Acting for Love & Money provides insight, exercises, and inspiration to all of us who are involved, interested, and passionate about what we do. If you want to work and win at auditions and you are serious about this industry, buy, steal, or borrow this book and use it!

— Peter Barlow FRSA (Fellow of the Royal Society of Arts), Chair of Conference of Drama Schools

Dedication

With special thanks to:
Freda Kosmin
Monty Hall
Kara Holland
Ty Laforest
Marissa Guerrero-Longoria
Christina Romero
Aaron Schmidt

Table of Contents

Introduction

All of the material in this book was formed during workshops conducted by Paul Gleason and Gavin Levy with participants of the Paul Gleason Theatre in Hollywood. Three hundred hours of recorded sessions were edited by Gavin Levy to create this book. It has taken a total of three years to put together. Although these exercises include material from a great number of workshops, they strictly adhere to specific dramatic content.

How to Use This Book

You are an actor if for no other reason than because you say you are; thus begins your journey. The purpose of this book is not to teach acting, but to show you how to study acting and how to synthesize it to make it more accessible to you. People who think acting is a way to make money in a short time probably shouldn't read this book. The reason we didn't call this book *Acting for Money & Love* is because you can't do it for money first. In order to put up with the number of hours, days, weeks, and years it takes to become a good actor, you have to have passion. You have to love it.

We're interested in addressing acting as a profession. In order for it to be a profession, there are agents, attorneys, contracts, and money. The only reason you are able to put up with all the challenges and rejection that an acting career will bring is because you have such a love for it. *Acting for Love & Money* shows you how to connect the craft to the industry. It indicates why you have to be wise enough, passionate enough, and driven enough to do so. This book will hopefully not be just a book, but instead a companion for you.

We wanted to make this book actor-friendly so that you are able to work through it in a practical, efficient, and enjoyable manner. To achieve this, we have broken it down into a number of sections so that it is best able to suit your needs in getting precisely what you need at any given moment. The problem with a number of books on acting is that an actor cannot comprehend them, and they are, therefore, of no value to the actor whatsoever. If you cannot comprehend this book, if it doesn't do anything for you, or if we cannot work together, then please spend your money on another acting book that works for you.

There is a danger in working with these exercises or any others in which the teacher is not there to walk alongside you, so be aware of this. Even though these exercises have been worked many thousands of times before, it is possible that not all of them will fit you. We wanted to create a book that would enhance your career, not interfere with your career. This book is for those who identify themselves as actors.

One of the purposes of this book is to find exercises that are so primary that they immediately affect your whole system. This does not mean these exercises are simple. On the contrary, they are often complex and profound. We are not asking you to go through this book and do the exercises in the precise order in which they are presented. We want you to pick the exercises you need on a particular day and give you a full workout of your *instrument*. Try an exercise, and if you do not understand it at first reading, skip to the next exercise. Later you can come back to that exercise and you will have a clearer understanding.

With each exercise we have given you specific expected results and a description of what it is working on. It is necessary that, as an actor, you know why you are doing an exercise and what it is going to do for you. If you decide not to work on your instrument, you have as much chance to work professionally or make acting a career as you do to win the lottery. Many of these exercises can be completed in a matter of minutes or a matter of hours — such is the versatility of the material. This is not a sit-down-on-the-couch-and-read book, but a get-up-and-do book. Having said that, many of the *Food for Thought* sections may compel you to stop, sit down, and consider what is being said. It is a blend between doing and reviewing that not only guides you through the steps, but also encourages you to do your own thinking and make your own discoveries.

At times you may find that you do not always understand the vocabulary used in this text. This is done intentionally — you should make the effort to research the meaning of any language with which you are not familiar. In terms of the text, Sanford Meisner says, "The text is like a canoe, and the river on which it sits is the emotion."[1] If you look at all great actors, you will see that they have an amazing command and understanding of vocabulary, and so should you.

Many of these exercises you can do on your own, which means you can give yourself no excuse. *A word of warning:* Some of these exercises are so profound and so revealing that you may discover that you are really not prepared for a career in acting. This book is concerned with the career of an actor. It is designed for the working professional and the aspiring actor to incorporate its principles into daily life. This book considers the actor's point of view as well as those of the audience, casting director, and director. If you want to play at acting or win the lottery, this book is not for you. This book is for dedicated actors looking to be in major productions, on major television shows, or in major movies. It is our wish that your life as an actor becomes a lifestyle and a way of being, for this is where you will truly make the discoveries. This book does not profess a specific technique, except perhaps an *everyman technique,* which means that we have taken what we can from every great acting teacher, past and present, to give you the tools to eventually formulate your own technique.

One final word of warning: This book is not meant to be read from beginning to end. To attempt to read this book in such a fashion will cause it to become a chore rather than a pleasure. If that is what you are looking for, then please close this book and save your time and energy. Your acting career is going to take many twists and turns and so does this book. It is written so that you can open it up to any chapter, page, or paragraph that is relevant to your specific needs in any given moment. One week you may be interested in the audition chapter and you may find one particular paragraph that necessitates your attention that day. The next month you might choose to focus on the imagination chapter. This book enables you to take responsibility for your own acting career.

You will discover that some points are stated in slightly altered form again and again so that you may begin to question whether you are receiving really anything new. This is consciously done to make sure necessary points really hit home. The hope is that if one observation doesn't quite affect you, another one will. We make no apology for this approach.

You will notice a *Food for Thought* is followed immediately by another *Food for Thought* paragraph in which the passages between the two are not necessarily linked even though they are both related to the same chapter heading. This isn't a book to be picked up and finished in a week. You might read one *Food for Thought* one day and let it sink in for two or three days. It is our sincere desire that this book become tattered, used, and dog-eared. Otherwise, it is of no use to you. Remember, you are living your dream. Don't miss it!

---

1. Sanford Meisner and Denise Longwell, *Sanford Meisner on Acting* (New York: Random House, 1987), 115.

Look Who's Talking

This book is based on the workshops we conducted. During the observed exercises, actors were also encouraged to comment. You will be able to identify these points when you see ACTOR: You will also find that in many cases only a small sample of the conversation with an actor has been included. This is so you have an idea where a diagnosis or discussion might go, but because the results may apply specifically to that actor, we thought it would be redundant to include the entire conversation here. We wanted to use two voices so that you got insights from more than one person. This has specifically been done to highlight the fact that, in your acting career, you are going to hear numerous voices in regards to your work, many of which will contradict each other. We want you to get used to the idea of receiving different opinions.

Food for Thought

The *Food for Thought* sections contain many insights or observations made in regard to acting. They are interwoven throughout the book and between the exercises in no particular order. Each *Food for Thought* makes a specific point for your benefit. They are there for you to do with them as you please.

The Ingredients

This section explains the exercise in detail. It gives you a step-by-step explanation of what to do and how to do it. On many occasions you will see interactive conversations between the teacher and the actors participating in the exercise. This is a useful way to share each exercise and allows you to see any challenges or feedback given by the teacher or the actors involved.

The Diagnosis

This section explains why you are being asked to participate in this exercise in the first place, as well as the benefits of each exercise. It is not limited to these observations, as you may find many more than the ones we give you. While we may tell you the benefits, you will only be able to discover for yourself by actively participating in the exercises.

Final Thoughts

In this section, we will sum up any thoughts to conclude each exercise. This section was written months after the rest of the book. The reason for this was to allow enough time to pass to add any new reflections that may have occurred or arisen. As an actor, it is going to be necessary at times to step back and review, and as authors of this book we thought it was also necessary that we took the time to step back and gather our thoughts.

Chapter 1:
Acting Is Not a Business,
but It Can Be Business-Like

1. A Way of Being

Food for Thought

You may take a workshop that is poor, but you are in that workshop because you can meet people who might give you work. In a number of cases, the purpose of teaching acting is to make it a business. The success of these businesses is cash flow, not the product they turn out. As long as you understand that these classes have nothing to do with acting, then you are OK. But if you don't understand, then we have great concern for you because your imagination and your talent will be subjected to getting the job. You must understand that if you go into the class where the teacher is no good and the majority of the people are not ever going to be successful in the industry, it will actually damage you as an actor. Know exactly why you are doing what you are doing.

Food for Thought

As an actor you're going to be asked to lie, cheat, steal, and murder. You're going to have to take your clothes off, you're going to have to make a complete fool of yourself, and you'll have to be anything and everything mankind has ever been. A famous Hollywood legend made her entire career by making a complete fool of herself and she was brilliant at it. She had taken away all limitations on her acting, so the possibilities were boundless.

The Ingredients

What we would like you to do is draw a circle on a page so that it looks like a pie. We would like you to cut that pie down the middle simply by drawing a line down the center.

We want you to label the left side *Life*. Make a list of everything that entails your private life, such as family, going to dinner, entertainment, playing sports, marriage, doing your laundry, driving to the bank, getting your car repaired, and cleaning your apartment. The right side should be labeled *Acting*. This is anything you do related to your acting or about your career. Make a list of everything related to these things, such as rehearsals, headshots, watching quality plays or movies, reading plays or scripts, watching famous actors or teachers on the Internet, meeting with an agent, resumés, working on a play or movie, taking a class, working on your instrument, etc. What we want you to do now is calculate roughly how many hours a day it takes you to do all those things. If you add up both sides, do you still have a little bit of time left over?

Observed Exercise

PAUL: What I would like you to do is draw a circle on a page so that it looks like a pie. I would like you to cut that pie down the middle simply by drawing a line down the center ...

ACTOR: OK.

PAUL: If you add up both sides, do you still have a little bit of time left over?

ACTOR: Not a whole lot.

PAUL: But you do have some.

ACTOR: Yeah.

PAUL: Well, you shouldn't have any.

ACTOR: Oh, OK. I sleep sometimes.

PAUL: In the first circle you probably had enough hours to do everything you wanted on both sides. This is probably because you are dedicating pitifully few hours to your acting, while the vast majority of hours are going to *Life.* Now I want you to draw a second circle and draw a very tiny slice, a little slice of pie. In that tiny space (ten percent) fits all of your life. Everything on the other side of the pie (ninety percent) is the time and energy you should be spending on acting.

ACTOR: Good.

PAUL: If you cannot fill that pie, you do not know enough about acting. Some actors say, "Paul, that is not possible." It's possible if you have other people to do all of that other stuff for you. Famous movie stars have private cooks, personal trainers, and cleaners. Everything is done for them so they can focus on their careers.

ACTOR: Wow.

GAVIN: As Stephen R. Covey says, "I want it now. People want this and want that now."[2] You cannot necessarily do all of this immediately or have all the things other actors have right away, but there is nothing to stop you from working toward these goals right away. If you start creating your pie like this now, you will begin to create a compounding effect in the right direction.

Food for Thought

The idea is to find a teacher who walks with you. The danger for the actor is that there always will be charlatans. There are some teachers who are brilliant, some charismatic, some who are business people, and some who are a combination or none of these. There are some teachers who have tried to be actors and failed, and now they are trying to be teachers and failing. As an actor, you have to know what a teacher is going to give you. You are intelligent, so make informed decisions when choosing a teacher.

Food for Thought

A colleague of mine was in the gym one day doing sit-ups and he was eavesdropping on a conversation between two actors. He said one turned to the other one and said, "I've got to get back into acting class! I really do have to get back into acting class, I need to do that." And the young man went on to add, "Because socially and for networking purposes it would be a good thing." My colleague said, after hearing this, he was bathed in disappointment. It is so sad and disturbing for me to hear an actor using words like "socializing" and "networking" in terms of going to class. I would respond to this actor by saying that the only thing that is good for you in class is to learn how to act; that is why it is an acting class. This is not a class in socializing or networking, because surely there are other places where you can do this. Why would you socialize and network with pilots if you didn't know how to fly a plane? Why would you network and socialize with writers if you are not a writer? Why would you network and socialize with actors unless you are a highly developed actor? An acting class is for one thing and one thing alone: to practice acting. If the main advantage of going to that class is networking, don't call it an acting class, call it a networking class. Don't mix yourself up. There are many ways to socialize outside of your acting class. Socializing and networking take away from why you should be there and the results that will follow.

Many actors are not particularly social, and they relish the fact that they can go home,

---

2. Stephen R. Covey, *The 7 Habits of Highly Effective People* (New York: Free Press, 1989) 8.

recuperate, and then go back to acting. Teaching classes is a business and teachers want to make a living, so they will often allow people to be in the class who are social butterflies and who are only interested in networking. I think that this is unfortunate, and if this continues, I think you should find another class. Here is the reason why: If you're paying a large amount of money for a class that's three hours long and an hour and a half of that is networking and socializing, then you are not getting your money's worth. Do not allow the wool to be pulled over your eyes. What is the main thrust of the acting class? If it's not acting, get out quick!

The Diagnosis

We have never heard of any successful actor who was able to split the pie down the middle. This is a real wake-up exercise, because if you are not willing to do what it takes, you are going to realize that you are in the wrong career. If your hours away from acting are more than those dedicated to acting and you are competing with actors who have a pie with one tiny slice for *Life* and one huge piece for *Acting,* do the math, which of you is going to be more successful?

You may say that the more you can spend on these things the happier you are. You do have to pay rent, you do have to buy groceries, and have some kind of day job to survive, so you will work towards it one step at a time. To be a successful actor you have to be completely self-centered and completely self-absorbed. If you were going to parachute out of a plane, it would seem that the moment you jump out of that plane the only person you are thinking about is yourself. In order to be successful you must spend so much time at your craft, and you must be comfortable thinking about yourself.

Don't limit your acting to a classroom or a workshop. You can work an acting exercise while you are climbing a hill or while you are at the doctor's office. You can be driving in your car and thinking about an audition you are going to — just watch the road! We have said that you should watch film and theatre on a regular basis, but not just watch it, really understand it. Civilians see what they want to see, and actors see what's really there. If you do this, you will start to discover what great acting is and you will start to discover what poor acting is. In regards to great actors, Giovanni Potiero says of Elenora Duse in his book, *Duse on Tour,* "Loyal admirers discovered something new with every performance and she herself treated every successive performance in the same role as if it were opening night."[3]

Successful actors, without exception, cut their pie in the way we have shown you — with a small slice for everything else. Whether you can see it or not, they are spending ninety percent of their time in acting and concerned with themselves. They are concerned with how they walk, how they talk, their weight (they have special diets), they read certain things, and they develop new skills. You must do this. At first you may not be able to fill your whole time with acting. However, as you start to train yourself in this way, there are so many things to get done in acting that there are not enough hours in the day to get them all done. You need to walk like an actor, talk like an actor, and dress like an actor. You also have to get used to being looked at and start making eye contact with the public as much as possible. As an actor you must train yourself to do this, and you must train yourself not to blink when holding a conversation. You have to be so much an actor that when you walk into a supermarket or a park, people should come up to you and ask if you are an actor. You must adapt to a way of being that works for an actor and be that twenty-four-seven.

You can't look like an actor part of the time, and you can't sound like an actor part of the time. Stars have a team around them to help them think of themselves. They have a hairdresser, a chef, a personal trainer, a driver; they have a full entourage to take away any distractions

---

3. Giovanni Pontiero, *Duse on Tour: Guido Noccioli's Diaries* (Amherst: The University of Massachusetts Press, 1982) 27.

that can interfere with their acting. As Vladimir Sokoloff said, "Acting is the only way I am able to live. I wanted to be everybody, and I wanted to be everything. One life is not enough."[4] You need every hour available to you to be an actor. Or as Robert Brustein says, "Actors don't keep the same schedules as normal people. They sleep late and stay up late, turn night into day and day into night."[5]

You see, there are so many things linked to acting that the list is never-ending. This may seem daunting, but actually it highlights that only those who are passionate about what they do can really sustain this for any given length of time. The question that then begs to be asked is, "Is that person you?" You may not be able to cut your pie this way from the very beginning, but you can start working towards this one step at a time. As Suze Orman explains, "The most important thing to remember is that whatever your goal, step by step, you can take charge of your destiny and achieve financial freedom. The power is within you."[6] As an actor, you either win the lottery or you take compounding steps to create your own destiny.

Food for Thought

When I was touring a show in London, I visited one of the most famous dance schools in the world, which had a brochure that said, "Your son's career in dance." Boys were taken on at the age of eleven and this brochure explained to the parents what they could expect, what chances he had, what he must do, and what they must do. This school has one of the highest success rates for creating famous, world-class dancers. What interested me was that this school thought it important enough to address the subject of students studying at any age and to explain their chances of a professional career. I personally do not know any acting schools or colleges that approach this topic thoroughly enough. A good rule of thumb is to speak to graduates from any acting program one or two years after they graduated to find out how industry-ready their school made them. As Andrew Reilly explains, "While professional training programs in this country are turning out some fine actors, most of them don't have the faintest idea how to get started in the business."[7]

Food for Thought

I always find speaking with an aspiring actor uplifting as well as perplexing. What can you say that can guide and advise this traveling warrior? Huffing and puffing off to war without armor or a map, the aspirant already has the only ingredient necessary: instinctive blind ambition. It is a good thing his eyes aren't open yet, for the sight of it is fearsome. Blindness of this ilk isn't so bad because it makes the traveler more sensitive to all the hazards that surround him. The bruises he or she will get along the way are heralded as accomplishments. If they are the result of an honest fight, the bruised ego will heal quickly. I guess it is what is called *experience*. No teacher, no scene partner, no director, no production is anymore than an influence, an aroma the actor picks up, or something to tint the personality for a while. Then does the young actor need any of this? Probably not, all you need is a mirror and a logbook. Those become your only training manual and someone to carry them for you so you can travel light. The person to carry them for you is the person to seek out. You can travel light and not be tormented by this curtain called knowledge, which is a burden that absolutely must be put aside when you go to battle or performance. King Arthur had Merlin, and every great actor has this force behind them that we shall call a *prod*. A prod supports, angers, inflames, irritates, riles, ruffles, induces, motivates, and compels the warrior to move forward. Rod Steiger once said, "The actor must not answer what they do as an actor, but

---

4. Lillian Ross, Helen Ross, *The Player* (New York: Simon and Schuster, 1961), 310.
5. Robert Brustein, *Letters to a Young Actor* (New York: Basic Books, 2005), 9.
6. Suze Orman, *9 Steps to Financial Freedom* (New York: Three Rivers Press, 2006), 7.
7. Andrew Reilly, *An Actor's Business* (Florida: Venture Press, 1996), 9.

why they must follow this career." He said the length of pause between the question and the answer would be the tempo of their career. Acting is an art form, not a business, but it can be business-like. Be aware of those numerous showcases, lectures, and seminars that make someone spend a lot of money while offering nothing of much use to the actor. There are many workshops given by SAG, AFTRA, and Equity giving plenty of information for a nominal fee. Look for things like this, not a class or an agent that promises to make you a star or even a mild success. That's your job, although it may not be your quest. Paul talks about many different facets that make up the actor's journey, yet he quickly addresses the need for instinctive blind ambition. Passion and ambition are two key ingredients that will allow you to stay motivated throughout.

Final Thoughts

There are other people who stand in front of audiences. Some we would call personalities, some we would call products, and some we would call saleable commodities. They are what they are with no training, with no preparation, and they are hired that way. They hired under the terms *what you see is what you get.*

Just like any other profession, you must do it twenty-four-seven. Some professions require you only to go to work for eight hours. Acting is not about how many hours you work for somebody else. Acting is about how many hours you work for yourself. The more hours you work for yourself, the more likely you are to be a good actor. It does not mean it will sell necessarily, but if you are striving to be a good actor, then you must put in more time than anyone else. It appears to be a selfish profession, but it is not selfish, it is a constant self-awareness. It is also important to point out that being a good person has nothing to do with acting — that's up to you. Life can sometimes get in the way, but the actor has to find a way around this, through this, or over this. As Milton Katselas says, "You may think you're not an artist. You are. Everyone is, or can be, but it all depends on how you deal with your life."[8]

2. Acting All the Way

Food for Thought

When you are selling a house the realtor, generally speaking, doesn't care what the house looks like. The realtor doesn't care if the people selling it get too much or too little money, and the realtor doesn't care if the people who buy it like it. The realtor doesn't care about any of this. The realtor just says, "I sell houses, I make commissions." Then there are those who fix houses who say, "I can make that property a great deal more valuable than it already is." Agents, if they are good, don't care what the product looks like, and they don't care what they sell it for, they just care that they sell it. They will sell it for as low or as high as they can get. Your agent theoretically talks to every producer, every casting director, and every director in town. If you are up for a job and you are not a star, the studio offers you X amount, and your agent asks for twice as much, what are the chances of him getting this for you? The chances are zero! Why is that? It is because he cannot afford to insult or anger the producers or directors. He will sell you more often than not for less than he could get. If you want to work the craft of acting and work professionally, you cannot forget to research and become thoroughly familiar with the business side of acting. Agents rarely try to push your salary up unless you are very famous. You might be saying, "I have no interest in the business of acting," and yet if you don't embrace it, it may become your undoing.

Food for Thought

Agents and managers have nothing to do with acting. They do not have to know how to

---

8. Milton Katselas, *Dreams into Action* (California: Dove Books, 1996), Foreword.

act, and they do not have to know who can act. An agent sells apples every day, and if he has the most expensive apples in town, he is only going to sell them occasionally. A grocery store does not care what kind of apples it sells, it just cares what kind of apples the public buys. Agents generally don't know anything about acting. They don't have to know anything about acting, and they don't particularly want to know anything about acting. They often, particularly if they are very young, think they know something about acting. Sometimes they have immature, unfinished egos and continue to think they know something about acting. The agents that have been in business forever often love acting and say, "He is really good. She is really good. She doesn't seem to know what she is talking about." They then send the actor to someone whether it is an acting coach, voice coach, or an Alexander coach. They can do this because they know experts in the acting field with whom they have built relationships, and they don't presume to teach acting themselves! Think about this: Would you allow your pet's vet to operate on you personally? Why would you take acting advice from someone who has absolutely no training or background in the field of acting? A good agent may point you in the right direction and recommend experts for you to go to. As for critiquing your acting, one would hope they would leave well enough alone.

The Ingredients

What we would like you to do is start thinking about acting all the time. We would like for you to start to integrate acting into most of your thoughts. When you are having a conversation, even if it has nothing whatsoever to do with acting, in your mind we want you to make the connections to acting. This is not something to do for a few minutes or a few hours, but something we want you to do for the rest of your life. If you start off with it as an exercise, then eventually, just like everything else in this book, it will become automatic for you. Inventors and creators spend many thousands of hours thinking about the field they love.

Food for Thought

We think it is a waste of time to go to a class and study with a teacher because you think that teacher has connections in the business. Even though that may be true, they cannot get you anywhere unless you are highly trained and they won't because it will besmirch their own profession. If you decided you wanted to get near somebody who might get you work, it is best that you go first and for a long time to someone that can really teach you the craft of acting. Then when you know you are very good, take the other class for the reason you were going to take it in the first place. Take it not to learn anything, but take it in order to get close to work. Why is anybody going to put you up for work or let you get work on their name if you are not the best person in town or not the best person in class? You have to be the best person possible auditioning. That is what you are up against. No matter what connections you have, you can do yourself great damage by going to an audition that you are not prepared for. Showing a product that is not only unfinished but that has not even begun yet is a dangerous road to take. When there is somebody before and after you who is better than you because they are more highly trained, you will not fair well.

It appears that there is a back door open to famous personalities, singers, models, sport types, and high profile people. It would be best to examine that again. One of two things has happened: they have some training or are currently training as an actor even when it is not made public, or they get the job because they don't have training and that is the only job they get. Not only is it the only job they get, it is much harder for them to get the next job because they convince people that they have no talent. To get a job before you have technique is running the risk of convincing people you have no talent. Consider your personal priorities. If they have nothing to do with acting, then why are you pursuing a career in acting?

Food for Thought

Other people go to work forty hours a week, and an actor should make a business of going to work at least that much. It is fair for us to ask "Why not?" if somebody doesn't think of acting twenty-four-seven in ways such as, "Can people hear me? Am I speaking clearly? Do I have a regionalism in my voice? Am I always communicating to tell a story?" Is it narcissistic for actors to be looking at themselves in the mirror or is it part of what you should be doing? We think it is part of what you should be doing. We think it is part of the process of being an actor. Are you obsessed with acting? Does it occupy a great deal of your time, thoughts, and energy?

The Diagnosis

You may not agree with this exercise, or you may say, "I'm an actor and I don't think about acting all the time," or, "I can't imagine why you would encourage us to do that because it would be so limiting." Of course it isn't. You have to ask yourself, "Do I think about acting all the time? Am I happy to think about acting all the time?" The reason we say this is because all of the really successful actors we have ever known don't talk about anything but acting all day long. Have you thought about that?

ACTOR 1: Oh yeah, I even try to force myself to be interested in other things.

ACTOR 2: I think about acting a lot but not all the time.

PAUL: We have to be very careful with definitions because they can be misinterpreted; however, if I tell you that if you do not think about acting all the time you are not going to be a professional actor, that is true. You can then choose to become a recreational actor. If your friends tell you to stop talking about acting then perhaps you should change your friends.

GAVIN: You want to do the things that will enhance your acting and your acting career.

Food for Thought

Casting directors, agents, and managers always like to see a resumé that says that you have worked in New York or London. They assume that if you have been an actor in New York or London you have had to play by some of the rules, although this may not be a correct assumption. What they are really impressed in is that you are an *actor*, not just a *product*. The product is very limited, where an actor can do anything and be anyone. A product is someone who simply looks like somebody.

Agents are in the business of marketing products, and they will have a certain amount of product on their shelf. They keep the products that sell and toss those that don't. They will not make you a better actor and they will not access your talent. Often, products are hired and then fired because someone figures out there is nothing inside. To be a working actor you must also learn the industry inside out, because whether you like it or not, it is your responsibility. If you are a fine co-actor who is not on top of the industry, you will stay a fine, unemployed actor. We are saying you have to have both pieces and not one or the other.

Food for Thought

When casting shows I had a colleague who would go through the headshots after the auditions and say, "Quickly look through everybody here and see if there is one person in your mind that without a doubt belongs here. It has to be unanimous." We would sometimes pick one, or possibly even two, but there would always be at least one actor we all agreed on. We were not auditioning for the best person. We were auditioning for people who are involved in the business that we certainly agreed our colleagues would want to work with. You are constantly working on your instrument so that you are going to be that individual.

Final Thoughts

When we say to be a great actor is to think of acting all the time and you say, "What a bore," then you need to rethink your career. If you are to be a successful actor, you are thinking about acting twenty-four-seven. Integrate exercises into your life, such as those in this book, until they cease to be exercises for you. In time, the exercises can become part of who you are.

3. Home

Food for Thought

What the audience thinks about you is none of your business and you don't want it to be. How they feel when you are in front of them is your business, and you want to know exactly how they feel. You want to be in as much control as is humanly possible and then even more so. It is the audience that will remember you or forget you, or vanish you into oblivion or immortalize you.

Food for Thought

One of the most famous people in the history of Hollywood as a writer, director, actor, and personality did a magic show in Vegas to earn money. He did it because he was destitute, even with all that fame and glory. Those who skyrocket to the top can also catapult to the bottom.

Ingredients

Here is a little exercise that has very practical implications. If you are moving to a new city to pursue your acting, what we would like you to do is move your home. You have not moved to a new place unless you have moved your home there. If you leave your hometown and leave all your furniture, etc. behind, it is as if you are saying, "I'll be back." If you don't want to take these things with you, then you need to find a way to emotionally separate yourself from the possessions and, to some extent, the people you have left behind. There is a famous story of a captain who burned all his ships before facing the enemy. His men knew that if they did not defeat the enemy they would all die. They had systematically burnt their bridges. They won the battle.

Food for Thought

Some actors are being paid an enormous amount of money. Just divide the number of workdays into that one person's salary for an idea. Every minute wasted is a great deal of money wasted, and so directors have every right to rant and rave and expect from you only professionalism and your full focus and attention at all times. Those who pull the strings will tell you that it is those who are capable of playing according to the rules that will get the job. Not the greatest, not the most well endowed, not the best trained, not the easiest to get along with, but simply those who are capable of doing what needs to get done will get the job. Theatre and film are the major pieces of the actor's work and yet they are worlds apart in terms of economic gain. We also want to be careful when we talk about films. Let's call them what they really are, which is *motion pictures*. In other words, it is one picture moving to another picture, moving to another picture. It is a picture that can be an art form in itself. It's amazing to think that motion pictures are tens of thousands of single pictures, each one composed in color, size, etc. This then is the art of the cinematographer, the editor, and the director. They decide what materials they require to build that picture. Even with all of this the actor is still talking to the audience and the audience is still watching the actor. In this respect, film and television are the same. When you go to a play you are looking at set design, costume design, the lighting, the sound, etc. You are still looking at all of these elements, but perhaps we are not as aware of it. Perhaps we are not as aware as when we see special effects in a motion picture. Your professionalism is of the utmost importance, not only in terms of your performance but also in the enormous sums of money your professionalism could save a studio. As Thomas W. Babson says, "The major difference between theatre and film can be traced to one source: money."[9]

Food for Thought

We are interested in the actor, the process of acting, the product of acting, and the result of acting. That is what we are interested in. In order for you to be an actor you have to be able to use your body, your emotions, and your imagination. If anything distracts you from that such as money, relationships, or drugs, then you are minimizing your chances for success. The actor must live in a creative state and be aware of anything that is taking him away from this.

The Diagnosis

The only way you can search for something is when you are free to search for it and when you are mobile to search for it. You can't search for something if you don't go to where you are supposed to be looking for it. If when you get there you are distracted by other things, you still can't look for it. That is why we will sometimes tell an actor, "You are very talented, but you are very fragile. You don't belong here because you don't want it. There is something about you that is not going to pursue a career in acting." Thomas Wolfe wrote a very famous novel called *You Can't Go Home Again,* and what he meant was that as you continue this pursuit of excellence, your home changes. One of the difficulties of being an artist is that you must live where you can search for excellence. You cannot search for excellence anywhere and everywhere. There are certain places that you have to go. Wherever you identify that you can, that is your home. Actors, when they begin their career, have to make a decision to joyfully search for excellence. If they look inside themselves they will know that it's their home because it's the place they most feel at home. It's the place they feel most calm and completed, and they feel like they can do what they're meant to do.

One of the challenges for a number of actors is they don't adapt to their new environment. There is a story I know of two actors who would go to the grocery store just down the street from them and they always got two Cokes. They would go to the checkout stand and the checkout person would say, "Wouldn't you like to buy a six pack? It's a little cheaper." And their response was, "No, because I might be going back to New York tomorrow." It got huge laughs, because everybody is going back to New York tomorrow. An actor's home is something they probably shouldn't discuss with other people. At the beginning of your career you may not have a home, you may be looking for a home, and then you may have a home base. You may not live in your home base all the time, but you have a home base. It is going to take some courage to move to your new home, and it is going to take even more courage to stay there.

Food for Thought

The world abounds in wonderful acting teachers. Jerzy Grotowski says, "The actor who undertakes an act of self-penetration, who reveals himself and sacrifices the innermost part of himself — the most painful, that which is not intended for the eyes of the world, must be able to manifest the least impulse. He must be able to express, through sound and movement, those impulses which waver on the borderline between dream and reality."[10] Are you willing to seek out that teacher, or are you willing to go where that teacher is? There are also a number

---

9. Thomas W. Babson, *The Actor's Choice: The Transition from Stage to Screen* (New Hampshire: Heinemann Press, 1996), 2.

10. Jerzy Grotowski, *Towards a Poor Theatre* (London: Methuen, 1991), 35.

of acting teachers who should not be teaching acting. As the saying goes, "talk is cheap," but it can be dangerous, detrimental, and destructive to your acting career. That is why we say to seek out the wonderful teachers as opposed to parting with your money and trusting anyone who calls themselves an acting coach.

Food for Thought

Sometimes you will hear it said that the actors in New York are better actors than those in Los Angeles, and that the actors in London are better than those in New York. It is interesting that a number of actors who work in New York go there from Los Angeles and vice versa. A number of actors who work in London have come from all over England and were not all born there. Before we can argue, we have to define our terms. Actors have to move where they can be themselves and where people speak their language, by this we mean of the actor. Fine actors come from all over the globe, but the money, the studios, and the production companies are mainly limited to a finite number of acting hubs.

Final Thoughts

Major careers can happen in this day and age in many places such as Los Angeles, London, Moscow, New York, Paris, Tokyo, Bollywood, Berlin, and all kinds of places. If you are pursuing a career in one of those places or another well-known place and you understand that in that place you can have a career that you can earn a living and that can give you the fame and fortune you seek, then stay there. Don't go looking, because you are already home.

The majority of people who are creative come from other places. They do move to an acting center to study and to work. You cannot have a major career in a place that is not doing major theatre, film, or television. Once you become famous, you can travel with a company. Remember that company starts in a major acting hub and goes on what we call *location* and then they come back. They take you with them. Maybe sometime when you are a very famous actor you can live wherever you want. This is not when you are *trying* for a major career, it is when you *have* a major career.

The following is the worst thing you can do and we hear it being done all the time. People tell us they are in Los Angeles and they say, "I am going to New York for a couple of weeks to see how it is and audition for shows." We don't think it's hard to understand that every casting director and everybody in New York can tell if you have come from another city for three weeks. If you walk into that audition and look like that is where you want to be even if you have just arrived in that city, they will be fine with that. You have to go in as though you are saying, "This is the only place in the world for me," because you are meeting people for whom that is true. How dare you visit their house and say, "I want to be in your show, and if you don't give it to me I'll go home." This has to be your home. People do it the other way and come from New York to Los Angeles when they already have a wonderful career in New York. They say, "I think I'll try to be in film." They wonder why Los Angeles isn't interested in them. Los Angeles isn't interested in them because everybody knows they are talented, but when they go to another place, they are not successful because of one thing: that's not where they want to be. If you want to work in London you have to say in your heart of hearts, "This is the only place I want to live, and when I am successful here I will go out for short times to other places." Every successful actor will tell you, "This is the only place for me!" A place where you feel miserable and unhappy most of the time is unlikely to allow you to do creative or fulfilling work.

4. Ask a Question
Food for Thought

Most acting schools and universities don't teach you how to become a saleable commodity. Most professional classes in major cities don't teach you how to act, but the main thrust of the classes is how to be a saleable commodity. It is like when you take a monologue or scene study class and you get to pick your own scene, and the scene doesn't fit you. It is like trying to wear a dress or suit that doesn't fit you because the dress or suit was not made for you. In your acting career you are never going to get to pick your own scenes. The only person responsible for your success or your growth or your knowledge in an acting class is you. A teacher is not responsible for that. Be very careful when choosing where to learn your craft. You should know why you are going to that teacher and exactly what you are looking to get from them. It is your time and money, so do not be afraid to say, "This is not the right fit for me," and then proceed to find a teacher or school that is.

Food for Thought

Sometimes a director may rant and rave and lose his or her temper. You may feel they are being unreasonable, and you may feel they are being unfair, but people are paying a lot of money to watch you perform whether it is at the movies or at the theatre. I remember working with a famous director who told us, "I know I am difficult, at the same time you force me to show you my reviews. Do you want to win a Tony? Do you want to win an Academy Award?" And whose time do you think is being wasted if you think he's doing it simply to be a jerk? Continue to be a professional actor throughout your career.

The Ingredients

In this exercise the actor is asked to prepare three questions in regards to acting or industry-related questions. What this exercise is going to dissect and cover is how to ask a proper question.

ACTOR: Question 1, *What would you say is the difference between intelligent, creative acting versus overthinking?*

PAUL: If you are questioning this, it means you haven't studied acting long enough or lived long enough, each of which is called experience.

ACTOR: Question 2, *How does an actor snap into a character faster?*

PAUL: This is called practice.

ACTOR: Question 3, *How can I find an agent or manager who wants to work with me and understands the roles that I want and are best suited for me?*

PAUL: This is not a valid or logical question because it doesn't make sense at all. It makes you sound very naïve. The answer to all three of these questions is practice. These are enormous questions to ask. It's like saying, "How do I win an Oscar?" If you are going to ask a question successfully you have to establish a connection between you and the person you are asking and that is your responsibility. You need to make sure you are looking in their direction as opposed to the floor or ceiling. You have to state the question slowly and clearly. Watch them very carefully to see if they are following what you are saying.

GAVIN: Before you can *ask* a question, you have to learn *how to* ask a question. Create one new question on acting every week. You are learning to ask a better question.

Food for Thought

On occasion I have asked an aspiring actor why they want to be an actor. Instead of saying, "the rush you can get from a performance," I have heard it said, "I like being in front of people. I want lots of money and nice clothes." And I say, "That's all? You really want to act for money, food, and clothes? That's all? You really want to settle for that?" They don't know what I'm talking about, but an *actor* knows what I'm talking about. The possibilities of what acting can give to you are limitless.

Food for Thought

Sometimes when you audition for a part and they say you have to be over eighteen, this is not because of a social or moral obligation in regards to the role. It just costs money to have schooling provided for you, etc., and they don't want to have to deal with the hassle or the expense. There are some examples of actors under eighteen being cast in these roles by using the creativity of their imagination.

The Diagnosis

The more poetic a question gets the more it tends to entertain us instead of inform us. Often you can't answer a question because you haven't been given any information. So when we say, "There are no small parts, only small actors," we are very entertained, but we get no information from it whatsoever. You are going to get informed by asking yourself the same five questions, which are: who, what, why, when, and where. The immediacy of those five questions will be the best manager you've ever had.

When you ask a question, you ask a question because you want an answer. You understand the question, and you understand it so well that you don't really care if the person you are asking understands the question. If a person cannot quite follow your question, they will answer very quickly and they will answer with whatever is on their mind that day. The worst question you can possibly ask a director is, "What do you want me to do with this part?" Your questions need to be purposeful and to the point. A question for the sake of a question is redundant, but a good question is invaluable.

Food for Thought

Wages and self-respect are important things in acting and to the actor. We need wages to pay the rent, but we need self-respect to live happily. Neither one of them has anything to do with acting, other than the fact that if we do not have enough to pay our bills we may not be allowed to act. If we are in a financial situation that is not well, then we may not be able to act. If we are in an emotional or a personal situation in which we are not well, then it will stop us from acting. This would therefore contradict every actor's desire, or as Michael Bofshever says, "What every actor wants to do is to act. That is the plain and simple fact of the matter."[11]

While a lack of financial planning or having little money is not part of your acting, consider how the lack of it may affect you and your work. As Robert T. Kiyosaki says, "Money is only an idea. If you want more money, simply change your thinking."[12] When you study acting, it is your responsibility to make what you think acting, and not confuse other things. You work on your emotional, personal, and financial situation in order to allow your body to work. If you allow yourself to be physically ill, mentally ill, or financially ill, then you will have to get well before you can act to your true potential. Let's make no bones about it, you can be financially ill.

Food for Thought

As an actor, you have to be healthy. Many times you could be on a movie set for a great deal of hours, and you have to have the stamina for that. You have to be healthy because enormous sums of money are at stake.

---

11. Michael Bofshever, *Your Face Looks Familiar* (New Hampshire: Heineman, 2006), 91.
12. Robert T. Kiyosaki and Sharon L. Lechter, *Rich Dad, Poor Dad* (New York: Warner Books, 1998), 195.

Final Thoughts

It is interesting to us how often actors come up with questions and yet they give no information to help answer the question. It is amazing how often an actor asks a question when they are not really interested in getting the real answer. This is as much basic acting as anything in the world because it is also what you need to know when dealing with a director, casting director, producer, and so on. Great teachers and great directors seem to be annoyed and impatient by unintelligent or naïve questions. Teachers who answer them generally aren't very good teachers. The reason is because a good teacher does not want you to think too much about the wrong thing. There is so much "stuff" that can get in your way that you want to create as clear and as direct a path as is humanly possible.

5. In Search of Excellence

The Ingredients

We decided we wanted to have a discussion with a person not involved in the field of acting. We were privileged to talk to a great man who in his time was right at the very top of the entertainment field and known and liked by audiences worldwide. His understanding of the audience makes him a vitally important resource for the actor. The interview was two hours in length, what follows is an edited version of the discussion. The questions were asked by both of us, and in the spirit of this book we have decided not to indicate who asked what.

The Discussion

MONTY HALL: (Inspired by a Rudyard Kipling poem) "If you realize that the name of the game is rejection, if you can keep your head while you are getting all these rejections, if you can take adverse reactions, and face adversity, if you have the talent and are ready to persevere, continue and brush aside all those negative qualities, then you have a chance. If you can't, don't lead yourself into a life of despair."

INTERVIEWER: Talk a little about the audition process.

MONTY HALL: When people come to audition for me and they come into the office, I look for something. I look for something in that person that has potential. If I find that potential, that's what I want to work with. If a man comes to me and wants to be a game show host, first of all, I take a look at his appearance. Has he got the appearance of a host? Are people going to accept him? Are they going to take him into their homes as the host? Is he pleasant? Does he have a good personality? Does he know his craft? A famous comedian who was a good friend of mine saw me at a club once and said, "You know, I watch your show everyday and I noticed you never take a close up." I said, "That's right." He asked, "Why?" I said, "I want to see her reaction. I'm there, I'm the constant, and the contestant is the variable." If you are confident enough to make all those around you look good, then you will look good. I once had a man come to me who believed he was hired because he was a star. He thought the show was entirely about him, and so we couldn't use him.

INTERVIEWER: Where else have you seen this?

MONTY HALL: Every situation comedy show that is successful the star makes everyone around them a star. They know how to share it, and by making everyone around them funny, they shine. When the star wants all the laughs it will never work.

INTERVIEWER: How important is an agent?

MONTY HALL: An agent is someone who can sell a star and not an unknown.

INTERVIEWER: What advice would you give to someone looking to succeed in the entertainment industry?

MONTY HALL: I have had kids come to me for at least forty years and say, "I want to emcee a game show." I tell them, "You have to do the work just like an actor, just like a singer. You've got to practice, you've got to learn, and you've got to study. You are not going to start out with a network show. You have to pay your dues. You have to learn to work on-set or on-stage with people. Start out in a smaller city and learn your craft, then move to a slightly bigger city and work there for a while. By the time you arrive in Los Angeles or New York you can say, 'Here's my film, here's what I've done. I've come with a track record.' This is the first piece of advice. The second piece of advice is you are in a business called rejection and you have to get used to it. If a guy says you're not going to make it, you shrug your shoulders and keep going. If you have talent, when that talent and perseverance intersect with that one lucky moment, your whole life changes." Some people are overnight successes and some people will wait ten or fifteen years for overnight success.

A colleague of mine was a comedian doing a spot in Vegas. He comes into my dressing room and he's crying, and I say, "Why are you crying?" He says, "I just met this guy at the Sahara hotel who said to me, 'Get out of this business, you're never going to make it!'" I say, "You're not going to quit this business until you say to yourself, 'I'm through,' not when he says you're through!" This all stems from the fact that you have talent. If you don't have talent, then this is all water under the bridge. If you're a doctor, people will beat a path to your door. If you're a lawyer, they'll beat a path to your door. We don't *have* a profession, we *call it* a profession. Our profession is called unemployment, which is interrupted spasmodically by bursts of employment.

INTERVIEWER: What are some of the biggest challenges you see for those seeking to break into the entertainment industry?

MONTY HALL: I'll go from my own personal history. I was working in Toronto and when television came in, I immediately got a show and then I got a second show. All of a sudden, I had no shows. So I went to New York in the 1950s and I was an unknown. The first thing you had to do was try to meet somebody. After pursuing it for some time, I finally got to meet somebody. He said to me, "Sit here in my office for awhile." He was in his office doing business and I sat in the corner like little Jack Horner. A funny thing happened, he said, "What are you doing for dinner, kid?" He took a shine to me only because I was persistent and I was there. He gave me a shot at doing a show, which led to other shows. I was in the right place at the right time, but only because I got up and made twenty phone calls like I did every other day. Maybe the first ninety-nine people will throw you out of their office, but here was the hundredth person. I was ready. I wasn't a kid off the street. I had done hundreds and hundreds of shows in Canada, but in New York it was starting all over again. You have to be recognized, that's the most important thing, getting in to be recognized. After many, many months I opened up *Life* magazine and they were interviewing the head of NBC. I sent him a telegram telling him about myself. Monday morning, the phone rings. His secretary phoned me to say that he wanted to see me. I go to his office and he says, "You got ten minutes, because I've got to catch a plane to the coast." I gave him my ten minutes worth. He told his assistant, "Get him in to see anybody he wants to in this building." His assistant said, "Who do you want to see?" I said, "Everybody." They got me in to see all of these producers. I got nothing from that. It was the first break of my life and I ended up with nothing. I could have taken the first plane back to Toronto and hid under the covers. It broke my heart, but I said to myself, "No sir, I'm gonna stick it out!" The only person that succeeds in this business is the guy who's got guts.

INTERVIEWER: Did your career come in part because you were open to possibilities?

MONTY HALL: When I came to New York I was a sportscaster and emcee and a producer.

So I got a game show. Now the game show wasn't at the top of my list. I could have said, "No, I'm not going to do it until they give me a bigger show," but I wanted to work. I created a show with a colleague called *Let's Make a Deal*. NBC likes the show. They say, "Whose going to emcee the show?" My colleague tells them I am. And they said, "Well, we'd like to have our guy do it." And my colleague told them they either use me or there is no show. He stood up for me. He said, "He created it and he's the perfect man for the job."

INTERVIEWER: What made you decide you wanted to be in entertainment?

MONTY HALL: When I was very young my mother was an actress and I would sometimes be in one of her plays. I was the kid who sat at the end of the table. In college, I got the lead in a play and it was a huge hit. Now I got a job at the radio station. I was head of the barn dance program, square dancing, sports. I did everything, and what training that was. At the same time, I was doing the army show, you know, like the USO. The training I got was terrific. Then the manager of the radio said to me, "I think you should go. I think you should go to Toronto. You are going places, but you won't go anywhere if you stick around this town." So I go home, I say to my folks, "I'm going to Toronto, then I'm going to go to Montreal and see what's happening there, and then I'm going to go to New York." And my grandfather said, "And then you come home to Winnipeg." I said, "No, Grandpa, I'm never coming back." I worked in Toronto, had two offers from Montreal, and then I said, "I'm going to New York and I'm gonna kill them!" And when I finally go to New York they said, "Who are you?"

INTERVIEWER: How does a career in entertainment affect family life and personal life?

MONTY HALL: Good question. I was living in Toronto and had radio and television work and my wife says to me, "Why don't you go to New York and try your luck there?" At this time my children are five and three. My wife says, "You go and I'll be a mother and a father to these kids." It took a lot of guts. So I go and I'm getting nothing. What I don't know is that while I'm in New York my daughter was hemorrhaging from appendicitis, and they took her back to surgery and she made it through OK. My wife is twenty-seven and she never told me. She knew that if she called me I'd come running home and that would be the end of my career in New York. That was the turning point in my life.

INTERVIEWER: Then what happens?

MONTY HALL: After six months I would come home for one week to be with my wife and kids, and I would go to New York for a week. When I was home I would write a one page memo called *A Memo from Monty*. It had a stick figure with a guy with a microphone and I sent it to all of these people I couldn't get in to see. The memo was things that had happened to me that week in New York: people I ran into, interesting stories and vignettes, and so on. I did this for a number of months and then I got a phone call from the program manager of NBC and he said, "Where's the memo? I didn't get it this week?" I said, "I didn't think anybody was reading it." He said, "I read it all the time! What are you doing for lunch? Come and meet me." I lunched with him at the Rockefeller Center in a big restaurant there. He said, "I'm having trouble with a show and I want you to go look at it." I watched it every day for a week and think I could have got four post graduate degrees for the thesis I wrote on that show and what it needed. I got a phone call, "I want you for that show. I want you to emcee it and I want you to produce it. When can you start to work?" Six months later I sold my house in Toronto and moved my family down to New York where I'd rented a house. I picked up my family at the airport, say good-bye to the moving van, the phone rings, I pick up the phone, it's NBC, "Your show has been canceled." I had just moved my wife and kids to my new country and my new city and my show was canceled.

INTERVIEWER: What did you do?

MONTY HALL: I said to my wife, "We're going to Florida for a vacation. I'm thumbing my nose at them right now. They are not going to beat me down."

INTERVIEWER: You had to step back?

MONTY HALL: If you get sent back to square one you have to have guts, you have to start knocking on doors again. Three years later I had two network shows and I lost both because they wanted to give those to big stars. I was back to square one again. I would make a living here and make a living there.

INTERVIEWER: Can you talk about building relationships?

MONTY HALL: I used to go to NBC and sit with the guys and have lunch with them even though I didn't have a job. Sending my memo every week was building relationships. This is what you have to do. When a guy comes 'round to me and says, "I'm an emcee!" I say, "Oh yeah? Where have you been, what have you done, show me what you've done." There is a big difference between show business and other professions. If you study to become a doctor and finish your training and do your internship, work a little and in nine years you are a doctor, no one can take that away from you. You can't say that about show business, because nine years later you can be back to square one. You are only as good as the work you have right now. An actor must act, a writer must write. You have to find a way.

INTERVIEWER: Talk about the importance of location.

MONTY HALL: I had a famous actor from Canada come down and stay with me in New York looking for work, and two weeks later he went home. I had the number one singer in Canada come and bunk with me looking for work in New York, two days later he left a note that said, "I couldn't take it, I'm leaving." I thought, "Here I am walking the streets, and you are running home." I said to myself, "I'm not going back." When I was walking the streets of New York, I was befriended by a guy at NBC. I was in his office when the phone rang. He said, "Listen. I just got a call from Connecticut and a hurricane has left devastation there and they are going to do a telethon next weekend. You're an emcee, how about hosting that telethon?" I said, "Sure, I'll emcee for you." Are you in the right place at the right time? If I would have stayed in a small town, I know I could have had a safe job, but I knew that that was not my life, and not my career.

INTERVIEWER: How did you know?

MONTY HALL: I said to myself, "If I can prove myself in New York, why don't I go for it to the best of my ability? If I don't make it I'll fall back, but you've got to fire before you fall back." For many years I had it, I lost it, I had it, and I lost it. You have got to believe in yourself. If you were to ask me how many times I was right in my life and how many times I was wrong, I would say it was pretty even. I think that courage is the most important thing you need provided you have the talent. Show business is the toughest business you can be in. One out of a hundred of you will have a chance. Do you like the odds? If you don't like the odds, go into another profession. There is one chance in a hundred again that you will get in and stay with it. So realize again that you have to be one of thousands of people who come to the big city. Take a look at how many people we have at the top of the industry. There is no substitute for talent or courage. People talk about luck, but luck will only happen if you stick it out.

Chapter 2:
The Audience

6. Gathering 2

(See Gathering on page 94 before participating in this exercise.)

Food for Thought

A play or script is not a play or movie until it is being performed in front of an audience. In other words, what it was intended to be. Whenever you see that we have referred to the audience, we are talking about any audience, whether a live audience or an audience at the movie theatre. As Simon Callow so eloquently puts it, "It's a pretty old arrangement, an actor and an audience, and we're not going to let it die."[13]

Food for Thought

In acting, if a tree falls in the forest and no one is there to hear it, does it make a sound? In acting, the actor requires an audience.

The Ingredients

What we would like you to do is when you are out and about, whether it be in a café or looking across the street, we want you to start to gather people with your eyes. We want you to gather people on a regular basis wherever you may be. Do not use your arms as you did in part one, but simply use your eyes and your intentions. This must not be confused with getting attention and wanting to be seen. You don't want people to think that you are accosting them or coming on to them. So this has to be a very quiet thing in your mind. When you see a person you want to gather, in your mind pull that person towards you and then embrace them, not literally. Like many of the exercises in this book, there is no need to plan this exercise ahead of time. You can work it in, sporadically, to your day-to-day living.

Food for Thought

"The instrument of the actor is himself. The actor must have a double personality. The first self works upon the second self until it is transfigured. Thence, an ideal personage is evolved in short until from himself he has made his work of art."[14] The famous French actor Constant Coquelin challenges you to give a different answer other than his. He goes on to say, "If you have no more consciousness where you are and what you are doing, you have ceased to be an actor."[15] This is what Coquelin says about an actor losing awareness of the audience and their surroundings on-stage. We should not be so high and mighty as to pass quick judgment over such a statement, for Coquelin is considered by many to be one of the greatest actors of his day. What he is saying is that the actor is two people: the person playing the instrument and the instrument being played. There is a great line in *Inherit the Wind* where a reporter is told words to the effect of, "Some people look for God too high up and too far away."

---

13. Simon Callow, *Being an Actor* (New York: Picador, 1984), 347.
14. Constant Coquelin, *Harpers New Monthly Magazine Volume LXXIV*, (New York: Harper and Brothers Publishers, 1887), 894.
15. Constant Coquelin, 906.

We seem to think that actors are supposed to lose themselves in the part and not be burdened by or be aware of the audience, not pander to the audience, not cater to them, not play for them alone, but remain true to themselves. By definition this is not acting. It takes two people to be an actor, and you have to have the actor telling the story and the person the story is being told to. There also has to be an action and reaction constantly between the two. You should never forget your audience and that you are there for them. If you totally lose yourself in the part it is called madness, self-indulgent, or bad acting. The admiration for acting is between the actor and the instrument. It is the actor's respect for his instrument and his understanding of the instrument that is of the utmost importance. If the actor trains the instrument with esteem, knowledge of being, and knowledge of what he is trying to get to the audience, he is thus automatically aware of the audience. You have to be prepared to see what came before, in order to strive for what is yet to come.

Food for Thought

Every acting exercise deals with perception because what it brings about allows us to perceive things differently. It is not that the audience is interested in what we are perceiving, it is that they are interested that we are perceiving something. Your performance doesn't end with momentum, it begins there.

The Diagnosis

What are you there for? Whether it be film, television, theatre, or the Internet, you are there to gather the audience. When actors hide behind their character, when actors wait for the audience to come to them, they wonder why it never happens. Cavemen were the first actors and they attracted someone to their story. Not only did they want to tell a story, but they attracted someone to listen. So the instinct was to gather them.

There is a vast difference between getting attention and gathering a person. When you gather a person they come with or without their own permission. They come willingly, joyfully, and then they come running at full speed. When they leave the theatre or the movie they want to come back. Nothing is more thrilling to each and every individual than to feel that they have been recognized and gathered by the actor. An actor transcends all fears, all prejudices, everything. You must experience at least one time what it is to be gathered by a great actor. Great actors always refer to the other actors who have inspired them, or should we say *gathered* them. Great actors make each and every single person in the audience feel like they know who they are as individuals. There are people who have a very natural bent for gathering people, and you must not allow anyone to talk you out of it or misunderstand it. It is absolutely the most wonderful thing in the world. Remember this book is about gathering people, about being in front of people. Develop the ability to gather people and to draw them in, then you can also use these skills when meeting agents, directors, and auditioning.

Food for Thought

You are not convincing the audience who the character is, but rather who you want them to be, and who you say they are. *Hello, Dolly!* was played by Carol Channing, Phyllis Diller, Pearl Bailey, and Ginger Rogers. If you have any idea who these people are you will know that they are not alike in any way, shape, or form. Each one of them convinced us that they were Dolly. The character is who they are because that's who you say they are, and that's your shining moment. First you have to get the part and then you finesse your way into the role.

Food for Thought

We would love it if audiences wanted to hear the story, but not all audiences want to hear them. Successful actors want to tell the story so much that their enthusiasm and their mastery of their art make the audience want to hear the story. We have seen performances where we have said, "For no reason other than the actors' enthusiasm, I think I want to hear this story." Now they have us in the place of most importance. They have us in a place where we, as an audience, want to hear the story. Not only do you have to be good, you have to be better than good. You have to make the audience want to hear the story. It is not necessarily the story but the way you tell the story that draws the audience in to you. This is why the same story, play, or movie can be heard over and over again.

Final Thoughts

A good acting exercise is something that you can do all the time. This exercise entails learning to look around the world and gather those things that you want. The hard part is gathering things to yourself that you don't want, because an actor will be portraying people who are not them and who they don't entirely approve of. This exercise is gathering things without a judgment of whether you want them or not. Integrate gathering into your daily living because the advantages will be numerous.

7. The "I Am" Exercise

Food for Thought

There are many kinds of actors. The only kind worth anything at all is a working actor who spends every single second they can on their acting. There are a number of famous movie directors who consider a movie and don't do the movie until they know how to make it interesting to the audience. In other words, they want to make the audience listen. Many actors are opposed to the statement, "How do I make the audience want to hear this story?" They see it as a kind of pandering to the audience. It is true, it doesn't matter how you define it, and yet it is needed. It doesn't matter if you want to or not, what matters is you want to tell a story, and you use every bit of your art. All art has a technique, but art is greater than the technique because art is the sum total of the technique. Technique comes in parts, bits, and pieces. Sometimes a director will turn down a movie because they don't see all the pieces fitting together. Perhaps they did not get the actors they wanted or the screenplay wasn't fashioned in a way that suited their needs. They are congruent and absolute in getting precisely what they need to make the project work.

Food for Thought

An actor must say as often as they can, "Why do I want to tell this story?" Even if they know why they have to say it again, and again, and again because it renews them, it refreshes them, and it gives them more breadth. Some actors are talking to themselves, some actors are talking to the wind, and some actors seem to be talking to no one. Who are you telling the story for? Great actors always talk to the audience. Every great storyteller makes you want to hear their story. The Pied Piper of Hamelin said, "You have a problem with vermin, now I'm going to get rid of your problem." They didn't pay him and so he said, "I'm going to make all of the children want to follow me." He was a great storyteller. He could pipe in such a delicious manner and in such an inclusive manner that you had to follow him. We have both been in readings where playwrights have been asked, "Who is your audience?" and the playwrights replied they hadn't given it much thought. They often created material that seemed unfocused with no clear direction.

The Ingredients

What we would like you to do is get together with another group of actors. Perform a scene or monologue for them. Once you are finished, everybody in the room decides to be you and they recount the performance of the scene you have just done. They then proceed to say how you felt, each saying one or two things. They may say, "I am John and I am very nervous, and I cannot remember my lines," "I am John and I am in the middle of my scene and I'm afraid I'm going to forget something," "I am John and I feel very angry tonight," or, "I am John and I feel stagnant and unmotivated in my performance tonight." You could also do this for audition practice. The other actors can watch you and they may say things like, "I am John and I don't really want to get up in front of the casting director," "I am John and I don't feel prepared for this," or, "I am John and I feel very comfortable and relaxed around the casting director." Not everything they say is necessarily a negative critique. It is anything that they observe about you and your performance. It is important to remember that each sentence starts with "I am." Once you have finished, switch out, have the other actors do the same thing. This exercise will be of more value to you if you work with a group of actors as opposed to one. This way you will be able to get a whole range of feedback instead of just a limited response.

Food for Thought

It is your job as an actor to be able to image the set you are on. How many actors working in a scene study class can tell you what the entire room is supposed to look like? They may know there is a table, but if asked how big the room is supposed to be, they couldn't tell you. The attention to detail is a very important part of the actor's work not just in terms of your character, but also in every aspect of the movie or play you are working on. When an actor chooses not to get specific, then they are creating a series of generalities in their own imagination. If the actor does not believe, then why would an audience?

On the topic of scene study, an actor should not be in a scene study class until they know how to act. How can you teach an actor how to put something together when they don't know the elements they are putting together?

Food for Thought

Some of the greatest actors of all time have said, "I invented myself, and I invented acting, and I didn't study with anyone. I made it all up myself. I never really had any formal training." But we're telling you the training they had was far greater than the class you're going to. They were on-stage or screen with other actors every second of their life. They were saying, "What works for that actor?" and, "I love to affect the audience." They made a conscious effort to pull the audience in, and to give in to the audience. There are a number of great actors throughout history who have claimed to use no technique in regards to their acting process. On occasion, an actor can be so good that technique is virtually instinctive and automatic for them. They have technique, they just never recognized it as such.

The Diagnosis

What this exercise teaches you is that you can say, "That is what I was thinking." Or you may say, "That is not at all what I was thinking. Why on earth would you think I was thinking that?" The exercise doesn't teach you about you, and it doesn't teach you what they think your thinking is. The exercise simply teaches you that when people watch you, they think they know what you're thinking. The wonderful part of this is that people, when they look at you, think they know what you're thinking. That means that you are in control of what they think they are thinking. As a non-actor, you can look across at them and say, "She's very angry. She's very unhappy. She's very confused. She's very mature for her age." Very often, you will be right, because you are good at recognizing traits in other people. An actor is creating a part that has never been there before. The "I am" exercise simply teaches you one of the most important tools in acting. If the audience is capable of thinking, look at the advantage it gives: you are now in control of what the audience thinks. You are in control of what the audience thinks you are thinking. You will know that you are successful when they come back and say, "I really related to that. That character was so angry." And you say, "Thank you," when indeed you were so happy you could hardly keep yourself from giggling. You were having so much fun playing the part.

By the way, if you are an actor, if you act, you should be having the best time of your life. Live audiences do not just apply to the theatre, as Robert Benedetti points out, "Performing in a sitcom is very close to acting in a fairly broad comedy in the live theatre. The similarity starts with the fact that an audience is present."[16] Whether it be television, theatre, or film, an audience is always present in some way or other. The more tools you have in your toolbox, the wider your range and versatility as an actor. This exercise has profound value and reminds you not to forget your audience, less they forget you.

Food for Thought

How many of you have ever read a program during a play? If your audience is reading during your performance, or eating popcorn and talking, it's your fault. If your performance is engaging, your audience will be engaged.

Food for Thought

I knew an actress who campaigned for a part that she was totally wrong for. She had to campaign endlessly just to get the audition. She auditioned for them and they said, "Well, we are just going to have to change the part." Notice I didn't say, "Well, you've got the part." They said something far more important, they said, "We are going to have to change the part because we want a compelling person. We want a person who has passion. We want a person who will be wonderful in front of an audience. We don't know that some to-die-for lady is going to have any of those things. We don't want an actor who can play anger or who can play lust. Anger and lust are just poor substitutes for passion. We've got it right here. We have already looked at everybody in the category we want and we can't find what we need. What we really need is someone who can wow an audience." This actress was no beauty; however, she became a celebrated Broadway star and it was all of her own doing. If your audition is at nine a.m., then get up at six a.m. This is part of your pre-audition preparation. When you read a book or go to a seminar related to positive thinking, many people will say, "Yes, I know all that." The challenge is many of them don't follow through with what they know. Many actors tell us, "I know all that." In regards to audition preparation, the challenge is that many of them are not following through on what they know. If you look at this book and say, "That is really important, useful, and beneficial to me," and do nothing with it, then you are wasting your time.

Final Thoughts

The "I am" exercise is very simple and to the point. It simply points out to the actor that every single person in the audience thinks they know what you are thinking. If an audience thinks they know what you are thinking, then it stands to reason that you can control what they think they are thinking, and that, my dear friends, is called acting. Whether they are watching you live or on the big screen, never forget that the audience is part of the ensemble.

8. Template

Food for Thought

As an actor, you want to arrest your audience so that they only do what you want them to do. A great actor tells an audience when to laugh and cry, and they do so with great power. The actor can *expect* something from the audience, but they must *demand* it. They take away

---

16. Robert Benedetti, *Action!: Acting for Film and Television* (USA: Pearson Education Inc., 2006), 69.

the audience's freedom, which is willingly given. At the end of the play or movie the actor gives the audience back their freedom and they go home. The audience is begging the actor to draw them in. As Robert Edmond Jones says, "In the theatre, as in life, we try first of all to free ourselves, as far as we can, from our own limitations. Then we can begin to practice this noble magical art."[17]

Food for Thought

Your acting career is a risk in that you cannot be certain it will turn out exactly how you envisioned it. You move out to a big city and leave all your friends and support networks behind. This is a calculated risk that many aspiring actors may never be willing to take. Every time you go to an audition you take the risk of being told, "No thank you." Every time you are on television or in a movie you take the risk of being criticized for your performance by the audience. Being an actor is full of risks that you have to be willing to take! You have to take risks today, tomorrow, and for the rest of your career.

The Ingredients

Here is an exercise we would like you to do that will work well for you to practice with two other actors. Take a piece of paper and somewhere towards the top of the page draw a circle, and somewhere towards the bottom draw a triangle. Now take two other pieces of paper and cut out two templates so that if you put the first template (piece of paper) on top of the original page only the circle would be showing, and if you put the second template over the original page only the triangle would be showing. Now do this experiment with two actor friends. Ask them to close their eyes and have the first actor open their eyes, look at the first template, and ask them to remember what they see. Ask them not to say it out loud, but remember what they saw.

PAUL: *(Does the experiment and asks the ACTORS to opens their eyes.)* What did you see?

ACTOR 1: A circle.

PAUL: What do you see?

ACTOR 2: A triangle.

PAUL: How can that be? You both looked at the same piece of paper.

GAVIN: Even if the actors figure out you are changing the templates, this exercise is still a great metaphor for the actor.

Food for Thought

When an individual enters the room it dislodges some of the air and it is as if we become aware of their presence. Imagine what can happen when an actor enters the stage or a set. Think about when you have said, "I could feel the performance." This is when the actor is reaching out to you. The actor is embracing and arresting you so that you can actually taste the performance. Think of the potential understanding and influence this gives you over the audience.

Food for Thought

The greatest dramatic illusion is when the audience doesn't know it is an illusion. In the history of the world have there ever been two people who were exactly alike in every way? It is also worth noting that each actor playing a part is going to play it through a different instrument. The variables in a human being are unfathomable. While playing a part an actor may feel that they are connecting the physical to the vocal; however, the vocal is already physical.

---

17. Robert Edmond Jones, *The Dramatic Imagination* (New York: Theatre Arts Books, 1969), 23.

There are a lot of things we do that we have to become aware of doing. The audience does not have to become aware of us doing it, they have to become aware of the result of us doing it. We do want the audience to relate to what they see because if they don't relate to it they cannot be affected by it. Plays and movies do not become classics because of the universality in them, they become classics because the current public deems them to be, or votes them to be so. It is important to note that popularity is not fixed. We have been led to believe that Shakespeare has always been popular, and that simply isn't true. It has often been said that it is lonely at the top of the popularity pole. The price one pays for fame and fortune can be a costly one. As Julie Burchill explains when talking about female movie stars of yesterday, "Veronica Lake, Peggie Castle, Susan Shaw, and Gale Russell died of drink; Francois Dorlec, Jayne Mansfield, and Belinda Lee died in car crashes; Maria Montez drowned in her bath and Natalie Wood drowned in the Atlantic while drunk."[18] As the famous child star Hayley Mills said in a 1986 interview, "Hollywood is full of wonderful, colorful gilded cages with unhappy little birds inside."[19]

The Diagnosis

PAUL: Until you can look through the same template you cannot see what each other sees, do you understand?

ACTOR: Yes.

PAUL: Until you can look through the same template of a great teacher or a great actor, you can't see what they see. When you say, "They are wrong!" you are right, because the frame of reference does not exist for you yet. You say you saw a circle, and she says, "You couldn't have seen a circle, I was looking at the same piece of paper that you were." That is the quickest way to tell you that we all look at life through different templates.

A variation on this exercise would be to draw a black shield on one side of a piece of paper and a gold shield on the other side of the same piece of paper. You proceed with the exercise in the same way as before, except instead of using a template you simply flip the piece of paper over. The shield story comes from a famous medieval tale where two knights almost fought to the death over what they could and could not see.

ACTOR: How do you get the right template?

PAUL: You seek out the greatest teachers and greatest actors you can find, whether it be through technology or in person, and you learn from them as much as you can until you make it your own.

GAVIN: When you are good, no matter what people say, they are hiring you because you are good, period!

Food for Thought

From the moment we are born most of us are to some extent actors, because for the first six months of our lives we have an audience. As you get older, people entertain you by entertaining themselves or by taking you to something. In other words, you then become a captive and involuntary audience. By observing the world around you, you are part of an audience every day of your life.

Food for Thought

An actor watches a play differently than an audience. When an actor watches the play they hear something different than an audience. They hear in color, they hear in space, they

18. Julie Burchill, *Girls on Film* (New York: Pantheon Books, 1986), 60.
19. Hayley Mills talks about "The Parent Trap II" — 1986, http://www.youtube.com/watch?v=EXvJPLeaX7A.

hear in time, they hear in quantity, and they hear in quality. Now, if you don't understand any of these words, you're not an actor. That does not mean quit, that means researching and finding out whatever you need to find out for your acting.

Final Thoughts

We all see the same thing through a different template. Each person, by being independent and unique, is seeing things through a different template. Again, the actor transcends these. The actor has to take all of the templates off. That's actually going to be impossible, so you want to take as many as you can off so you are seeing what is sometimes called "the big picture."

At first, remind yourself that you have talked to somebody who has seen the same movie that you saw and they speak of it as though they saw a different movie. They did see a different movie, it's not in your imagination. They look at that movie through a different template, and they were listening to it through a different audio system than you were, so the two of you saw different movies. Great movies are great because they appear to be the same to everybody's template. That's what great movies do to transcend, to get to an audience. Great actors are the people who take all of the templates on and they see every possibility. Warn yourself that, in seeing something differently, you may think that different is the *other side* of the *same thing*. Remember, a coin has *two sides,* heads and tails. They are *two sides* of the *same coin. Templates* are *different,* not *two sides of the same.* If your template is not so rigid and fixed, then you are open to all templates that come your way.

9. A New Beginning

Food for Thought

Many politicians take voice and acting lessons, and many politicians we know will take what are called *accent reduction* classes. They do this so that their speech pattern becomes a more universal sound. If you can communicate with audiences universally, then your acting can reach them globally.

Food for Thought

The human being is the most advanced organism in the world. As opposed to being natural, acting is against your nature because in life, when you have too much stimulation, that is considered bad. Actors have to teach themselves to do something that is considered unnatural: they have to embrace stimulation on all levels. They don't run away from things, and they don't run away from an audience, even if they throw up before going on. Stage fright is natural. If you don't have stage fright, you have taught yourself to do something that is not natural. A hero is a person who is not afraid in battle. An actor is trained to do something that is against their nature, and it's the greatest high in the world to do it. Your blueprint on acting is inside you waiting to be discovered.

The Ingredients

For this exercise you will want to work with a partner. We want you to take a minute to think about a character that you have played before. What we want you to do is improvise a court scene where one of you will play the prosecutor and one of you will play the witness who saw your character. So you are not playing your character, but the witness of the character. The prosecutor can make up any wild scenario they choose and go out of their way to be impossibly difficult to disprove their case. Remember that this is a character that you already know about and you should take this into account when answering the questions.
PROSECUTOR: I can ask anything?

PAUL: You can ask anything, but you have to fire the questions.

PROSECUTOR: Does Sarah like to go out to parties?

WITNESS: She likes late-night parties.

PROSECUTOR: Does she like men?

WITNESS: She likes one man.

PROSECUTOR: Are you sure she only likes one man?

WITNESS: She's positive.

PROSECUTOR: Is he in love with her?

WITNESS: He does love her, but it's a complicated relationship.

PAUL: Good. Don't allow the witness to ramble and stick to short questions, and be relentless. *(Scene continues for ten minutes. Two more actors come on-stage and complete a new scene.)*

PAUL: Remember that the witness knows more about the character than the prosecutor ever will, because the prosecutor has never met them.

WITNESS: Are we making up the scenario?

PAUL: Good question. Try to keep your answers as they would relate to the character. A second phase of this exercise is to have the prosecutor ask, "What else do you know about Sarah?"

GAVIN: Continue to ask this same question over and over again. Once the scene is over, change places.

Food for Thought

I grew up in the era where directors and producers were all bullies. If you had a position of power, you were a bully. If you didn't have a position of power, you put up with bullies. We didn't have a different world to choose from, and the fact that they were this way makes absolutely no difference whatsoever. It's one way to play the game. We have to remember that actors have often been considered the bottom of the totem pole. We have been called low class people. When I came to Hollywood I couldn't get car insurance. What I got was assigned risk. In other words, they put your name in a bin and all insurance companies had to draw five out of this bin. The reason was that I was under twenty-six, I was living in Hollywood, I was single, and male, but the worst thing was I was an actor. Because I was an actor, it was virtually impossible to get insurance. What I am getting at is that even in those times when actors had been treated poorly, there have been successful actors and there have been audiences who were moved by them, who needed them, who were entertained by them, and who revered them, at least during the performance. It never ceases to amaze me what an actor has to go through in order to be an actor, and yet there has always been a need for actors, and there always will be.

Food for Thought

Talent is based entirely on the relationship you have with the audience. It is only important they are responding to you, it does not matter what their interpretation of that response is. Action and reaction is between you and the other actor. To take it one step further, it is, in a more subtle way, also between you and the audience. It is not enough to have talent. You have to have talent to handle the talent.

The Diagnosis

PAUL: Who is listening to the answers?

ACTORS: The jury and the judge.

PAUL: Who do you think the audience is?

ACTORS: The jury.

PAUL: The audience is the judge and the jury. It is the job of every actor to make and win their case. The interesting thing is great actors win their cases any way they can. They pull on your heartstrings, they lie, they cheat, and they steal.

WITNESS: When in reality I already know the character I am asked about. I think, "Why even ask the question?"

PAUL: When you do that you are not pursuing the part at all. You have made a decision and that's it. You've come to an end.

GAVIN: If you allow yourself to keep making discoveries you will surprise yourself and you will surprise us.

The best actor is also the best attorney. Well-established actors do not accept parts unless they think they can win the case. They say, "I don't think the audience or my fans will believe I'm that character." What if a screenwriter or playwright gives you a character and you say, "There is no way I can make this character interesting unless I stand off and say, 'I am going to convince you that this character is someone that you should think about.'" Great actors can convince us of anything.

A producer is like a judge in that he doesn't have to accept anybody at all, including the audience. At one point during this exercise you are asked to ask the same question over and over again. This is done to highlight to the actor the fact that some actors get one thing, bite on it, and pray for lockjaw instead of finding out more. It is the responsibility of the actor to convince the other actors, the producer, the director, and the audience of everything they do.

Food for Thought

PAUL: Before you started the scene you took a breath.

ACTOR: I wasn't aware I did that.

PAUL: That is logical. I mean, anybody needs a breath to start talking. Except I noticed a minute ago when I asked you your name and address you didn't take a breath. This is a common indicator of a novice actor to take a breath before the start of each scene. Actors often do something called *changing gears.* There is no reason for you to change gears when you act. That little breath you take before the scene tells the audience there is a change in the actor, and you are changing gears. If you watch great actors you won't see them change gears.

GAVIN: The reason for your preparation is so that the audience never sees your preparation.

Food for Thought

A discovery of character: Every time you feel something that seems unpredictable, wrong, or unfamiliar, that's a discovery of the character. It is a discovery of the character because it is not a discovery of you. If you say, "I have felt that before," then you are not acting. In fact, you are doing what the audience says. They look and say, "I recognize that experience," but at the same time they say, "But I've never seen it that way." The more you step into the known the more you want to step into the unknown.

Final Thoughts

We talk about results and it is also important to talk about how we get them. The way a great actor gets results is through investigation or information gathering. The greatest artists in the world are always convincing someone of something. An actor's job is not just the suspension of disbelief, it is belief. When we look at a great work of art we don't have to suspend anything because we believe something. The test of true art is when it convinces us and has nothing to do with whether it is right or wrong. In order to convince us you have to investigate something and it is up to you to find out. That is the simplest definition of art.

10. Day's Journey

Food for Thought

Even in a really bad play or movie, even with a really bad script, you must show the audience something they wouldn't have known had they not seen you. These are the timeless actors who are loved by generations.

Food for Thought

You must always know more about the character than the audience, and you must always find new things. If an audience says, "I know somebody exactly like that!" some actors feel very complimented. You should want someone to say, "I've never seen anyone like that in my whole life!" That's when you are successful. Particularly if someone says, "I've never seen that Hamlet in my entire life. I've seen eighteen Hamlets and I've never seen a Hamlet like that in my life." If every performance were exactly the same, why would we ever want to see the same play done twice? It would mean *Romeo and Juliet* would have ceased to be performed hundreds of years ago.

The Ingredients

What we would like you to do is when you are walking with a friend or when you are driving with a friend in a route you know they travel often, look around and see if you can find something that you bet they have never seen before. Perhaps you could pick out a coffee shop that they have never seen before, or maybe a grocery store, or a bench, or a tree. It is important that it is a route that they have taken quite often, and then you can have them do the same thing to you. It would be a good idea to do this exercise with a fellow actor so that you can both get the benefits, but a non-actor friend will do just fine. We have the ability to block out a lot of our environment, but the actor wants to absorb their environment.

Food for Thought

Symmetry actually means a kind of balance. In that balanced state we don't make discoveries because part of the definition of balance is that it comes to rest. One of the greatest discoveries of the actor is that they never come to rest. That's what we mean when we say, "There is an edge to their performance, and it's spontaneous." A see-saw that becomes balanced no longer becomes spontaneous. It just sits where it is. It is not that we are unbalanced, it's that we want balance moment-by-moment. The only way we can do that is to have no reference to balance. The one thing that is great about the best actors is that they seem still, confident, relaxed, and yet there is vibrancy to them, an energy to them that is spellbinding. In terms of stillness Jon Jory says, "It can be sexy to do less. If there isn't a lot of movement, what there is can startle."[20] This is because they are moving moment-to-moment, thought-to-thought, and each time they move to a new thought it becomes balanced. As soon as it becomes balanced they have moved on to a new thought.

It takes enormous energy to do a three hour performance. Balance is a way of calming us, but an actor doesn't want to be calmed. The audience didn't come to see you rest, they came to see you struggle. The conflict is often compared to mean fighting, but for the character it means never quite being able to find the right thing. There is a constant search. I have seen great actors in the same show many times, and yet it is always fascinating because they never found the right way in one performance. If they found the right way, I would never go back

---

20. Jon Jory, *Tips: Ideas for Directors* (New Hampshire: Smith and Kraus, 2002), 190.

to see it. I didn't go to see what they found, I went to see them searching for something. We went to a play where the acting was sincere and heartfelt, but something was lacking. The actors forgot what they were searching for, and so did we. Paul turned to me and said, "Well, I guess sometimes sincerity is not enough."

Food for Thought

A great performance is when an actor answers every question an audience could ever ask. I'm very vexed and unsettled if I walk out of a performance and I've got questions that haven't been answered. When I see a consummate performance I walk out of that show feeling every question I could possibly have has been answered. A great actor can create a performance that is so complete they sense every possible question that the audience has. Now you go back again with a new set of questions and you say, "Ah ha, now I am prepared and you can't possibly get ahead of me this time," and if they are a great actor they will answer all of your questions again. Think about the times when you have left a movie speechless with nothing to say. Perhaps it's because the actor's performance has left you with nothing left to say. A successful show is one that continues to grow. It never stays static. When I see a great performance of a play I have seen before I forget the previous play.

The Diagnosis

There is so much in acting that we don't see unless somebody points it out. There is so much in acting we don't hear unless somebody points it out. There is so much in acting we don't feel unless someone points it out. If you have the same way of walking or driving to some destination everyday, we bet you any amount of money that we could ride with you or walk with you and show you something that you have never seen before.

To be an actor you have to see what audiences never see, and you have to show them more than they could possibly see. You have to hear more than they ever will hear in the word, and you must give more sound to the word than they can possibly hear. If you are an actor, the words actually have a taste. If you are an actor, the words actually have a physical feeling. The audience doesn't know you can taste that word. The audience doesn't know that you can feel where your tongue is on the gum ridge behind your upper teeth when you pronounce certain words. You, on the other hand, are very aware of it because those are your tools. You are trying to find a way to make them want to hear the story, and they don't know that all five senses are working in a way greater than theirs, and in much more volume than theirs. Think about when you have finished a performance and your friends said, "That was really good." You were disappointed because you felt that they had not articulated more. It is not their job to understand or be aware of every nuance, every sound, or the ingredients that make up the performance. It is your job.

Food for Thought

I have been inspired by acting in every form. I have cried and been vexed in children's theatre. Children's theatre or movies does not mean that they're not for adults. It means they are accessible by children. Very famous actors have done performances for young audiences and been brilliant. Slapstick comedy has a brilliant message: it shows us the potential consequence of our actions. We can see a show that is entertaining and call it as such. This is entertainment for entertainment's sake and not necessarily good acting. It can be enjoyable, it can be highly amusing, it can also have nothing whatsoever to do with the craft of acting.

Food for Thought

Most audiences are somewhere in between *infatuated* with the actor, which means it doesn't matter what you do, and *hostile* towards the actor, which also means it doesn't matter what you do. As an actor, you will face directors who are either hostile or infatuated by you.

Both are a great danger to you because they are a distraction. It is important to recognize the different facets that influence and affect the actor's performance.

Final Thoughts

Has anybody ever said to you, "Didn't you see that?" Well, we think differently, therefore we see differently. Always use your friends as a creative resource, and remember the greatest resource an actor has is they are seeing infinite possibilities and infinite things. While using your friends as a creative resource, it is a very simple to say, "What do you see over there?" Keep asking them until they point out something you haven't already seen. You will now not only know everything you know, you know everything they know, and now you know more than both of you. You are continuing to grow as an actor and utilizing the resources around you.

Chapter 3:
Technology and Information for the Actor

11. Technology and the Actor

Food for Thought

When you find the sameness between two great teachers, that's technique. When you find the difference between them, that's publicity. Whether you want to accept it or not, all great teachers are after the same thing. The thing that makes them different is that they are finding it a different way. If you find the sameness of any two great teachers you have found a universal truth in acting. It is the publicity machine that will tell you that there is only one actor who can perform in that particular way. You waste so much time saying, "If you will only look at me you will know how talented I am." They are hiring you to do what they want. They are not hiring you to do what you want. There was a day when you could have a really bad teacher who was very persuasive, and they could talk anybody into anything, including a very bad technique. There is no excuse to have a bad teacher anymore because of technology. By watching master's classes of great teachers and actors such as Uta Hagen, Sanford Meisner, Michael Chekhov, and Lee Strasburg on the Internet and reading the works of great teachers and great actors, you will begin to know a good teacher when you find one. An actor is also able to watch a whole plethora of actors talk about their craft on the show *Inside the Actor's Studio*. You cannot always tell a good or bad teacher immediately, so give a fair amount of time to make a judgment.

Food for Thought

There is more work in acting now than there has ever been in the history of the world. I ran into a colleague the other day whose profession is teaching people how to make movies with their cell phones. With all the advanced technology the market for film has expanded ten-fold. There are also many more networks and cable channels expanding the demand and variety of programs being made, which translates to more work for the actor. There are more theatres in the world today than there have ever been. Almost every major city in the United States now has a fine arts center with a philharmonic hall, a large stage for music and opera, and a smaller stage for musicals and plays. This, in turn, translates into more work for the actor. Small, forty-nine seat and ninety-nine seat theatres are capable of doing international quality theatre. The likes of Brecht, Grotowski, and Stanislavski enjoyed working with spaces such as these. This means that if you are performing a play in a small theatre, it may still have a much bigger reach than you could imagine. This also means your success as a performer can happen anywhere. This, again, means if you want to be an actor, there is more opportunity in performing than at any other time in history. When an actor says, "There is no work," they are really creating a self-fulfilling prophecy. There is always work because some actors are always working. Something is always being produced, and something is always being created.

The Ingredients

This exercise is quite simple as it is easily accessible. What we would like you to do is take advantage of all the different forms of technology in order to enhance your awareness of acting. For instance, there are so many stations on television that you can see current actors, historic performances, and performances coming from all over the world, twenty-four-seven. You can find documentaries about great acting teachers as well as acting teachers who are no longer alive. You can watch historical dramatized accounts of accomplished actors, directors, and producers' lives. You can find all these things and you will also find differences in terminologies and phrases used in different acting capitals of the world. It is a good exercise to get acting books by teachers such as Stanislavski, Meyerhold, Strasberg, Adler, Hagen, Boloslavsky, Artaud, and Grotowski. You can also read books on German acting, French acting, Kabuki theatre, and so on and so on. Your job when reading these works is not to find the differences between them, but to find the similarities between their work. With so much technology at your fingertips you can learn as much or as little about your craft as you choose. Take full advantage of the incredible resources that are out there for you.

Food for Thought

Hollywood is abounding with people who come from little tiny towns, or what Marshall Mclewan predicted in the sixties as "A Global Village" has come about. He said words to the effect of, "Television will change the face of the earth," and he was right. What he didn't anticipate was that the Internet did it even more. Acting is now available and great actors are now available to everybody, whether it is on television, Internet, satellite, or any other form of technology. There are such great books on acting and there have historically been such magnificent teachers, but you had to be there. You had to have their set of circumstances. What did all these great teachers need? Who was their audience? Who were they speaking to? How were they speaking? What were the important things in their lives? How did they earn a living? What was their society like? Their work was so brilliant and it came about because of their needs. The second thing was they were geniuses and the work came about because of their talent. If we ignore the circumstances that they had, we are misled to believe that everything they taught is because of their genius. Very little of what they taught came from their genius. It came from their need. They said, "What do I need from this actor or this performance?" We have to look at their time, circumstances, and what came before. There are so many misinterpretations and misconceptions of what is being said, and why it was said, and in what context it was said. This is why, in the end, the actors must become their own guide, and use what works for them individually.

Food for Thought

Human beings are only able to process so much stimulation. What is relevant is how we process things. We are delighted to say there are some performances on-stage, screen, and television that, with the combination of set, lights, performance, costumes, makeup, body language, words, choreography, and all the things that could possibly stimulate us, they actually *over* stimulate us. They do this until we laugh, cry, are spellbound, or worn out. We are constantly bombarded with stimulation, which leads to desensitization. The role of the actor has now become that much more challenging.

The Diagnosis

It used to be that if you wanted to see the world's most famous actor you had to go to a major city, or you had to wait until they came to your city once in your lifetime. Theatres used to advertise, "A once-in-a-lifetime opportunity to see this famous actor," and it was. Now, because of technology, there are opportunities galore to see any actor or performance you wish. A lot of charlatans used to be able to tell you, "It's my way because I tell you so." Since they didn't have the ability to look up things, they didn't have the chance to be at the performance, to be at the rehearsal, or to read the book. Actors had less maneuverability in terms of resources. Because there is the technical availability of so much airtime with hundreds of channels, they look for anything and everything to fill this time, much to our advantage.

They film rehearsals, interview actors, directors, writers, producers, etc. Now you can see everything possible about the show — where the writer was brought up, who the writer was married to, what they do for fun. All of these things are very useable to the actor because you can find out what works, what is true, and what is myth.

Many years ago acting teachers would tell you something that wasn't true, and very often they believed it to be true. The challenge was they had never seen the performer, they had never been in the rehearsals, and they had never met the director. Now you can meet all the living playwrights, screenwriters, all the directors, the producers, and all the actors. You can meet all of the people connected with motion picture, television, and stage because of the abundant availability through technology. Now you can see the greatest actors giving the greatest performances twenty-four-seven. You can also see them doing things that are just sheer entertainment, so it explains to you and redefines to you that being a great actor does not exclude you from being a great entertainer, even though they can be two different things. You can see actors in dance contests or running marathons so they don't become the distant gods and goddesses that can never be understood. They show you how similar they are to you, so it can give you great confidence and great knowledge. What this exercise also encourages you to do is be aware that knowledge is available to us twenty-four-seven. Very few people can have power over you. In this exercise you are also asked to read books by great teachers. There is no question or doubt that they are all talking about great performances.

There are only a few things that make up a great performance. It is like colors: The whole world of color comes from three primary colors. Why does anybody think that acting has any more than that? There are a few basic things in acting and an infinite number of ways to use them. If you study painting and you started with *tertiary,* which is a greater combination, then you would never understand how they were made, you would skip the primary ingredients. When you skip to the end of great performances and you don't know the ingredients that make it, this can lead to a great deal of confusion. The same ingredients make all great acting whether it is Russian, English, American, French, or Japanese. Gavin Levy says, "You may find an acting book that gives you a whole new approach to your work. If you live in an area where there are few resources for the actor, then bring the resources to you."[21]

Food for Thought

In relation to working on film, Ian Bernard says, "I will leave you with one thought about film and television acting: nothing is forever. But once you've committed a performance to film, it will seem like it."[22] Jeremiah Comey says about film, "On-stage it is almost impossible to achieve films' intense intimacy."[23] Great film actors say, "I know what the audience is going to think at this precise moment." Great film actors say to directors, "My public wants me to do this." Great actors are doing things that their audiences are never going to be able to do. The audience gets to do these things through them. The audience is given the opportunity to live vicariously through the actor. Perhaps this is one reason why people enjoy watching the same movie again and again.

Food for Thought

We hear some actors say that they love film because you can do another take. We hear other actors say they hate film because you can do another take. If you have developed a technique of start, stop, start, stop, then it will not matter whether you have to work a scene for two hours or two seconds. It is more difficult to have to start the whole process again every two minutes. You can learn to do it, it just tends to tire you more. It is easier to do a three and

21. Gavin Levy, *Acting Games for Individual Performers* (Colorado: Meriwether Publishing, 2007), 203.
22. Ian Bernard, *Film and Television Acting* (Boston: Focal Press, 1998), 46.
23. Jeremiah Comey. *The Art of Film Acting* (London: Focal Press, 2002), Intro.

a half hour play than it is to do a film because starting and stopping is exhausting. This is why in film, stage, and television one can't be better than the other. The main technical difference between them is that you start and stop in bigger or smaller segments. (See exercise Begin Again on page 178.) As Amy Ryan says in regards to the theatre, "I will add one thing: The stage takes unbelievable stamina and strength, and even though you're only working two hours a night, it's really your whole day and probably one of the most exhausting things you can do."[24] Whether you want to be a film, television, or stage actor it requires an enormous amount of dedication and stamina.

Final Thoughts

We hope you are fortunate enough to study with somebody who is a genius teacher or to work with a director who is a genius director. By the way, the world abounds in such people. If you stay in acting and get yourself around like you should, you should come in contact with these very wonderful people. The great advantage of working with a genius is their genius. There are also disadvantages in working with them because, since they are a genius, they do not need a very wide vocabulary to do what they do. The greatest painters in the world are only dealing with three basic colors. If you ask them what colors they are using they will tell you, "Three." That is wonderful if they are going to show you how to use them. The language a genius uses is usually much more limited, much more terse, much more to the point, and much simpler than what the rest of the world uses. If you read three different books on acting by three different geniuses it will say the same thing three different ways. It will confuse you because you will think that one of them is right and two of them are wrong. It isn't true. All three of them are right. In order to understand a simple truth you have to read it in as many ways as you can. Knowledge is not the difference between two things, it is when you find the sameness between two things. Geniuses often seem to be a little odd or a little unusual. They are highly independent and their time is taken up by their thoughts. The last thing on their mind is correct social etiquette.

12. Sound Off

Food for Thought

The reason there were such great stars at the end of the nineteenth and early part of the twentieth century was that if you went to the theatre and saw them perform, you only saw them once in your entire life. If you didn't live in New York, London, Paris, or maybe Chicago, then you probably only got one opportunity to see them. They didn't play the provinces. Now you can see every famous actor you want, and you can see hundreds of internationally known actors at any moment by turning on your television. The interesting thing is you can see so many, but you probably don't know seventy-five percent of them, but before everybody knew who Sarah Bernhardt, Elenora Duse, Edwin Booth, and David Garrick were. You may or may not know who these actors are, if you don't, then find out, because they are part of your heritage as an actor.

Food for Thought

You may feel a camera technique class is the real thing, but it is not. It is a guarded situation and an opinionated situation. It has none of the pressures or immediate needs of the moment of a real film or television show. A professional actor is someone who is performing on-stage or on-camera. A student actor is someone who is not performing on-stage or on-camera. Even if they are the best actor in the class and a scriptwriter comes and says, "That's wonderful. I want you for my next movie." Or the producer comes and says, "We want to build a series around you." Until that series is made or until that movie is made, you are a student actor. So

---

24. Ben Affleck, *Interview* (New York: Brant Publications, Inc., November 2007), 46.

why go to class? You go to class to learn technique. A beginning actor will say, "Whenever you are ready." A professional actor will say, "I was ready years ago." When you do a scene in an acting class it should make you a better actor. It should not simply make the scene better. If the scene gets better and you didn't become a better actor, then you didn't learn anything. Every class should make you a better actor until you become a good actor. There is such a thing as a good acting class, there is such a thing as a professional student, and the professional student will never have an acting career as long as he or she is a professional student.

The Ingredients

Get in the habit of watching very famous performances that are done on film or television. Watch them all the way through. Then watch it next time all the way through without any sound. This sounds quite simple, but it is, in fact, quite a difficult exercise to do. You could also do this at the movies or a play by wearing earplugs.

Food for Thought

Actors hear all kinds of advice on what kind of parts they should and should not accept. We know a film where a famous actress only appeared in a six-minute scene and won an academy award. It is only when you are in a specific situation that you will be able to make a decision based on all the facts that are presented to you. Because no two situations are exactly alike, specific advice may do you a disservice instead of serving your specific needs in that situation.

Food for Thought

Is a film the work of the actor, or the work of an editor and director? That is a dicey question. Actors have made many discoveries by asking questions and continuing to ask them.

The Diagnosis

When you watch the acting without sound you will notice who the better actors are. When we watch a very good production it is often produced so well that the costumes are good, the scenery is good, and the cinematography is good. However, when the film or play is saying something wonderful and the movie or play has a number of wonderful merits to it, particularly the dialogue, we forgive a lot of things such as poor acting, poor direction, and a poor set. We've got so many things to pick from when we watch a good production that if three or four things fail, we just pick another one and we have a wonderful time. When you turn the sound off you no longer have what sometimes is a distraction of the music, of the sound of the voice, or of the vocal enhancement. You are now watching the body language of actors. You will find that some actors are not giving the right body language. They are saying, "I believe in what I am doing," but the body language is telling you nothing whatsoever. When you watch it with no dialogue you will also find out that some actors have trouble wearing certain costumes. You will be able to say to yourself, "That actor doesn't like that costume." What we say in the business is, "The costume is wearing the actor." You are discovering whether the actor has the ability and the desire to communicate.

Food for Thought

You must work on your instrument specifically because you are an actor. We have heard on many occasions, "Oh, when I get a job I will start doing it. When I get a movie or a Broadway show, I will take three or four months to prepare myself." You must have a regime that you do every single day. When you do that, you will be more prepared. Your preparation offscreen or off-stage is what will prepare you when you are on. As James Gandolfini says in the book *Acting Teachers of America,* "You don't need more than five minutes to prepare in film work, especially since they don't give you more than five minutes. It's true you have to shift gears and get going."[25] You have to be able to adapt to the situation at hand, whatever it may be.

Food for Thought

It's fun to watch a channel that shows only classic movies because they do the original promo for the film too. "Now we are going to see Jeffery what's-his-name who is going to be the next romantic lead all America is waiting to see." And I say to myself, "Whatever happened to Jeffery what's-his-name? I never saw him before or since." For a split second somebody saw something in that actor and then it disappeared.

Final Thoughts

The great advantage that actors did not have until the twentieth century is now we can see the layers that an actor has. We can see the layers of things an actor does as the layers of reality, the layers of perception. In television and film we are given the opportunity of seeing an actor in a way that we cannot see them on-stage. By turning down the volume you can see what causes the body language. You are actually seeing an actor think. When you can hear them, sometimes words and the flexibility of their voice is so entertaining that you miss the thing that is most entertaining. The most entertaining thing that an actor does is what causes them to do what you see. When you turn the sound off you begin to see what causes them to do that. If acting is "doing," then it is of value to you to know as much as you can about the "doing."

13. Acting Is Everywhere

Food for Thought

We would like to think that a sleeping actor is more prepared in that state than a non-actor. In our heart of hearts we really believe that if you are destined to be an actor, you will be a fine actor. There are people who are not destined to be an actor who technically learn how to be in front of a camera or on-stage. Being prepared can also mean you are ready when opportunity comes your way.

Food for Thought

Major studios will not make a picture until they are almost certain of the profit margins before they start the picture. Here it is in your face, and no one is denying it. If you are looking to play major roles in the movies, then you have to fit or be molded into their profit margin equation.

The Ingredients

PAUL: First of all, you have an assignment. Are you on the Internet?

ACTOR: Yes.

PAUL: This is your assignment: Go onto the Internet at least five days a week and search for "acting." You will come up with more than you can look at in a year, I guarantee you. There are some very well-known sites where you can watch videos for free all about acting, on acting, by great actors, and by great teachers. Keep a list of all the things you have watched. Have you ever gone on the Internet and watched recordings of great actors?

ACTOR: No, I've never done it before.

PAUL: For instance, you can go on YouTube and watch Michael Caine, "Acting In Film Part 1-6," for free, or you can watch Sanford Meisner working with his actors, and you can see Uta Hagen working with her actors.

---

25. Ronald Rand & Luigi Scorcia, *Acting Teachers of America* (New York: Allworth Press, 2007), 51.

GAVIN: The opportunities available to you through technology are unlimited. Technology has become a very important tool to the actor.

Food for Thought

Great camera technique is not great acting, it is great camera technique.

Food for Thought

Every time you feel comfortable, or you finally feel you've got it right, you must be wrong. This is because every moment that you are acting must be unfamiliar to you. Once you learn to get comfortable with being in a state of unfamiliar, it is the most exciting and freeing thing in the world. Who else gets to do that? Who else gets to have a different experience every single day? Actors do not just crave being in front of cameras and being on a stage because they want people to see them. When they are on-camera or on-stage they get the luxury of experiencing something they have never experienced before. You may be on a set or watching a play and seeing performances that appear stale, uninteresting, and totally unbelievable. You say to yourself that they cannot possibly be doing any of the things mentioned here, and you are probably right.

The Diagnosis

The purpose of this assignment is to see good acting as much as you can and to go on to the Internet everyday and see great acting. Watch Uta Hagen, watch Sandy Meisner, watch Grotowski, watch Strasberg, and watch everybody. Do you realize that right at this moment you can study with some of the greatest acting teachers who ever lived? For the first time in history you have the ability to study with almost all of the greatest teachers who ever lived, everyday! If you are not doing it, perhaps it is because nobody has required it of you before. It finally puts the control in the hands of the actor. The control of technique, the control of you getting good, is in your hands. Getting better is the simplest thing in the world, but it doesn't make it good. Watch great actors as often as you can and you will see good. You can watch almost all of the greatest actors that have ever walked the face of the earth.

If you want to work you have to be good. If you are not good you might be lucky, and you might get a few crumbs in your life. You might even have a semi-career as a product, but everyone knows you are not good. Do you understand what we are saying? This is an assignment that makes you good, and you should not be interested in settling for being better. People insist on getting better, and why would you waste your time settling for this? You avoid getting good and you satisfy yourself by getting better. If you do this assignment on a continual basis, then eventually you will start to see things that you have never seen before. Just look at what you could do if you didn't say, "I like this great teacher better than this great teacher." Why don't you look and see how together they can make you good? Look at each person and say, "That from her could make me good, that from him could make me good," and take from them as much as you can. You have to find a way to perceive what is good. If you look at these great teachers long enough, if you listen to what they are saying long enough, if you find out and discover what is the same in them, then eventually you will get good.

What we are getting at is you now know how to go in the direction of good. It's not for you to decide or define what good is, it's for you to discover and recognize what good is. Do you know how much time and money you would have had to spend before to see everything? With the advancement of technology you can practically bring everything to your own doorstep. The advice of many of the greatest acting teachers who have ever lived, and many of the greatest actors who have ever lived, is there for the taking. Do everything in your power to walk down the right street rather than getting constantly pulled in the wrong direction.

Food for Thought

In discussing theatre, Antonin Artaud says in his book *The Theatre and Its Double,* "Therefore I propose a theatre where violent physical images pulverize, mesmerize the audience's sensibilities, caught in the drama as if in a vortex of higher forces."[26] The actor in a film has such a sense of the audience. The leap of faith is that when an audience is sitting in their homes or at the theatre, they believe that the actor they are looking at is speaking to them. Why do we think the art of acting is different on film (notice we did not say the *technicalities*)? A painter is talking to an audience and they are not there, the composer is talking to an audience and they are not there. In terms of film, the painter, the composer, and the actor are all the same because they are all talking to someone who is not there. By a leap of faith, technique, and an understanding of technique, they have to speak to that audience. The camera lens is as much your audience as the stage in front of it can be an audience of millions.

Food for Thought

I know many actors who have been handed scene changes while the audience is sitting there and they are about to go on-camera. One of my colleagues quickly went into the ladies room with the other actor and ran the lines. There was no rehearsal, no blocking, and they did it the first time on-camera in front of an audience. When we talk about preparation, do you hear what we are saying? An actor is preparing every day of their life. Background work is not an actor and is not a performer because they will take absolutely anybody — they don't care. Many aspiring actors turn their noses up at background work, and I do not want to encourage you to make a career of this; however, let's take stock of the situation. Don't kid yourself, here is your choice: You can go to an on-camera workshop or you can work background on a movie set. If you have a choice, where are you going to learn the most? Everything that is happening on the film set is happening for real, and under real circumstances. You have the opportunity to be in the real situation. If you do work background on a set, pick up everything you can and pay attention to as much as you can. You need to know exactly why you are doing it. We are in no way recommending you spend an extended period of time doing this, but you can certainly add it to your preparation. Someone is always going to tell you, "Do this, don't do that." In the end you are going to have to decide what is of most value and most benefit to you.

Final Thoughts

Go on the Internet and search acting on any and all search engines. Then it is up to you to find the one that gives you the most answers. Think of the possibilities available to you that were not available to the millions of actors who came before you.

---

26. Antonin Artaud, *The Theatre and Its Double* (London: Calder Publications Ltd., 1993), 63.

Chapter 4:
Fix Yourself, Then Use Yourself

14. Energy In, Energy Out

Food for Thought

Most senior actors are so accomplished in their technique that they stick exclusively to their technique. An accomplished actor wants to give every ounce of their energy, every moment to the production. Sometimes actors seem unsociable, but they are not unsociable at all, they are just doing their work. Novice or young actors sometimes get caught up in the social and it is their acting that suffers. There is also the young actor who says, "I'm going to put every effort I have into the part and nothing else. I'm not going to worry about my social standing, or my intelligence. I'm just going to concentrate on the part." Very often they look like a loner, and unsociable. They are unsociable because they are there to work. They are called a working actor, not a social actor, and not a posing actor. The actor must ask not only, "What do I want, and what does the character want?" but, "How do I make the audience listen?" The work it takes to create a great part takes all of the actor's focus and concentration.

Food for Thought

Science now tells us that, medically speaking, only about one person in a hundred thousand can think two thoughts at the same time. Most of us can only think one thought at a time; however, we get so we can alternate between these thoughts so rapidly as if there is electricity, or a line of energy between them. When an actor is thinking, they are not thinking two thoughts at the same time; therefore, the actor learns to alternate between thoughts so rapidly that they appear to become one, and that, my dears, is called *subtext*. Some actors are open and able to move between their thoughts so rapidly that we say, "How could she do so many things, think so many things at one time?" I have seen actors on-stage and thought to myself, "They are thinking so loud that they are shouting at me!" Alternating between thoughts at a rapid pace opens the pathway for a heightened imagination.

The Ingredients

In this exercise we want you to look at an object or a person and think of energy going from your body toward it. Now let's do a little thing to prove that this exists. Take your hand and put the flat part of your palm as close as you can to your cheek without actually touching your cheek. Now, when you get pretty close you will eventually begin to feel heat. I'm not quite sure whether the heat is going from your hand to your face or from your face to the hand. However, what I do know is that something called heat is going from one place to another. Something is always going towards you and something is always going from you. As actors we have to take that heat and we have to get in control of it. Now if you take your hand way out to the side, still facing your cheek, you may find you cannot feel the heat. Go to where you can feel the heat and start to move your hand further and further away. Whenever you find you can't feel the heat, stay right there and practice. Say to yourself, "I'm going to intensify the energy coming from my hand to my face. I'm going to intensify the energy going from my face to my hand."

Now I want you to work this with a partner. Stand very close and face your partner. I want you to look at your partner and draw their energy towards you, just by using your thoughts. As you look at them, I want you to think, "energy in," or "energy out." Then I want you to send energy to them just by using your thoughts. I want you to do both. See if you can also feel the heat from your partner to you. If you find it is working well, you can stand further apart and continue. There is no time limit, you can work for thirty seconds or five minutes just going back and forth. If you are on your own, then you can simply work the hand to the cheek part of this exercise. Stay very focused for this exercise so you can experience it with maximum effect. If you do half an exercise you will only experience half of the results.

Food for Thought

There is a story about a very famous writer who, on her deathbed, said words to the effect of, "What's the answer?" Everyone looked at each other and didn't know what to say, and she said, "Alright then, then what's the question?" and died. In other words, she was creating that energy until she died. This is why you can see famous actors in movies, in the West End of London, and on Broadway well into their eighties. These actors never let up, and they never stop being an actor.

Food for Thought

I remember a very distinguished lady who saw Nureyev, the famous ballet star, in one of his later performances and she said, "You know, he doesn't have what he had before. He wasn't really very good." I missed my opportunity to say, "That's all right that you say that, but do you realize that you are speaking about one of the greatest dancers that ever lived in the history of dance? Do you realize that? Tell me that you realize that before you tell me that he's not very good. Are you saying he's not very good for one of the most famous dancers in the history of the world?" You often hear people who don't know what they are talking about if they don't know what acting is. By the way, these types of people are usually networking and socializing, so you need to take everything they say very cautiously and lightly. If a person is misinformed, but is insistent they are right, you may choose to let them think they are right. Use your energy wisely and put it where it is of most benefit to you. Pick your battles.

The Diagnosis

I have to assume that if I had enough heat in me it would go from me to the audience, and if I had enough strength I could pull the heat from them. Isn't it interesting that when you walk past a person you might say to yourself, "She is really hot." I can only assume that you were getting heat from that person. We also say things such as, "I was in this meeting and things really heated up." When you are working with other actors during a performance you might really feel very attracted to them or you may feel repulsed by them; however, these are luxuries the actor cannot afford. As an actor, you have to act on what you notice and use it. Actors need to be completely aware of everything around them and also be in control of everything around them. Famous musicians have stopped in the middle of performances and asked the audience to give them their attention. I have seen actors stop in the middle of a performance and say, "Stop talking." I don't know whether I approve of it, but I have witnessed it. In this exercise you are making something happen between you and another, and acting is when something happens between you and another person. You have to make an audience love you, hate you, be confused by you, be repulsed by you, and there is a technique for doing this. If you cannot activate the audience's interest, you will never get to this stage. If there is no energy between you and your audience, then you are not acting. You cannot push your performance upon the audience, you must allow it to be absorbed and engulfed by them so they can respond in kind.

Food for Thought

I like the word *decompress* much better than the word *relax,* because the word relax is more often than not interpreted to mean *collapse.* Collapse also disallows energy from moving through the body. Occasionally I say to the actor, "Now I am going to ask you to do something that you can do only for this moment and that you must not do ever again. I want you to collapse the arm. I've tried everything else and it hasn't worked. You're trying so hard to help me that we are just not communicating. I am just going to ask you to collapse that arm." I don't want an actor, as a general rule, to collapse, because to collapse is to take energy out of the actor. The actor discovers what not to do on both a physical and visceral level.

Food for Thought

We often hear people say, "Acting is larger than life," or "Acting is a heightened reality," but to a great actor it is not. That is who they are, and where they live all the time. When they go to a party they are that way, when they go shopping they are that way. Most successful actors cannot be anything else. It's amazing that so many actors walk in to start a scene or an audition, and when they talk about acting they sound so passionate, so excited, so engaging, and then they begin the scene and they start to mumble, they pause, and all their passion and energy disappears. Unfortunately, many actors are smaller than life, in a diminished reality. This is a serious malaise and disastrous for actors because it's wrong and it's not going to get anyone anywhere. When asked the question, "What is acting?" you will most likely find a hundred definitions from a hundred different actors. Ivana Chubuck points out that acting is, "A complex and elusive art to define."[27]

Final Thoughts

An actor is an athlete physically, emotionally, and intellectually. Each and every exercise must increase the potential of at least one of these areas. Although this exercise begins as a physical exercise, the actor will find that it will quickly move into an emotional exercise as the actor feels the connection between himself and others. The actor's intellect and imagination will be stimulated by the limitless choices of any situation. This exercise gives the actor the potential to grow and explore physically.

15. Scanning the Body

Food for Thought

By beginning over and over continuously we have a fresh energy. One second after we begin, it begins to deteriorate. The simplest thing in the world is to begin again. You are continuing to start with a clean slate.

Food for Thought

If you went to an acting school and learned to act, and then you went to sleep one night and when you woke up your head and mind were in a different person's body, you would have to learn all over because your thoughts wouldn't work from that body. Try this: go from driving a car, to riding a bicycle, to roller skating, to skateboarding, to running, to skiing, to climbing a mountain, and to stilts. Do this with the same mind, the same body, the same education, the same desires, the same passions, and you'd have to learn to use your body differently. Coordination is an ongoing process because we are not highly coordinated in all that we do.

---

27. Ivana Chubuck, *The Power of the Actor* (New York: Gotham Books, 2004), Intro.

The Ingredients

This exercise is inspired by the work of Moshe Feldenkrais. Find a place on the floor, and lie on your back. Put your feet a little wider than your hips. Put your arms five or six inches away from your hips, moving them up towards your ears. Be aware of what is going on in your body and ask yourself "How do my legs feel? How do my shoulders feel?" etc.

You may notice that one shoulder is higher off the ground than the other, but don't try to fix it because nothing is wrong. Just imagine you have two fingers at your spine and that you are going to push those fingers up the length of your body to the top of your head. Take about ten seconds to do this, and when you have done that, use your imagination to push them back down the other way. Now, start with the fingers at your right hip and push them down towards your heel, going down the length of your leg. Some people like to flex their foot just as they are passing the heel. Once you get all the way down the length of one leg, send them back up the leg towards the hip. Now do the same thing with your other leg. Now put two fingers in your right shoulder coming down towards the middle finger. Just send the energy down that arm, and when it's done, turn it around and send it back up the other way. Do this with the other arm. There's no hurry to do this.

We want you to get up now, but we don't want you to disturb anything, so we want you to roll to one side or the other and get into a fetal position. Then gently come up on your knees and move up slowly so that you end up sitting with your legs crossed. Use your arms to carefully push yourself up. There are only three things you can do with any technique: You can stretch, strengthen, and coordinate. Processing moving a muscle is a thought that is literally returned back to the brain to say "I did what you asked me to do." By centering the body, you simply put yourself in more of a connective state to use for whatever it needs to do. In terms of body awareness, Litz Pisk comments, "You inhabit your body by your presence in it and by your awareness of it."[28] Paul uses this exercise in part to have his actors become centered, balanced, and aware. This is an excellent exercise for actors to find themselves in a creative state.

Food for Thought

When an actor is embarrassed to do a scene, a role, or an acting exercise it is a sign of a weakness in their acting because an actor shouldn't be embarrassed to do anything. You have to be the actor who says, "I can do that." You want to make sure that you don't learn to out-think yourself. As the famous director Peter Brooke says, "It is always a mistake for actors to begin their work with intellectual discussion, as the rational mind is not nearly as potent an instrument of discovery as the more secret faculties of intuition."[29]

Food for Thought

Isn't it absurd that actors are often encouraged to only study one technique and nothing else? Famous Broadway directors once went to visit Stanislavski and watch him work. As the story goes, Stanislavski turned to them and said, "I hope you are not doing what I'm doing. I hope you are creating your own work and finding new things." Great people change their minds because they continue to grow. As Lee Strasberg said in regards to his own journey, "I was still obsessed with finding out as much as I could about the problem of the actor. Even today there is still no serious history of acting, so I had to search for and find my way through material largely on my own."[30] Open up to all the resources available to you as an actor. Why limit yourself to only one technique when there are so many pearls waiting for you just around the corner? We are of the belief of the *everyman* technique. During your lifetime,

---

28. Litz Pisk, *The Actor and His Body* (New York: Theatre Arts Books, 1976), 11.
29. Alison Hodge, *Twentieth Century Actor Training* (New York: Routledge, 2000), 179.
30. Lee Strasberg, *A Dream of Passion*, (New York: A Plume Book, 1987), 29.

become familiar with as many techniques as possible, use what works, and disregard the rest. All great acting teachers want you to reach the point where you are able to become your own teacher. Now you have to decide what it is going to take to allow that to become a possibility. Your search and growth as an actor should never end, as is mentioned in the book *The Japanese Stage,* "The theatre ... is, even now, evolving by the moment."[31]

The Diagnosis

PAUL: Now I want you to ask yourself, "Do I feel any different from when I started this exercise?" How do you feel more different?

ACTOR 1: I feel more light and aware of myself.

PAUL: Anything you can do to get out of your own way is a positive step. How do you feel different?

ACTOR 2: I have much more body to surface ratio on the ground.

PAUL: I see. Here is a fun thing to think about: I have people say to me, "I have a natural curve in my back." I say, "Why don't you think about this, if you took all the muscles out of your back, would it still be in that state or would it fall down to the floor?" It's the muscles that are keeping it held in that state and most of us don't even know that. How do you feel?

ACTOR 3: I feel much more centered.

PAUL: So notice the difference and whatever the difference is between this and that is what you learned. The point is I never ask questions I do not know the answer to or I would not be a very good teacher. So I will ask you the question so that you feel your answers.

GAVIN: Paul makes an excellent point here. He chooses not to give his actors all the answers. Instead, he lets them make their own discoveries so that they can become independent, freethinking actors. He is not looking to create robots, but rather actors who know how to think for themselves. In respect to answers Joseph Chaikin says, "The best answers are those that destroy the question."[32]

Food for Thought

The idea of acting for some actors is to isolate. They tell themselves, "Now I'm speaking, now I'm moving, now I'm motivated, now I'm thinking, and now I'm releasing." They do not act holistically. Instead of giving a flow to their bodies, they stop almost everything in their body in order to act. When you do that your body has decided you are more real, you are in the moment, and you're more serious than if you are keeping everything from happening. That is not stillness, it is inhibiting you as an actor. You have to have fluidity about you so that your mind and body can move in any direction.

Food for Thought

I used to take a group of actors into schools to give an example of what acting was as a technique, a profession, and an art form. By engaging the different elements that make up your acting you can develop all these areas simultaneously. I once had a group of five actors. Of them, one became a famous director, one married the cop who held John Lennon as he died, and one became a famous actor. We asked the children a simple question, "What do actors use to paint?" They said, "Their bodies." We asked them, "What do they paint on?" They said, "Air and space." And then I said, "What do they measure with?" A young boy raised his hand and all the actors looked at me and looked at the boy because they didn't have a clear answer in their own minds. The boy said, "They measure with time." And he was

31. Ronald Cavaye, Paul Griffith, Akihiko Senda, *A Guide to the Japanese Stage,* (Tokyo: Kodansha International Ltd., 2004), 19.

32. Joseph Chaikin, *The Presence of the Actor* (New York: Theatre Communications Group, 1972), 161.

absolutely right. He just overwhelmed me, and it was the most electrifying moment. We say that an actor must have good timing and yet we have no idea what we are talking about. It's the time it takes to get from one word to another word.

Final Thoughts

Remember that an actor is an athlete physically, emotionally, and intellectually. By the time the audience sees the result of the actor's work, three things have happened: first the thought, then the energy created by the thought, and then the action created by the energy sent to the body. These three things require an extraordinary coordination. This exercise is a simple warm-up in coordinating thought, energy, and action. If it appears simple, it should, so that it can simply open the body. In terms of thought, emotion, and the body, Peter Brook says, "For an actor's intentions to be perfectly clear, within intellectual alertness, true feelings and a balanced and tuned body, the three elements — thought, emotion, body — must be in perfect harmony."[33] Practice, practice, and practice until it becomes automatic for you.

16. Six Awarenesses

Food for Thought

PAUL: If you are standing in the center of the room and your body is pretty well-balanced, which direction can you most likely walk in?

ACTOR: Straight ahead.

PAUL: Any direction. Balance is balance is balance is balance. You have so much going for you because nobody is like you.

GAVIN: Your body and mind have the potential to move in any direction.

Food for Thought

There are some books where the title is so brilliant that the title is fuller than anything that can be in the book. My favorite book title is called *Beyond Freedom and Dignity,* by B.F. Skinner. I love this book title because acting is beyond freedom and dignity. Part of your search takes you beyond. There is no freedom in fear, prejudice, or hate. An actor has to train in such a way that at least on occasion they can be beyond freedom and dignity. You take an acting class because you are looking for freedom, or you take a part in a movie because you are looking for dignity. What would it be like if you didn't have those burdens? The reason great actors are great is because they go beyond freedom and dignity. They don't have time to pause. Great actors don't worry about being free, they just are free. Beyond freedom is when it doesn't even cross your mind. With consistent work, effort, and discovery you can get to the place where freedom and dignity become automatic for you.

The Ingredients

This exercise should follow Energy In, Energy Out. In this exercise, you are going to work with six kinds of awareness. Being aware of something does not mean you have to be right about something, just aware. In order to keep from being judgmental, you are only allowed to use one word. For this exercise, sit opposite a partner so that you are facing one another. This exercise is divided into six stages. Do not skip a step, but rather work through the exercise in its entirety.

External Awareness

The first part is external awareness. You are going to look at your partner and say out loud the awareness you have of them externally. *External awareness* is anything you *see* in one

---

33. Peter Brook, *The Open Door* (New York: Anchor Books, 1993), 19.

word. These are based on their body, what they are wearing, facial expressions, and so on. You have to do them all in one word so you cannot say, "You blink a lot," or "You are wearing a green T-shirt." Rather, you would say, "Blink, green." We only want you to use one word because when you use sentences you become so bogged down with detail that you are no longer aware of the person. You and your partner are going to make your awareness at the same time because you have to exercise your body to get used to making these perceptions without waiting your turn. Allow your vision to become very general so that it encompasses the whole person. If I say, "You are wearing a T-shirt" that is not awareness, it's description that is judging and analyzing. You do not have to work at the same pace as your partner — there is no prize for being first.

ACTOR 1: Elbow, stripe, eye, nose, reflection, neck, ear, tilt, hair, sit, shoulder, lips, beard, shadow, reflection.

ACTOR 2: *(Simultaneously as ACTOR 1)* Red, slant, eye, shirt, leg, hair, sliver, scowl, lines, silver, neck, bumps.

PAUL: Now what you just did was practicing, not judging and analyzing.

Internal Awareness

In this part I am going to use words that some people call emotions, some people call judgments, and some people call psychology. This is why I ask you to use only one word as opposed to, "You look like you are concerned about something right now." This is judging and analyzing, and I have no right to say that because I am not a doctor and there is no need to say it. *Internal awareness* is anything that comes to you or that crosses your mind, not anything you figure out. You are only to use one word at a time as in External Awareness, and this time it is based on how you think the actor facing you ticks.

If you allow it, things will pop in your mind that you had no idea were there, and this is because you have taken away any filters to block this. You don't want rational things, you want random things.

ACTOR 1: Quiet, thoughtful, resistant, blocked, grief, concerned, trying, thoughts, here, happy, confused, perplexed.

ACTOR 2: *(Simultaneously as ACTOR 1)* Comfort, satisfied, thoughtful, pensive, open, caring, alone, insightful, aware, simplistic, kind, attention, pensive.

GAVIN: If you were to write down everything you just said you would most likely say, "Did I say that?" You are trying to not judge and analyze, so in a way you are aiming to not be aware of what you are saying. You are only to be aware of the internal reactions of the person opposite you.

External Awareness of Self

PAUL: I want you to look at your partner here, and while you are looking at your partner you are going to do external awareness of yourself.

ACTOR 1: Hand, knees, squint, stomach, breath, lips, hips, knees, breathe, shoulders, stomach, throat.

ACTOR 2: *(Simultaneously as ACTOR 1)* Knees, nose, eyelids, mouth, nostrils, tears, breathe, arms, hair, lips, gums, ankle.

Internal Awareness of Self

Now you are going to make internal observations of yourself. Be very careful here not to ask yourself, "How do I feel today?" What you are doing here is simply saying words that cross your mind. When we start this exercise, we are all guarded because of what life has taught us and the influence of the environment in which we live such as, "I don't want to tell you secrets I have. I don't want to tell you what my emotion is at the moment," because we have been taught not to tell people any of these things. As you practice this you are just going to say aloud the words about your own internal feelings. Remember, no judging, no analyzing, and saying only one word keeps us from editorializing.

ACTOR 1: Fun, troubled, temper, amused, perplexed, thoughtful, unhappy, wise.

ACTOR 2: *(Simultaneously as ACTOR 1)* Alive, inquisitive, shocking, internal, devastated, gullible, fear, simplistic.

PAUL: Jean-Paul Sartre, the famous playwright, lived in France during the time of the Nazi occupation. In regards to influences on our lives, Dorothy McCall quotes Sartre as saying, "It is neither our fault nor our merit if we lived in a time when torture was a daily fact. Chateaubriant, Oradour, the Rue des Saussaies, Tulle, Dachau, and Auschwitz have all demonstrated to us that Evil is not an appearance, that knowing its cause does not dispel it."[34]

GAVIN: Some people use the phrase, "larger than life," yet nothing is larger than life.

External Awareness of the Audience

External awareness of the audience is drawn from anybody who is not your scene partner. If you are on-stage, then everyone else on the stage with you who is not your scene partner is the audience. The same applies to when you are on a set. As your scene partner changes in each scene, so does the audience, and this builds threads between all of you. Augusto Boal explains the relationship between the actor and the audience when he states, "In the theatre of the oppressed, the oppressed are the subject. Theatre is their language."[35]

As you are on a set or stage you can make observations of the audience. You might notice a lot of people in the audience wearing blue and the word "blue" crosses your mind. Remember, the audience is anyone on the stage or set who is not your scene partner. You can also work this exercise if you are in a coffee shop by yourself. Simply choose a scene partner and make everyone else the audience. They do not have to know they are your scene partner.

Internal Awareness of the Audience

Internal awareness of the audience is done in the same way as Internal Awareness of Self, except this time anyone who is not your scene partner is the audience. This means you can have multiple awarenesses of different people at the same time.

Food for Thought

An actor may not need sincerity or even integrity in their social life, but they do need it in their art. I've known famous actors to lie, cheat, steal, to be heavily on drugs, or to not pay attention to their own mental and physical health, but when they acted they were perfect in their integrity, they were perfect in their intent, and they had no thought in their mind but to act. By the way, these kinds of actors don't go to class to network or be social. The most an individual who takes a class for their resumé could hope to be is a saleable commodity. We don't know why you want to be an actor. We don't know if you love acting, but you do.

Food for Thought

Great actors and great acting is great actors and great acting. To be a great actor you have to do very dangerous things. You have to think thoughts and do things that are not socially or morally acceptable, and you have to let those things course through your body. You have to let those thoughts be in your mind when you are constantly told by everybody

---

34. Dorothy McCall, *The Theatre of Jean-Paul Sartre* (New York: Columbia University Press, 1969), 43.
35. Augusto Boal, *The Rainbow of Desire* (London: Routledge, 1995), 188.

not to think or be that. Great acting teachers and great acting coaches will coach anybody in any part because it is acting. Somebody once asked me, "Why don't we have great actors anymore?" There are possibly more great actors today than ever before. Somebody asked me once, "Why aren't there more people like Plato, Aristotle, and Socrates today?" I said, "There are hundreds and thousands of people like them today. In the world of that day there were so few people like them, so it was very easy to see them." You have to have an extremely wide, extremely deep comfort zone.

The Diagnosis

You are asked to make your awareness at the same time as your partner. One of the reasons for this is related to when you are working on a scene or a performance, where some actors actually wait for their turn. In other words, they may think, "You say your line and then I'll say my line, now I'm talking, and now I'm waiting." You can't do that. You have to act all the time so that when you are not talking, you are actively listening and responding to what is being said.

In each part of this exercise you are being asked to not judge or analyze. Everything in our life teaches us to judge and analyze, and as an actor you want thoughts to cross your mind randomly. We want to exercise it in this way so that we can put ourselves in a state to accept things randomly. How can an actor be creative unless they can accept things randomly, not rationally? Acting is not a rational thing, it's a random thing, so practice at being random. Random thoughts can lead to a further utilization of your imagination. As imagination is vital to the actor, this can only be of benefit to you.

In regards to Internal Awareness, think about a time in life, when perhaps you were at a party, and you met someone and you said to yourself, "I don't know why I don't trust them." In other words, you have made an internal awareness, or *trust*. Because acting is pretty much against anything we have been taught socially, think about this: You are not supposed to speak every thought that crosses your mind. If we are not allowed to speak it, most of the time we stop ourselves from thinking. But if you start exercising by letting anything cross your mind, then as you are acting and playing the part, things will begin to impulsively cross your mind during a performance. You will start to find that if you utilize the exercise often enough, you will start to make discoveries in your characters while performing.

The reason awareness will cross your mind is because you are feeding those vibes, those words, those thoughts, and because you are able to accept random thoughts you are able to make discoveries that you have not made before. When you get a technique that works for you in your acting you will find yourself saying, "I can't wait to play that role, it doesn't frighten me, because my mind and body are ready, and I can't wait to see what will happen when I play that role."

You may already have a scene partner, yet choose to make someone else your scene partner. In other words, just because you are talking to someone, it does not necessarily make them your scene partner. Let's say you have gone out with a friend and you are talking to him, but behind you is a really striking woman. In your mind she is now your scene partner.

Think about how you can apply this to any scene you are in. Talking to someone does not necessarily make them your scene partner. In this exercise you are not being asked to act logically, but to act emotionally, by instinct and by the moment. An actor who says they are giving the exact same performance each night is incorrect because you are not the exact same person today that you were yesterday. It is not good enough that an actor works with these exercises, but it is also necessary that you see the relevance to your life and how they integrate into your work as an actor.

Food for Thought

An acting class should prominently be about the use of the instrument, not the result of the use. If an athlete keeps running every day, eventually they will reach a plateau. If, on the other hand, they break down the different elements of what it is to run by lifting weights, eating right, sleeping right, clearing their mind, and training right, then eventually they will get faster. This is because they have worked on the nature of the instrument. For a certain period of time very good acting schools would say "We will not allow you to do scenes or a play. We are only going to work on the body, the voice, and the nature of the instrument during this time." We think the mistake that can be made is that they go through the motions, and at the end of the year, or however long it is, you are allowed to go ahead even if the instrument is not ready. Because you are not ready, when you go ahead you will not be very good at what you are doing. Then they will say, "You are a very nice person, the problem is you're just not talented." And that is, to quote Shakespeare, "The most unkindest cut of all." It is also incorrect and brutal because we know many people who weren't good at one time and then became brilliant afterward. That is because they concentrated on the use of the instrument. A personal trainer will help you to put extra focus on the areas of your body that are the weakest. Diagnose which areas of your acting are the weakest and put extra time, effort, and focus here.

Food for Thought

Acting activates every cell, nerve, neuron, and everything that happened to your DNA a million years ago as well as everything that will happen a million years from now. If we didn't believe that, we wouldn't be interested in acting. If acting didn't include something more than we could ever comprehend, we don't think we would want to pursue it. Acting is so incredible that it gives an audience the potential to experience anything that will ever happen in the history of the world. That is why we call acting *the human condition*. It takes an incredible amount of intensity and passion to truly be an actor.

Final Thoughts

Science tells us that a person is only capable of thinking one thought at a time, beyond that there may be one person in a hundred thousand who can think more than one thought at a time. This exercise trains the ability to alternate between thoughts, between the six awarenesses. As the actor repeats the exercise they develop the ability to alternate between all of these thoughts so rapidly that it appears to the audience, and perhaps to the actor themselves, that they are thinking all of these thoughts simultaneously. Actually, they are practicing alternating between thoughts. What we call subtext, depth, and creative spirit is really an actor alternating between numerous thoughts so rapidly that we can't keep up with them and we are overwhelmed by their performance. You are training your mind to be open to a constant flow of thoughts, which in turn creates a flow of ideas.

17. Child's Play

Food for Thought

What do you do if the director or script supervisor says it is written "huh" and you cannot change it? You have a dilemma sometimes in life where you are right and the director can be wrong. You have to learn to handle it at that moment. Remember, part of acting is learning how to adapt to any given situation. The point is, even if the playwright or screenwriter said, "I want it pronounced *huh*," he has no right to say that, because it is not a word. He has a right to have you say every word the way it is written, but "huh" is not a word, it is a sound.

If a director or anyone else insists you do that, then they are asking you to do it as you and not the character. By letting the entire line influence the sounds you make would not be the sounds you would make under those circumstances, they would be the sounds the character would make under those circumstances. You have a right, at that point, to say to a director, "I don't know how to make that sound." If he is that specific, and has an exact idea in mind, then it is what you will have to do. It is hard to do that sometimes, but that is the art of acting. See how you can naturally integrate sounds into a performance as we do in life.

Food for Thought

Child actors are, generally speaking, people who want to act and who want to tell stories at a very young age. Not only do they want to tell stories, they recognize that they have a certain success at it, so they repeat it. Children don't repeat an awful lot of things where they don't have success. Adults are the ones who repeat things when they are not successful. Children are better coordinated than adults. As they get older they think they have lost it but they haven't, it is just that their mind and coordination is now in a different body. As children we are generally uninhibited with vast imaginations. It is only as young adults that we seem to subdue what was given to us by Mother Nature. The actors cannot afford to allow their creativity and imaginations to be suppressed.

The Ingredients

Here is another exercise that you can do on your own or with friends. It is going to appear to be fun and games, although you are working on your instrument, so it is not just fun and games. What we want you to do is hand clapping games. If you are by yourself, you can sit with a chair up close to a wall. If you have a friend, then you can stand or sit facing each other. Start off with a very simple clapping rhythm and then allow them to become more elaborate. Once you have done the activity for a minute or so, add a monologue, scene, poem, or dialogue at the same time. You can make the songs up or use well-known ones, such as, "A sailor went to sea, to see what he could see, see, see. But all that he could see, see, see was the bottom of the deep blue sea, sea, sea." You can also get a jump rope and do jump rope rhymes as well. You can also make a hopscotch grid and play hopscotch. In reference to playing, Viola Spolin, the theatre games guru says, "Let the playing build up your inner strength, your vast incredible potential."[36] It starts with the games first, then gradually add your monologue or scene into what you are doing. Do not stop the game to do the monologue, it should be happening simultaneously. You must have the ability to multitask.

Food for Thought

The only way you can create is if you and those who you are working with can agree on a common language. A very famous acting teacher once said, "Theatre is not about conflict, it is about agreement." There is conflict in the story, but actors aren't better when they don't get along, they are better when they find something to agree on. Surround yourself with and seek out like-minded people. Seek out really good actors, alive or dead, and borrow from them.

Food for Thought

It's difficult to devote yourself to anything that has a serious technique and a challenge to it because to get it takes concentration, devotion, and enormous repetition. A big challenge is that nobody is going to demand that you do it. It's easier to work in a factory because you go and you do the same things every day. Many people say they would never want to do a job like that, and yet factory workers can be healthier than many because they have

---

36 Viola Spolin, *Theatre Games for the Lone Actor* (Illinois: Northwestern University Press, 2001), 5.

scheduled lives. They repeat exactly the same thing every day and they learn to like it. Great artists mysteriously, magnificently make a decision to live an artist life under any condition. Once they have made that decision, the repetition of it becomes not only easy, but also joyful. When you get success, when you begin to build technique from the repetition, then it gets rather like working out at a gym and you get the equivalent of endorphins. In the best of terms, it's addicting. If you follow a particular regimen in studying acting, your body, your mind, your heart, and your soul will begin to crave that. It not only becomes easier, it becomes something you love and can't live without. If your first thought of acting was, "It's probably an easy way to make a lot of money," we probably wouldn't have anything else to talk about. Acting is a noble art, a noble profession, and actors have made enormous contributions to societies and cultures across the globe.

The Diagnosis

Exercises such as these can be a great warm-up for you to do. These exercises are telling your body that it must work for you whenever you speak, and that is why you are asked to add the dialogue. We are taught not to bang, make noise, or be very physical, so we become disconnected from our bodies. Think about the small child who is banging on the floor and having fun when she is told by her mother, "Stop doing that!" What they should do if it starts driving them crazy is do it with you. We have to learn this. At first you may think, "I can do the clapping or I can do the dialogue, and in order to do the dialogue I have to concentrate." No, in order to do the dialogue you have to stop thinking and this exercise encourages you in this direction. Your muscles have to get a new relationship with you. This exercise encourages you to multitask and work on more than one thing at the same time. Think about this: To stand on one foot uses numerous muscles, it does not just use one muscle. For you to stand on one foot, your muscles are making all kinds of adjustments to stay there. Think for a moment about all of the things you have to do on a set or stage. You cannot do them all at once, but you can move between them at lightning speed.

Food for Thought

Do you know how many potential distractions there are on-set? As Stanislavski says in reference to creativity, "When you look for something you have lost, more often than not you find it in an unexpected place. The same is true with creativeness. You must send your scouting mind off in all directions."[37] If you have not already, develop a keen and inquisitive mind.

Food for Thought

Once our body is matured and has stopped growing it is still many more years until our brain has stopped growing and maturing. The human body has organs that mature at different rates. When a baby is born the reason it can't eat certain foods is because its system is not completed inside yet. The only time that you can use your body the same way two days in a row is if there's not a possibility that it has changed or has grown. Later in life your body begins to deteriorate and you have to learn it all over again, because you are dealing with a different body. The complexities of the human body mean the possibilities are endless.

Final Thoughts

Some research has implied that one of the reasons some children do not mature evenly or properly is that they haven't done the full spectrum of motion that other children have done. Many of the games children play are very important for coordination of mind and body. The purpose of children's games is to give children coordination and to challenge them. An adult may have more trouble than they think doing, "Pat-a-cake, pat-a-cake." Don't think that these are just for a child. They are also excellent for the coordination of the actor. Children remind

---

37. Constantin Stanislavski, *Creating a Role* (New York: Routledge, 1961), 11.

us how to pretend. They pretend with such congruency and a vivid imagination that we forget they are pretending.

18. Sing Us a Song

Food for Thought

The best part of teaching, metaphorically speaking, is locking somebody up because you are going to change their perceptions. Teaching is behavior modification whether you do it yourself or not. A good teacher enables the actor to make shifts in awareness.

Food for Thought

When you work with an exercise, make sure you work it to the best of your ability. If you do a little percentage of an exercise you are not only *not* doing the exercise at all, you are training yourself to do it *incorrectly*. If you do less than one hundred percent, you are training yourself to do the exercise improperly. If you find you are doing an exercise and it's not working, stop doing that exercise until you are at a level of understanding as to where it can be effective for you. When you teach your body something incorrectly, that's what it's going to do. Once you have learned an exercise incorrectly it is going to be that much more difficult to unlearn it. These exercises are designed for you to work at your own pace to create the maximum benefits.

The Ingredients

In this exercise you are asked to sing a song; however, it is not about singing, it's not about training your voice. It has to do with the coordination of your muscles and your emotion. We would like you to spend at least five or ten minutes on this exercise. This exercise is not as beneficial for trained singers because they know how to block things. What we would like you to do is sing a song one note at a time, and hold each note you sing until you run out of breath. Then pause, let air come into your body, and sing the next note until you run out of breath. You also have to do this at your maximum level of projection without straining or damaging your throat. To do this with a complete song would take a very long time. We advise you to pick a short song or just work with part of a song. If you pick Handel's *Messiah* you will be there the rest of your life!

PAUL: Who would like to have a go?

ACTOR: I'll have a go. Can I sing "Happy Birthday?"

PAUL: No, do you know anything else? How about, *Oh, What a Beautiful Morning?*

ACTOR: I know a little bit of that.

PAUL: *(Sings a few lines of the song.)* Let your arms hang down and loose. Now, in this position, you have no defense. An actor must be defenseless.

ACTOR: Ooooh! *(Sings on one breath.)* Whaaaat!

PAUL: Louder. Louder. Louder. Loud as you can. Next word try to make twice as loud as that. *(ACTOR sings a word.)* Louder, louder, louder. Beeeeutiful! Louder, louder, really loud! *(ACTOR sings another word.)* Louder, louder, much louder. Pick a note quite a bit higher. Better, come on and let it grow and grow and grow. Did that note hurt your throat a little bit, or did it tickle a little bit? OK, you were very wise to stop for a moment. Now pick a comfortable note, find a friendly vowel and a friendly place in your voice and start there. OK, go ahead. *(ACTOR sings a word.)* Louder, louder, much louder. For some reason or other, you can't make it as loud as I think you could. I think right now you have the ability to go much louder. Think that you have long underwear or long johns on, and I want you in your mind's imagination to unbutton all of those buttons and let your stomach fall out.

(ACTOR sings.) There you go, louder, let it keep getting louder. I also think you can hold it longer. *(ACTOR sings another word.)* Better, louder, better. Now some way or other you found a way to make it louder and hold it longer without having vocal training and without hurting your voice. You also gave more thought to your breath. I want to stress again that this is not a singing exercise. This exercise is also great to do with a large group of actors observing because they can begin to see an emotional release and a different kind of coordination. This exercise also works very well for you to do by yourself at home. Remember, I have stated you must work each word on one continual breath at your loudest possible volume. It does not work if you are humming a tune to yourself in the car. You have to go full out. Soon after you start this exercise, something in your body, and your mind, and your emotion will tell you that you want to stop, that you don't want to go on, and it's of benefit to know these things in advance. It's fun for you to learn this, to say, "That doesn't sound logical," and then get up and do it and find out by yourself.

GAVIN: Notice that you are asked to go full out in this exercise. Sometimes you will hear an actor say, "I am saving it for the performance." The challenge is that by the time they get to perform, they forget what they were saving.

Food for Thought

Talent is the passion of human spirit. If an actor is well-trained, passion flows through the entire body and the discoveries become body languages. People have been killed just for mentioning that they are an actor. Nobody said that acting must be renewed. Nobody said that movies, television, or plays have to continue, because sometimes they don't. If you look at financial records for large cities or studios, they might say action is doing well, musicals are doing well, comedies are doing poorly, dramas are doing poorly, etc. The actor is not interested in the financial returns to these studios or cities because it is not what they do for a living. Actors are interested to know that thirty comedies were produced by a studio last year and only eleven this year. Ultimately, acting exists because of the passion of people who want to be actors. Anything we love we justify as needed because we want it to be needed. When everything else around you appears to be falling into disarray, your passion can still be alive and kicking.

Food for Thought

When you read about or observe exercises, the better you get and the more skill you will have at those exercises. You'll be putting them in an order that works for you. You will not do them from exercise one to twenty, you will make up the order. The problem is with thinking about exercises as having an order in which they should be done. The experienced actor, when they get very experienced and trained, will from that point to the rest of their life rarely do anything but the simplest exercises. Actors do this because they are not using the simple exercises in performance. Ian Watson describes the work of the famous Italian director Eugenio Barba by saying, "Since the exercises are less important than how the actor chooses to use them in training for Barba, he has not developed a prescribed body of exercises or systematic hierarchy of information that a neophyte actor has to master in order to perform."[38] You are creating the *everyman technique,* which in effect is the technique specifically tailored for you.

The Diagnosis

The amazing thing with this exercise is that some kind of release happens through your body. Some places where tension is held because of society, thoughts, or perceptions have stopped or slowed you down from feeling something or functioning in a certain way. Let us give you an example of what we mean here. Let us say society teaches you that spitting is a

---

38. Alison Hodge, 212.

terrible, gross habit. If you have a part in an old Western and have to spit into a spittoon, you might not do it because you have been told it's wrong. Even more profoundly, the muscles have rarely done it, and it may surprise you to know that some people can't spit. They actually have to be taught how to spit with conviction. This exercise aims to bring about coordination within the body. The point of this exercise is to make your body more responsive to your thoughts. You might think that touching or talking to someone you barely know is wrong, but an actor cannot think like this because your character might not think like this.

You have to be open to anything and everything. One thing this exercise allows your body to do is to respond in a clear way without judgment. You won't make any of these discoveries by reading this book, just get up and work through the exercises! If you ask an actor, "How are you planning your career?" the first thing they do is get defensive. Nothing frightens an actor, and nothing can make an actor defensive because they cannot respond to their thoughts. This is one of the great things happening in this exercise.

Let me give you another way in which this exercise is useful. A primary difference between a very experienced actor and a very inexperienced actor is that an inexperienced actor is in their body, their mind, and their emotions can build up. Some of it is stage fright, but more than that, the majority of it is what they have been taught not to do or think. An experienced actor has many years of training and dedication, and now they have jumped that hurdle. They can say or think anything, and this gives them a tremendous range and flexibility. This exercise is a step in the direction of training your body and mind to let go of your restrictions. It brings about a release and it allows you to think any thought, to make any sound — it is so simple. As you work with this exercise, you will find that your body will start to give up things that held it back. It will start to take away emotional and physical barriers. As a working actor, you cannot have any barriers that get in the way of your work. You have to be capable of doing anything and everything it takes to win.

Food for Thought

Actors are often told that they need to get rid of tension. I have seen ballerinas hold their arms out for fifteen minutes without any tension. There is a difference between tension and collapsing. As an actor we do not want you to collapse, but let go. To relax completely will create lethargy in the body. That is not a conducive place from which to work.

Food for Thought

Get lines from your play or lines that you are going to have to say to somebody and slip them into a conversation. It's a great exercise. If you take lines from a script such as, "Yeah, and then I jumped backwards four times and had to blow my nose," you may wonder how you are going to drop that into a conversation. Just try one day and you may find that nobody notices it. See how acting can be integrated into your lifestyle. It is important for the actor to realize that you can work on your acting whenever and wherever you choose. This can open up a whole new set of possibilities for the actor. As Uta Hagen explains, "When you look at paintings, put yourself into them instead of looking at them."[39] In other words, integrate your acting into many areas of your life.

Final Thoughts

An actor cannot be limited by habits. The only way of breaking these habits is to do something to the body that doesn't allow it to respond in any way that it has ever responded before. One way to do that is to sing a song one note at a time and hold it for as long as you can. This exercise not only has nothing to do with singing, but it will also most likely not work with a highly trained singer because they can do this effortlessly. This exercise is one way of

---

39. Uta Hagen, *Respect for Acting* (New York: Macmillan Publishing Company, 1973), 31.

acting the habits in your body and you telling your body, "I will not let you do anything I do not want you to do." When it is functioning with no habits, your body is open to respond in different ways. It is open to discovering new ways of solving problems, new ways of thinking about things, new ways of breathing, and new ways of using your imagination. We have often seen actors get very irritable, and we have often seen actors cry simply because their body is not used to doing what it is told. This is an exercise to get you out of your limited habits and into infinite possibility. This exercise may make you feel silly, or ridiculous, or humiliated, which you must get over immediately, if not sooner, in order to study acting. As your instrument begins to break through barriers, it will begin to become more responsive to the stimuli around it.

19. Body Bio

Food for Thought

Acting is perhaps the only art form where your limitation becomes your uniqueness. The actor's greatest contribution to the arts is their uniqueness. What an actor is trying to do is build a technique on their body. You can't build a four-minute mile on everyone's body, you can't build a famous basketball player on everybody's body, but you can build a brilliant actor on anybody's body. We have all sizes, shapes, and all kinds of people acting. There are people much too short, much too big, much too beautiful, much too homely, and yet people such as these have always had a special way of presenting themselves and thus become actors. Good actors come in all shapes and sizes. Good actors are very beautiful and not so beautiful.

Food for Thought

We know in physical therapy that the body is made up of corresponding muscles that keep it in balance. If one muscle is weakened by an accident or by an illness, not only does that muscle have to be strengthened, but the counter muscle to it also has to be strengthened. People that develop one muscle doing only one activity will often weaken another part of their body. Perhaps you have a strong voice or your movements are well-coordinated. Learn to strengthen the weakest areas of your instrument so you can become rounded.

The Ingredients

What we would like you to do is take a piece of paper and a pencil and stand in front of a mirror. On one side of the page we would like you to write everything that you like about yourself. On the other side of the page write everything that you don't like about yourself, but that column has two sides. It's got everything that you don't like about yourself *and* what can be done about it. Basically, you have, "What I Like" and "What I Don't Like and What can be Done about It." When you are writing down things you dislike, do not worry about whether there is something that can be done about it. Do not say, "I shouldn't dislike that because nothing can be done about it" Be honest with yourself.

Study your body and what it's really capable of, what it really looks like, what instruments you have, what attributes you have, and what failings you have. You may say "I like my hair color, it really suits me. I like my feet and their shape. I like my eyes and the way they catch the light. I like my lips, which are full." You may say, "I don't like my toenails because they are dirty and uneven. I don't like my belly. I don't like my ears. I don't like my teeth because they stick out too much. I don't like my thighs." Now you want to say what can be done about it. "Toenails: Get them manicured. Belly: Exercise more. Nose: Save money to get it changed." Now you have taken care of that. When you are not thinking about your nose, people are not looking at your nose. In other words, decide what can be done and what cannot be changed, and learn to live with those parts.

We gave you a few short examples, but you can go into great detail with this exercise, and you can say everything you like or dislike about your hair. The next step to this exercise is to stand in front of a mirror and do the exercise with your clothes off. You are going to do exactly the same thing, except this time you are naked and are looking at your entire body. If you are uncomfortable standing in front of a mirror naked looking at your entire body, toenail by toenail, then you might have trouble being an actor. The next step to this exercise is to sit down with a very good friend or another actor and tell them what you like or dislike about yourself and how you are going to fix it. You are not asking for their opinion about you. It is also important that you work with a person you trust. Once you have finished, you can alternate.

As the final part of this exercise, we would like you to take your list and read it to a blank wall. If you do not have a partner, then you can move straight to this stage. We are not recommending you get plastic surgery. In certain circumstances, corrective surgery may be of benefit to you. The challenge for an actor who engages in a lot of plastic surgery is they are unable to move many of their facial muscles to their full extent. Think about how that would affect the work of the actor. Remember that this exercise is encouraging you to be who you are, not someone else.

Food for Thought

Muscles are dumb, but nervous systems are brilliant, and nervous systems are sensitive. Muscles are so dumb that if you take two needles, put them more than six inches apart, touch them to a person's back, and you ask the person how many needles there are, they will always say one. The muscles do not compute the difference. While the human body is quite incredible, it also has the ability to create dysfunction and adapt to dysfunction. When you take away the dysfunction you will become you once more.

Food for Thought

It's a good thing to remember along the way as you study acting that a place is created for you where you can do very dangerous things in a very safe place. What appears dangerous to one person appears child's play to another, and what appears very personal to one person is impersonal to another, so it is up to you. When looking for a class, look for a place where you believe you could do things that appear dangerous to you. You must be able to find a place outside of your apartment where you can do things with no restrictions, where you can yell and scream and cry. Acting is always an extreme, and when an actor sits very still without uttering a sound it can be an enormously aggressive movement for an actor. For somebody else it would be nothing. Acting allows us to go from inside ourselves to exploding outwards. When an actor is very still on-stage they are radiating with love, radiating with rage, or radiating in listening. They must be on the verge of exploding and allowing it to go out, or why would anyone want to watch them? Actors constantly want to put themselves in situations where they can unleash themselves. Find safe environments in which you can do this on a regular basis. How will it happen during a performance if you don't create the potential in other areas of your life?

The Diagnosis

You may not like this exercise and you may find it intrusive, but unfortunately you are in a business that does this all the time. If you think you can get by without doing this, then you are kidding yourself. Don't kid yourself if you don't notice it. It's not because you haven't seen it, it's that you are avoiding looking at it. Therefore, it will show in the audition, which has nothing to do with acting, but has to do with selling yourself. Auditions are not about selling your talent, yet actors walk in and say, "If you would only look at my talent!" You are selling the package, and you are saying, "Please buy this package." Unfortunately, many actors walk in saying, "I have a right to be in this room, you owe me something because I'm in this room." There are thousands of actors who wanted to get to that audition, and you have the advantage of being in the room. Now you have to ask yourself, "What is it I really want out of this?" and then get it.

The point of the body bio is actually to learn how to be yourself. This exercise has just as much effect on those people we might consider as "beautiful" as everyone else. In other words, they have just as many hang-ups as the rest of us. Part of this exercise asks you to go through your likes and dislikes with another person. The reason you have been asked to do this is because you may find they are totally unaware of your ears, or your nose, or your mole, and that you are much more aware of these things than anyone else. As you are recording this information on a piece of paper, we want you to get used to the idea of recording information. The best book on acting is your own personal journal, day-by-day-by-day on acting. That's the best book on acting because it is the only book on acting written in your language. In this exercise, even if you do not have a way of changing something, you can always change your attitude. If you feel you are too short, for instance, you could put lifts in your shoes, but you could also say "I can live with this. It's not such a big deal." If you go to an audition and don't get the part you could say, "I did my best and learned a lot." In other words, when there is nothing you can do to change the situation, it is yourself you have to change. It is better to put your time and energy into supporting your career rather than sabotaging it. You are not being asked to see what you want or what you don't want, but what is there. What we are saying is that you have to learn a way of preparing yourself and you have to do it on a daily basis.

Food for Thought

Every technique on acting is about two different people who exist in the body of one person. It's about the person who had certain needs, and it's about a genius. You can put them the other way around if you want to, but it's about a genius who had certain needs. Their technique did not come from their genius, it came from their needs. As their needs changed, their exercises changed. We have no idea what the specific needs of the actor using this book are. A book such as this can be of great benefit to you, but it cannot be a substitute for a great teacher. Only when you have a great teacher can you get specific diagnoses and exercises that will work specifically on your instrument and its needs at that precise moment. Actors are like snowflakes, no two are exactly the same.

Food for Thought

It is interesting to note that the last part of your body to grow is your brain. It is said that it will be fully developed by the time you are thirty-five-years-old. It is interesting that we can utilize the creative spirit before our bodies are fully grown. Those who prematurely leave the field of acting may never have realized their true potential. As a famous acting coach supposedly once said, "Life is a losing game, and you might as well enjoy it."

Final Thoughts

We have all sorts of phrases such as, "don't be vain," "beauty is only skin deep," and "don't get caught up in yourself." Men are told they shouldn't objectify women and vice versa. The person you know who seems to stare at the mirror incessantly is probably the person who sees less of themselves than anybody else in the world. The person who stares in the mirror all of the time has trained themselves to see only what they want to see. This exercise is to train you to get used to and comfortable with thinking of your body as a tool. It also allows you to think about how you can improve it, such as developing a desire to go to the gym. It is saying, "What can I do to improve it, and what can I do to make it do what I want it to do as an actor?" Look at yourself and say, "What advantages do I have, and how can I turn the rest of this instrument into just as much of an advantage?" You are what you think you are, especially when this is followed through by taking action.

Chapter 5:
Sound and Vocal Levels

20. Directing the Voice

Food for Thought

Once, at the end of a voice lesson my acting coach asked me where I was going next. I told her I was going to a dance class and she said to me, "Your friends will ask you whether you have a cold. Tell them yes, because they are going to notice something different in your voice. If you explain to them what is different and how you did it, you will go back to your old habits, or they will talk you out of your newfound voice." Sure enough, when I went to class they asked me if I had a cold, I said yes, and nothing more was said. From that day on my voice stayed that way and got stronger and stronger, and no one teased me or told me I was putting on airs, or trying to be different. What she was really saying was learn right now not to discuss your growth as an actor with anybody. What you are doing now is more you than anything you have ever done before. By choosing not to conform to your environment or surroundings, you may find you become a more accessible instrument.

Food for Thought

You have to be careful of emulating others. A famous Welsh singer was once asked about how he developed his wonderful singing voice. He said words to the effect of, "As a young man I would go out to the pastures and yell at the cows." As Jules Renard once said, "Look for the ridiculous in everything and you will find it."[40] Now if you go out and yell at cows you will most likely injure your voice. You're going to have to find out what works for you, and not what works for someone else. This is why we have said we would like you to ultimately develop your own technique that works for you specifically.

The Ingredients

We are going to give you a little exercise now so that no matter where you are you will be heard. You are going to learn how to direct your voice. You are going to consciously direct your voice. What we want you to do is walk around and talk to some people in the room. If you are by yourself, then speak out loud as if there were other people there.

Observed Exercise

PAUL: I want you to look at your fellow actors, know where they are, and then walk around and direct your voice to them. *(ACTORS continue exercise.)* You do not have to be standing anywhere near them to accomplish this. Direct your voice and your thoughts to them. Next I want you to hold your hands as close as you can to your face without touching. Do you feel something? Of course you do, it's heat. Now, I don't know if the heat is coming from my hand to my face or my face to my hand, but what I do know is that something is moving away from my body. And so when an audience member says, "I could feel that performance going right through me," they are right.

ACTOR: That is really powerful.

---

40. Augusten Burroughs, *Running with Scissors* (New York: St. Martin's Press, 2002), Preface.

PAUL: And that is what we mean when we say that an actor must project. It is to direct your whole being towards that person, audience, or camera. *(At this point PAUL directs one of the actors.)* What I would like you to do is go to the end of the room and talk to yourself. OK, now I want you to talk to us, and really direct your thoughts to, "I am talking to all of you." Now talk to yourself. It's just the greatest experience. Let's have another actor go in there, and I'm going to say "Talk to yourself," and I want you to also talk to us. Now, it's not necessary at all that you face us. In fact, sometimes you get a better feel for the exercise if at the beginning you don't. The most important thing in an exercise is how you feel, and not how we feel or want you to feel. You can practice this exercise all day long. It's great fun.

GAVIN: If you go to the gym one time, you won't get the results you're looking for. You will have to go back again and again and again. This is a great exercise that you will want to revisit frequently.

Food for Thought

One of my old students became a Broadway success. Sometime later she was going to teach a class for me. Her husband came to me and said she would only teach for me if she were the only one teaching voice. I said that was not possible. I said, "We bring in the best possible teachers, and we bring them in to promote and enhance the careers of the actors." She reluctantly said, "Alright." Suffice to say, she came to me after that session and said, "Everybody is coming to me for private lessons and I didn't suggest it to anyone." What had happened was that actors recognized excellence. I only brought in teachers whose own career was in search of excellence. It seems so obvious, and yet too few of us spend our lives in search of excellence.

Food for Thought

Some actors are lazy with their words and their projection and are difficult to understand. An audience is not going to strain itself to hear or understand you, so you had better be audible. Some actors will say, "This is my acting voice and this is my normal voice." You should only have one voice that is clear and vibrant. You can practice this wherever you go so now you can work on your acting twenty-four-seven. You know the actors that do this because people will turn and say, "Oh, he/she is obviously an actor." Good, this is what you want them to say, and you want every cell in your body to know that you are an actor. As Higgins points out in *Pygmalion*, "I've taught her to speak properly; and she has strict orders as to her behavior. She's to keep to two subjects: the weather and everybody's health."[41] You cannot be a part-time actor, but must be one twenty-four-seven. If working on your instrument is integrated into your lifestyle, then it becomes who you are.

The Diagnosis

If you could get a little sound gauge, it would show you how the sound levels have changed and you can actually feel the difference when you direct your voice. The smallest level of sound we can make is called a *phoneme*, not a syllable or a consonant. It drives me crazy when people are talking to me, yet they're not talking to me. And then I say, "What?" and they start shouting louder. I say, "You know, you really don't need to yell at me." Sometimes an actor will be auditioning in front of a casting director and they will virtually be shouting so as to make sure that every word is heard. Unfortunately, they are only standing two feet away and giving the casting director a headache. This is unlikely to get them the job. If they learn how to direct their voice, their resonance will travel quite comfortably with little effort.

Here is the problem that takes place in theatre and in classes: the misinterpretation of what theatre is about. Some instructors view the fourth wall as your protection from the audience.

41. Bernard Shaw, *Pygmalion* (London: Penguin Books, 1956), 71.

You don't want to be protected from the audience, you want to embrace the audience. You do not want to be protected from the camera, you want to fall in love with the camera.

When you really get good at this exercise, you won't change the volume at all. I do not even want you to think about that, at this stage, which will happen all by itself. Thinking about changing your volume is a good lesson of what not to do. One day you will notice your volume, and it is at this point that technique has taken over. Having a clear, enunciated voice is so important for the actor, and as Cicely Berry so eloquently puts it, "I know a great many people worry deeply about how they speak and how they sound, and that this anxiety often stops them expressing themselves as fully as they would wish."[42]

Food for Thought

I once coached an actor who was tall, good looking, wonderfully built, wonderfully coordinated, and had a big voice. I said to him, "You know you really should do musicals." He said, "Paul, I just want to stand very still and act." Most actors would like to stand and act if they could. Go and research great actors and you will find at some point in their lifetime they have done a performance that involved dancing. They refuse to limit themselves or their career.

Food for Thought

When a director or instructor talks about loud and soft, what they are really talking about is resonance and supporting the voice. When working with a director or instructor, you need to be able to work very specifically. Do not come up with your own slant of what you think they want, just listen very carefully and give them exactly what they want. Having a flexible voice is not only important in terms of your audience, it is also important in terms of communication with your fellow actors. As Ed Hooks says, "Speaking a line is like tossing a ball; you have to make sure the other actor catches it."[43]

Final Thoughts

My only concern regarding actors studying with the protégés of great teachers is that the great teacher who developed the exercise did so by need of the actor in front of them, or the production they were doing. In other words, they developed it because of some creative or technical need of the moment. When the protégé is teaching, they often do not understand the need that the teacher or great master had when they created this. The need is often very simple.

I often ask actors to look at me when they are talking to me — it is just common courtesy. Then I realized that it is not that I wanted them to look at me, it is that I wanted them to think of me. It appears to me that when they are talking to me, they are thinking of something else. That is how this exercise was developed, out of a need. I realized that, in order to direct your voice, you have to put the thought of it in some direction. I asked an actor to say what they had to say twenty feet away, and when they directed it towards me, I could hear them clearly without them raising the volume. If your intent is to be heard, you will be heard. With technique and an awareness of your audience you will be heard and understood. A microphone can pick up anything you say on-camera, but you still have to be understood.

---

42. Cicely Berry, *Your Voice and How to Use It* (London: Harrap Limited, 1990), 7.
43. Ed Hooks, *The Actor's Field Guide* (New York: Watson-Guptill publications, 2004), 114.

21. The Whisper Exercise

Food for Thought

For a number of actors, as soon as they start acting, they have trained themselves to drop their voice because it feels more natural, more sincere, it doesn't feel put on, and it doesn't feel affected. The problem with this is it has no vibrancy, and they are not even pronouncing their words clearly. Remember, in life we only have to say a couple of words and the other person will generally know what the rest of the sentence is whether you have pronounced it correctly or not. Actors have given fine performances that are softly spoken, and yet because of their technique, every word could be clearly understood.

Food for Thought

There are a lot of warm-up exercises given to acting, but they will never replace experts in that field. There are many things you should do and certain things you must do. A book on acting may give you a voice exercise, but only an expert on voice can diagnose you. After watching you they are able to prescribe a certain exercise for you, and then they have to watch you do it to make sure you are doing it correctly. Approach your acting from all sides of the equation.

The Ingredients

What we would like you to do is stand with your feet about shoulder width apart and let your hands dangle by your sides. It is better to wear loose fitting clothing for this exercise. We would like you now to lengthen your spine, and to do this imagine there is a button towards the back of your head in a similar position to where it would be on a beanie. It is that button that is floating up towards the sky, and as you think about your head floating up and lengthening towards the sky, you can also think about your spine lengthening. Imagine from the base of your spine (the tail bone) is a kind of fountain and as it goes up it branches out of your armpits and shoulders like a fountain. You are thinking of the head floating upwards and the spine lengthening and widening. You could also imagine you have a string attached to the top of your head that is elongating your spine as held by a puppeteer. Your head is not forward and it is not back. You should notice now that your weight is slightly on your heels, not forward on your toes. If it is forward on your toes, you will have to use muscles on the back of your legs to keep balance, which in turn will create unnecessary tension. Think that you have on a pair of long johns and in your mind's eye you undo the front buttons so that it opens up from your belly button right towards your groin and the top of your legs. This in turn will allow your stomach to hang out and fall forward. By letting your muscles go in this way you are going to find that air is sucked into your body rather than you trying to force air in. You are not drawing air into your body, and you are not forcing air into your body. It is being sucked in all by itself. As Michael McCallion points out, "If you have ensured that your basic use is working for you rather than against you, then in the course of using the voice normally you will experience no difficulty with the breath."[44] Remember that relaxation has dynamics to it, and is not the same as collapse. Collapsing is heavy and relaxation is light.

We want you now to let your stomach suck air in whether it be through your nose or mouth. When you think your stomach had done it, we want you to count from one to five in a whisper. So here we go, head lifted, spine lengthening and widening, weight on the heels, let the stomach fall forward, know that there is air in your lungs, count from one to five in a whisper. When you get done with that take a breath, allowing the air to fill your lungs, and now count from one to six. Try to let one number flow to the next number so that they are not staccato. The rhythm should be a nice pace, not too slow.

---

44. Michael McCallion, *The Voice Book* (London: Faber and Faber, 1988), 39.

As you continue to work with this exercise, allow your mouth to open so that you feel like you are exercising your lips and your tongue. If you find tension in your jaw, don't reach out and touch it, just think, "Is my jaw tight?" If it is, let your mouth hang open like you are going to drool and let your stomach hang out. Continue in this way, each time adding a number and go as far as you can comfortably, remembering to do so at a whisper. You should be able to get to fifteen on your first day, or maybe twenty; however, if your maximum is six, then aim for seven the next time. Remember that a whisper is a sound that does not voice in a projected fashion and should only be heard by you or an individual standing in the immediate vicinity.

Work only with a sufficient amount of breath. In other words, you do not need a great deal of air to count to five or six, but by the time you reach eleven or twelve you will find the muscles of the stomach going in ever so slightly to help you. Once you have practiced this exercise once or twice, you can then do it anywhere you like. You can do it on a bus, in a subway, or while in line at the grocery store. Allow yourself to be working on your acting wherever you are.

Food for Thought

Stage shows often bring in voice coaches just because that is part of the rehearsal. In the movie *Cabaret* they set up a little conservatory for everybody in the movie. The actors in the movie had a variety of lessons during the preparation of the movie. Dedication and hard work are key ingredients to your acting career.

Food for Thought

I used to teach acting to opera singers. I told them, "You study acting so that when you sing opera you have been influenced by acting." You wear it like an aroma. You are influenced by those who teach you. The actor is influenced by the environment in which they live and, like a sponge, soaks everything up.

The Diagnosis

The purpose of this exercise is to create a freer way of breathing and a way of relaxing things that cannot harm you so that you are not damaging your vocal chords or tensing your jaw. One of the benefits of this exercise is to encourage you to let go of unnecessary tensions and have body awareness. The problem is that we are so taken with having perfect abs that we want to pull our stomachs in, but an actor has to breathe differently from other people to be able to use their instrument to its full potential.

In this exercise you are asked to whisper, and this is because you are only being asked to work on your breathing. Another reason is that when we speak out loud, we tend to want to make a sound that we want to hear, or a voice that we think our friends or a director might want to hear. This exercise allows you to work with speaking and breathing without judging and analyzing. We want you to realize something we think you should find in this exercise once you are complete. What do you notice about your voice now? Do you notice that it is slightly more colorful and slightly lower or more grounded? We say this, concerned that you might assume from the get-go that you know what an exercise does and that you think if you know what an exercise brings you to, then you start at the end. That would be like starting from the end result instead of finding and discovering through the work.

You may find that your voice is lower. This exercise did not lower your voice, that is your natural voice. Because of tension in the muscles we tend to speak higher. This exercise can be very useful when you are at an audition and you are waiting outside, because when you are not vocalizing, you can work when other people are around and not draw attention to yourself. Generally, if you were doing this exercise in an audition waiting room, people will simply assume you are going over your lines.

The reason you go from a lower number to a higher number is that you are increasing your capacity for speaking. You can take some dialogue of a long speech or monologue and do as much of the dialogue or the speech without taking a breath. It is better to do this with a piece you are not actually using so that it is just a practice exercise. If you practice this, you will find that over time you will be able to do very long speeches in one breath. Let us say you are in a scene where you are arguing with your boyfriend or girlfriend. You have a very long sentence that, when said in one breath, can be really powerful and build the scene. Unfortunately, you do not have breath control and you have to keep pausing for breath. The sentence now sounds choppy and your argument with your boyfriend or girlfriend loses its intensity and actually sounds weaker. The importance of working with the breath, therefore, has very practical and real uses for you. Watch your friends who are not actors and they will take breaths all over the place. In fact, where they take a breath confuses you in what they mean.

Sometimes you will see actors on television or in a movie and you will be aware they are speaking softly and yet you can understand every word they are saying. They have adapted to the medium they are working with, and yet with the versatility and range of their voice they are able to do so and still be perfectly understood. Don't fall into the habit of thinking TV and film is simply a soft voice. It is still a supported and clearly understood voice. It is more important that an actor is breathing diaphragmatically rather than actually knowing what diaphragmatic breathing actually is.

Generally speaking, when an actor is taught an accent for a movie, they are taught a less authentic version. A colleague of ours was the dialect coach on a movie where the American actors required French accents. Once seeing these wonderful authentic sounding French accents the producers asked him to, "Water down the French accents so that they could be easily understood by an American audience." Accept that in specific character situations directors always want their actors to be clearly understood by the audience.

The importance of voice in terms of communication is a vital tool of the actor. As Sue Jennings says in her book *Remedial Drama*, "Language, which enabled man to control his environment, to share himself and information with others, also caused him sometimes to lose touch with himself and, at times, caused him to lose touch with his significant others. Language in its distortions caused problems in communication."[45]

Food for Thought

It is interesting to note, for instance, that if you have a low voice, it means that your vocal folds have to be more relaxed and they have to be working less. You have to understand your voice in order to be able to use your voice effectively. You do not necessarily have to lose your accent, but you may have to go to an accent reduction coach. In professional life, another actor has the right to say to you "You must not give me direction, I don't want direction from you." In real life, you don't give the other actors suggestions or direction. You may feel you do not have to have a projected voice for film and television. You do, however, have to have a certain quality to your voice. As Susan Blu and Molly Ann Mullin point out, "If you were blessed with the power of speech, you already have something about your natural voice that makes it different and special. In fact, your voice is unique; no one has one identical to yours."[46]

Food for Thought

This is what actors do: they go to an audition and the director or casting director says, "I would like you to do this." And the actor says, "No, no, no, I've got this good idea and can

---

45. Sue Jennings, *Remedial Drama* (London: Pitman Publishing, 1973), v.
46. Susan Blu, Molly Ann Mullin, *Word of Mouth*, (Los Angles: Pomegranate Press, 1996), 14.

I just try that?" What was the first word the actor just said? The first word the actor said was "No." The point is that, even when it is said vocally, you may not hear it. You may not have heard it, but they did!

Final Thoughts

Voice and diction are a very important part of acting. If we can't hear it, if we can't understand it, then it is only pantomime and it's not acting the spoken word. It is necessary for you to have an expert, or a specialist, all your life. You should have on file the name of a voice specialist who teaches voice only and a laryngologist who can treat and look after the health of your voice.

In class, the actor must do simple voice warm-ups. You can do some of these by yourself, and in order for them not to be misinterpreted, they must be kept very simple. This exercise tends to relax all the muscles that are needed in speech. It also helps build up greater lung capacity and the ability to do longer and longer lines without taking a breath. Young actors often think that if they think in pauses, starts, and stops it will be interesting for the audience. It isn't. It's just annoying and distracting to the audience. Actors, as opposed to non-actors, speak very long lines in one breath, the rule often being to finish a thought on one breath. The exercises Boomlay and Whispering should be done together as they complement each other. Turn the volume down to low on your television set while watching your favorite show, and you may find you quickly lose interest. Why should it be any different when an audience is watching you?

22. Falling Inflection

Food for Thought

A lot of actors are not getting what they should out of vocal training. The reason is that they go to a voice class and say, "I'll stop acting, and I'll study this." And then when you start to act you wonder why it doesn't work. It is because you never did it to begin with. When you study voice, you are not doing things that you would do as an actor. In fact, you stop doing them. You say, "I must be in an ordinary state because I am learning vocal exercises, not acting wrong." You must now go back to your vocal classes and say, without telling anyone, "I must be an actor while doing vocal exercises so that when I am acting my body will relate to these exercises." If you don't do this, you will find yourself saying, "This exercise is of no use to me at all because I can't use it."

When you are studying voice and diction you have to stay in a high functioning state. Do you think about a character you are playing while in voice class? You should! When you go to a voice class, you go as a performer. You have to be an actor twenty-four-seven. When you are acting, all of the pieces have to come together. It would be wise to seize any opportunities to allow all these pieces to come together at every possible moment.

Food for Thought

We think that perhaps acting is the only art form you can work on one hundred percent of the time, if you choose to. You can walk down the street and focus on your breathing. You can sit on the bus and work on your posture. You can work on a character wherever you choose. You can memorize lines lying down and whispering them practically in your sleep. There is not a moment of your existence in which you cannot work on your acting, if you choose to.

We want you to think about all the times you have told yourself that you couldn't work on your acting because you were not in a production or a class at that time. You can work on your instrument any time you like because it will follow you wherever you go. As Michael

Caine tells us, "If you really want to become an actor, but only providing that acting doesn't interfere with your golf game, your political ambitions, and your sex life, you don't really want to become an actor. Not only is acting more than a part-time job, its more than a full-time job, it's a full-time obsession."[47]

The Ingredients

This exercise works well with a partner and is an excellent way of developing a falling inflection. An *inflection* is basically a slide of the voice upwards or downwards, in the case of falling inflections it applies to downwards. A falling inflection is also generally used to give strong emphasis to a word. What we would like you to do is turn to any page in a film or play script and read a short sentence out loud. Your partner should then respond with a question. Go back and forth a few times where you repeat the sentence and they respond with the question. Look to use a falling inflection when answering these questions.

ACTOR: Dry up, will you.

PAUL: Do what?

ACTOR: Dry up, will you.

PAUL: OK, now just say the first two words and drop the rest. Do what?

ACTOR: Dry up.

PAUL: Do what?

ACTOR: Dry up.

PAUL: In this exercise you have to go through your dialogue and find a way to make every line the answer to a question. When you get to respond to the question simply by giving the answer it becomes so easy to do the line. Do another line.

ACTOR: Never said there was.

PAUL: Never said what?

ACTOR: Never said there was.

PAUL: Cut it down so that you are simply answering the question. Never said what?

ACTOR: There was.

PAUL: You see the feeling you get from it?

GAVIN: It appears more effortless as if you are less concerned about getting it right.

ACTOR: I feel that. I said he's dead and long dead.

PAUL: He's what?

ACTOR: Long dead.

PAUL: Isn't that astonishing. Notice the feeling each time you finish with a falling inflection. Now what I would like you to do is do a whole sentence, and then when I ask you a question, I want you to do the line again, but start it with, "I said."

ACTOR: We think bad of losing him.

PAUL: What did you say?

ACTOR: I said we think bad of losing him.

PAUL: Isn't that ten times the reading you had a moment ago? Do another one.

ACTOR: Do you mean the boy's adopted?

ACTOR: What did you say?

ACTOR: I said do you mean the boy's adopted?

PAUL: Great, and you see how you're automatically starting to use a falling inflection? In this

---

47. Michael Caine, *Acting in Film* (New York: Applause, 1997), Introduction.

exercise you are learning to just answer questions. It doesn't matter which line you use as long as you answer the question.

GAVIN: If you are working alone you can ask the question silently and answer the question yourself.

Food for Thought

My brother once asked me, "What do you teach when you teach acting?" I said, "Well, I teach people how to speak clearly." And he said, "That's what I thought." Sometimes you just tell people what they want to hear. As the saying goes, pick your battles.

Food for Thought

I was coaching a very famous American actor for a classical role in London in the 1960s. The British press said of him, "He speaks the language well." That was the entire review. They didn't say, "He is a great actor." They simply said, "He speaks the language well." For an American, you couldn't get a better review for the classics. He and I would go and see movies or plays so that he could hear the sounds that I wanted him to recognize. This was a world-renowned actor who continuously looked for every opportunity to work on his instrument.

The Diagnosis

An actor's voice has to have shape to it. It has to have highs and lows in inflection. It has to have timing. I have heard actors say on a number of occasions, "You don't need voice training for film and television." There are numerous shows and movies that use regional dialects. I would say, personally, that the actor wants to start with a clean slate. You want your voice to have the flexibility and range to go in any direction you choose so that you can get cast in a whole range of parts, and therefore increase your marketability.

There are some sounds in other languages that simply don't exist in English. Until you have a standard, you have no reference point. In order to speak any dialect it takes muscle, and it takes exercise of that muscle. When you start from standard speech you are exercising muscles that will allow you to exercise unique or specialized muscles to do a dialect. Don't kid yourself that you can do a dialect just by hearing it if you do not have the muscles to do it.

In a vast generality, a falling inflection is stronger than a rising inflection. If you listen to actors no matter how flexible their voice is, they particularly end serious thoughts with falling inflections. We use a rising inflection to indicate a question, and we don't need to because the words and the sentence explain to us that it is a question. People that we take more seriously seem to use more falling inflections. Perhaps you can utilize falling inflections in audition situations.

Generalizing, we might even say that men seem to be more masculine the more falling inflections they use. Women seem to be more serious the more falling inflections they use. Women seem to be a little more scatterbrained the more rising inflections they use. A falling inflection indicates that you are relaxed and in control of the situation. As you develop the flexibility in your voice you will become more interesting to listen to. Understanding inflections cannot only help you create a character, but it also has to do with how you are accepted in the world.

We say great actors listen, well that's not enough because they are sometimes listening while they are waiting for their turn to speak. It's not that great actors listen, it's that great actors answer the questions. Great actors answer the questions that great writers ask.

When explaining the purpose behind this exercise it is also worth saying, "You had to be there." In other words, the best way for us to explain the benefit of these exercises is for you to experience them. Generally, when we speak we can get accused of not thinking before we speak, but when we ask a quick question we often answer it quickly without thinking.

What we are doing is answering without lying and without preparation. This exercise encourages muscles in our body to work in an automatic and coordinated way.

Food for Thought
People are enormously affected by how you speak. You can probably get almost anything in the world by how you speak. You can get a better job, you can get a better place in the line, you can get more attention, or you can get a callback based on how you speak. We can't emphasize enough the benefits of voice and the actor. All you have is you, so make the most of you.

Food for Thought
Don't let people make you who they define you as. Don't let your teacher define you. Don't let your friends or other actors define you. Only you define you. A great teacher made the most wonderful observation one day. A young man got up and did a scene, when he was done she looked at him and said, "If you speak like less than a man, you will be less than a man." That was the whole critique. If you speak like less than an actor, you will be less than an actor. It's not demanding. It's not putting on airs. It's what you learn and the time you spend on your instrument. If you are a young or inexperienced actor and if you are around great actors and if you work in this manner, they will embrace you. If you don't, they will simply ignore you. We are interested in acting and the actor. It is our sincere hope that you are too.

Final Thoughts
We use pitch to comment on the word, give our interpretation about the word, or to show our feelings about the word. A falling inflection generally means, "I mean it," or "I'm done," or "Listen to me," or "I am sure of what I am saying." It therefore becomes a stronger way of expressing oneself. If you start paying attention in movies, you will notice you hear a lot of falling inflections. We want to make sure you understand that a falling inflection does not mean dropping the ends of your sentences to where you are not understood.

23. In a Word

Food for Thought
It is said that you know you can speak a language fluently when you can think in that language. I used to think when I learned to speak French I would think in French. Then one day I started to think in French. And then I realized I don't think in English, I don't think in any language. I think in impulses. I've an impulse to say something, and if you do something, it changes my impulse. Great actors live in the impulse of random thoughts.

Food for Thought
Great actors speak the language of an actor. Once you speak the language, you continue to work the instrument to keep in shape and to learn. A number of people who call themselves actors don't speak the language. Imagine going to Italy and being told, "We're going to speak to you in Italian. From now on there will be no English spoken until you speak Italian. If you don't know how to say coffee you ain't getting your coffee tomorrow morning." You have to speak the language of the actor. This does not simply mean buying a book of dramatic terms. It also means thinking, breathing, and dreaming in the language of the actor.

The Ingredients
What we would like you to do in this exercise is start with a monologue or scene that you have learned. We want you to stay consistent with using your voice and not create a voice for your acting. We want you to speak rather slowly, loudly, and let out every word and

syllable in a continuous flow. If your thoughts change, if the functioning in your body changes, your voice may change to a point. Be careful not to rush through this exercise. It should still be an interesting voice, a supported voice, and a resonating voice.

ACTOR: His, li-ttle, face —

PAUL: Much too fast, it's not supported, and there is no resonance. I would also like you to make it a little less stilted and staccato. OK, off you go.

ACTOR: His, li-ttle, face, was, co-vered, with, cho-co-late, I took, a hand-ker-chief, out, of, my, purse, and —

PAUL: That's good. Now see if you can actually support your voice throughout. Keep your voice colorful throughout, it sounds good now, but it can get better. As you continue, let go and surrender any tensions in your body, and you will probably find your voice drops lower. Stand on two feet, and keep your body supported with your back lengthening. Continue louder than you may think, stronger than you may think, and even more than you may think.

ACTOR: And wet-ted, it, with, my, tongue, to, clean, his face, he, pulled, a-way, from, me, no, I, pulled, him, back.

PAUL: Good, that's good. It is not completely in your mouth yet, but it is coming. Very nice. A variation of this exercise is to go through your monologue and do just the vowels. As you do this they should morph into one sound.

ACTOR: Ayyyy, eeee, iiii, ayyyy, eeee, ayyyy, ooooh.

PAUL: Good. You can vary this yet again by just pronouncing the consonants.

ACTOR: Mmmm, ssss, wwww, tttt.

PAUL: Once you have worked with just the vowels and the consonants, go back to working with the whole words.

GAVIN: This exercise is going to take a great deal of patience and concentration, so be patient with yourself.

Food for Thought

I used to have a friend who was blind who would direct shows. If I said I was going to the theatre to watch a play, he would say, "Oh, can I go with you?" If we went to a dance concert, he would go backstage afterwards and talk to the dancers as though he had seen it. He would tell them which part of the show was best and so on. He would get that from the words they said, and from words I said. He had this enormous sensitivity. He would direct shows and say, "This is what I want to hear, and this is what I want you to be."

I once said, "Have you ever been able to see?" He said, "No." I said, "Then how do you know the difference between red and green?" He said, "By how people describe them. I have always been blind, Paul, and so I listened to what people said about them." The loss of one sense heightens the abilities of the other senses.

Food for Thought

There is an artist by the name of Robert Henri Lipica, and he said some of the following words about art. We have ad-libbed some connections to the field of acting. "The object of painting a picture is not to make a picture. The object of acting is not to make a play or movie; however, it is not unreasonable that that may sound ridiculous. The object, which is that of every true work of art, including acting, is the attainment of a state of being, a state of high functioning, a more than ordinary moment of existence."

A great teacher is only an influence, an aroma, something that tints your personality for a while. Judy Garland, Edith Piaf, and Billie Holiday all died before fifty, and all were the most famous female performers living at that time. These women lived in a high state of functioning, and yet it is not for everybody. It can be a difficult place to be. If you live in this state, it is very difficult to exist with people who aren't in this state. A number of these people become drug addicts, alcoholics, or recluses. As you move towards a high state of functioning, understand that you are opening yourself to a whole world of possibilities.

The Diagnosis

One of the purposes in this exercise is to remind you that you only have one voice, and while the situation and character may change, there is no such thing as your acting voice and your regular voice. They are one and the same.

We want you to "fix you" so that nothing changes when you start to act, and you do not suddenly adopt affectations to your voice. A director wants to understand every word you say the first time you speak. If that is not you, they would rather take the person who does it the first time.

In this exercise you may be good, and you may be better than when you first began. In school, you are rarely told that's not good enough, and yet that is what they are often saying when you leave the audition room. They are not going to say he or she has improved. They want you to be that good the first time you open your mouth. They are not interested in what you think. They want to know if, technically, you can be consistent.

Another aim of this exercise is to put the musculature of the words into your mouth when you speak. When you go to an audition, get the sides as soon as possible so that you can get the words into your mouth. An actor's body doesn't twitch, wander, and do all kinds of unnecessary things. In this exercise, you are being asked to pronounce every syllable in one continuous flow. We always have actors take all of the punctuation out of lines so that they do not get caught up in punctuation and grammar. We do not speak in grammatically correct sentences. By taking out the grammar and punctuation, you are able to work without judging, analyzing, and getting in your own way.

When you look at an exercise such as this, you realize there is a great deal of preparation involved and you might not like this. Stanislavski would sometimes take months or years to direct a play, and was, on a number of occasions, asked if he could speed the process up. He replied with words to the effect of he could put a play together in five or six weeks if he didn't have to keep stopping to teach the actors how to act. This exercise is an acting workout for the musculature of your mouth. When you go to the gym to do a workout, you don't just go one time, but go back again and again to stay in shape. You have also been asked not to rush this exercise. An actor may, because of nerves, rush their way through an audition and say, "Thank God it's over!" What they don't realize is the casting director is saying exactly the same thing about your performance.

Food for Thought

Try to use words that propel you to continue your search. The things you have been taught that are the best are the things that you forget. They become part of you. They encourage you to search and your search will only happen alone. It won't happen with me, it won't happen with your scene partner, and it won't happen with the love of your life. Your search will only happen with you. Are you too fragile to be an actor? Do you have any desire to be an actor? You have to take this journey by yourself. Even when you are surrounded by an entire ensemble, you are still alone. It is your search, your discoveries, and your professionalism that will follow you wherever you go.

Food for Thought

The word *sustain* is what confuses us, because we actually don't sustain a note. We don't actually sustain a performance. The secret that we have that the audience doesn't know, and some of our colleagues don't know, is we begin again an infinite number of times. If you say, "To be or not to be," every time you can, you begin the performance all over again. As though the performance starts on the word "to," and then the performance starts on the word "be," etc. Try this yourself as if with each word you are beginning again. Even though you may have done the same show, with the same lines, hundreds of times, it must appear as if it is the very first time you have uttered the words, the thoughts, the reactions.

Final Thoughts

An actor often thinks that words are only broken up into vowels and consonants, so this is what they practice. Actually, there are smaller sounds than consonants and there are smaller sounds than vowels called *phonemes.* These are the smallest units of utterances a person can make. We build up very bad habits of moving from one sound to the other. Our friends have a shorthand way of talking, and we have to develop this slang that keeps us from pronouncing our words fully. This exercise makes you aware of the need to speak clearly and audibly. It is simply an exercise in exercising the muscle of your voice and, indeed, your whole body to utter sounds that, when put together, make words. When a great playwright or screenwriter gives you sounds, you're able to derive the most invention from the sounds. We have often heard actors say, "Those sounds are delicious." Not only can they speak them, but they can taste them. Enjoy the words that come out of your mouth, so that others may do the same.

24. Walk and Talk

Food for Thought

I once heard it said by a colleague of mine that it had been found that scientists only really knew how to communicate with other scientists. I said, "Your point? I don't really understand your point? Why should they be able to talk to anybody else?" An actor should want to and be able to communicate with those involved in their craft or industry on a constant basis. Those who love acting constantly talk about, think about, and dream about acting.

Food for Thought

Be careful with exercises, because if you take an exercise into rehearsal or performance and you are not comfortable or adept at it, you will stop doing the performance and start concentrating on the exercise. The exercise has to be such an action that you just fall into it. Sometimes an actor is so proud of their vocal abilities that it becomes the main focus of their intent and all meaning is lost.

The Ingredients

Here is a variation of the Whisper Exercise. What we would like you to do to begin this exercise is start walking around the room. As you are walking slowly around the room and really giving very little thought to the fact that you are walking around the room, we want you to put both your thumbs on your navel, so your fingers are pointing to the ground. We want you to think of releasing the muscles that are directly beneath your fingers so that your belly is falling out. Once you've thought about that, keep walking, and then just let your arms hang down to the side. Now you know what muscles are relaxing. As you continue to breathe, just be aware that the process of breathing is not sucking air into the body. As you release the muscles below your navel the air will automatically be sucked in to your body, and you don't have to think of taking a breath.

What we would like you to do now is count from one to ten in a whisper on one breath. Once you have done that, forget the whole thing and start over. Walk around. Let the muscles fall down below your navel. Let air be sucked into your body, and this time you count to eleven. Walk around for a while, then, if you want to, for variation, come to a standstill. Let the muscles relax, suck air into your body, and count to thirteen. As you are counting, start to walk again, just by impulse.

Once you have done that, forget about everything. Continue to do this on your own until you get to twenty, or anything that seems to use up all the breath. It may be fifteen or it may be thirty. When you have done this, sit down for a moment in a chair, and while you are sitting down, think back on how it felt and what the discoveries were. Did the muscle feel different? Were you walking more easily? Was it harder to walk? Did you get heavier, or did you get lighter? When you have done that, forget everything, get up, and start over; only this time you are going to count out loud from one to ten. If you find that you are talking in a monotone without much effort, then let it go up and down and around almost like you are singing a song that the pitches change. Continue in this manner up to twenty or wherever you can on one breath. You are learning to control the breath, and you are learning to work with the breath. You are becoming aware of the breath so that eventually it will become automatic for you.

Food for Thought

All child stars, no matter how successful they were, have to learn to act all over again. One would think they are headed that way because, as they get older, they lose their naiveté. That is not why. It's because when they are a child their surroundings applied to their proportions. As they get older their body is no longer in the same proportion. A very small child can lean forward and put their head on the ground, but an adult has trouble putting their hands on the ground. When the proportions are that tremendously different, then the coordination will be different. As they get older, a person does not always continue to learn coordination. Adaptation will always be necessary for you.

Food for Thought

In life, we tell people not to stutter when they are talking. Isn't it interesting how many things we tell people not to do in life that, if we are telling a story, we should do. We are trying to do what a person does because of their circumstances. When you are younger, you put a lot of sounds in because of immaturity. As you get older, because you are told not to, you stop making those sounds. They are part of the richness of our language, so much so that there is even a language in Africa where they make clicks for communication. There are many contradictions between life and the life of the actor, and you have to learn how to skip over that.

The Diagnosis

All acting exercises are a form of investigation, discovery, and coordination. You are investigating your body, discovering things about your body that you don't know, and coordinating it by the fact that you are doing something. Coordination comes last because you should not become self-conscious of coordination. Once you become self-conscious of coordination you don't discover anything by using it. If you do something and are just open to discovery, you will find that your body will do things you didn't know it could do.

In this exercise you are asked to start over, and the best way to do any exercise is to start over many times. Think about when you perform in a play. You have to start over numerous times. On a movie set you will most likely have to start the scene over many times. If you did a play for a year, the show would be the same, but each performance would be ever so slightly different from the last.

In this exercise you were asked to ask yourself a number of questions. None of the things are better than the others. The best thing is for you to discover differences in all of those. See how your voice feels after this exercise. Your voice may sound like it has more volume, and this means that more muscles will be engaged. Whenever you think about volume, understand that your voice gets more volume when it has more muscles engaged. The volume of your acting is the number of muscles that work at any given moment.

Food for Thought

The greatest actors in the world look at each other and say, "How did you do that?" One of the greatest pianists who ever lived was ninety-five-years-old, and after a performance a composer who had won seven Academy Awards called him and said, "How did you do that?" and he said, "I just found it." He kept walking down the right street all his life. He would never have found it walking down the wrong street. All the actors who don't make it either walk down the wrong street accidentally or are led down the wrong street by people, or they refuse to walk down the right street. There is a never-ending search for these great artists.

Food for Thought

The biggest mistake actors ever do in acting class is to not learn how to act. They learn how to do everything else. They learn how take a picture, write a resumé, network, and who the top casting directors are, but they don't learn how to act! All these things are necessary alongside your acting, not instead of.

Final Thoughts

It's alright to do an exercise simplistically in order to learn the components of the exercise. Remember, simplistically means overly simple. In the case of the actor it means it's so simple that you most probably won't be doing much of anything. Any exercise you can, start by sitting, standing, or lying down quietly, and thinking of the exercise. The exercise only works if it's attached to the kind of movement we need. Actors walk as they talk. Theatre has a rule where we say, "Don't walk and talk," but there are a lot of lines we walk and move on. On film you may not always be moving due to a camera shot or specific angle. Almost every exercise in this book, or any acting book, you could do while you are walking, sitting, or lying down. Then you're telling your body silently and firmly that this is something to use while you're acting. Otherwise, your body tends to think that you can only use that exercise when you're not acting. An actor who pretends to think, pretends to imagine, or pretends is simply going through the motions and is creating patterns of behavior that may be difficult to change, especially when it comes to the performance.

25. Boomlay Boomlay Boomlay Boom

Food for Thought

The person who studies all their life but never does anything is called untalented. The person who doesn't study and becomes a famous person is therefore called talented. Don't you think that's unfair? If you don't recognize these you do not exist. You haven't started. It is unfair for you not to recognize how to take your acting and career to its highest outcome.

Food for Thought

There is no reason to study acting if we have not defined our terms.

The Ingredients

What we would like you to do is start to walk around the room or space and say "Boomlay, boomlay, boomlay, boommmm." Allow the boom to end on a hum so that your lips are tingling. Stay on this boom as long as you can, and use the breath. Use a big booming voice for this exercise. Keep the whole thing moving fairly briskly and together. Each time you start a new "boomlay" take it up a half step so that you are going higher and higher. When you get as high as you can comfortably, we want you to go down half a step each time. Be careful you do not run out of breath too quick — take a bigger breath and hold it longer. There should be no pushing or straining of your voice at any point during this exercise. If you find yourself doing these things then stop, adapt, and start again.

Food for Thought

In order to become an actor, you have to devote your life to acting, just as you can't study math and science as well as eighteen other subjects. Musicians, artists, and dancers don't perfect their crafts through a general education, and neither can the actor. There are exceptions to this, just as there always will be exceptions to every rule.

Food for Thought

Every technique has rope exercises that you do every single day, and what we want is that if every other art form has it, then acting should as well. We love an actor to be independent, to be able to independently act. The ultimate goal is for each actor to become his or her own coach. As Ernesto Rossi commented to Stanislavski, "Mm-a! If there is no great artist near you whom you can trust, I can recommend only one teacher: You, yourself."[48]

The Diagnosis

Part of this exercise is working with the pitch of your voice, which incidentally is in your mouth and your throat. Now you know a new way of experimenting with changing the shape of the inside of your mouth in order to change and to influence the pitch — that is called speaking. It is the shape of the inside of your mouth that makes the sound and gives the sound shape. In very simple terms, this exercise warms up your voice, and it gets some resonance in your voice. If you work enough with this exercise, the vocal folds will become more relaxed and will almost collapse. You may find this exercise challenging if your muscles have not done this before, so this exercise is also adding an extra degree of coordination. In this exercise you are actually humming, and humming is an excellent way to get resonance and depth to your voice. You can practice humming wherever you go. Some of you may think you have a pitch problem, when in fact what you have is a coordination of muscle problem. You can work on your muscles for control of your pitch. Continue to work with this exercise and other exercises to work on your voice. Part of the strength of this exercise is its simplicity. Simple things in acting can oftentimes be most effective.

Food for Thought

A famous director used to start each rehearsal by saying to his actors, "We don't know anything." He explained that, as we work together, we find out what our needs are. He was also saying that nothing is bad, because if something is bad we can't do it. An actor must be able to do absolutely anything that is required.

Food for Thought

Since acting has not changed, what's the difference between then and now? The difference is that there is a technique for acting. Anyone can act and anyone can run, but not anyone can run a four-minute mile, and not anybody can be a brilliant actor. There is a technique for acting. If you understand what we're saying, we don't need to say it to you. If you don't understand what we're saying, we shouldn't be saying it to you. Acting is a technique that you should practice every day. You do it because you want to, because you have to, and not because we are asking you to.

Final Thoughts

All the kind of sounds that great actors make may not be so thrilling to the audience such as the variations in their voice, the shape of vowels, and the flexibilities of highs and lows in the voice. The audience does not always realize how fragile and delicate the voice is. One

---

48. David Allen, *Stanislavski for Beginners* (London: Writers and Readers Publishing, 1999), 31.

should never do a vocal exercise that has any possibility of being strenuous, strident, or causing any kind of tension without a highly trained vocal coach. The danger of getting a book on vocal production is that if the exercise is done the slightest bit wrong, it can damage the voice. To the other extreme, it can confuse a person until they don't know how to use the voice. A piano can be played four ways: loud, soft, fast, slow, and a multitude of variations of these. The voice is, without doubt, the most versatile, and has more potential than any instrument that will ever be invented by man. To give a voice exercise in a book, it is absolutely necessary that it is so simple that it simply gives you a little bit more. This is something anybody could do — your mother, your brother, your neighbors, or anybody. It will just help them to have a healthy voice all of their lives.

Many people, as they get older, talk more softly because they have not done simple exercises all of their lives. For more complex voice work, you should go to a voice specialist who can help you make it the fabulous instrument that has flexibility and variety. This exercise is named after a poem that contains the words "boomlay, boomlay, boomlay, boom." It was given to me by my voice teacher. She had found something that was poetic, simple, and everybody who studied with her was always given this exercise at the start of each class. You may believe that film actors are not vocally trained because of microphones and so forth. All great actors are acutely aware of the importance of a versatile and audible voice.

Chapter 6:
The Storyteller

26. Over the Top
Food for Thought

We sometimes want to go back to a play or movie, not necessarily because we want to hear that story again, but because we just want to hear that actor tell it. We want to hear them tell it again and again. It's like the little kids sitting at the feet of a storyteller in the library on a Saturday morning who says, "What story shall I tell today?" And they tell one that has been heard twenty times before. Do the children want to be told the story again, or do they want to hear that person tell the story? If you want to be successful with producers, if you learn to be an actor where people desire to come back to hear the story again, there is nothing more economically sound to a producer than an actor that can do that. Does an actor ever think of that? We would think that an actor says, "I would like everybody to come and see this play ... once." We don't know how many actors say, "My success is not how well I tell the story, but how often I can get the audience to return to hear me tell the story." You are not responsible for the lights, you are not responsible for the sets, the costume, for box office, publicity, or bringing the audience in there, but once the audience is in there, you are responsible for making them want to hear you tell the story. This is probably the most neglected part of an actor's study. The actor approaches each part in their own way, and the actor approaches each part in his or her own time.

Food for Thought

(ACTOR gets up and performs a monologue.)

PAUL: What would your next step have been? The thing that the actor wants to hear is, "How did you do that?"

ACTOR 1: I know what I needed to make that better, I needed another minute to myself for preparation.

ACTOR 2: You have to learn to break that contract. Stop telling yourself you need that minute of time and dive into it.

PAUL: I love to see an actor explain why something I have given them is so much better than I knew. I made up the contract exercise and I have never used it in a situation such as this, I love it! You understand what she is saying: You need to break that contract. In other words, when the casting director or director doesn't say, "Take a moment" or "Start when you're ready," you have to be able to say to yourself, "I don't need that time." Your audition should tell us anything that's good about you and nothing that's bad about you. That's all we want to see. Some actors say, "I'm saving the best for last." Next! I want the best before you get here.

GAVIN: If you can only do the scene with a specific preparation and a specific period of time, then you have created a limitation.

The Ingredients

This exercise is called Over the Top. In this exercise you are going to do a scene or monologue and you are going to do it totally over the top. You could do the scene as if your character has gone quite mad or has lost their mind. We want you to do this and we want you to do whatever in your mind is a ridiculous extreme. If you want, you can use a nursery rhyme such as *Jack and Jill,* or anything you want. You can scream it, you can run around and beat things, and you can make the biggest and most disturbing sound and motions that you can. It will work best if it is loud and extreme. The loudest it goes will be unpleasant and be everything in the world that you would never do. If you are in front of a class, you must do it until you actually think you have disturbed them. If you do it at home, then you must do it till you actually disturb yourself in some manner. You may not want to do this in class. If not, find a gymnasium or an open field somewhere that you can do it.

As a reminder, it is big and foolish with extreme sounds and extreme motions. Do it on a continual basis, because the nature of acting is for your body to be in a state that is so far more extreme than anybody else that you have a different relationship to life. In this exercise you can scream and yell and gurgle and tear things and beat things up (objects, not people).

Another form of this exercise that I have used many times in class is to take a great big newspaper and roll it up until you form two rather hefty bats. Then, as you do your scene, monologue, or song, you simply beat them on the table or floor, somewhere, as hard as you can and with all your strength.

PAUL: *(Gives ACTOR the two pieces of newspaper rolled up in each hand.)* OK, I want you to take this and this. I want you to beat the floor. You can beat the chair. You can beat the table and anything you want. Start your scene from the beginning and I want you to spend a great deal of time just beating these things up as much as you can. *(ACTOR starts scene.)* OK, keep beating things even when you are in between thoughts. You are associating your dialogue with the beating, so I want you to take time to beat with the newspapers and not speaking. *(ACTOR continues.)* What's that? You are either going to beat it or not. OK, this time as you work, I am going to say "dialogue" or "no dialogue" and you are going to keep the beating with the newspapers throughout. I want you to swack, really beat with those! *(ACTOR starts scene again.)* Dialogue, no dialogue, dialogue, no dialogue, dialogue, no dialogue, dialogue, no dialogue, dialogue. *(PAUL lets scene continue with all the dialogue through the second half of the scene.)* Start over!

GAVIN: Think of the times you need enormous amounts of stamina, and this exercise is no exception. You need an instrument that is prepared for any situation at any given moment.

Food for Thought

A great director will not tell you what to do. They will help you discover your image. They hire you because they like your image. If they are trying to change the image, then they hired the wrong person and you're going to get in trouble. A great director will keep at you because of what they see in you, not to be like them. It never ceases to intrigue us as to how many actors get plastic surgery so that they can look like somebody else.

Food for Thought

Haven't you seen an actor and said, "Every time they do a new movie, I just have to go and see it!" It doesn't matter what the story is.

One day I was sitting alone and I thought to myself, "I think I will go to a movie tonight, but tonight I want to see really good acting." I picked a movie that was not that interesting, but the performances were so wonderful. I was glued to my seat. I have seen actors who, for a bit of fun, read names out of a phone book and were so compelling that the audience was saying, "Would you please read one more name, just one more." It's like the first time you eat chocolate — you feel like you cannot have enough. Storytellers can tell us anything and we are enthralled by it. If they tell us a complex story somehow it becomes simple. If they tell us a dangerous story, somehow they give us a safety net. They make us feel happy, safe, amused, and constantly surprise us with what seems like an infinite number of changes. Great acting is constantly falling into a new beginning, a new moment.

The Diagnosis

The purpose of having you beat with newspapers is so that your muscles feel what it's like to be used that way. We are told not to do things like that in polite society. If you are going to ride with the Hell's Angels, you are going to have to get used to the sound of their motorcycles. We want to give you the potential reactions to this exercise so you are somewhat prepared for what may follow. One actor, after completing this exercise, said words to the effect of, "I've never experienced anything like that in my life, and I love it!" Another actor said, "I've never experienced anything like that in my life, and I hate it!" The point is that actors have to deal with passions and with extremes. There are very few places where we are allowed to do extremes in life, and yet an actor has to experience them. If an actor is not comfortable with them, they will lose track of what they are doing. An actor can be in the middle of a scene or in performance and break their ankle and not know until the end of the performance, so we know that passion in acting can anesthetize. We don't want it to, yet we want passion to make us more sensitive, not less. This exercise, when worked to its full potential, will change you on a molecular level. We go to theatre or movies to increase the molecular activity in our being.

ACTOR: When do you stop working on these exercises?

PAUL: Never. The actor is working on their instrument for the entirety of their life. Your aim is not to get better, but good. Once you're good, your aim is to stay good. A catharsis releases energy within you. This exercise does something very different. This exercise teaches you to create energy. There is a big difference, a huge difference. That is why an actor at their worst drunken state can still give an amazing performance.

GAVIN: You want to be able to have an unlimited number of experiences in your life. Always be looking for new opportunities to create new experiences. An actor with limited experiences will have a limited toolbox from which to work.

Food for Thought

An actor works with such extremities because it is only in that state that you are likely to make the greatest character discoveries. The reason we act is because of the discoveries we make in the midst of acting. Acting is not talking about the performance tomorrow or thinking about the performance you did yesterday. It's not about yesterday. Acting has never been about yesterday or tomorrow. What we mean by "in the moment" and "now" is that while you are in that state, something crosses your mind that you have never thought of. You are going to create a situation in which you predictably think of something that you couldn't think of, and this great, seeming contradiction is what makes acting so special. That's why some actors are able to play the same character on and off for their entire life. As a director I have often said to an actor, "In my wildest imagination, I could never have come up with that. I can lead you there." It's why I love teaching and directing so much. If a director shows an actor everything they want them to do, they are missing an opportunity. They are not utilizing the abilities or capabilities of the actor.

Food for Thought

It would be great if we could say that actors respect one another, but they often do not, and they often do not respect themselves. The biggest word in acting is being *responsible*. An actor must be responsible. By taking responsibility for everything in your life you will become a more empowered individual.

Final Thoughts

Acting is relative. If acting takes only two people, a speaker and a listener, then we suppose there is a potential of a little bit of acting in every moment of our day. One of the big differences is the skill in which it is done and to what degree. The world often teaches us to be smaller than life, but on the other hand, some acting teachers often ask us to be larger than life. The only way we can be as large as life is to be familiar with that. Too many actors seem to think that the softer they talk, the less they feel, and the less they move, the more sincere they are. This is not the case. They are just boring. This exercise helps you to get a new relationship and a new frame of reference. The audience sees great intensity. They see things bigger than they are used to, as big as life itself. Acting as a sport requires intensity and bigness, and you can't do that until you are familiar with it. This exercise takes away all boundaries so you can experience what it is like to work without boundaries.

27. Impulse

Food for Thought

When looking at titles for acting exercises, I like titles that are accessible rather than poetic, esoteric, or only known by a select few. I like a title that is so clear that it would be just as clear to a non-actor as to an actor. It is not always possible to do this, but for the most part it is possible. Sometimes a title is so advanced it is simply referring to the knowledge we already have. We have broken this book down into sections so that you can find what you are looking for in its simplest form.

Food for Thought

I have always said that acting takes an actor telling a story and another person to listen. Let's take it one step further and say somebody talks and somebody listens. Does that mean we are acting all of our lives? Yes. What is the difference between a performance on-stage and talking on the street with a friend? Magnification. Young children don't know the difference of being on-stage or on-camera and off. They don't know the difference of anything. There is no difference in anything in their life. Children live moment to moment, living through impulsive and imaginary behavior. It is important for actors to rekindle this within themselves.

The Ingredients

Here's a little exercise you can do. One day, step away to watch yourself and listen to yourself speak. You might be saying, "I have to do more laundry soon. I don't like doing laundry because I find it tedious, etc." Ask yourself, "Who are those words coming from? They just seem to come out word after word after word. They have flexibilities, highs and lows, they are fast and slow, full of emotion, laughter, and anger. Where is that coming from? Where are these words coming out of my mouth coming from?" These words come out because you have an impulse. What you do is you stand across the room and in your imagination you watch yourself moving and you watch yourself talking. You begin to listen to yourself as you would listen to another person talking to you. You are paying attention to your words verbally, but also to the words that are being said through your thoughts. You are not judging them, you are just aware of them.

Food for Thought

If you are a gardener and someone says, "What do you grow?" You tell them, "I raise radishes, tomatoes, and avocados." If you're a builder and someone says, "What do you do?" You say, "I build houses." When you're actor, first of all, someone should look at you and say, "Are you an actor?" If they do, say, "What do you do?" It's not a proper answer to say, "I act." The proper answer is to say, "I become people I am not." This is the most basic part of acting. Acting is storytelling, but it goes beyond that because the actors in the film or play become people they are not. If a person asks you, "Are you an actor?" it is because every essence of your being tells them that is so.

Food for Thought

An actor might say, "Part of my unique way of acting is that I wander all over the stage when I'm talking." That's not a unique way of acting, and that's not acting. Can you imagine a basketball player saying, "Part of my unique way of making a basket is to dribble the ball and not throw it"? It makes that much sense. It is an example of how actors are bringing a language in to acting other than acting. Some classes will allow it because of finances, or because the teacher knows no better. It is really difficult to teach. Teaching is not an easy thing to do. You will find, if you have not already, that everyone has an opinion, but not everyone has an informed opinion.

The Diagnosis

Some people have an impulse to talk, and some people have an impulse not to talk. Some people have an impulse to talk, but they hold it in because of those around them who might disapprove. They arrest and stop their impulses. It's called *arrested development.*

We must keep going back to basics in every acting class on every occasion. Medical science has said at one time or another that the only difference between paranoid schizophrenia and what an actor does is that an actor does it on purpose. Both of them share the phenomenon of being across the room looking at themselves. You can't predict every word, and learn every word, and the tempo of the person talking to you. An actor has to begin to look at themselves as someone else talking. An actor must be two people and must be able to step out of themselves because, as a person, they couldn't do these things. As a person they couldn't do these things because there are some awful things a character must do and say. Think about some of the terrible actions committed by a character and things you have heard said by an array of characters at the movies. Can you imagine if these actions and all these views were held by the actor personally? Hamlet says terrible things to his mother. In traditional productions he frightens Ophelia, his girlfriend, and in traditional performances there is a scene in which he threatens to cause her personal discredit. In other words, he comes onto her in such an unpleasant manner that it drives her away.

Food for Thought

Sometimes a director might cast an actor and say, "You know, they're not very bright." I used to think they were being rude; however, they weren't. They were saying, "Look how talented they are. They are not a philosopher, a writer, or a mathematician, but they are a fabulous actor." The flipside is you can be in a class for twenty years. You can understand everything the teacher is sharing right up to the very last detail, and you could write a doctoral thesis, but not be a good actor. You will want to decide, if you have not already, what your contribution to the field of acting is going to be.

Food for Thought

Some people say you are either born an actor or you are not. You know it because you pursue acting. You pursue it relentlessly, you pursue it doggedly, and you refuse to pursue anything else no matter what your friends say. No matter what society says, you keep on going because it is what you have decided you must do, because it is what you are destined to do. There is often no clear logic to why actors pursue acting in this way, yet pursue it they must.

Final Thoughts

We are sure you have heard it said that you only speak a language when you can think in that language. We beg to differ. We think in impulses, and we have an impulse to say something. The words flow out simply because we have a language on which to put those impulses. A beginning actor will say, "I know what I want the audience to see now," and we have to take it into a language. We think they will understand, as a good actor simply does. The only people I know who think in the language they speak are liars. Other people only speak in impulses. The challenge for the actor is that impulses are not premeditated and your character's dialogue usually is.

28. Punctuation Out

Food for Thought

If you are cast, you do not pick your scene, your costume, your makeup, your setting, your director, or the other actors. All of these things are done without your permission. It seems to us there is a great deception in a scene study class that asks you to do all of these things yourself. This book is for actors who are professional or aspire to a professional life. While you may think that what we say is being unfair, that is not our concern. Our concern is that you understand and are thoroughly prepared for the professional life of an actor. You have to be prepared so that when opportunity comes your way, you are ready for it. This work is specifically for actors who want to become or are already professional actors. While you can learn wonderful and creative things in some acting courses, it does not mean they will be useful or practical to you as a professional actor. It does not mean it is incorrect, it means it is not preparation for a professional acting career.

Food for Thought

Learn how to adjust yourself. Many people cannot. Many people say, "Let me do it the way I am." And I will say, "Unless you are willing to make an adjustment, you will never be a successful actor." If you are able to adapt, you will become a more malleable actor.

The Ingredients

If you are working with a script or a monologue, type or cross out punctuation so that you don't have a habit of falsely pausing at a comma and pausing a little longer at periods. What we want you to do is work the piece without the punctuation given. What we want you to do is work with the piece without paying attention to the punctuation and allowing it to fall where it may. At first you may find this a challenge, but with practice you may find it quite a freeing experience. You may find you are not tangled up in the punctuation, which may allow the dialogue to flow.

Many acting teachers have come upon this exercise by themselves and so it has popped up all over the place. One of the reasons that we see a number of exercises by different teachers that are similar is that everybody came to the same conclusion. There are some exercises that are just universal no matter what language you are speaking. Some directors will follow the stage directions verbatim, but in your mind or in the script cross them out. For auditions you might choose to follow the directions in your sides, but in your mind create a freedom where you can be less predictable.

Food for Thought

There is no difference between a great actor and a sociopath except that one is a madman. What an actor does is sociopathic. A sociopath does not know he's lying. What are actors taught to do? They are taught to believe what they are doing, and what they're doing is not them. Perhaps it becomes clearer as to why actors can be called odd, peculiar, or eccentric.

Food for Thought

Actors are trained to accept and process any and all kinds of stimulation. In this respect, actors have to be without reference to anything. That is rather heroic because many people you meet will tell you it is not good to be stimulated past a certain degree. Some will also say it is not morally right to be stimulated in some manner. In almost every profession and sport in the world we choose what to accept as stimulation and what not to. What does it mean to see a performance that is heroic? It means that the person in front of us has allowed themselves to accept any and all kinds of stimulation. By being sponge-like you are prepared to take in anything and everything. If it does not suit your needs, you can always ring it out.

The Diagnosis

In this exercise we tell the actor to actually understand something when it's written as opposed to when it's spontaneous from the actor. When it's spontaneous from you, you understand it by your intention. When you speak spontaneously it is not necessary for a person to be able to read or write in order to speak very well. We know, for instance, that the Greeks were highly advanced and intellectual, and yet the majority of them could not read or write. When we speak, we don't speak with any particular nod to punctuation. The only purpose of punctuation is so that we can translate the code back with passion. If we haven't learned grammar, then we speak with no association with grammar, yet we can express ourselves very well because we are with a group of people that understands the language we are using. If we have different grammar from a different group of people, then it becomes a language in itself. If you are with other people that speak the same way, then it is proper grammar as far as they are concerned. When a person speaks to us, we generally understand what they are saying because of their intention and the words they use.

You want to fix your muscles and then use intention. When you are acting, the muscles are there for you so that no matter what your intention is, they will come up with the greatest muscular potential of that intention. We do not speak in sentences with correct punctuation. We do not always pause or speak in complete sentences, and neither does this exercise. When words are written on a page they are not words, they are codes. They might as well be Xs and Ys. They could be anything. You must be able to look at the words on the page and say, "These are not the words on the page, these are symbols that represent words in my mind." It appalls us when an actor tells a teacher, "Pause for a comma, pause for a period." We have witnessed teachers saying this when the purpose of this punctuation is to break the code. Once we have broken code we can pause anywhere we want to according to our own passion.

Food for Thought

To become an actor you have to become yourself, and when you become yourself you may not become a star. Success is surrender. When we work with actors, we find we often stop them on a number of occasions. This is not because they are doing something wrong, but because they are not being themselves. You want to find a way to make your instrument the best possible instrument it can be. If you become yourself you may not be a star, but you *can* be an actor. If you do not become yourself, the most you can hope for is to be a saleable commodity, a personality, an object, a fifteen minutes of fame, or certainly a product of some kind.

Actors often want to do it backwards. They say, "It doesn't matter what I look like. If I'm too short I'll wear lifts. If I'm too tall I'll slump. If I'm not beautiful, I'll try to be beautiful." You are working backwards! And then you try to fit yourself into something that somebody else did and was successful doing. It is great to be around successful actors whom you can learn and grow from, but you must not try to be them because we already have them, and now we want to find you. When you work an exercise such as this you may feel you have to unlearn things, but we would rather you think of it as creating a blank slate on which you can now create anything new. Learning to be yourself is one of the most challenging things an actor will ever do, and yet the results can be so devastatingly beautiful.

Food for Thought

Can you remember a situation where somebody was telling you a story, then they pause for a minute, and you said, "Wait, don't stop, don't stop, I want to hear the rest!" That's because they have told a story in such an entertaining, infectious, and passionate manner that you want to hear the complete story. A good actor does this automatically because they love to communicate stories.

Final Thoughts

Book after book, time after time, class after class briefly reminds us that what is written on a page is actually a code. Punctuation on a page is the equivalent of hieroglyphics or pictures. Punctuation is saying this is where the thought starts and this is where it stops. The actor cannot be thinking, "Oh, this sentence begins with a capital letter." When we talk, we do not talk in punctuation. If you want to be a good actor, write out your script with no punctuation. Look at it and you will begin to say, "What do I mean? Where do I mean that?" Your pauses will come where you want them to, not where grammar dictates them. Take the punctuation out of this paragraph and say it in your own way.

29. Alternating between Thoughts, or The Intent Exercise

Food for Thought

When you tell an actor to do something, you know they are wrong when they gasp before the first sentence. If you say "scene" or "action" and they suddenly gasp, the whole scene is wrong. We do it out of nervousness. It is our way of taking care of ourselves before starting a scene. We don't need it.

PAUL: Where did you live before you came to California?

ACTOR: Brooklyn.

PAUL: Did you like it there?

ACTOR: It's a great place.

PAUL: Yes, we never take a breath if we are asked a question, but some way or another we get the oxygen we need. We don't make a sudden gasp. Very nervous, frightened, or insecure people will, but normally we don't do it. It's a dead giveaway that the instrument has not been prepared adequately. It's the funniest thing in the world because if you go to an audition and gasp before you begin, you won't get the job. It's as simple as that. The casting director doing the hiring is never going to know why they won't hire you, they just won't hire you.

GAVIN: It's funny because sometimes what we think of as preparation is overly prepared, and thus becomes stagnate, artificial, and unbelievable.

Food for Thought

When you do exercises successfully you will recognize your own success. You will be excited by your own success. You will be joyful, and it will also give you more confidence in yourself. Then you will begin to think you are talented, and so will the people you audition for. All of this can begin with a simple exercise. The importance of an exercise is the value you give it. If it influences your acting in a good way, if it influences your career in a good way, then it is of value.

The Ingredients

What we would like you to do in this exercise is have a monologue or scene of some sort, preferably one you have not worked before, and without any thought to anything we want you to say the words. Then you are going to alternate between thoughts, so we want you to read the scene and talk to someone at almost the same time. We say *almost the same time* because most of us can only hold one thought in our head at any given moment.

PAUL: Tell me, who you are going to talk to?

ACTOR: My brother.

PAUL: So as you read this, you are going to be having a separate conversation with your brother internally. You are going to be morphing in and out between the two conversations. In other words, we will not hear that dialogue with your brother, but you will. You have to have a certain attention to the piece you are reading in order to speak it out loud. The reason I am asking you to have a separate conversation is so that you are able to think about something that doesn't have anything to do with this play or script. Your intention is to talk to your brother, not to read this. That is secondary. It is very important that you remember this. The most important part of this exercise is the conversation with your brother. You just happen to be reading or performing the scene at almost the same time. Go ahead.

ACTOR: I always worry that people aren't going to like me when I go to a party. *(ACTOR continues with the scene.)*

PAUL: That's very good work, but be careful that you stay true to your intentions. The intention you chose was, "I intend to speak to my brother." I saw it working. Those wonderful dramatic pauses were happening because you had to stop what you were doing and talk to your brother for a little bit. Go on.

ACTOR: I have to keep from feeling that the whole world is against me. *(Continues.)*

PAUL: Tell me a little about the conversation you had with your brother.

ACTOR: I told him that I got worried going to parties and that it wasn't fair and that I felt the whole world was against me at times.

PAUL: OK, so you somewhat tailored it to what you were saying in the scene?

ACTOR: Yeah, that's what I thought you wanted.

GAVIN: Can you simultaneously have a totally separate conversation that has nothing to do with the scene?

PAUL: Actually, *that's* what I wanted.

ACTOR: Oh, I didn't realize that's what you wanted me to do.

PAUL: What you did was have a specific, preconceived conversation with your brother. You had a conversation you intended. Isn't it interesting that an intent exercise keeps you from doing things you intend because you choose what you are going to intend and that keeps you from manipulating anything else? A very clean way of doing this exercise is to talk to them as you know them.

ACTOR: I didn't see that the first time. I didn't know I was supposed to do that.

PAUL: Now you have learned the difference between what you thought I wanted and what I actually wanted.

We thought it was very important to leave this little bit of conversation in because we wanted to show the potential confusion an actor can have when working with a teacher. If we had not gone back through this, the actor would have been doing the exercise incorrectly.

It was still getting some results, but not to the exercise's potential. This is why you hear it said that it is better to be with a teacher who can guide you specifically rather than working with a book. Of course we want you to work with this book, but we want you to be aware of the pitfalls, shortcomings, and misunderstandings that can arise when you are not actually there. As we have just shown here, misunderstandings can arise even when you are there with the teacher. I think the conversation works better if it has nothing to do with the play. This is particularly the case in the early stages, because if you do it the other way, you are making too many decisions about the play, and that is what you don't want to do. Experienced actors at table readings will try not to make any concrete decisions about the characters.

You may be wondering why we do not include the entire conversation with each actor. The reason is that it would take up hundreds of extra pages. It is also because we want to hint what each actor has discovered while allowing you to work these exercises and draw your own conclusions.

Food for Thought

All great performers do pretty much the same thing. It's just like all great bicycle riders peddle pretty much the same way. You stretch, strengthen, coordinate, and then you adapt. Sarah Bernhardt at the end of her career was giving magnificent performances and she did have to make a slight adaptation, she only had one leg! The challenges you will face if you are a good actor will only spur you on.

Food for Thought

The human being is the most advanced organism in the world. As opposed to being natural, acting is against your nature because in life, when you have too much stimulation, that is considered bad. Actors have to teach themselves to do something that is considered unnatural — they have to embrace stimulation on all levels. They don't run away from things, and they don't run away from an audience even if they throw up before going on. Stage fright is natural. If you don't have stage fright you have taught yourself to do something that is not natural. A hero is a person who is not afraid in battle. An actor is trained to do something that is against their nature, and it's the greatest high in the world to do it. Your blueprint on acting is inside you waiting to be discovered.

The Diagnosis

When a person speaks to us, we understand what they are saying because of their intention and the words they use. Generally speaking, we understand other people quite well even though we don't always understand all the words they are saying, perhaps due to their dialect or slang. We understand because of the intention and you have to reverse that process. You have to look at the script and find your intention at any given moment. It is even better to say, "What is my intention when I say these words?" As you continue with the dialogue you can ask, "Is this still my intention?" And if it's not, then it's changed. In order to do the exercise and understand it, we generally isolate it and then we go back and incorporate it — that's the nature of an exercise. A personal trainer will get you to isolate the muscles you are working with so that you get into the habit of doing that. In this exercise you have to move between the scene and the other conversation you are having. You have to move between thoughts. Acting is not picking up a ball and holding it, or a medicine ball that I throw and you catch. It's juggling many, and you can practice these things everyday.

This exercise is also the simplest form of intention rather than anything that might be called motivation. You have to focus on two entirely separate conversations and you may find that you pause in certain places. The staggering and stuttering can be golden and can also be described as discovery of character. If this happens because of the work, then it will be a discovery for you. This is one of the most beneficial exercises in terms of blind faith that you can do — anything creative is. One of the definitions for the word *creative* is unexpected. If we expect it, we don't call it creative, do we? We would then call it mechanical. Society always steers you away from being creative and doing things unexpectedly. Antonin Artaud is discussed by Gabriela Stoppelman when she says, "Artaud turned society's accepted idea upside-down. He said that, 'the soul is born of the body, and not the body of the soul.'"[49] In this exercise you have to multitask throughout, and while you are having your internal conversation, you are also reading the dialogue on the page. The actor is constantly multitasking, whether it be on-stage or camera or off, it is an integral part of your life.

Food for Thought

Sometimes we have to refer to other techniques because acting has not clarified itself as much as it should. Acting remains mysterious. Some actors and teachers seem to revel in the fact that you can't quite explain it. Subjectivity in art creates potential for great art and great confusion.

Food for Thought

Work a scene or a monologue, and while you do it take your shoe off, take the shoelace completely out of the shoe. You then put the shoelace completely back in the shoe while you are doing the monologue. It forces you to use both sides of your brain. In time, the actor finds the ability within themselves to stop struggling.

Final Thoughts

When we talk to another person, we generally do it spontaneously, without inhibition or self-consciousness. You just talk and the words come out. As soon as we begin to work with dialogue, we fill ourselves with all kinds of thoughts that wouldn't be happening if we were just talking to somebody naturally. It even surprises me that you are taught in an acting class to think the thoughts you are going to think while you're speaking. Now we have doubled up the limitations of thought. Self-conscious thought displaces imagination. Haven't you ever talked to somebody and thought how bright you were for what you just said? Any exercise is so that you go on-stage or set and do nothing.

Remember, every exercise in this book is a functional exercise. Function in your best way and the best function of our body is when we are happy, healthy, full of energy, and talking to someone we like to talk to. Not when we're trying to explain why we shouldn't get a traffic ticket or something like that. The best acting is when you are saying something so magnificent and you're the only one who gets to say it at that moment. How can you get the body in that state? In this exercise you are switching between two separate conversations and you are keeping the body on its toes in order to function the way it wants to function. You are taking away your automatic intentions in order to discover new ones.

30. Teach Yourself

Food for Thought

When a person tells you something is not possible, what they are telling you is that their imagination is tight. When you have done a number of exercises, no exercise is by definition complete, and no exercise actually completes anything. Exercises are often given as if they complete, finish, or correct something. Exercises are by definition a small part of something you will never be able to see. Instead of looking for the results, instead of looking for the moment, be in the moment you are in.

---

49. Gabriela Stoppelman, *Artaud for Beginners* (New York: Writers and Readers Publishing, 1998), 134.

Food for Thought

We must remember to be accurate in our use of words in any profession. The word *actor* means a person who tells stories to an audience, who shows an audience something they have never seen, or who shows an audience something they never imagined could be. This can only be done by constant work, constant revelation, and constant practice. In terms of acting and making theatre, Luke Dixon quotes Athol Fugard when he says, "All you need to make theatre is three things: an actor, a space, and a pair of ears."[50] You have probably been told by friends and family at some stage to, "Get a real job." Acting has the potential to entertain, change, and influence lives. What can be more real than that?

The Ingredients

This is an exercise where you become the teacher, and while you are acting, you can interrupt yourself and say, "That's not how I meant to say it, I meant it this way, let me do it once more." Or "Oh, now I see, I didn't see until I did it, now I see how it should be. This is the way it should be," until you get what you want or until you get what you think is the best you can do. For this exercise you can either work with a scene or monologue you know or you can read a scene from a script or play.

PAUL: Since I did not ask you to bring a monologue with you, I am going to have you look at the page. Read this scene for me. *(Gives ACTOR scene and indicates where to begin.)* I am going to demand that you have a life and energy to you. I am going to demand that you are in a state of readiness and alertness before you look down at the script. OK, you can begin.

ACTOR: OK, when I was ten or eleven I had my tonsils out.

PAUL: Slow down a little.

ACTOR: It's not me if I talk slower.

PAUL: That's fine, I want you to speak with your voice and not your mannerisms, big difference.

ACTOR: When I was ten or eleven ... that, didn't feel right. When I was ten or eleven ... I wouldn't do it like that.

PAUL: Good, start again.

ACTOR: OK, when I was ten or eleven I had my tonsils out. My dad was on a business trip ... I read that weird. I wanted it to be more sincere. OK, when I was ten or eleven I had my tonsils out. My dad was on a business trip, and I wanted my dad to see it, so I asked the doctor ... I wanted to respond differently there, I would like it to be more caring.

PAUL: It distracts you, doesn't it? You have to stop what you are doing to listen to yourself.

ACTOR: Yeah, it's a little difficult.

PAUL: Good, so remember you can stop yourself wherever you want and self-teach or correct. "Oh, I said that too fast, I'll slow it down. Oh, that wasn't the idea I had in mind, this is how I wanted to do it, etc." Good, read this piece.

ACTOR: That's not funny, do you want me to tell you something weird that happened to me? Ahhhh, I know I'm using a backup plan, it's an easy go-to.

PAUL: Is there a better way you can do it or would like to do it?

ACTOR: Yes, I wish I had more time to read it over.

PAUL: But you don't.

ACTOR: But I don't. That's not funny, do you want me to tell you something weird that happened to me?

---

50. Luke Dixon, *Play Acting* (London: Methuen, 2003), 178.

PAUL: In this exercise there will be a number of times when you get frustrated with yourself, and you may find that you demand a better answer of yourself. What I would like you to do is help yourself along, and when you find a resistance, wait for a better response. When you wait a moment you will find you stop fighting yourself, you are not defensive, and you will come up with a better way to teach yourself.

GAVIN: At the end of the day, every actor must become their own teacher.

Food for Thought

An actor should be the most empathetic person in the world. You want to cultivate that more and less on your intellect. You recognize it and you allow it to pass through you. Allow it to take you over. What we are talking about is making you and your instrument better, stronger, and more accessible. This is in order to increase your ability and to use your talent. To us, good actors are all doing exactly the same thing. When looking at great actors, rather than looking at what is different in them, start looking at what is the same in them. It is necessary to observe others in order to learn from them. In the book, *Twentieth Century Actor Training,* Peter Thomson says, "The Brechtian actor's training begins with the observation of the outside world."[51] Darryl Hickman says, "True actors instinctively mimic their fellow humans, recreate the everydayness and the addition of the natural world."[52] You must continue to use your powers of observation and gesticulation on an ongoing basis.

Food for Thought

As a young man I worked with a very famous actor and was told, "When he comes in the building, never say anything to him! Don't say good morning, don't say good afternoon, and just don't speak to him ever!" Now the reason was he was saying, "I've got a lot of work to do, I've got a very short time to do it, and I do not have a moment to waste." Some actors may appear rude or obnoxious on-set, and perhaps they are. There is also the likelihood that they are preparing their instrument and have no time for distractions.

The Diagnosis

During this exercise some actors commented that they were just given the script and they didn't even have time to get a grasp of the character. However, there will be times when you don't have a chance to get a grasp of the character. In these circumstances, go in there, do something very dangerous, and trust your instinct. As you work exercises, you are going to find that you process things faster. What this exercise allows you to do is to create spontaneity about you. You have to be spontaneous because in an audition you do not know what the casting director or director wants. You don't know what they are looking for, and you do not know what they want. This is part of the reason why very famous actors do not audition very often, they say, "My people will talk to your people." A famous actor gets that consideration, but anybody other than a very famous actor would not get that. You are there simply to please the casting director.

A reason this exercise asks you to work with a monologue from a scene or play is because they work by themselves and you don't need a scene partner. As you continue to work with and teach yourself, you will start to become a more trained and experienced you. It's one thing to have interesting ideas. It is another thing to be fully available to them. A number of actors who have been in a series for a long time are sometimes given the opportunity to direct an episode or two. It's figured that they're on-set everyday, and they know the ropes. What they are really saying is this show could go on without a director because everyone knows exactly what they are doing. WE want you to be confident enough in yourself and your work to know exactly what you are doing.

---

51. Alison Hodge, 104.
52. Darryl Hickman, *The Unconscious Actor* (Canada: Small Mountain Press, 2007), 26.

It is worth noting that the role of the director as we know it only really goes back to the nineteenth century. When looking at the role of the director Harold Clurman says, "The Director must be an organizer, a teacher, a politician, a psychic detective, a lay analyst, a technician, a creative being. He must inspire confidence."[53]

Food for Thought

The only thing we learn is the difference between two things.

Food for Thought

Society gives us all kinds of social guidelines that say we are not supposed to do this because it's rude, it's illegal, etc. We are constantly told not to do things and not to look at people, but on-stage we must do it. Since our whole life has been telling us not to do this, it's very difficult to do. As Ann Brebner says, "Everyone, from time to time, trips over unfinished emotional business from the past. For those of us who are actors, those stumbling blocks have a profound effect on the quality of our work and on our ability to develop our craft to its greatest state of grace."[54] Because of this, the beginning exercises are the ones that are least invasive to you as an actor. Some actors want to skip the basics and go straight to the good stuff, but the basics is the good stuff, it's your foundation on which you can build.

Final Thoughts

Teachers can very often demonstrate something better than the student can do it. It is easier because they are not performing, they are teaching. This exercise points out that when an actor acts like they would when teaching someone else, suddenly the intimidation goes away and they feel a freedom and pleasure at showing us what they intended or what they thought should be done. It is that simple. When you are acting, you tend to be intimidated by or worried about what people are seeing. When you are a teacher, you don't worry about what people are seeing because if you make a mistake, you just do it over. You say, "That's not what I meant." Actors must realize that no matter what they do, they can still do it again, and again, and again. You may come across a teacher who has a god complex, where in their own eyes they can say or do no wrong. It is your responsibility to question what they are saying until it sits well with you.

31. Release of Reaction

Food for Thought

Exercises don't work unless you are absolutely sure what the exercise is doing. All great acting exercises should be able to be done in some way or other by you alone if the intent is to use them for the rest of your life. It is about being specific with your work rather than accepting generalities.

Food for Thought

A number of the terms we use in acting today came from psychology and have only been around since the twentieth century. An actor who was alive before this time didn't even have the vocabulary that we have today. He didn't say, "What's the psychological significance for that?" Words such as *morose, depressed,* or *motivation* hadn't been conceived yet. Acting terminology can be an actor's best friend, and it can also be the actor's worst enemy. Don't get too stuck on this term or that term to the point that it confines you and your acting. Remember that different directors use the same acting terminology with a different interpretation.

---

53. Harold Clurman, On Directing (New York: Macmillan Publishing,1972), 14.
54. Ann Brebner, Setting Free the Actor (California: Mercury House, 1990), xiii.

The Ingredients

What we would like you to do in this exercise runs along similar lines to Over the Top. That is, while you are doing a scene, do any thought that crosses your mind or any impulse you have. Don't look and see if this fits into the scene. Just do any impulse you have. You might burp, you might hiccup, or you might jump at any moment. You have to be careful not to worry too much about words. If we say, "You are doing it too fast," we may mean you look nervous. What we want is a performance, a piece of art. Sometimes you might do this exercise in front of a class, or you might choose to go out in the middle of an open field because it is difficult to do. Do not worry about your audience at all. If you have one, it is their responsibility to get out of the way, not yours. You can come up and look as if you are going to punch us if it takes you there.

(ACTOR starts to perform a scene.)

PAUL: Don't hold back. If you're crying, then go with it. *(ACTOR keeps going.)* Bigger, bigger, more! Go! It's hard work. It's fun, but it's hard work. *(ACTOR continues.)* Why are you looking at me all the time? Get involved in what you are doing. You're avoiding a lot of this. The reason you are avoiding it is not because you have made a decision, but because it is unfamiliar to you. Another reason is you are prejudging from your own life. Perhaps it's not safe or good, and so it feels a little uncomfortable. Go ahead. *(ACTOR continues to end of scene and is somewhat exhausted.)* Take a seat for a moment, put you head down between your legs, just lean forward and rest your torso on your knees. Lean forward as far as you can go comfortably. *(One minute goes by.)* OK, stand up and begin the scene again.

GAVIN: There is a great physical intensity to this exercise. When you see a great actor give a great performance, they seem to have intensity about them that goes on forever.

Food for Thought

Is there any reason to believe that cavemen could not act as well as we can now? There is a reason to believe that cavemen could not play the piano because they did not have one. As far as we can see in everything we've ever studied, the only art form that wasn't invented was acting. We do not see any difference in acting now than it was with the cavemen. Cavemen were naked in a cave. They didn't need clothing, and one of those cavemen who had a minute left over was a storyteller. He didn't just want to tell a story, but to communicate with the person beside him. As Oscar Brockett explains, "Relating and listening to stories are seen as fundamental human pleasures. Thus, the recalling of an event, a hunt, battle, or other feat is elaborated through the narrator's pantomime and impersonation and eventually through each role being assumed by a different person."[55] Since the beginning of our existence it seems we have always had a desire to communicate and share stories with one another.

Food for Thought

The interesting part of a fall is that between A and B you give up any tension. In a fall, in a split second you give everything up and then you regain it on the other end. A moment of inspiration is like falling, the point of no return.

The Diagnosis

PAUL: You will never in your life be able to do what you did when you first started the scene today because you have changed the whole function of your body. You have changed on a molecular level. A lot of things happened today, more than I could possibly describe, and more than you think you saw. That is the magic and joy of being an actor. There is no

---

55. Oscar G. Brockett, *History of the Theatre* (Austin, Texas: A Viacom Company, 1999), 6.

way to describe what you look like at this precise moment in time. Tell me how you feel about what you have just done. I'm not looking for you to tell me anything, there is not a right or wrong answer. The only reason I would ask you the question is so that you can hear yourself talking. There is a very big, important thing here: When I ask you to talk about the work you have just done, it is so you can feel yourself expressing and it will lock it in, and it will make it clearer for you. It means you will own it for the rest of your life.

ACTOR: I found that, at times, I was so engaged that it was hard to continue speaking.

PAUL: You see, by doing basic exercises like this, you function clearer. This exercise changes the way you function and kinetically you will never be quite the same.

ACTOR: I felt free.

PAUL: It's so wonderful to hear that.

ACTOR: At the same time, I felt really connected with the character.

PAUL: When an actor has truly experienced an exercise, there comes a time where they start talking and they can't make sense. We just saw a little bit of that in you. That's a wonderful thing, and when you notice that in yourself you are on the right track.

ACTOR: I felt I was very engaged in the moment.

PAUL: What an actor experiences is nothing like anybody who is not an actor ever experiences. If a non-actor says, "I feel free," it's an entirely different thing, because what it does is it releases them, and what it does for the actor is it teaches you to use your body in a creative state. The only problem is that this is more addictive than any drug known in history. It activates endorphins throughout your body and makes you want to do it again. In this exercise you encouraged yourself to allow anything to happen. I just can't say often enough — you look like an entirely different entity. I can actually see somebody I have never seen. When you are functioning like this I can see you and not see you.

GAVIN: This exercise allows the actor to strip away what is unnecessary so that by the end of it we see you. This sounds very simple, yet it is one of the biggest challenges an actor will face. We spend our whole lives hiding behind masks that the actor must strip away.

Food for Thought

The sign of a good teacher is one who gives all of their secrets away. A good instructor will beg, borrow, or steal from other teachers.

Food for Thought

When we say "Think outside the box" we are burdening ourselves with a box. If someone says to me, "Think outside the box," I say to them, "What box?" What we *should* say is, "Think beyond the box." Occasionally we have advisers who say, "You have to move on." I never like that. There is nothing more exciting to me than the moment I'm in. There isn't anything else but the moment I'm in. To tell an actor to move beyond something means it has infinite possibilities for direction and discovery. To move forward means in front of your nose, and to move beyond forward means it radiates in all directions. Why think outside the box when you can live outside the box?

Final Thoughts

What most people, other than actors, call *maturity*, we would call *restricted behavior*. After all, we are faced with all sorts of catch phrases: don't lose control, think before you speak, and don't talk foolishly. If we learn how to restrict ourselves from doing all of these things, then we are often called mature. But we certainly can't be an actor in this state. An actor must be familiar with their body, the order in which we use muscles, and the ability to let our muscles follow anything our imagination might imagine.

In this exercise, you might find that you start crying out of nowhere. Actors call such an event a *golden moment*. We would call it *release of reaction.* You are telling yourself that you are going to allow any kind of reaction to that moment or to your scene partner. Your reactions are uninhibited and arrive moment to moment. You have to allow yourself any kind of reaction to how the costume feels on you, to the atmosphere, or the heat or coolness in the room. This is only able to happen if you are a fully functioning actor. You will, as an experienced actor, begin to process this, but you have to have something to use.

I sometimes watch an actor and think, "How did they think that? Whatever gave them that thought?" Bad acting is easy to define, but great acting is a whole different matter entirely. I've asked many actors after a release of reaction, their golden moment, "Why did you do this?" They will often turn and say to me, "I don't know, it just happened." Let's practice "it just happened." Great actors and great teachers often delved further into their approach to acting after they had a eureka! moment, not before it. These actors become intrigued in finding out how they did what they just did.

Chapter 7:
A Magnetic Personality

32. Gathering

Food for Thought

I remember seeing a performance by a world-famous clown who did some of the most brilliant acting I have ever seen. There was a spotlight on the ground (a follow spot), he went to the edge, and began to sweep it up. As he swept it up he made it smaller. Then he made it smaller, and smaller, and smaller. Thousands of people watched him in rapt attention. Suddenly it was silent, everything had stopped, the orchestra had stopped, the venders had stopped, and everyone was watching him. At the end he took a little dustpan to sweep up the last drop. It wasn't just great performing. There was something that I was learning about life as I was watching him. That was theatre of consequence. Great performances can touch us, move us, and influence our lives. In reference to clowning Jacques Lecoq points out, "Research for one's own clown begins by looking for one's ridiculous side."[56] Discover all facets of your personality by stretching them so that you can be aware of them.

Food for Thought

Some actors wallow in a role. They either make decisions too quickly or make no decisions at all, instead of pursuing, pursuing, pursuing. Have the courage to go beyond the character. As the famous philosopher Derrida says, "A transcendental signified is a meaning that lies beyond everything in the whole universe."[57]

The Ingredients

I formed this exercise after talking to a well-known actress who told me she was working on a play with an actor who did not know what he was doing. When I asked her how she coped with this she said, "I spent the entire performance gathering the audience." It was as if she said to the audience, "Excuse me, there is a play going on here, and if you all come along and follow me, I will tell you all about it."

In gathering, you walk towards the audience and you gather them. Imagine that I am bringing my arms in towards my chest and walking towards the audience in the form of a self-embrace. I just gathered them. I didn't snap my fingers to get their attention, but instead I really gathered them.

What we want you to do now is, one at a time, walk from the other end of the room, turn to face us, walk towards us, and gather us. First, gather your own thoughts, and then gather our energy, our thoughts, and our being. If you are doing this exercise by yourself, simply use your imagination as if your audience were there.

PAUL: That was good, but you know what? I would suggest to you, as you approach, that you just get stronger at gathering and take more time.

ACTOR: Can I try it again?

PAUL: Oh, you like it, don't you?

---

56. Jacques Lecoq, *The Moving Body* (New York: A Theatre Arts Book, 1997), 145.
57. Jim Powell, *Derrida for Beginners* (New York: Writers And Readers Publishing, 1997), 35.

ACTOR: I felt like I rushed it.

PAUL: Yeah, you're right, you did a little bit ... go ahead. Now that was better because you set it up. You set it up before you used your arms. And, by the way, the arms are just a teaching aid. Look at an object in the room and feel like you can bring this object towards you. You can will it towards you or you can embrace it as though it's moving towards you. You can also do this exercise with a friend by standing about fifteen feet apart and facing one another. Have them gather you and then you can gather them. You can practice this exercise wherever you are. If you are sitting in a café with a friend, you can look at them and, without taking your arms out to the side and by using your thoughts, gather them up toward you. You will know it is working when you notice that your friends are giving you all of their attention. Actors proceed by gathering us with their intent, their thoughts, and their eyes.

GAVIN: The specific physical action of gathering is more of a metaphor that works very well at the beginning, and then the actor is asked to strip this away and simply gather us by their intent. This is a very important point because it means an actor can gather their audience in any moment of any scene and in any situation.

Food for Thought

It is interesting to note that if an actor has their own star on Hollywood Boulevard it is because they, themselves, their manager, or an organization sends in a request and then they pay for the costs and for the ceremony. It is perfectly acceptable because it is a publicity expense. It is good to know how things are done even if you do not always understand why things are done.

Food for Thought

When you see a star at openings or on a red carpet we wouldn't believe it if you said you didn't feel they were gathering you. You will find that many of the top stars have a magnetic personality that draws you in. It is energy that they have practiced all of their lives. Haven't you, at one time, had somebody look directly at the camera and you said, "My god, they know me!" Great actors have a presence in any room, any venue, and any location.

The Diagnosis

You, as an actor, must have the ability to gather a hostile audience. Acting is when there is something happening between you (the actor) and the observer or audience. As an audience member you have fifty percent of the power to make it acting. If I am flipping through my cell phone or reading the back of my candy packet, then what is happening in the movie or on-stage at that precise moment ceases to be acting to me. It doesn't matter whose fault it is. It is still your responsibility as an actor to compel the audience to pay attention!

This is an exercise that, with practice, becomes an automatic action that gathers your audience in. By gathering people on a regular basis you create a stage or scene presence. Stage presence is something that radiates from your body, and it is something you draw to your body from the audience. Your mother, the police, and society tell you to leave people alone; however, acting tells you just the opposite. As Margie Haber says, "Every audition you go on increases your odds of winning a part, each reading gets you closer to booking a job. Actors often ask me if they should audition for a part that is not right for them and I always tell them, 'yes!'"[58]

Society will teach you to have personal space, but when an actor is performing they no longer have personal space. As you walk into the room and face the audition panel, you

---

58. Margie Haber and Barbara Babchick, *How to Get the Part*, (New York: Lone Eagle Publishing Company, 1999), 9.

gather them. Getting the part is not just fun. Getting the part is like winning the lottery. It's a rush, and it is actually doing the work that is the fun part. Kenneth Branagh talks about his own experiences as an actor when he says, "I still felt compelled to be more than just an actor, and I felt almost guilty at the fun I had making, *Coming Through* and *Ghosts*."[59]

I don't work on the audition, I work on the attitude of the person going in to the audition. Everything that you have heard of as *talent* is based on technique, and everything comes from technique. When I see an actor whose performance does not turn me on that night, and then they just suck me in, I love that. I say to myself, "Look at that, look what they've just done. I've no reason to like them or like the play or anything else, and it's just fabulous because they are a good actor."

This applies as much to films as it does to theatre. Think of a time when you have seen a movie that you thought was mediocre, and most of the acting was, at best, average. Then think about that one actor who stood out for you whose performance you were drawn into. What was it that they did that grabbed and demanded your attention? Part of the answer is that they gathered you in. In regards to not gathering the audience, Michael Caine explains, "If you catch somebody 'acting' in a movie, that actor is doing it wrong."[60] I saw an actor who was playing Dracula and with one glance he bit everybody in the audience before he bit his victim. That's acting. As Michael Checkhov says on his work with the actor, "The 'charisma' of an actor or actress on-stage and screen corresponds to the degree of purely invisible radiation he or she is able to achieve. Some people have this ability naturally; others need to spend a good deal of time radiating in order to develop it."[61]

Food for Thought

Has anybody thought of the fact that you would like your audience to see the same performance whether it's on stage or on television or on film numerous times, or do you all think you want everybody to come just once to your performance? Wouldn't you like everybody to want to come and see it ten times? How often do you pull an audience in to see you do the same performance? Every time you hear a great actor tell a story you hear something you didn't hear before, because it is so rich. A performance that is so engaging, so strong, will make you want to come back to it again and again throughout your life. If you see a show at the end of its run, then it is the experience that will stay with you for the rest of your life.

Food for Thought

An actor may see an incredible performance and say, "I can't figure out how she does that!" As an audience they say, "I don't care how she does that, I just care that she does it."

Final Thoughts

We have to continually remind ourselves that we are talking about an actor as a creative artist, not as a saleable commodity or a personality. The gathering exercise came out of the practical need of an actor while she was on-stage and was later turned into an exercise. It's a reminder that an actor can find exercises by themselves by simply asking themselves, "What do I need at this moment?" You make discoveries because of your practical need to do so.

---

59. Kenneth Branagh, *Beginning* (New York: St Martin's Press, 1989), 169.
60. Michael Caine, 4.
61. Michael Chekhov, *On the Technique of Acting* (New York: Harper Collins, 1985), xli.

33. Plumb Line

Food for Thought

A famous actor was given an exercise where he was asked to live in his home naked for two months and he did. He did it because it made him aware of things in a different way. He had learned to literally strip himself bare and be an open book.

Food for Thought

People do not get fired because they are not talented. They get fired because they do not do what's asked of them. If you are in a general audition, watch to see who the worst one in the room is and then go stand by them. Even if you are average you will shine next to them. We want you to be a smart, intelligent, talented, streetwise actor.

The Ingredients

We want you to take a piece of string that is about two feet in length and tie a small weight of some sort to the end. Gravity will pull it towards the ground and the line between the bottom and the top is called a *plumb line*. It is absolutely balanced according to gravity. If you hold that string in front of you, then the opposites of everything on that string are equal. When your body is in balance, it is in symmetry. If you do not have a string, then hold out the hand you write with straight in front of you and imagine that the string is in that hand. What we would like you to do is go up on your tiptoes and come back down again. As you go up, be careful not to overcompensate by leaning forward. As you come down, we want you to keep thinking up. We want you to repeat this action a few times while keeping your arm out in front of you and your plumb line perfectly balanced. What we would like you to do is think of the plumb line going two ways — both upwards and with gravity. What we have to think of is that we are one of the forces in the plumb line. What's the other force?

ACTOR: Gravity.

PAUL: That's right, it's gravity. Keep your arm held out at all times. As you keep your arm out, you may start to feel a burning in your shoulder, this is because you are gripping with those muscles of your rotator cuff and you need to let them go. At this point, I want you to recite a scene or a monologue while going up and down on your toes. Once you get to the end of the monologue you can repeat it. *(ACTOR keeps on working.)* Kudos! You recognize the work and you recognize it within yourself. Anytime you find yourself forgetting about your plumb line, I want you to stop and then resume.

ACTOR: I was losing it in the middle of words and I was trying to continue. I was wondering if I should start from the beginning or continue on from where I left off?

PAUL: You can do either. For now, stop and start over again, but eventually you want to continue. Remember you have to sustain a performance on-stage no matter what. The more you practice this, the more you will be able to sustain it. If you are balanced, this exercise won't take much energy. When you are doing it correctly it is because of *thought* instead of *action*.

GAVIN: In order to get good at this exercise you are going to have to start out as a pragmatist. The better you get, the more you will be able to adapt instinctively.

Food for Thought

There must be a place that you go to shop for groceries or for clothes or for hardware. You go there if you need to, if it is in your neighborhood, and you go there often. Because you go there often you know where everything is. That is what acting is like. You have to build your own warehouse, and you have to know where things are. We don't know many actors who know how to access the tools that they need and should have in their warehouse. If you said, "I bought a new light fixture and I want to put it on the wall," you need to have an idea of where the tools are to do that. You have to put screws in, you have to fit it a certain way, and you have to connect it to electricity. Actors say, "If I could just get a good script, if I could just get a good director, if I could just get a good scene partner, and if I could just get a break." That's kind of like saying, "If I could just get a house, I know I would have a beautiful house." Then you say, "It needs to be painted," and we say, "Do you have any idea where the paint is, where the paint store is, and what the best colors are?" "No, but I'll find out," you might say. You should already know, and you should already have the necessary tools. An experienced actor looks at a part and says, "I know where to shop for the things that this character needs. Not only can I go to the store for it, I know which aisle that it is on." The more you work on your instrument, the more you will be able to expand your toolbox. The more you have in that toolbox the more accessible your instrument will become.

Food for Thought

There is a wonderful story of a very famous actor who, at a young age, was in a play where he had a tendency to giggle. He was working alongside two very accomplished actors and they didn't like that. It annoyed them. They cured him of it in a purposeful fashion. They went on-stage knowing his weaknesses and did everything in the world to make him laugh, until it was serious and he almost made a complete fool of himself. He finally had to give up the giggling because he couldn't act, and he realized it was getting in the way.

Laughter can also be beneficial to the actor as Viola Spolin explains, "When laughter is moderate and enjoyable, it is useful. It most often denotes a breakthrough. It will help, not impede the work. When it has elements of hysteria in it, however, it will prove destructive and must be carefully handled by the director."[62] In terms of humor, Andy Goldberg says, "Humor comes from specifics. Try to zero in on the particulars of real-life situations, whether they're big events or small ones."[63]

A famous teacher was working with an actor and told her, "You didn't do that well." The actor said, "I took a real glass to a real water cooler, and I really poured water, and I really drank it. How could anything I did have been wrong?" And the teacher said, "You didn't want it." This was a simple answer, but we have to be simplistic because we have to get to simple things in order to get to the complex things. Reality on-stage or film can never quite be the same as that of real life as much as we might believe it should be. As Stella Adler says, "Truth on the stage is not quite the truth in life. It is always more or less than life. On-stage, you never do exactly what you do in life."[64] Part of your responsibility in acting is knowing how to solve problems at any given moment.

The Diagnosis

This exercise can cause an immediate emotional reaction from you, and that is good. It also means you have to be satisfied with, "I'm going to think that until it works." When you think something and nothing happens, you wait until it does. If you look up the word *balance* in the dictionary, it will say something like, "A state of equilibrium or parity."[65] Yoga, Alexander, Pilates, and Feldenkrais are popular because they all address balance. When you are in balance you have the potential to do anything. The plumb line is a straight line and everything around on all sides of that straight line is equal to what is opposite. Gravity is taken care of for us, but in order to glide up we have to think up. The only thing that helps you balance at first is thought. The string is what ties life and you together. Life will do its thing without any help from you whatsoever. It is also worth noting that the purpose of the knees

62. Viola Spolin, *Improvisation for the Theatre* (Illinois: Northwestern University Press, 1963), 343.
63. Andy Goldberg, *Improv Comedy* (California: Samuel French Trade, 1991), 5.
64. Stella Adler, *The Technique of Acting* (New York: Bantam Books, 1988), 62.
65. David Jost, *The American Heritage College Dictionary* (New York: Houghton Mifflin Company, 1997), 103.

and the hips is to lower and raise your torso. The difference between going up on your toes and coming down is only embellishment or choreography.

When you are doing this exercise correctly we can see you thinking. This exercise will almost automatically enable you to look at people in a more direct way. This is not only important, but also invaluable for you in many aspects of your career. You are not commanding their attention, you are engaging them. People love to be engaged. In this exercise, you have to make adjustments. That is like life, where you are constantly having to make adjustments. Sometimes you see movie stars who appear to be gliding across the room. As they are walking it is most likely that they are consciously or subconsciously thinking it up.

Food for Thought

You may think that you want to be able to take what is practical from your training and use it, and this is a good point. While a technique may be of great benefit, it is without a doubt the man or woman behind the technique that really makes it what it is. Unfortunately, when you study with a disciple or other individual, what you will always be missing are the originator's personal insights. These are priceless. We are not saying don't go to college, but as a professional actor, it is not going to be a significant advantage for you. If you are in college and working with this book, these comments might concern you. It is better that you hear them now than when you are looking for work and discovering this reality for yourself.

Food for Thought

Never do something because you expect something in return. Instead of saying, "What can I take?" ask yourself, "What am I bringing to the situation?" As Ingrid Bergman explains, "What you bring to a part is what you have within you. It's your very first intuition about a part that comes out in the end."[66]

Final Thoughts

This exercise is important because it helps you to balance your body according to gravity. You have to use thought in order to achieve this because thought is your being. What this exercise highlights is that the potential of thought already exists and that imagination is the actor's key. The challenge is to keep working and practicing this exercise with the plumb line. This exercise is encouraging your body to get used to working in balance. Some people call this organic, but if it is not organic it is balance because organic doesn't take thought. Actors are constantly being asked to work on things that their bodies are not used to. The key is to allow your body to become used to these things.

34. Unmask Yourself

Food for Thought

We do have a good expression in acting, "Leave it outside." Even though actors say they are concentrating, focused, and working on their instrument, they make the mistake of bringing in stuff to the rehearsal. This will confuse you, others, and your performance. If you are strong and you are not confused, then you won't confuse other people. If you are not strong and unable to leave your personal life outside, my colleagues will say, "They've lost their talent, I was wrong to cast them." Or the director will say, "I don't think you are ever going to understand this part." One of the biggest challenges of the actor is to leave everything outside of acting that needs to stay outside of acting.

---

66. Lillian Ross and Helen Ross, *The Player* (New York: Limelight Edition, 1984), 38.

Food for Thought

The most profound exercise you can do in acting is the one you are doing right now. The most profound moment in rehearsal is the moment you are in right now. The most frightening, terrifying thing of acting is to know that every single moment you are acting is the most profound of your life, and if it isn't, then you are not acting. We can choose to show up to a rehearsal or filming and sit on the sidelines. Once you get the part, what are you going to do with it? It is your foundation that will allow you to take the part to the next level.

The Ingredients

What we would like you to do is go to a store that sells costumes, masks, etc. Buy a couple of cheap masks or you can simply do this exercise in the store. There are clear plastic masks that have lips and eyes painted on them. What is good about these is that, because they are clear plastic, when you put the mask on, you see the features and the expression of the mask, but you see your own skin through the plastic. There is a melding of you and the mask. The mask has an expression that you've never had before. If you cannot find these, buy any masks that take your fancy. Some masks will just show the upper side of your face or the lower side of your face, or only the left side or right side. All of these will give you a sense of who you have never been before.

To start, put a mask on and do not look in the mirror. It is important that your mask has eyes so you can see. When your mask is securely on, look in the mirror and see somebody that you are not. Let that affect you, and you may find that you have a startled reaction, and you should. Let yourself feel what it is to be something that you are not. This exercise may be interesting to do in the store because you will also be able to gauge the reactions of those in the store as you walk around with the mask on.

Food for Thought

Every word you read, every note you hear, and every odor you smell should tell you something about acting. You can practice acting any time, anywhere, and if you want to, twenty-four hours a day. If acting is in your blood, you won't have a choice but to practice it wherever you go.

Food for Thought

When studying acting, the biggest turn off for an actor is when she doesn't immediately see how it applies to her.

The Diagnosis

You must be able to find a way to teach yourself or bring about a situation in which you look in the mirror and see a person that you have never seen before. An actor has to experience and be comfortable with the fact that people are looking at them. Here is a very big point: When people look at you, they are going to look at a character that you have created, that is because you have allowed your body to look like something it is not, and to do something it is not. The actor has to put the phrase "without reference to" to everything they do because you are going to play liars, cheaters, thieves, lovers, geniuses, dunces, kings, queens, and any gender. Like when you are wearing a mask, you have to get comfortable with people seeing somebody you are not. Somebody who is not an actor does not have to be this. They can have people look at them and see that that's who they are. They rarely, if ever, look in the mirror and see somebody they've never seen, or have any need to be familiar with being somebody else.

Have you ever looked on television or in a paper and said, "I'm awfully glad I'm not that person." You say to yourself, "I wouldn't want people to see me in that way." A great step is to look at a person that you would not want to be and try to step into that person. When you look in the mirror it's not just that you feel what that person feels, but that you look in the mirror and you see that person. Believe me, if you look in the mirror and see somebody that you have never seen before, you will instantly get the feeling of what it is like to be that person. You have to be able to look in the mirror and see somebody you have never seen before. Experience not somebody you are trying or wishing to be, but somebody that you actually believe when you look in the mirror so that you are startled. Then you have to walk around with that person, and you will begin to learn things about that character that you had no idea existed. You believe so deeply that you say, "That's not me." We have heard of great actors who have said, after seeing themselves on film, with a delight in their voice, "That's not me." They are admiring their own work because they are saying, "There is nothing about that person that reminds me of myself. I have been successful, I have created something, and I've allowed myself to experience a character."

The most profound things are always the most simple. The most profound thing in the mask exercise is that you're experiencing seeing yourself. As Betty Edwards explains, "Drawing is not really very difficult. Seeing is the problem, or to be more specific, shifting to a particular way of seeing."[67] It's yet another way for you to experience all of the five senses and to allow yourself to be someone you have never known or have never seen. You are not the character in the movie, series, or play, and you have to be comfortable being someone you have never been before. Most of us are a little apprehensive, frightened, or unsure of ourselves if we are in an unfamiliar situation. An actor must be in an unfamiliar situation all the time. An actor is not acting as soon as what they are doing becomes familiar. An actor has an enormous task because they constantly, moment-by-moment, must be experiencing something that is not familiar to them.

Food for Thought

A very famous actor did a film in which he brought a book of things that he had handwritten about the character that was hundreds of pages in length. He handed it to the director on the first day, and the director said, "Thank you very much," and threw it on the table. This is exactly what the actor had wanted him to do. Can you imagine how long it took him to write this handwritten book on his character? Then people watch his performance and say, "Why is he so interesting?" What my colleagues call *talent* you can do. There are no secret shortcuts to acting. It takes work. Plan to take the long way home.

Food for Thought

I have seen great performances that moved me to tears, threatened me, delighted me, and made me laugh, all the while being well aware of the fact that as I was watching it I personally didn't like the actor who was having this impact on me. And yet there is no limit to what I was capable of experiencing because of the strength of their acting and their technique. Great performances go beyond the individual, they are able to take us and transport us somewhere else.

Final Thoughts

What the audience sees is a creation of the actors and their own imaginations. Growing up society teaches us, "Don't be something you are not, just be yourself." Telling an actor to "just be yourself" is like telling an actor not to act. The actor's job is to be something they are not. It is something they have never seen and probably never will, because an actor can never quite be an audience to their own performance. The actor has to get used to people seeing them as they aren't. A young actor has an ego where he wants everybody to know who he is. As an actor progresses, he or she wants only someone to see the creation. It is not the body you *are*, it is the body you have *created*. It's not who you are, it's who you imagine you are.

---

67. Betty Edwards, *Drawing on the Right Side of the Brain* (Canada: Penguin Putnam Inc., 1999), 4.

35. Throw It Away

Food for Thought

I once saw a very famous actor in a performance. He was so astonishing in the first few minutes that I thought surely the play was going to be a disaster. No one I've ever seen could keep up that kind of energy and spontaneity for that length of time. It's not humanly possible, and of course he proved me wrong. For four hours he had greater, and greater, and greater intensity. This is why we say, "Give everything you've got in the first second and pray to god you find more." If you ever perform in theatre, and I hope you do, you have to have the physical stamina that goes with it.

Food for Thought

You have to go into each performance knowing you are going to activate the emotions of the people you are acting for. The next step is to know how to orchestrate the emotions that you have displayed – that's technique. As John Harrop puts it, "Discussion of the acting process usually resolves itself into the received dichotomy of emotion versus technique."[68]

The Ingredients

In this exercise you are going to do a ritual where you throw away things that are unnecessary to you. What I would like you to do is think of a contract that you have made with somebody. When I was young I told my mother, "I don't think kids should smoke." We didn't ever talk about it, so when I did became a smoker for a period of time I had trouble smoking in front of my mother. When I finally did, she looked very disapproving of it. It led me to believe that I had made a contract with my mother that I wouldn't smoke.

We want you to think of some contract, no matter how silly or simple it might be. It doesn't have to be soul-searching. Perhaps you told a friend you would never drink again, or swear, or eat dairy products, or wear jeans, or take the dog for a walk. It has to have been a contract you made with somebody and one that you probably should not have made because there was no reason. We want you to think of a contract you made that you didn't keep because you decided you didn't want to do it. It is probably a contract that you made without giving much thought to at the time. What we want you to do now is write the contract down on a piece of paper then take the piece of paper, rip it in half, and break that contract. We want you to make a ritual out of this. Whenever you have a contract that does not serve you, write it down and rip it up. This does not mean that you had to have sat down together and written out a contract. It is simply something that you see as being a contract, an agreement that was verbal or even nonverbal.

Food for Thought

There is a huge difference between acting and non-acting communication. It is as big as the difference for a pianist playing chopsticks and playing a concerto. An actor actually has to learn not to use much body language, and to relax their body so much that their body is very subtle. The reason body language is so big in a non-actor is that subconsciously and consciously they realize that, at times, the person they are communicating with does not completely understand what they are saying through their dialogue alone. Because nonverbal communication plays such an enormous and vital role in our communication with others, an actor must become a connoisseur.

Food for Thought

We think acting is the only art form you can work on one hundred percent of the time if you choose. You can walk down the street and focus on your breathing, you can sit on the

---

68. John Harrop, *Acting* (London: Routledge 1992), 4.

bus and work on your posture, you can work on a character wherever you choose, and you can memorize lines lying down and whispering them practically in your sleep. There is not a moment of your existence in which you cannot work on your acting if you choose. We want you to think about all the times you have told yourself that you couldn't work on your acting because you were not in a production or a class at that time. You can work on your instrument any time you like because it will follow you wherever you go. As Michael Caine tells us, "If you really want to become an actor, but only providing that acting doesn't interfere with your golf game, your political ambitions, and your sex life, you don't really want to become an actor. Not only is acting more than a part-time job, it's more than a full-time job, it's a full-time obsession."[69]

The Diagnosis

What you have to learn how to do is break contracts. What happens is that somewhere down the line you have decided something or made an agreement. Perhaps you decided you are always nervous when you go to an audition, and when you have decided something it is the same thing as making a contract. Perhaps you have said, "Every time it is opening night I throw up." That is a contract. You cannot be fabulous if you have inadvertently made contracts that hinder your acting. If you have to think all things and do all things and you've made contracts not to do all things, then how can you be an actor? Let us say a person said, "I am going to be a gymnast, but I refuse to wear those tights." You say, "You cannot tell me that in order to be a gymnast I have to wear tights." It's not whether you are right or wrong. It's that you have made a contract that inhibits you from doing what you have been asked to do.

Successful actors break contracts all the time. They are not being bad, what they are saying is, "I know there is always a danger when I have a contract that is keeping me from doing the part whole, so I will break it." If people tell me to be quiet in a restaurant, I don't do it. I don't make contracts with anybody at anytime. It makes them look anti-social and difficult. They're generally not anti-social, even if they are a little overzealous about their careers.

Successful actors have in some form or other taken the contract that says, "I care what people think," and ripped it up. They are saying, "In order for me to be able to do something, I can't have that thought in my head." Any time you find there is anything that you have to fix in yourself or do in order to get to acting, think of it in these terms, "If I have to break this in order to get where I need to be, so be it." Try not to have any contracts that stop you or slow you down. You have to be able to take away every defense you have, this is so you can do a very dangerous thing in a very safe place. By placing limitations around yourself, you have created limitations. Your craft cannot afford these, and your industry will not suffer these either. If you are flexible and malleable, you will function that much better.

Food for Thought

If you are reading this, you are an actor now. The reason we say this is because you are what you think you are. You are what your intent is. You are an actor from the beginning, and what you are doing is refining the instrument. What is the difference between a good guitar and one that is poorly made? What's the difference between a toy guitar and a concert guitar? There is no difference. They're both guitars. What's the difference between a beginning actor and a senior actor? What we are saying is you are an actor, and one day, with commitment and the way you are working, you will become a good actor, or maybe even a wonderful actor. As Friedrich Durrenmatt, whose influence over German theatre is unquestioned, explains, "To be taken seriously is one thing, to be taken deadly seriously, quite another."[70] There are good chefs and bad chefs, there are good mechanics and bad mechanics, and there are good actors and bad actors.

---

69. Michael Caine, Introduction.

Food for Thought

You can have bad manners and still be a successful actor. You have to either have talent so great that people will hire you in spite of it, or you have to be making a great deal of money for someone. Even those people who do get away with it don't get away with it for very long.

Final Thoughts

When was the last time someone said to you, "I promise, I'll never do that again"? We are so quick to say, "In order to please you, I promise not to do anything that would displease you." Almost everything we do would displease somebody! What we don't realize is that we have made a contract that stops us from doing certain things. In order to be an actor you have to have the ability to rip up these contracts. You are not doing it to defy somebody, or hurt somebody's feelings, or to disagree with somebody. You're doing it so that your body retains the capacity it had before you made that contract. When you tear up a contract, promise yourself that you don't have to keep that contract anymore. Remember that contracts most of us make are contracts that we write. You have a choice. Remember, if you tore up a contract that you really liked, you can make the contract again later. You may make contracts to free yourself, when in fact you are virtually tying yourself up in knots. You are putting hurdles and barriers in the path of your acting.

36. Using Senses to Make Sense

Food for Thought

When an actor is very, very good, people recognize that right away. They also say things like, "You are so funny. Oh, but that is so easy for you." Or, "You play such a wonderful array of different characters ... Oh, but that is so easy for you." This underestimates the enormous thought, effort, time, and technique it takes to go step-by-step to reach these great heights. It is a masterful actor who makes everything look so easy and effortless that, as we watch the performance, we forget that it is a performance in the first place and we are transformed to wherever they want us to be.

Food for Thought

Each year, near the end of the Academy Awards, there is a list of names and pictures of actors who have died in the last year. I sadly mourn these many great artists who had long and distinguished careers. There were also a few very young actors who had already given amazing performances and now they are gone forever. I realized that the senior actors had not only continued to show up, but they liked every moment of what they were doing. It is my belief that the young actors had access to great passion and technique within themselves but did not like acting. They were only intoxicated by passion. So between the moments of passion they looked for ways to avoid their dislikes. And now they and their talents are gone forever. Again, you must show up and you must like what you are doing. Notice I did not say "love what you are doing," that is a form of passion. As I am sure you have heard many times before, acting is truly not a job but a lifestyle.

The Ingredients

In this exercise you are asked to explore all five senses in a different way.

---

70. Friedrich Durrenmatt, *The Theatre of Friedrich Durrenmatt* (London: Oswald Wolff Publishers & Humanities Press Inc., 1980), 9.

Taste

What we would like you to do is fast for a period of at least twenty-four hours. The only thing you are allowed to have during this period is fluids. Please make sure you are in good health and have you doctor's permission to do this activity. You can also experience a lack of taste when you have a bad cold. Be delighted that, for one moment, you know what it is like to not be able to taste because you know you will get it back.

Feel

You are going to be given two possibilities in this section. The first is to walk around your house naked for a period of at least three days, whenever you are home. If you have roommates, then perhaps you can limit this to your own bedroom.

The second is called a *sensory deprivation tank* where the ratio of salt to water is so great that when you get in there you float. It looks like a big bathtub and you are in darkness and you hear nothing. For actors, this would be a very beneficial experience. Some would describe it as an enlightened bliss state as in Zen, Buddhism, and Hinduism.

See

For this exercise we would like you to do a blind walk. It would not be a bad idea to set up everything carefully in your apartment and become blind for at least one hour. You can do this at night by turning off all the lights, or you could also cover your eyes with a blindfold. Do not just sit down but complete a number of tasks such as tying your shoelaces, washing the dishes, cleaning the floor, etc. You could also have a friend lead you around their apartment or in an unknown place. Avoid places such as in the street where there are dangers such as traffic.

Hear

In this section take away your hearing for a minimum of one hour, and then proceed with tasks as in the Sight section. You can do this by wearing earplugs.

Smell

Taking away a sense of smell is more complex, but when you have a cold you will be able to experience this quite well. You can also sniff coffee beans for a moment, which tends to clear the palate.

Food for Thought

There is a famous TV series that has now ended that had numerous stars appear on its show. There were other shows they could have done but many chose to appear on the same show. These are some of the greatest stars living today. They are actors who like to work.

Food for Thought

If anybody ever asks you, "If you get to the top, do you think you'll be able to handle it?" or if anybody says to you, "Are you sure you want that lifestyle?" walk away from them very quickly and never look over your shoulder. It has nothing to do with your life or anything else. It will only confuse you. If a person asks you one of those questions, you are around the wrong person. The only people who would ask you those types of questions are those who are trying to make you look a fool mostly out of jealousy and sometimes out of fear. Do not let anyone steal your dreams.

The Diagnosis

This exercise makes you aware of things in a different way. When you put on the same clothes in the same way every day and you go in the same room with all your same defenses, you are not stretching the boundaries. If you complete the section on fasting, you will find that this breaks up your routine of eating meals at specific times. You may find you stop going in the kitchen because you have no reason to go into the kitchen. You may also find this exercise revealing and thought provoking. By working with your senses you listen to things in a different way. You see things in a different way. It can change your life around in what you wear, in how you talk, etc.

What this exercise allows you to do is to understand things differently. In the naked exercise we are not used to being naked outside of the bath or shower and perhaps in bed. We are not used to being naked in the living room, the kitchen, etc. We begin to see things differently, feel things differently, because our awareness has changed. These are not silly exercises. Rather, they are an absolute must for the actor.

We mentioned the sensory deprivation tanks but we prefer to call this *sensory enhancement* because when you take away things to that extreme, your senses are actually enhanced. Doing these exercises with the senses is not the most important thing. The most important thing is what it teaches you. You have to tell the audience, show them, let them smell, let them hear, let them experience something that they have never heard, something that they have never experienced, and without you they would never have experienced that. Become intimately familiar with your senses, because you will be using them throughout your acting career.

Food for Thought

Anytime a person asks you to explain yourself, it means that you have something that they want and never will have.

Food for Thought

There was a founder of a famous agency who used to come and lecture for me to the actors. He would say, "I'm talking to you because I am the founder of an agency with many big stars and none of you here will ever be with our agency. But send us a card every month and tell us what you're doing." Big stars, when they were not big stars, knew how to send cards, how to network, how to get invites to the country club, to go to the right lunches, and to be invited to the right parties.

Final Thoughts

You should understand exactly what this exercise is about. For instance, "I want that so bad I can taste it!" The success of this book and the success of your career will be how fast you relate to everything around you. Think about how this exercise integrates into your life, "Something doesn't smell right. I can't believe what I hear." If you say, "I can't believe what I hear," you are using the senses to make sense. A famous actress once said, "The sweet smell of success is the world's greatest deodorant." As you enter any space, you are using your sense to compute your surroundings. As you work on-set or on-stage you will be integrating your senses in a very visceral way. We are exactly where we are supposed to be when we are there.

Chapter 8:
Auditioning

37. To Be an Actor, or Not To Be

Food for Thought

Accomplished actors campaign for the part. They go to everyone and anyone who can help them get the part they are after. I remember a big star who wanted to audition for a show. She had her agent talk to the director, who said, "No, she's wrong for it." She had her agent call again and they said, "No, we're not going to see her." She had her agent call again and they continued to say, "No!" She went to the studio herself and said, "I'm a star, you have to give me the courtesy of letting me audition!" And she campaigned for it, and she got an audition, and she got the lead in the movie. It takes a certain type of conviction to see things through to their conclusion.

Food for Thought

Every time you go to an audition, how many times do you say, "It wasn't quite clear which room I had to go to and where I had to go to sign in." You tell yourself it is their fault. Do you think these things don't affect you as an actor? How often do you get there and you don't know which gate to go through, and when you do find out, they ask you to park four blocks away? Why don't you go the day before, see where the gate is, try to find out where exactly in the building your audition will be held, and get as much information as you can? You familiarize yourself with everything, and when you go in you have an entirely different body language. To be a compelling personality you have to appear secure and relaxed. We are not talking about "talent," we are talking about campaigning for the part and "I want to get the job!" Do a test run for your audition, because it will be too late to do a test run after your audition is over! If there are people who upset you the tiniest bit, such as family, friends, or a landlord, don't talk to them that day. This is preparing your body and yourself for the audition. If you have ever been to an audition and wished you could do it all again, wished you would have said something different, done something different, then that is your preparation.

The Ingredients

This is an exercise you can do all by yourself in a few seconds. You can take both hands and put them straight out, horizontally, in front of you so that the little fingers of each hand are touching. They should now look somewhat like a flat plate, palms up, with the thumbs stretched way out to the sides. With your hands in that position, say, "In my head, in my heart, in my mind, and most of all in my art, my hands will always be like this." Close your hands and make two fists. Then open them all the way back up and close them into two fists again. Now open them all the way back up. When you go to an audition, your hand is somewhere between the open hand and the fist. What each actor has to learn is to open your hand on a continual basis, metaphorically speaking, as if to say, "I want more!" There is a poem that says something like, if you ask for a penny, a penny is all you will get. What are you asking for?

Food for Thought

You have to be well coordinated in every aspect. Art equals coordination. Every single time we have heard a director or casting director talk about talent it was a kind of coordination they were really talking about. Each actor should strive to unleash their talent to its true potential. As Sean Penn says in the *Los Angeles Times*, "I'm disappointed in actors who become models and journalists who become contest-show hosts. What disappoints me the most is somebody who can do something well and does not do it."[71] To reach your true potential is no easy task.

Food for Thought

I once asked an actress who was studying with me who was rather plain looking to put on pounds of makeup and to walk to Hollywood and Vine and back. I also told her to get three bras that would hold her three different ways. I told her to wear the one that she thought was the most provocative. When I saw her next I asked how it went. She said, "I have never had people whistle at me before in my life, it was terrific!" A year before she had auditioned for a major Los Angeles company. They were not interested. This time I sent her back with this new look and she got in. The reason they hired her is because I changed her bra and her makeup. What I discovered is that what my colleagues call "talent" can be taught. The challenge is oftentimes they cannot figure out what they want you to do, but they want it all the same. If they don't see it with you, they will say you are not talented.

I am not telling every actress to cake themselves in makeup. I am giving an example of how I specifically diagnosed this particular actress. For any actor who is not booking auditions, you will want to diagnose the areas of specific concern that apply to you. When you work with a great teacher they are able to diagnose your strengths and weaknesses as they apply to you.

The Diagnosis

To an actor, no part of you should be closed off. You should be open to every eventuality. In this exercise, your hands are open as if to say "I want more, and I am receptive to everything." When your hand is completely open, you are ready to do anything asked of you, and to use every bit of your mind, your talent, and your creativity to run as fast as you can, and to please as much as you can. The more you close your hands, the less you are willing to do this. When your hands are completely open, you are able to do both what is asked of you and what you ask of yourself. Your potential is unlimited.

As soon as you close your hands and say, "No, no, no, let me show you something I want to do!" you have lost. It's like a universal law, and it is worth noting that the best exercises to affirm this are the most simple to do. You can do the simplest exercises for the rest of your life and keep your instrument ready and willing. If you practice this simple exercise before every audition, whether it be physically or in your imagination, what you will find yourself saying is, "I want to be that available." And any time you disagree, forget that they are there, or do something that you just have to do without saying, "Is this what you want of me?" know that you are, metaphorically speaking, closing your fists. This could be in the form of extraneous movements. Perhaps when you are asked to do something by the casting director that you don't want to do you automatically cross your arms without realizing it. It sends a signal of negative energy. At that point the casting director says, "There is something I don't like about this actor." You see, the actor who has trained himself or herself not to work this way looks more prepared and more available. Don't forget that the casting director is also a human being and any negative signals you give off will be recorded in one way or another. Think of a time when you have been to a party, walked into the room, and seen somebody who, for

---

71. Joe Donnelly, *LA Weekly* (Los Angeles: LA Weekly, 2007), 43.

some reason, you had no desire to speak to. Now think about the person who you are dying to run over and speak to. This is who the casting director wants to see when you walk in the room.

While this exercise is very basic, to actually follow it through is very difficult. In this exercise you are being asked to do something that is going to change your everyday life, so who you are is going to become different. What you do and how you do it is going to become different. It's going to become more saleable, more professional, and more believable. It's going to be more of an actor and less of a civilian.

Food for Thought

Why is there any argument or debate about going to an audition when the only reason you go to an audition is to get the job? Make a study of how to get the job. This is called preparing for the job. Become a professional auditioner. You've got to get the work in order to work.

Food for Thought

We think that the audition is over by the time they are aware of you. As Mari Lyn Henry and Lynne Rogers explain, "Did you know that studies have proved that within seven seconds your appearance will indicate your financial stability, education, trustworthiness, social position, level of sophistication, marital status, success, moral character, occupation and lifestyle?"[72] If we make people gods when we go into the audition, then that is the problem. You have to do exercises to improve. Every technique has exercises. There are many facets to your craft and you want to learn to connect each one so that they can work as one.

Final Thoughts

We must remind people that spirituality and ritual are not the same. A ritual is simply something that one goes through that helps them think and function more clearly. All great actors I know have some kind of ritual they do at the theatre or on-set. This exercise falls in the category of ritual and is meant to be so simple that it allows you to think your own thoughts and attain your own answers without the help or influence of anyone else. What you find in this exercise is that you can accept more with an open hand than you can with a closed fist. You should make up a series of your own rituals that help to keep every part of you available. Many rehearsals have rituals. The purpose of a ritual is to get you to repeat something until you have an understanding of it. Look at rituals as a way of getting out of habits and allowing you to be open and receiving to more. The more you repeat something, the more it will become automatic for you.

38. Falling in Line

Food for Thought

When you are auditioning for a part they may see you some of the time or all of the time, and you don't want them to see one second of you less than a professional. Remember that when you are auditioning the tiniest little thing might make all the difference, so we want to address the tiniest little thing. When working on a character one has to find the specifics of that character. When you are going for an audition be as prepared, aware, and as detailed as is possible.

---

72. Mari Lyn Henry and Lynne Rogers, *How to be a Working Actor* (New York: Watson-Guptill Publications, 2000), 129.

Food for Thought

In professional acting you are going to be called in and you are going to be cast by a professional casting director in a part that they need. They will call you in and they will decide whether you are the type to play it. They will let you read something, possibly from the script. Oftentimes it is just a few words, and not the whole thing. Most times you will not have had the opportunity to read the whole script ahead of time. This is professional life. If you are auditioning for television or film, the camera lens in now your best friend and you will want to get very well acquainted.

The Ingredients

What we would like you to do is find a space in the room and just start walking around in any direction you choose. Walk at a comfortable and easy pace. At some point I am going to come around and ask you, one by one, to fall in line with another actor. When I do this, I want you to walk alongside them at the rhythm, pace, and tempo they are walking so that you are walking and moving together. At some point I will come over and ask you to start walking in line with a different actor, and you will simply move over to them and repeat the process.

PAUL: *(ACTORS start to walk around the room and gradually find a partner. This continues for the next three minutes, alternating partners.)* Do you feel as if you are sharing energy with the other person? Do you feel a compatibility with the other person?

ACTOR 1: It makes me feel connected with them, as if I know them better than I actually do.

PAUL: It is as if you have created a form of synergy between you.

ACTOR 2: I feel a little uncomfortable, actually.

PAUL: That is because you are not used to *walking in line* with another person. By falling in line you begin to create a feeling of familiarity between you. If you go to an audition you also want to create that feeling of familiarity immediately, that feeling of rapport. Practice this exercise with other actors on your own time. The more you practice, the better you will get and the more awareness you will develop.

GAVIN: This exercise is really simple, yet it will give you a strong visceral experience. As you walk side by side with other actors, you will find you start to build rapport. This isn't only useful, it is paramount for you to develop rapport with the casting director, other actors, and have a sense of awareness at every audition you go to.

Food for Thought

The color white is white. If we take the color gray, for example, it is not a different color, it is that we've added something to white. What we are trying to do is to get white, white. When we go to a paint store and ask for different types of white it is an oxymoron. They are all white with different colors added to them. If, for instance, you want a super white, that is white with a little blue in it. An actor has to learn how to get white before they can start adding other things to their acting. When a director watches an audition they say, "They're doing the same lines, they moved in a similar fashion. Oh, that one's more talented than the rest." And we would say, "No, they added things to their performance and they are so subtle you can't see them. You think you are seeing something you are not seeing." If you never learn the fundamentals and basics in acting, you are just making your task that much more difficult. You never have a place from which to begin.

Food for Thought

When you are under pressure everything that is said to you sounds like gibberish. Even if you are really focusing it's as if nothing being said to you makes any sense. This may happen at an audition, on a set, or when you are receiving some sort of direction. You are going to have to get used to pressure. Those observing may say things like, "What's wrong with him, can't he take direction?" Think about the individual on a game show going for a large sum of money. They are given a relatively easy question and they get it wrong. Afterwards, they kick themselves because they knew the answer. It was not the question but the enormous amount of pressure that caused the error. You are going to have to embrace these pressure situations because you will be involved in them on a regular basis. You do not have the luxury of allowing them to affect your work. This is why it is so important that you have the ability to work with a clean slate.

The Diagnosis

You are going to have to get used to *falling in line* with casting agents, directors, and other actors. This exercise is really a metaphor to let you taste what it feels like to walk in line with another. When you go to an audition you have to mentally be able to fall in line with the casting agent or director. Every one of you can remember a time when you said to yourself, "I gave them everything they asked for, and I don't understand why I didn't get it." Did you ask yourself what kind of mood they were in that day? Did you ask yourself how many people they had already seen before you? Did you listen to every word they spoke to you? Did you give them exactly what they asked for?

Some actors go into an audition and say, consciously or subconsciously, "No, no, no, let me show you what I can do!" or "I've got an idea here, and I know you're going to love it." If you do that, you will not get the part. You might feel they are taking away from what you can do. Tough, you'll just have to get used to it. They are not interested in what *you* want to show them. They are interested in what *they* want you to show them. You are going to go to all types of auditions, and you are going to face a lot of rejection. You have to find a way to deal with it. You have to have the knowledge, the strength, the will, and the coordination that your body is able to deal with.

In this exercise you are being asked to literally walk along with another actor, and when you are at an audition, you have to metaphorically walk alongside the casting director. Oftentimes the actor is not speaking the same language, they misinterpret, and are not walking with the director. This is their downfall. When Lewis Funke interviewed Dustin Hoffman the following was said in regards to rejection, "I had auditions at the Actors Studio and never could get past the first audition."[73] We all know how Hoffmann handled rejection – he never let it get in his way. We are not telling you that if you follow the advice given in this exercise that you are certain to get the part. It is, however, another important advantage that you will have over many actors who are not doing this. Why not stack the odds in your favor instead of against?

Food for Thought

Some actors will say in an audition with great pride, "I've just flown in from Los Angeles. I'll only be here for a month, and I really want to get a Broadway show." They have no idea that the people auditioning them are saying, "We'd rather get somebody who lives here. You are not making any commitment to us at all." They know they want somebody good, but they don't know which of the good ones they want. The only individuals this can genuinely work for are established stars. Quite often they don't actually audition, but will say, "OK, I will have my people talk to your people." If an individual wanted to learn about health and nutrition, they would find a great deal of contradictory advice, and so it is for the actor. With every example or piece of advice that you are given on acting, good or bad, there will always be at least one example to contradict that. Perhaps one of the most wonderful or awful things

---

73. Lewis Funke, *Actors Talk about Theatre* (United States: Dramatic Publishing Company, 1977), 15.

about acting is the subjectivity of it all, and yet we would like your journey to be as smooth, direct, and focused as possible.

Food for Thought

During the auditioning process, some drama schools in Europe have asked the actors to take all of their clothes off. What they are really saying is, "At this very beginning we can see whether you have been taught to be so judgmental. If you cannot take your clothes off or if you are so restrained that you hesitate, we can tell how much you have been damaged or restrained by your life up until now. We want to know if you can do what we think is required of an actor." It is not that you have to be naked, it is that you have to be instantly responsive. As Nicolas Cage explains, "I want to become more and more naked as an artist."[74] You can't be defensive and you can't have hang-ups. It has often been very popular to take your clothes off on-stage because it is very theatrical and we don't see it all the time. You are not being advised to run outside and take your clothes off. You are not being encouraged to take your clothes off at any audition you go to. This advice is in regards to legitimate auditions, often at world-renowned settings. Do not take your clothes off just because you are asked to do so. There are many predators out their looking to play on your desperation to be a star, but this has nothing to do with what is being discussed here.

Final Thoughts

The French writer Camus said, "Do not lead, I may not want to follow. Do not follow, I may not want to lead. Just walk beside me and be my friend." For the actor, this is another very strong, powerful exercise. We tend to use the word *synergistic* as though it is a poetic term, when indeed we know that it is a very accurate word. When two things are in sync and working in tandem, the strength, imagination, and emotion are greater than the sum of the two total parts. This is an exercise that allows the actor to partner with anyone and anything, and you are working synergistically so that anything that anyone has ever done can be part of you. This exercise encourages you not to relate to a part, but to relate to any part. A civilian can be one with a person they admire, but an actor has to be one with everyone. This exercise allows you to experience and build rapport with any individual you encounter.

39. The Animation Exercise

Food for Thought

What we are looking for in an audition is someone who is searching for excellence. Haven't you gone to an audition and said, "Why did they take them?" The reason is that their whole way of living is in search of excellence. If you are simply in search of excellence, you will never find it, but you will always enjoy the search. If you are told, "If you have not found excellence, maybe you should search for something else," and you follow their advice not only will you not be a successful actor, you will not be a successful anything. As soon as you give up the search, your whole being becomes less interesting. Think about a character who is determined, inquisitive, and passionate in their quest. We are right there with them and we root for them all the way. You want to find the passion in your search for excellence in your own journey.

Food for Thought

I only want one job. If there is only one job, I want that one! Actors are trying to work too generally, and they go to an audition too generally. Actors brag about how many auditions they went to that week, they say things like, "I did a great thing. I went to five auditions this

---

74. Kathryn Marie Bild, *The Actor's Quotation Book*, (New Hampshire: Smith and Kraus, 2003), 21.

week." They never tell me, "I'm campaigning for a job." Famous actors and great actors look at one thing at a time. They don't look at a general career — ever. When you tell people you are an actor, director, and writer, it tends to make it hard for people to take you seriously. You may have a passion for all these areas, but if you introduce yourself this way it tends to dilute the impact. What is your main goal and main area of focus?

The Ingredients

What we would like you to do is choose a scene or a monologue you are working on. Now we would like you to stand in front of a mirror as you do your scene or monologue and smile until you are showing all of your teeth. If you are working with another actor, you can have them observe you. If ever your lips touch for more than a split second you have to start over. In other words, there should never be a time when you completely close your mouth. We are not looking for the meaning in the scene. We are looking at the objectives of the exercise. You may find that you have to say the words rather briskly and go quickly. It's going to be tougher than you think. This is not primarily a voice exercise, although it may increase your ability to enunciate. If this exercise was to do your scene and animate your face, all you would do is make faces and grimace. It has to be taken away until it doesn't apply, until it can't be used, until it is so simple and so concentrated that you can't relate it to something. As you read this exercise, put a big smile across your face. You should be able to feel your facial muscles working. If by the time you finish this exercise your facial muscles don't ache or at the very least tingle, you need to work for a bigger, more pronounced smile next time.

Food for Thought

When you are campaigning for a role it means a kind of preparation, but it also means a greater preparation than anybody else will ever do, and that's who gets the job. It's the kind of preparation that is not generally taught in acting schools. I knew a well-known star who was preparing for an audition for a major role. She found out ahead of time where the auditions were going to be held. She happened to know the stage manager and she called a week ahead and said, "I'm going to an audition next Wednesday. My audition is at twelve o'clock, and I hear that there is no one going before me. Can I possibly come in and get on the stage an hour before he arrives?" Of course this is highly irregular, but he is a friend and he says, "Be my guest." She trudges in there, parks, walks in, and does her audition on the stage for forty-five minutes over and over and over before the director arrives. She then leaves, and fifteen minutes later she walks in as if she is just arriving and she auditions and gets the part. Why? She is completely familiar and comfortable with her surroundings. Every essence of your being has to want to get the part.

Food for Thought

In regards to the audition process, you may get a lot of benefit from going to a commercial workshop or researching what a commercial workshop teaches. They don't teach you how to act, they don't teach you how to breathe, but they do teach you how to present yourself as a commodity. Commercial workshops are about getting the job, and acting workshops are about acting. An acting workshop might give you the contact on where the job is, but it doesn't teach you how to go after the job. Getting the job is not about talent. Getting the job is not about getting better, it's about being good from the start. As Squire Fridelly explains, "Actors make as much money acting in television commercials as they make acting in movies and television combined."[75]

It is not enough to do a better job than you did last time. When you go to the audition they are not going to say, "They are better." You have to be good from the start. The result is good or it's not a result, or it's in progress. If you do something and it is better, you still haven't got

---

75. Squire Fridelly, *Acting in Television Commercials for Fun and Profit,* (New York: Three Rivers Press, 1986), 2.

the result you were looking for yet. Actors often go into auditions knowing what they want instead of saying, "What do *they* want?" We go to acting class to practice acting. We don't go to practice auditioning. Auditioning is different than acting, and you need to incorporate the audition process into your life as well as the acting process. One day you are going to figure out there is a *meat rack*. I was working with a young actor who came back from an audition looking rather shaken. I said, "What happened?" He said, "I saw the meat rack today. I went into an audition and I saw six people who looked exactly like me." It is our desire to see you be a good actor and a working actor. You have to learn to get by all the gatekeepers of the world.

The Diagnosis

We worked this exercise with an actor who had very little malleability in his facial muscles. He came back a few days later and said, "You must be right, because all the muscles around my mouth were sore." What we are doing is creating flexibility in the facial muscles so that your face is able to respond to your thoughts. It is not that your face is necessarily more animated; rather, it is more responsive to your thoughts. Some actors think that smiling too much makes them look like a fool and that when they don't smile they will be taken more seriously. They think that if they look somber, they will look older, more mature, and thus more intelligent. These actors will then direct themselves into when to use certain facial muscles and it becomes wooden rather than being spontaneous. As we have said, this is not a voice exercise as much as it is a muscle exercise. When you are in film with all the close-ups, the audience is going to be watching the body language of your face. This exercise helps you to create a fuller range of expression. As Carlton Colyer says, "Movies and television are much more a visual medium of expression than they are a verbal means of expression."[76] Some actors will, unfortunately, look in the mirror and decide what they want people to see. Most people who are not actors have very little expression in their face. Go back and look at your friends again. This is why we have all seen someone who we thought was not very attractive yet they were so versatile and animated that we thought, "That's a very attractive person." Great actors are so versatile that we very rarely get to see what they look like, but we get to see what they are doing, and, as an actor, you do not want people to see what you look like.

Food for Thought

Some actors walk in to an audition and say, "What would you like me to do?" This is one of the most confrontational things you can say to a director or casting director because you are now putting the complete burden on them. You are basically saying, "I won't do anything until you tell me what to do," instead of saying, "Because I have had experience and am a professional actor, I know exactly what you want." You want to be exactly what they want to buy. If they don't know what they want, then you have to say through your thought process, "When I figure it out, I am going to be the thing that you want. I am the most malleable, adaptable actor you will find." If you walk in and say, "This is what the script means and this is exactly what I will show you," you are in trouble. Go in, be prepared to show good acting, put yourself in that state, and you will make discoveries together. Then they may ask you to do different things. You may walk in and they say, "Don't worry about the script. We are not doing that today, just walk for us." Now you are angry because you have prepared for the script. Remember that you are going to an audition for one reason and one reason only: get the job! If you want to be a working actor, then you have to master the technique of auditioning. You may feel it is beneath you, but think about the vital role auditioning plays in your career. Once you are an "A list" actor, then you can stop concerning yourself with auditioning, because chances are you won't have to.

---

76. Carlton Colyer, *The Art of Acting* (Colorado: Meriwether Publishing, 1989), 206.

Food for Thought

I had a colleague who had an audition for a big show that was touring and eventually going to Broadway. She had a long drive to make and for various reasons when she got there it was too late, and they were leaving. They were in the parking lot and she said, "I just got here, I'm terribly sorry, may I see you?" They said, "OK." They went back in and she got the part, and she went to Broadway. Actors often say, "I really want the part," this actress *really* wanted the part.

Final Thoughts

Great actors want to think and move randomly. What this exercise does is it gives your face animation even when you are still. You may also find that this exercise allows you to access more thoughts. Richard Brestoff, author of *The Actor's Wheel of Connection,* says, "When we watch great acting, it too disappears. We are so caught up in the struggles, actions, feelings, hopes, desires, defeats, successes, with the sheer motion and emotion of the character, that we cannot see the acting itself, the mechanism of it."[77] When we see great acting we are so moved by it and so influenced by it that it appears effortless.

40. Conversation with the Actor (Part 1)

Food for Thought

I know some famous actresses who, when they were starting out, were so good that casting directors would ask them to stay behind and read with the other actors auditioning. The casting directors had no intention of hiring them. The actresses recognized that they were being misused and made a pact not to "help out in this way again." If an actor takes all the rejection and frustration to heart, they will be like a stick that snaps in half. You have to find a way to brush things off so you are like a bendable straw that continues to bounce back.

Food for Thought

There is only one thing in the director's or casting director's estimation: You are either good or you are bad. Your willingness, forwardness, enthusiasm, and generosity needs to show. If they can see you, if they can see an open slate, then they can cast you. If they don't know what they are seeing, if their questions go unanswered, then you become a questionable risk.

The Ingredients

This section is a conversation held between Paul and one of the actors we worked with. The discussion was much longer than the one that will follow, but this is to give you a taste of the conversation. It has been included so as to highlight a discussion between the teacher and the actor. While this particular discussion, in part, applies to this particular actor, the questions raised can apply to any actor. We want you to continue to ask questions until you find a satisfactory answer that sits well with you.

Food for Thought

If you go to an audition that feels totally unprofessional, then you have to size up the situation and make a quick decision, because it may be a waste of your time. Look at the situation, and if need be, get out of the situation and protect yourself. A question to ask is "What can benefit me the most in this situation?" If your gut tells you something is not right, then it is not right. You might take on a role that not only damages your career, but places you in a box that you now cannot get out of. Think about actors whose work you know this has happened to. We want to make sure you see the practical implications of what is being said as opposed to the theoretical.

---

77. Richard Brestoff, *The Actor's Wheel of Connection,* (New Hampshire: Smith and Kraus, 2005), 1.

Food for Thought

It is also worth noting that sometimes at an audition you are buying the part. Imagine going to a Rolls-Royce dealership and the dealer says to himself, "Can you afford to look at this car? If you cannot afford to look at this car, I don't have time to look at you." When a star takes on a role, they have just brought the studio millions of dollars in box office sales — they've bought the part. In other words, they are saying, "My reputation, my life, and what I can bring to this movie is priceless to you." A great audition does not necessarily get you the part. You have to take into account all of the possible variables. We want you to make the connections between the craft of acting and the industry.

The Diagnosis

PAUL: What is acting?

ACTOR: Basically, telling a story to the audience and having the emotions of the scene picked up by the audience.

PAUL: What matters in acting?

ACTOR: The communication between the person doing the scene and the person who is watching.

PAUL: Then you and I agree because I would say that the definition of acting takes two people, one telling the story and one perceiving or hearing the story. If you don't have those two components, it's not acting.

ACTOR: I rarely personalize when I see other actors work.

PAUL: I think you personalize by definition. You implied earlier that when you enjoy an actor's work to the degree that if they were good enough at faking, you didn't care. I agree with you, and what you are also saying is that if they weren't good, you took it personally. This does not mean to be offended. It means to think of it on personal terms.

ACTOR: I love to talk about acting. It gets me excited a little bit. It feels like I'm refreshing all of the stuff that there is — the meat of everything.

PAUL: What did your initial acting training give you?

ACTOR: I was a very shy person and introverted. It actually threw me and jolted me.

PAUL: What do you mean by jolted?

ACTOR It opened me to this world of acting that I wasn't even aware of.

PAUL: So it was beneficial to you?

ACTOR: Yes.

PAUL: What is your purpose at the audition?

ACTOR: To bring an interesting, believable, convincing character.

PAUL: What else?

ACTOR: To react in the moment.

PAUL: Good, what else?

ACTOR: That I am confident and that I have the ability to take direction.

PAUL: OK, what else?

ACTOR: That I enjoy what I am doing, and that it will sell with me in it.

PAUL: There is a little tiny thing you didn't say: "The only reason I am there is to get the job."

GAVIN: It sounds obvious, doesn't it? As you read this you probably assume it is the first thing that will come out of your mouth, yet you will be surprised at how many actors forget to mention they want the job. Learn to put your focus where you want it to be so that you do not become clouded and unfocused.

Food for Thought

In an audition, what we are saying is, "As long as you do exactly what I ask you to do, I'm interested in knowing that it was uniquely done by you." You know we never need anything but what we need. If we need a triangle and you're a triangle, we take you. Do exactly what you are asked and they will say, "That actor really surprised me." And the reason is that there is nobody like you. Anyone who surprises you surprises themselves. In order to experience this, the actor must be fully available.

Food for Thought

Thomas Jefferson said that he never contradicted a man, that instead he would just ask them a series of questions. What questions do you ask yourself when going for an audition? Do you think you can get the job? Do you want the job? Why are you going to the audition? Do you like to please people, and do you attempt to please the casting director? We guarantee that most actors, if they are honest, will have to answer no to most of these questions. When you go to get the job say, "I want the job," not, "I want them to like me." Believe the part is already yours and feel good about it. Most actors will say, "I am not there to please the casting director, I'm there to show him my talent." We always hear actors say they have no idea who they are auditioning for. Even worse, we have actors say, "I had an audition and I have no idea who I auditioned for." Becoming an expert on auditioning and knowing the work of local casting directors is extremely important to your career as an actor.

Final Thoughts

When you ask an actor to talk about acting they usually don't talk about acting. They talk about why they feel good when they act. This shows that the actor is actually missing the point, and they are actually not answering the question. The question they are being asked to answer is "what is acting?" This can only be discussed between actors, an acting teacher, or someone who understands acting such as a director.

The greatest thing an actor has to learn to do is ask the specific question. An actor has to make a concerted effort to say, "What is it I want to know?" and to think, "Is this the question I am really asking?" When you are asked the question, "What is the main purpose of going to an audition?" you should only ever have one answer, "To get the job." Great actors sometimes seem to be impatient; however, they're not impatient, they're just wise and they know how to ask the right questions. It is only when you know how to ask the right questions that you get the right answers. A director may give you very specific direction, but if you are not quite focused you may totally miss the point of the question. The director may now think you cannot take direction and are not as talented as they first thought.

41. Dancing Like a Star

Food for Thought

The beginning is something that cannot be preceded, it must be followed. Think about how this applies to acting in terms of a movie, a play, or a scene. As Michael Shurtleff explains in his book *Audition*, "Every scene you will ever act begins in the middle, and it is up to you, the actor, to provide what comes before."[78]

Food for Thought

Look at different acting terminology used by different countries and cities. Actors use different expressions in different capitals of the world. Acting jargon comes from any group of people who work together and they develop a kind of slang or shortcut words for acting

---

78. Michael Shurtleff, *Audition* (New York: Bantam Book, 1978), 67.

terminology. Your job is to not only find the similarities between them, but also to find one thing that you think is very clever and how many different words or expressions there are for the same thing. An example would be the history of a character, back story, character background, or character exposition. Now see if you can find three other ways to say the same thing. The reason to do this is, for instance, when you go to an audition, class, or rehearsal you will know that is one of five ways to say the same thing, and you will clearly understand what is being said while others may not have the foggiest idea. The number of things that exist in acting are finite, and the number of words used to describe these things seems to be limitless. After we've used up the logical, we get poetic until finally we just get ridiculous and obscure. On a set there is terminology for you to get used to that is different from that of stage. Even though the technical language of the crew may not directly affect you, it can influence the outcome of the end result in some way and therefore is important for you to be aware of it.

The Ingredients

For this exercise you are going to learn how to break down a dance routine for an acting audition or for a performance. Follow this protocol any time you have to learn a dance routine.

1. You are going to start with the most basic thing, which is to clap out the rhythm of the routine. If you are at an audition and you want to be less obvious, you can simply tap the rhythm with one finger on your leg.

2. In order to learn a routine you break it down to its simplest form. The simplest form of movement in choreography is changes of weight, and everything after that is embellishment. Note the changes of weight.

3. Now you know the step, your hands know the step, now your hands need to teach it to your feet. Be aware that if the rhythm is a count of three, one-two-three, it will change the leading foot each time. Uneven will change the leading foot and even will always keep the same foot.

4. An embellishment is the flare that goes with the step. Give names to each piece of embellishment.

PAUL: As I dance the steps say the words out loud. *(PAUL dances a short routine.)*

ACTORS: Sun, closeness, dice, kick, humdrum.

Food for Thought

I sat in on many auditions and little did they know I wasn't watching the people auditioning. I was watching the people conducting the auditions. People say "Don't do that scene because everybody is doing that scene," but I say the opposite. Since everybody is doing that scene, they're going to look at you. If you do a scene that nobody knows, you are auditioning the playwright. Many actors say, "I know what you want, but let me show you what I think you want." They don't respond to that ever, ever, ever! Famous actresses have said to me, "I have just read for this famous director or playwright and she just wants me to do what she wants!" If you are auditioning without the desired outcome, it is time to reevaluate.

Food for Thought

If a large part of your potential to work is auditioning, then you should be practicing auditioning everyday. Do you get up every morning and pretend that you just got a call and that you've got an audition in one hour? You may be a darling person, but many actors turn up to auditions with very little experience or preparation. Your job is to activate the emotions of the people you are performing and auditioning for. When you activate an individual's imagination, you pique their interest. Auditions are unfair, barbaric, and have nothing to do with talent or acting. Professional acting also means professional auditioning.

The Diagnosis

Dancing is movement and coordination, and it is something that actors don't think of enough. You start by clapping the rhythm because your hands are more articulate than your feet because you use them all the time. It is also so that you can have your hands teach it to your feet. The lesson is you use what you're best at to teach anything in your body.

There is no way that you can escape choreography. It has been said that dancing does not contribute to acting. It doesn't. It contributes to the instrument of acting. You must take all of the physical things in the world that contribute to giving you a more flexible and malleable instrument. You may say, "I am an actor and I will never have to dance." Yet there are many great actors who have. I cannot tell you how many actors have gotten work this way. They went to the audition and said, "I watched, I clapped it out, and when I got up I did the most basic thing and they took me!"

GAVIN: In this exercise you are learning step-by-step. The main thing is you don't want to *do* the result. In acting we say don't *play* a result.

ACTOR: I discovered here that I have to start from the very beginning, and I now have to transfer that to my acting instead of assuming I know it all.

PAUL: Good for you. I am interested in the discoveries you make, and the fact that you can then apply them. You are learning to apply and adapt your technique to any situation that presents itself.

Food for Thought

Actors often say that when you go to an audition, "It's all about what you look like." We have talked about auditioning throughout this book, so let's talk a little more. People look at actors, so certainly at the beginning of your career what you look like is going to influence an audition. Just for openers, do you look healthy? You might have seen a famous star who died very young of drugs, and you might think that they got work because they were pale, delicate, fragile, and talented. They didn't. They were not delicate and they were not fragile, even though they may have played these types of characters. If you think they were, then they were more convincing actors than you know. If you look at famous stars you will find that they are driven, goal dominated, and had tunnel vision while achieving everything they wanted to achieve, and were always hungry for more.

Food for Thought

Never wear your own clothes to play a scene, because you will have no feeling of being a new character. You are burdened with your own clothes and with the sameness of the sound of your voice. You picked your clothes and you picked them to show people something. Try putting on a selection of clothes with your eyes closed just based on the feeling of how they felt. If you walk past a mirror hopefully you will say, "Who is that person?" The answer to it is, "That is a person I have created who has never been seen before any time, by anybody."

ACTOR: What can you do if you are in a play or movie where you have to wear the same clothes every day?

PAUL: Well, this is known by you and you don't have to tell anyone. You can change your underwear every day. You can do all kinds of things that every day when you step on-stage there is something that you have never experienced before. That is your food that feeds you to create your character.

GAVIN: If you decide to wear new clothes for every audition you might decide that this is impractical and too expensive. I know of actors who buy clothes for an audition and once it is over they take them back to the store. I am not in any way suggesting you do this, but this is something that is occasionally done by actors.

Final Thoughts

We think that dancing is something that some actors believe they will never have to do and, to a point, they are right. It is amazing how many famous actors have wonderfully trained singing voices. If you are a famous person, you will, in order to appear in front of as many audiences as possible, include musicals as part of your work, whether they be on-stage, film, television, or Internet. If you are a star, they will work the choreography around your potential. The one thing you have to know as a leading actor is how to take direction and dance also demands this. Choreography is an embellishment on direction, and there is no actor who isn't expected to understand stage and set direction. The more coordinated your instrument, the more you can maximize your potential to do or be anything.

42. Conversation with the Actor (Part 2)

Food for Thought

Margaret Emory points out that, "Agents recognize that getting auditions is critical to their own livelihoods, as well as their clients. After all, our daily bread, so to speak, comes from the commission earned on actor bookings, and those bookings are, for the most part, the direct result of the auditions we obtain for our clients."[79]

Food for Thought

ACTOR: Should you look into the eyes of the casting director at an audition?

PAUL: Sometimes it will make them self-conscious. They want to be free to watch you without being watched. Some casting directors actually prefer it. For the most part, you will find that they do not want you to look at them, but you should not make a conscious decision. You should adapt to the situation. Your body should tell you what to do. Some agents will say, "Don't look at me." Some agents will call and say they didn't like the fact you were looking in their eyes. You have to get by mirroring, by being empathetic to them, and you have to get a feeling as to whether you are disturbing them or not. I have often told actors to see a movie screen behind the director and see the whole scene you are doing on that movie screen. Then I found out some directors actually want that personal eye contact. That is why we talk about adaptation and adapting to the situation at hand. The only thing we're going to notice is if you make a conscious decision whether or not to look at me. This means that you are not available should I want to see something else. If everything you do is preconceived, then where is the room for adaptation and spontaneity?

GAVIN: In relation to auditioning, the only thing you should be doing is what pleases them and what makes them comfortable. It is your job to discover what this is for each situation.

The Ingredients

In this excerpt you are reading part of the conversation that took place between Paul and an actor. The actor was phoning to talk about an acting workshop he had just been to and how he felt about the experience. This had nothing to do with Paul. He was not there, and he had nothing to do with the actor's decision to take this class. Part of the reason this excerpt has been included is to show that we can talk about acting in any situation. We can find others who are like-minded and discuss our findings or our misgivings on acting no matter where we are. With today's technology you don't have to be in the same room, the same building, the same state, county, or the same country and you can still communicate about acting.

---

79. Margaret Emory, *Ask an Agent* (New York: Back Stage Books, 2005), 87.

Food for Thought

Go to auditions. Even if you do not get the part it is good practice for you. A studio once called me and said, "We need a short, brunette soprano and we're on the wire, who do you have?" We said, "Well, we're going to send over this tall, blond belter." She got the job. They didn't know what they wanted. Don't limit yourself, as Michael Shurtleff points out, "I think an actor should audition every damn chance he gets."[80] This may confuse you into thinking you should go into an audition and show them what you want. On the contrary, the actor Paul sent still followed direction, listened to the director, and still did what she was asked to do because this was how she had been trained. She just happened to be a tall, blond belter. When an actor is given direction, there are a number of important factors, such as taking direction.

Food for Thought

When you go to an audition, what obligation does the casting director or director have to you? Some might say that they don't have any other obligation to you than they would to any other human being. However, you need to take one more giant step in understanding the audition process. Let us say your house is on fire and the fire brigade has come to put it out, what obligation do they have in how they treat you? First, you would want them to save your house, and you are absolutely right. If you understand "house on fire," what you don't understand is why I am not asking you anything about you. The fire brigade is there to save the house and, provided you are safe, they have no obligation to you. You would simply want to get out of the way and let them do their job. If they ask you a question you would want to answer them as clearly, quickly, and efficiently as you can because you would know that all they want from you is the answer. This is exactly the same as an audition situation. They owe you absolutely nothing, and they have no obligation to give you anything. This is not because they are mean people, but perhaps they are very busy. Perhaps they have had a very long day, or perhaps they are there to cast a show and all they want from you is exactly what they ask of you.

Society may have taught you to stand up for your rights, but do not apply this to the audition situation. Get in, do what you are asked, and get out. They owe you absolutely nothing. If you understand this, then you understand something that many actors never will, which is to their enormous disadvantage. When an actor tries to bend themselves or mold themselves to be like someone else, this is a pitfall. We have already got one of them and don't need another. In an audition, they are looking for you. As Eric Morris points out, "There is no other person on this earth like you! I cannot emphasize this enough. You are as unique as your fingerprints, and your uniqueness is what you have to sell as an actor."[81] Hone in your auditioning skills and learn to read the nonverbal communication in the room. You are now leaps and bound ahead of the majority, provided you can act.

The Diagnosis

ACTOR: I enjoyed watching the performances of the other actors. I thought this lady was overwhelming in a good sense. She was extremely poised and unflappable.

PAUL: So it was the use of the instrument, not being tall, short, old, or young.

ACTOR: Totally, she introduced herself first and I thought, "What is she even doing here?" and fifteen minutes later I was watching her do a scene and thinking she is probably the best actor in here. It didn't matter what language she was speaking.

---

80. Michael Shurtleff, 27.
81. Eric Morris, *Being & Doing* (Los Angeles: A Whitehouse/Spelling Publication, 1981), 20.

PAUL: A good teacher speaks many languages. They never tell an actor to speak their language. When the body is functioning better, the actor is better understood.

ACTOR: So what you are saying comes with training?

PAUL: Absolutely, and when an actor is trying to be someone they are not, they look like a complete fool, or slightly amusing, or a complete liar.

ACTOR: When I took this class today the teacher said, "The decision is already made and I don't want you to even think about who you are or this audition."

PAUL: What do you think he meant by *the decision is already made?*

ACTOR: I think he just wanted us to be ourselves.

PAUL: The audition is over by the time they are aware of you.

ACTOR: I used to think that was preposterous. But now I realize how important it is to be on from the get-go.

PAUL: What did you think of your teacher?

ACTOR: I didn't think that one thing he said from start to finish was dubious. I once had a voice-over teacher who I knew was working a lot and could teach a lot, but I knew that fifty percent of what she said was out of line. I felt that it was an unpleasant experience. She actually taught me a couple of things, but not many things.

PAUL: You have to let those people go and don't get involved with them.

ACTOR: She used to humiliate actors in the class.

PAUL: Remember, I come from the *mean era,* and all those directors and choreographers were rude and intolerable. I came from the era when all of these directors and teachers were bullies. All of them. I worked with geniuses who were crazy, and you just let them be crazy. However, we knew that they had such genius that we skipped over that.

ACTOR: You didn't have to pay for the class, though.

PAUL: When we did a show, we paid with our soul.

ACTOR: *(Laughs.)* Yeah, that's an interesting answer. The class was so inspiring I really want to get into the class and do all of that.

PAUL: I had a colleague who worked in such a way that even though you were never right, you were also never wrong.

ACTOR: Yeah, this guy worked like that too. I didn't take offense or anything.

PAUL: You never got embarrassed, humiliated, or put off.

ACTOR: I'm interested in being in the intermediate class.

PAUL: I often recommend starting with a beginner's class no matter what their training. If you take the beginner's class, then you are working on your instrument every day. Work on yourself more than your performance.

ACTOR: I know I can be overzealous. Some of the work is not using the body.

PAUL: Good acting knows no boundaries, and good teaching and good performances know no boundaries. When I was growing up in Oregon our city didn't have television. It was like living in a cave. Famous movie actors would do movies on the radio. If you listened to these shows you would realize how amazing these people were. They actually got up and moved about.

ACTOR: Acting is an incredible thing.

PAUL: Yes it is.

GAVIN: I have a number of colleagues whom I talk with about acting until the wee hours of the morning. We get so caught up that we totally lose track of time. Paul and I often get together for many hours and discuss acting. Surround yourself with like-minded people, because it truly is an exhilarating experience.

Food for Thought

There is no difference between stage acting, film acting, and television acting. They may have different technicalities in dealing with presentation, but acting is acting. The word is *adaptation*. The greatest way to getting what you want is by adapting to the needs of the situation. This is simply the hardest part of acting because it is called experience. If you refuse to adapt, you will not get the part, or you will not fulfill any of your own desires within that part. An actor must adapt to every audition, rehearsal, every take, and to all aspects of their craft.

Food for Thought

Auditioning, by definition, is adapting to a situation. In an audition, you are anything you want to be. You are any character you want to be, and everything about you is whatever you want it to be. You arrive at the audition, quickly assess the situation, and say, "What have I got in my warehouse to show them?" The biggest problem that actors have in auditions is they say, "I want you to see me as I am." The person auditioning them, the casting director or the director, doesn't want that at all. Before you tell me, "The casting director or director did not tell me what they wanted," you should be able to discern from the situation what they want. The most successful actors can do that. Once you are a very famous actor you can say, "I don't have to do that for you anymore because you know my track record. You know that I can be anything that you want me to be." Before you are very famous you have to show them that you have the flexibility to be anything that they want you to be. Too many actors go to an audition and say to themselves, "I will learn everything I need during the audition." No, you go with a warehouse full of things that you learned. They are not interested in you. They are interested in your ability to be something you are not. You will get a lot of different advice from other actors about what you should and shouldn't do. Paul personally auditioned thousands of working actors over a number of decades. Make sure that the advice you are following is informed advice.

Final Thoughts

In my dialogue with actors I am always surprised that the revelation we come to is there at the beginning. It surprises me that it takes them even a minute to find it. What any actor wants at any age is to be creative, to be inventive, to have an imagination, to be balanced, and to be efficient at all of those things. Geniuses who work with directors, crews, choreographers, teachers, actors, composers, cinematographers, and set designers are able to do that. They often do something else simultaneously. They can be selfish, overbearing, and they can be mean, but we have to skip over all of these things and just take their genius. What they think of me is none of my business, and what I think of them is none of their business. If you can keep that in mind, then the only thing you are left with is creativity. I have seen actors turn to other actors and say, "I think the director hates me!" I have known that the director favored them over anyone else in the cast. I have also heard actors say, "Oh, the producers loved me!" I have known that they were not going to get the job. To spend any time at all trying to figure out what another person thinks of you is to take all of that precious time away from acting. If you are doing this while a director is watching you during an audition or performance, then you are going to look unhealthy and untalented. You look like you have no concentration and no talent because they can see that you're not concerned with what they're concerned with. Stress, worry, concern, and anxiety take an enormous amount of energy to muster up on an ongoing basis.

Chapter 9:
Imagination

43. Descriptive Imagination

Food for Thought

No exercise should change you, but every exercise should influence you. It is your limitations that stop you from reaching your greatest performances and from getting work. Actors are limited by tension, by what they have been told, and by the fact that no one has told them to be themselves. What is being said here is what my colleagues call *talent* can be taught. As Robert Cohen professes in his book *Acting One,* "The actor must learn to be free, free from physical and psychological inhibition, and must learn to enjoy that freedom. The actor must be free to think, feel, touch, and be touched. Above all, the actor's imagination must be unhindered."[82] As the great teacher and director Meyerhold says in this quote pulled by Robert Leach, "Training! Training! Training! But if it's the kind of training which exercises only the body and not the mind, then no, thank you!"[83] Work your entire being so that your whole system is engaged

Food for Thought

What is the difference between most actors and some enormously gifted actors? There are some actors that, by sheer fate, are built in such a way that they are exercising their imaginations in every moment. Maybe they have the ability to build a technique easier and faster. That doesn't work for most of us, as we need exercises that we can practice with our imagination. The imagination transcends the limitations of our bodies. Anybody can play at acting, but not anybody can be an actor. As Stanislavski said, "Technique exists above all for those who possess talent and inspiration."[84] Technique exists for those who have the determination and will to acquire it.

The Ingredients

We want you to imagine a rock that you have picked up on the beach. We want you to see this in your mind's eye with your eyes open, because as an actor you can't close your eyes during a performance when you want to see something. Imagine a stone. What color is it? What is it made of? What are the edges like? What is the texture? Once you have pictured one rock, we want you to picture a different one without losing the image of the first rock. You pick up one rock, examine it, and keep that image as you move on to the second rock.

Now you should have two rocks in your mind's eye at the same time, and you should see them as quite complete. Each time you pick up a new rock you are going to have to remind yourself to find the specifics. We want you to keep going and see how many rocks you can see with full description at the same time. In this exercise, each rock is like a unit that you can pile up. As you go to the next image, do not lose sight of the image you already have. We don't want you to end up with one image at a time, but many images at a time because that makes fuller acting. Remember you are being asked to hold the rocks, so you should also

---

82. Robert Cohen, *Acting One,* (California: Mayfield Publishing, 1984), 7.
83. Alison Hodge, 37.
84. Constantin Stanislavski, *An Actor's Handbook* (New York: Theatre Art Books, 1961), 139.

know their weight and texture. Eventually in your imagination you should be able to pick up twelve rocks at one time and be able to describe each one of them. You are going to find that during this exercise you will develop a specific feeling of concentration and focus. In this exercise you are creating a compound effect within your imagination.

Food for Thought

If actors only look for everything they are capable of, then they limit their imagination and they limit stretching themselves. As an actor, what you need to look at are the areas you are insufficient in, find out where your preparation is insufficient, and fix it. You cannot prepare in the moment if you haven't been preparing your entire life. As an actor, you can apply this to all areas of your life. As Rhonda Byrne explains, "The reason visualization is so powerful is because as you create pictures in your mind of seeing yourself with what it is you want, you are generating thought and feeling of having it now."[85] Be prepared to make change where change is necessary.

Food for Thought

Great actors often seem to be into their own work and appear difficult to work with. What they are doing is demanding that nothing get in the way of their imagination. They live in the state of imagination and spontaneity and they know how to access their imagination. They know that the study of acting and the study of creativity is endless. It is not important how you get there, as long as you get there.

The Diagnosis

The more rocks you can see at the same time, the more you are able to conceive of pictures in your mind. For example, if they are working on a beach scene they might say:

ACTOR: I went to the beach,

PAUL: What beach?

ACTOR: I don't know.

PAUL: What kind of beach was it? What color was the sand? Some beaches have white sand, golden sand ... did it have rocks?

ACTOR: What difference does it make?

PAUL: It makes all the difference in the world. When you say the line, "I just got back from the beach" you have to have a complete idea.

GAVIN: This exercise encourages you to use your imagination to see all of these things at once, instead of only individually. In other words, I can see the beach, I can see the ocean, I can see the children, I can see the seagulls, and I can see the sun setting, all at the same time.

An actor should have images every second while they are acting. When you are able to see what is happening in its entirety, it will have a physical and chemical effect on you as an actor. What you see or don't see will influence how you speak and how you move. The more images you are able to sustain at one time, the more it will effect your voice and your body language. When you are playing a character, you have to find the specific make up of that character. You have to build all the details that make that character in their entirety. As Moshe Feldenkrais explains, "I start each case as if it were my first, and ask more questions than any of my assistants or critics do."[86] For each character you play, start from scratch and picture all the images and details of that character.

---

85. Rhonda Byrne, *The Secret* (New York: Beyond Words Publishing, 2006), 81.
86. Moshe Feldenkrais, *The Case of Nora* (New York: Harper & Row Publishers, 1977), 27.

This exercise also professes the idea that what you see becomes thoughts and thoughts travel. Think about when you walked into a party and suddenly became irritable and said, "I'm not irritable." You look around the room and find somebody who came in with irritation. In other words, you caught their irritation.

This exercise also raises the idea of seeing what you need to see. Until you see acting the way other actors see it, until you see acting the way directors, set designers, and accomplished teachers see it, you are not acting yet. That might insult you, but do your parents understand acting the way you do? The point is, look at the people who can't see as much as you can. Then look to the other side at the actors who look at you and say, "I know you are a beginner." It's called experience. You learn by doing and working on-stage or screen.

An actor's imagination is their bread and butter, and they see images clearly in their mind to the point that, if they have prepared their instrument well, they are able to conjure up many thoughts in their mind simultaneously. You should not be so taken with the emotion that you have lost all imagery, because imagery and thoughts are what make your body move. Great actors have all kinds of images swirling around in their heads at the same time. They don't give up one to hold another. This exercise also demands your focus and concentration. If you are on a set and you see a fine actor who is absolutely focused and looks wonderfully prepared, you learn from that and are aware that it focuses everybody. Did you learn that this actor is like that twenty-four-seven? If you meet her for coffee, she is focused, not casual. She is living in this way every second of her life.

The whole point of this exercise and of your work as an actor is that you are preparing twenty-four-seven. Great actors are disciplined in everything that they do. As Robert Benedetti says, "Discipline is rooted in your respect for yourself, for your fellow workers, and for your work. Poor discipline is really a way of saying, 'I'm not worth it,' or 'This isn't worth it.' Discipline will come naturally if you can acknowledge the importance and seriousness of your work."[87] Great actors often ask for a script long before the first rehearsal so that they can exhaust it.

Food for Thought

You do not know anything about technique until you can say how Stanislavki, Uta Hagen, Lee Stresberg, Meisner, Meyerhold, Adler, Grotowski, Brecht, etc., are connected.

How can an actor say Meisner has nothing to offer unless they have explored Meisner's work? As Larry Silverberg says, "I also continually and ecstatically return to the classroom as acting coach, to share the brilliant process given to us by my teacher, the great acting teacher of our time, Sanford Meisner."[88] There is so much that has been discovered by these great teachers, why not take advantage of the *everyone approach?* Grab as much as you can from everyone, keep what works for you, and disregard the rest. In the end, each actor should be forming their own ideas, making their own choices, using their own imagination, and thus formulating a very individual technique that works for them.

Food for Thought

There are only thirty-six dramatic situations. You can go to the library and get the book called *The Thirty-Six Dramatic Situations*. Every play or script that has ever been written has to be a combination of these dramatic situations. We are therefore doomed to repeat ourselves. If it wasn't for fantasy and imagination, all plays and scripts that could have been written would already have been written. It is the subtle nuances that can take one situation and turn it into something totally out of the ordinary.

---

87. Robert L. Benedetti, *The Actor at Work* (New Jersey: Prentice-Hill, 1981), 3.
88. Larry Silverberg, *The Sanford Meisner Approach* (New Hampshire: Smith and Kraus, 1994), xvi.

Final Thoughts

A person can see many things at one time. If two people look at a landscape, one can probably see more simultaneously than another. An actor builds the ability to see more than most people and this allows their body to reflect what they see. This is an exercise in building the ability to see a great many things at one time. The more you can see, the more body language you will have. The audience will see an exciting result because they will see you with an athletic imagination, capable of seeing much more than they can. You are strengthening the muscles that make up your imagination.

44. Character Discoveries

Food for Thought

There is a very famous story about a famous actress who studied with a very famous instructor. She came to him after five years and she said, "You told me it would take me five years to become an actor." He said, "I was wrong. It's ten." You may have laughed when you read this, but now consider it in all seriousness. If it is going to be a ten year investment until you can call yourself a working actor and are able to pay your bills, is this something you are prepared for, or you are already in the middle of it and willing to it see through?

Food for Thought

Mysteriously, for no reason that can be explained by man, woman, or history, somebody says, "I want to act!" Why do you want to become an actor? The answer is because you are organically an actor. We identify with doctors, lawyers, and accountants in that we recognize them for who they are; however, many times an actor is left to identify themselves. You will face a lot of opposition from those around you, and from those you love. You may even find your parents full of support offering to pay for your acting training, but somewhere along the line they will say something like, "But you should get a second degree in accounting. You must have something to fall back on." If you are studying to be a doctor, an accountant, or an attorney, does anybody say, "You should study acting so you have something to fall back on,"? But everyone, including other actors, say you should have something to fall back on? Show us the world where actors are honored and supported in their endeavors. Think about the times a friend or relative has asked you, "What movies are you in at the moment?" You are left with a double conflict, one that is inflicted from within yourself and one from the people around you, oftentimes those closest to you.

The Ingredients

We want to tell you ahead of time why you are doing the exercise. It creates a little distance between you and the character so that you are objectively subjective.

PAUL: OK, tell me about a character you have enjoyed playing before.

ACTOR: I enjoyed playing Martha in *Cat on a Hot Tin Roof.*

PAUL: What I want you to do is walk around the space and take Martha with you. Using your imagination, show her around and just give her general overview of the place. You may find that she responds to you, and I want you to pay attention to that. You may find that she doesn't care to walk around, let her go wherever she goes. You do not have to vocalize any of this out loud. You can do all of this without comment to us. It is an internal conversation between the two of you. It's a bit like having an imaginary friend. When you are finished come back and join us. *(A period of five minutes passes.)* Did you find anything about Martha that you didn't anticipate?

ACTOR: When I first started the exercise I was taking her on a tour, but actually I found myself following her around the whole time. She just walked straight past me and I found myself following her.

PAUL: Did that teach you anything about her?

ACTOR: Yeah, I found that she was pretty assertive, confident, and wanted to get things her way. When she had enough of walking around, she just sat down and grabbed a beer.

PAUL: And what did you find out?

ACTOR: I found that having an imaginary friend really sparked my imagination. I found that learning specific things about her made her more vibrant and alive to me. I found out she likes people to be accommodating to her. I also know that she is older and so she would probably have trouble walking.

PAUL: Good, we have to be careful in this exercise not to use pre-thought. In other words, because she is older and an alcoholic, she will have problem walking upstairs. That's an actor's way of making logical deductions. So when you are talking about the exercise say, "She did this, she did that. I was annoyed with her when she did that." In that way you are really talking about a person and what they did at that precise moment.

ACTOR: OK, I had to be receptive about when she was getting bored with certain things. I started playing the piano and she got bored of this very quickly. I started to discover how I interacted with her.

PAUL: That's wonderful. What you told us just gave me material that I could use if I were directing you.

ACTOR: I like this exercise because it enables you not to intellectualize, but for the discoveries to come out physically and creatively.

PAUL: Good, I only want you to use this exercise if it works for you, and if you are getting something from it. I never believe an actor should work with an exercise simply because someone has told them to, but because it has true practical value to them.

GAVIN: Just because a teacher asks you to do something, that does not mean they are right. One exercise may help an actor immensely, while another actor may find it of no value. In the end, you take what works for you and disregard the rest. However, you have to understand what is being asked or being said before you can discard it.

PAUL: On the flipside, if you receive poor direction from a director, you may still have to give them what they want. It is then part of your job to finesse the situation so the directors feel they are getting what they ask for and you are still truthful to the scene.

Food for Thought

I was once rehearsing a scene with an actress at her apartment. At one point she left the room and I waited in the lounge. She came out and said, "Why didn't you follow me?" I said, "I thought you went to the bathroom." She said, "Well, what if I left the stage during the scene?" I said, "I'd stop the scene." She said, "Well, you have to learn to use it!" So I got really pissed. I was twenty-five. I asked the director if I could speak to him and I said, "I just want to tell you that if she gets up and leaves the stage, I'm going to stop the scene." He said, "Please don't do that." And then he devastated me when he said, "I always thought you had a sense of humor." He was really saying, "Be a professional actor." Be prepared to cope with any situation or any set of circumstances that come your way.

Food for Thought

You have to do every word like you just thought of it at that moment. You say, "How am I going to have a new thought for that?" That is the description of the result. You can't have a new thought every moment. That's not possible, but it's poetic. When an actor cannot do this, they think they are not talented. Nobody can have a brand new expression and epiphany every second. You can simply begin again as often as you want to. People will say, "I can't believe your intensity." Never tell them your secret. Your intensity is your commitment to what you are saying and what you are responding to.

The Diagnosis

This is a great way to do research on your characters instead of only reading the material and saying, "They are bitter. They have a quick temper, etc." With this exercise you are able to find out what they have to bring to the table. They may tell you things about themselves or you may make discoveries that you would never have got from the script.

This exercise asks you to take a character with you, and therefore sparks your imagination – technique simply accesses your imagination. The exciting thing about this exercise is that you are able to do this over a prolonged period of time and access your imagination continually. What is also interesting about this exercise is that you can take your character anywhere you want. You can take her home while you are driving in the car and you can take her to a party. You do not have to have her with you all day, but she can reappear any time you choose. Be open to it at any time during the day. If you hang around with a person long enough, you start to pick up habits of that person.

It is not enough to know about your character on an intellectual level, but also to live them on a visceral level. With this exercise you will begin to experience your character and create the character rather than allowing the character to create itself. It is also important to create a backstory for your character, such as where they came from, what happened in the past, etc. This gives you an advantage over other actors because you have inside information about your character that they don't have. The more you walk and talk with them, the more you will pick up their habits, even if you don't like them as a person. Once you pick up their habits, you are going to find that you start to act like them. What a lovely thought! It's basic, it's simple, it's rudimentary, and yet it is very, very effective. What a great exercise for the actor. It is simple, practical, and can be worked anytime and anywhere. It also naturally demands a degree of focus, concentration, and imagination from you so that you are able to communicate with and observe your character.

Food for Thought

In medicine they can say here's the order, here's the question, and here's the answer. But the difference is there are no absolute answers in acting. Acting is a discovery in every moment. If you have discovered yourself as an actor, now your troubles and woes have just begun. You are going to have to defend yourself, and believe us when we say defend yourself. You are going to have to rationalize why you have done something so foolish and why you have done something that may not exist except in your own imagination. In your imagination you can go anywhere and take your audience with you.

Food for Thought

I used to teach professional workshops to groups of twenty-two actors and after the course, at least one out of the twenty-two from each session would get a divorce. They finally found a place that said "We are entirely about you and your acting." We showed them how to fill their time entirely with acting. Some of them realized that they would have to get a divorce in order to follow their acting dreams fully. See the Pie exercise to cement what is being said here.

Final Thoughts

We were all told as children by our parents, "Don't hang around with those kids. I don't want you picking up their habits." Much of what we do is caused by our environment and we can use this to our advantage. We can hang around with the character and simply pick up the habits of that character. This exercise explores the concept that you tend to pick up habits, good and bad, from the people you hang around the most, or the people you admire, or the people who have the most control over you. You pick up these habits and you don't even notice you've done them. The actor wants to pick up the habits of a character rather than actually become them. Allow your character to sneak up on you and to come in through the side door rather than attacking you full on.

45. Up and Down

Food for Thought

There is a wonderful true story of a guy in Virginia who went to the doctor because he kept hearing voices. The doctor told him to write down what the voices were saying. What happened next was both logical and positive – he became a very famous author. He was not hearing voices. He was writing books. The difference between mental illness and creative thinking is that one is controllable and the other one isn't. Think of anyone you have known or heard about who is considered a genius. They are fairly close to being certifiable because the difference can be split. In order to be a genius one has to be willing to stretch the boundaries every second of their existence.

Food for Thought

When we are beginning we like a book on acting not because it teaches, but because it inspires.

The Ingredients

For this exercise you need to find an open space in a room. Stand where you have enough space around you so you can lay down when necessary. We want you to look at your age and your ability and find a way to safely get all the way down on the floor until you are actually lying on your back. Do it in whatever way is most comfortable for you. Use your hands, arms, or whatever is necessary for you to lie down comfortably. As soon as you are lying down find a way to safely and comfortably get up to a standing position. Now we're going to ask you to do something and you're going to have to make a judgment about yourself. You'll have to decide how old, how young, and how able you are to do it. We're going to ask you, in the safest way and the most pleasant way, to get down to the floor and on your back as quickly as possible. The first time you do it, don't do it too fast. Your body and you may consider that thirty seconds is quick, then somebody may decide that five seconds is quick. It's up to you. You really have to think about this and tell yourself this. You are not trying to get better at this. You're simply trying to do it. As you do this exercise don't tell your body what it must do, simply decide, "I'm going to get all the way down on the floor and onto my back. I'm going to get up off the floor until I'm standing." Do this for a couple of minutes or until you feel the body is prepared.

A variation you can do on this exercise is to lie down on your stomach instead of your back. You can also go down to your hands and knees so that perhaps your back is slightly arched and get up from there. Put together your own movement to vary this exercise. As you work with this exercise you have to have a good understanding of your own instrument in order to do it safely and efficiently.

Food for Thought

We have often heard famous schools say, "If you use what you are learning here to get on a television soap opera, then you have failed. You have failed us, you have accepted something that is beneath you, and you have accepted situations that will not allow you ever to do a great performance. It will harm you, and if you were on your way to becoming talented and successful and recognized as an artist, it will eat away and erode your talent." We hear actors say, "I don't want to do a soap," or "I don't want to do that movie because it is not worthy." What we are getting at it this: If you want to be an actor, you would do yourself well not to give soaps, television shows, movies, and theatre productions a second guess as to what you are and are not willing to do, because being an actor and acting is part of your everyday life. What they are saying is, "In order to be artistically healthy, you must feed yourself the ingredients that make for great acting." This simply is not true, even if we would like it to be so. Actors have walked on the greatest stages in the world drunk. There are more opportunities to be an actor in the world than there ever have been. A great actor wants to act every day of their life. A great actor wants to go to work every day. Acting is a lifestyle, a way of being, and you want to be doing it all the time. Every time you use your instrument you want to go back to basics: stretch, strengthen, coordinate, and discover. We have to separate the difference between a great performance, a great performer, and great material. You will learn something from every project you work on, even though not all of them will be your favorites.

Food for Thought

When somebody gets up and does a scene and nothing is happening, they are not making discoveries and it in turn becomes uninteresting to an audience. I was teaching a class and an actor did a scene in which, when he was done, I couldn't talk. If I talked I would have cried because I was overwhelmed. I said, "Yes, and we need to take a fifteen minute break. I would prefer that none of you talk to each other during the break." They came back and I said, "This is what you should do to an audience, this is what you should do to every audience." I've seen plays and movies that have driven me mad, frightened me, and riled me up. You want to affect your audience.

The Diagnosis

Acting is sound because we are dealing with words, and acting is simply body language when it has no sound. All words are the result of muscles moving; therefore all words carry with them a certain body language. All words have body language, but not all body language has sound. Remember, we have had brilliant silent film actors. We have all watched silent movies and cried, laughed, and experienced as much in as any other form of acting. Energy happens before muscles move, before energy comes a thought, and thought is equal to imagination. You can't have movement as a result of energy if something is standing between the energy and the movement. Imagination has been said many, many times before to be an actor's greatest tool. The purpose of a physical warm-up is to take away the potential of anything getting between a thought and energy and movement. If you stand up and lean forward and just let your hands fall down towards your toes, you're already stretching the body. If you simply walk around a room, you're already getting something out between energy and movement simply by walking. One would assume that any healthy person uses their imagination. It's entertaining, it's instructive, and it lets us go through a lot of things we don't have time to go through in reality or don't want to go through. Because the actor has to have a heightened imagination and because he has to speak and move, we have to do exercises that clear the path between imagination and movement.

Speaking is movement. We can forget that speaking requires muscular movement. The very act of doing this exercise, of lying on the floor and getting up, begins to warm up your body and give it coordination. When you lie on the floor you change your body's relationship to gravity and you change the circulation in the body. This exercise is good for a warm-up for singing, dancing, and acting. Remember, a good number of actors can sing, dance, and act to some degree. This exercise begins to ask the body to figure out how to coordinate certain moves. It asks the body to become familiar with itself. This exercise will also change your breathing patterns. What you have done in a wonderful way is enable your body to go through body language right now. The exercise becomes the most specific exercise in the world. While you might think this exercise engages the muscles of the body, it is quite the contrary. It shows you which muscles of the body are capable of being engaged. Two people standing beside one another will engage different muscles because different muscles are available to them. The more you do exercises such as this, the more muscles will become available to you. The more muscles that are available to you, the more your body can respond in subtle ways. An infinite variety and combination of body language creates a highly functional instrument.

Food for Thought

One of the most exciting things about acting is what is happening right now, at this very moment, in this very second. You cannot write about it or talk about it. You have to be there in that moment to experience it and that is the phenomenon of acting. We recognize that a book has its limitations, and there is no replacement for actually being there; however, there are some incredible resources all around.

Food for Thought

What is the difference between most actors and some enormously gifted actors? There are some actors who, by sheer fate, are built in such a way that they are acting and exercising their imaginations. Maybe they have the ability to build a technique easier and faster. That doesn't work for most of us as we need exercises that we can practice with our imagination. The imagination transcends the limitations of our bodies. Anybody can play at acting, but not anybody can be an actor. As Stanislavski said, "Technique exists above all for those who possess talent and inspiration."[89] Technique exists for those who have the determination and will to acquire it.

Final Thoughts

The older we get, the taller we get, the more difficult it is to fall down and get back up. An actor needs to master basic things such as to walk, to turn, and to stand. One way to retain the strength and dexterity of a child is to do a child's playful movement. Children have a game where at the end they all fall down. Nobody thinks that when the children are doing it they have to stand up in order to start the game over. They can do it for hours at a time and just have more fun than anything. We have to go back and regain the strength and agility of a child. Most great exercises are so simple that we either think they can't do anything for us or we entirely miss them. By practicing up and down you will find that you are able to memorize a script better, you understand the director better, audition better, and so on. When the instrument is tuned it can do everything better, including think. Your imagination is released when you are strong. When you watch them play, children have an unending, wonderful imaginations because all of their time and thoughts can be devoted only to imagination. As the body gets older it gets used to adaptations, which cause over-compensations. By working with very basic and rudimentary core exercises, you are learning to realign the body, which makes way for a freer, more capable instrument. It is necessary to be aware that dialogue is the last thing that happens between two people.

---

89. Constantin Stanislavski, 139.

46. Cross the Line

Food for Thought

You have to go into each performance knowing you are going to activate the emotions of the audience. The next step is to know how to organize the emotions that you have orchestrated – that's technique. As John Harrop puts it, "Discussion of the acting process usually resolves itself into the received dichotomy of emotion versus technique."[90]

Food for Thought

I once met an actress during an intermission of a play who came up to me and said, "I don't like this play." I said something that startled her, "You don't have the right to an opinion yet." I believe that I wasn't being harsh. How do you know that you don't like the play as an actor or you don't like the play as a civilian? Each and every one of us has cause to acknowledge the term *talk is cheap*.

The Ingredients

Whenever you have a moment when you can't think of anything to do or whenever there is a moment that you can't get beyond, whether it's being stuck how to work a script, preparing for an audition, or are at an impasse and having trouble moving beyond, then do a simple exercise. Take anything and draw a line on the floor. To do this you can use a rope, a piece of string, draw a line in the dirt, or use a piece of chalk. Draw this line in front of you, and then look at that line and decide whether you are going to step over it or not. If you step over it you have solved your problem. It might surprise you the number of times you look at the line and find you can't step over it, or you won't step over it. You really have to concentrate on what it is your crossing, "I don't know the part. I'm afraid of the audition. I'm afraid of filming. I'm afraid of opening night, etc." Whatever it is, you have to get beyond that and do a little ritual. It always works. Put down a straight line in front of you and concentrate on what it is that is restricting at that moment. While you are thinking of that, try to step over the line. There is something symbolic and ritualistic about this exercise, and yet it can be most effective.

Food for Thought

I want to have fun every second of my life, so if I look around and see that I'm not having fun, I say, "Stop!" This highlights that you are going to want to check in on yourself. It does not mean that every second of your acting career has to be fun, but if you're not enjoying any of it, then what are you doing it for? In terms of your career as an actor, Peter Jazwinski points out that, "Other than picking up this book, did you do anything else today to advance your acting career?"[91] If you didn't, then start now because somebody else is consistently doing something for their acting career.

Food for Thought

If exercises work for you, use them. If they don't, move on to ones that do. The only reason we say that is because we are not there to partner you in the exercise. The benefit of the exercise never comes until the exercise has been done on numerous occasions. What we mean is if you did an exercise every day for a year, you might realize the real importance of that exercise, and it would actually change you. If you did it for two years it would change you for the rest of your life. Be prepared to work on your instrument for the rest of your life.

The Diagnosis

An actor is a physical athlete, an emotional athlete, and an intellectual athlete, but the one thing we forget is that they have an athletic imagination. An actor has to stretch themselves

---

90. John Harrop, 4.
91. Peter Jazwinski, *Act Now!* (New York: Three Rivers Press, 2003), 5.

more physically than any other athlete because their work is unlimited. The actor has to stretch, strengthen, and coordinate their emotion. If you can't move beyond something, it means that part of you is not stretched. Something in your being is not stretched, something in your being is not strengthened, and something in your being is not coordinated. If you can step over the line, the impediment wasn't as bad as you thought. If you can't step over it, that's fine and good. The good thing is there are only three possibilities as to why you didn't step over the line: your emotion is not stretched, you don't have the strength to do that, or you don't have the coordination to put together what is needed to do whatever it is. When you have identified the problem you can say, "Now I have to stretch, strengthen, and coordinate so that the situation is no longer an issue." Now you know why you are in acting class. Now you know why you go back to the acting gym. The acting gym reminds you to continue to work with your instrument so that your muscles do not become weak and unused to where atrophy will follow. By continuing to work on your instrument you are creating muscle memory.

Food for Thought

There are some wonderful poetic myths about acting. They're great fun and they happen because of the work we do, but they don't get the work we do done. A director may have his actors sit around the table and do readings until they can't stand it any more or to where they are dying to jump to their feet and act, but this doesn't make the actors better. It is just a nice way to treat them because it challenges them. Good directors will use any means at their disposal to get the best results possible from their actors.

Food for Thought

A colleague of mine once told me the story of a famous director in France. He was working the actors extremely hard, and finally the stage manager said that the actors really should have a break. At this point the producer came over and said, "I can't tell you how happy we are to have you here and how stimulating you are for the actors. I only have one question: I don't understand how anything you are doing has anything to do with the play or is taking it in the direction where ultimately it must go?" And he replied, "I don't know, I haven't read the play yet." This was a true story. An actor is not the same as a non-actor. They are different because the actor lives in a life that is unfiltered. An actor may appear odd, different, extreme, and eccentric to others.

Final Thoughts

My mentor taught me never to ask a person to do something they cannot or will not do, and I've remembered that. I've also realized down the line that actors are constantly doing something they cannot or will not do. Since an actor is two people, the instrument accomplishing and creating the character, and the person telling the instrument what to do, it can be confusing. How, then, do we approach this as a simple exercise? It is not directorial or intellectual, but a very simple muscular exercise that will clue in the body, clue in the mind, and the heart, and the individual. The more you do the Cross the Line exercise, the more your body is open and willing to do anything. When you step over the line the physical part of your body says, "I can do anything I want to do. I can cross the line." You know the old expression "Don't cross the line"? Well, an actor must cross the line. Think of all the exciting actors you know and think while you are watching them they are constantly crossing the line. It may take time to find a mentor, but if you keep searching, you will find one. In the end the mentor will be you.

Chapter 10:
The Physical Actor

47. Breathe In and Out

Food for Thought

I once got an actor I was working with very angry, yet he did the scene and it was brilliant. He said, "You mean I have to get angry to be any good?" I thought, "You can't see it, can you?" I said to myself, "I don't seem to be able to get you there quickly any other way, so let's just take a short cut. I'll just prod you a little bit, get you angry, and that will give you performance energy, or close to it. You will do this with performance energy and you will be good. I don't want you to be angry all the time, that doesn't make any sense, but you see the kind of energy you have when you get angry? You need that energy all the time." Getting to this place is a challenge, and then to sustain this energy is an even greater challenge for the actor.

Food for Thought

There will always be wonderful actors who didn't study, but what they did do was create their own technique. Martha Graham was told to give up dancing because her legs were too short, so she made up her own technique and the rest, as they say, is history. There are actors who study all of their life and never get anything done and never do more than tiny bit parts professionally. Which one is most talented?

ACTOR: The actor who never studied?

PAUL: Neither one of them, that's the answer you're looking for. One is more coordinated in a specific area and they choose to be ambitious in that area. You have to recognize these two things. Once you recognize it you realize that you are somewhere in between. If you don't recognize it then you are nowhere, you don't exist, and you haven't been born yet.

GAVIN: Talent is not enough and hard work is not enough, so you need both. You need talent followed by consistent and neverending hard work.

The Ingredients

This exercise is very straightforward. What you are going to do is breathe in and out ten times. Each time you take a breath in, think a positive thought, and each time you breathe out, think a negative thought. You don't need to say a complete sentence. A word will suffice. An example of a positive thought could be "love," and a negative could be "fear." We think that you will be amazed at how quickly those thoughts come to you without any effort. You don't have to prepare your thought in advance. This is a primary exercise and there is nothing to prepare. Not only is it necessary *not* to say the thoughts out loud, but it is also *mandatory* not to say the thoughts out loud.

If you work this exercise with another actor you may not, *shall not, must not* say anything out loud because any exercise that intimidates you or restricts you should not be done.

You can do this exercise on your own or you can have another actor sit and observe you. If you are the observer, you want to find what the experience was like and not the specific thoughts that came to them. Go ahead and work on the exercise before reading further.

Don't force the thoughts in this exercise, but allow them to arrive.

PAUL: Tell me about it. What was the experience like?

ACTOR: It was very revealing when you said don't prepare and just see what comes to you. I thought I wasn't going to have to prepare instead of just letting thoughts come to me.

PAUL: Big key ... you presumed what the exercise was before you really knew.

ACTOR: Exactly, once I started, I didn't know what was coming, and I didn't know what the negative was going to be. I think that these words would not have come to me if I tried to plan.

PAUL: Did you give much thought to the way it very dramatically changed your breathing patterns?

ACTOR: I didn't focus on the breathing, but I knew I wanted to have enough time for each thought, and the breathing came automatically. I also found quite a lot of release coming from it, but it was effortless. I didn't have to dig emotionally or dig deep ... I didn't dig at all, really.

PAUL: That's a common reaction, and it is also interesting that a number of actors find they forget the negative thoughts when they have finished because they have gone. Your breathing got slower, your body calmed down, and your whole being looked more stable.

Food for Thought

The technique of acting is accumulated over a long period of time and can be more and more refined. I once saw a famous actress in her twilight years doing an exercise of throwing an imaginary ball back and forth with some actors from Yale. Though at an advanced age, she was wise enough to continue to practice this technique. This is a very simple exercise, showing us that this seasoned actress continued to go back to the basics throughout her life.

Food for Thought

A coach gives you exercises, but you do those exercises by yourself. The best exercises in the world are the ones you can do on your own. Think about the rehearsal process, in which you do the bulk of the work on your own time. This is what it means when the director asks you to come prepared.

The Diagnosis

In terms of the importance of breathing, John Miles-Brown says, "Good breathing is a fundamental requirement for voice productions and also for projecting the actor's speech."[92] This exercise is like clearing your sinuses, because breathing is in and out and thinking is in and out. We forget that we take thoughts in and we put thoughts out. This exercise encourages the flow of thoughts in and out, and consequently it encourages your imagination. You are your imagination, and great actors have more imagination than anyone in the audience.

In this exercise you are practicing your ability to think. In school we are taught how to think and to control the thinking. In acting, we are encouraged to free the thinking. School teaches us to control our thoughts so that we can think in an organized manner; however, an actor does not have to have an organized manner. Actually, they must think in a random manner so that any thought can come to them while playing this character. An actor must think in a uncontrolled, free, random way. When an actor goes on-stage, their awareness needs to be so much greater than the audience's. The part they are playing rushes through them with all kinds of random variations and thoughts. In order for this to happen the actor must have an enormous amount of trust in their instrument.

What an actor can do on-camera or stage is often illegal to do off-camera or stage. What an actor is allowed to do, is encouraged to do, and must do would often be illegal in daily

---

92. John Miles-Brown, *Acting: A Drama Studio Source Book* (London: Peter Owens Publishing, 2000), 27.

life. Historically, some of the greatest minds such as Copernicus and Socrates were imprisoned or even put to death just for thinking what they thought. If this is true, then an actor is fighting an uphill battle to let the thoughts that that character would think cross their minds. In the play *Medea*, Medea has the thought of killing her children. Can you imagine if the actress really thought about killing her own children to get back at her husband? If a woman in our society thought this out loud, her children would be taken from her because the fact that she *thought* it means she might act on it.

In society we are told what negative and positive thoughts are. In this exercise you are being asked not to block what is negative. Great actors insist on allowing their minds to have random thoughts, and they also insist on letting their minds think thoughts that are illegal or immoral. The actor has to have the ability to let any thought cross their mind. This exercise allows the actor to let negativity go and almost has a cleansing effect. It allows the actor to put their body and mind in a state of neutrality. If you have had a long and stressful day, you might find this exercise useful to work before a rehearsal or a performance. We are always looking for the practical implications of these exercises and not theoretical. As Deepak Chopra explains, "We all have the power to make reality. Why make it inside boundaries when the boundless is so near?"[93]

Food for Thought

Every time you feel comfortable or you finally feel you've got it right, you must be wrong. This is because every moment that you are acting must be unfamiliar to you. Once you learn to get comfortable with being in a state of unfamiliar, it is the most exciting and freeing thing in the world. Who else gets to do that? Who else gets to have a different experience every single day? Actors do not just crave being in front of cameras and being on a stage because they want people to see them. When they are on-camera or on-stage they get the luxury of experiencing something they have never experienced before. You may be on a set or watching a play and seeing performances that appear stale, uninteresting, and totally unbelievable. You say to yourself that they cannot possibly be doing any of the things mentioned here, and you are probably right.

Food for Thought

If you put on skis and go down a learning ramp, you may choose to say, "I am a skier!" and when asked why this is so, you may reply, "Because I have skis on!" And when you ask a number of people what makes you think that you are an actor, they say things like, "I'm doing a scene, I memorized my lines, I have a headshot, a commercial agent, and I took a class and the teacher told me I was getting better!" We would then ask, "Did the teacher ever say you were any good?" These things do not make an actor. The industry of acting is a vital part of your ability to get work, but it is not a substitute for acting.

Final Thoughts

This is an exercise that appears simple, as most good exercises do. If you do this exercise every day for one year, you will know what it means. If you do it for two years, other actors will know what it means. If you do it for three years, everybody will know what it means. Create longevity in your acting.

---

93. Deepak Chopra, *Journey into Healing* (New York: Harmony Books, 1994), 45.

48. Pre-Pre-Exercise

Food for Thought

Acting is the most intimate art form because it is the art form most easily confused with real life. The more intimate you are, the more colors you show. In the most physical of terms, the actor has to become intimate with their audience. Acting can be confused with real life in part because of its heightened realities.

Food for Thought

A world-renowned martial artist was once sent to me because he was being used for choreographed fights because he was an expert. The studio said, "We cannot understand a word he is saying, and he shows no feelings. He is just too cool." He came into my class and I had him get up in front of the class and teach us Taekwondo. Then I had him pretend that he was his teacher teaching him, and his teacher's teacher teaching his teacher. In any case, he went back to the studio after a couple of weeks and they said, "He doesn't have nearly as much of an accent, and he was much more open." When we first met he said words to the effect of, "I have no technique," and I said, "You introduced Taekwondo to the United States, you're one of the greatest technicians who ever lived. You usually only get one great technique in your entire life." Diagnose the specific situation in order to get the results. As you grow and learn, diagnose your own needs.

The Ingredients

What we would like you to do is sit down or walk around, whichever you prefer. At the end of each out breath, we want you to say the number one. We want to use your normal level of volume here. There is no need to attempt to create an even pattern for your breathing, just let it be where it is.

PAUL: *(ACTOR starts the breathing cycle.)* Keep your eyes closed.

ACTOR: One, one, two, one, three, one.

PAUL: Keep going, but move to a whisper now.

ACTOR: One, one, two, one, three, one.

PAUL: Now I would like you to do it again, and this time just think the number one and don't say it out loud. *(ACTOR works for another minute and goes through about four cycles.)* That was the best you have done so far. The biggest word to technique is patience. You will work this exercise by speaking, whispering, and thinking. I am not going to go through how you should be breathing here, but ask you to breathe in a comfortable fashion. Later, you can add another step where you work through this exercise with your eyes open. If you are working with a partner and you have your eyes open, try to engage them, try to interest them. This exercise is so basic that you might choose to pass over it. Please don't.

GAVIN: Great artists always go back to basics to remind their instrument of what it already knows.

Food for Thought

Some actors will get one line in a movie such as, "Hello, how do you do?" then they put on their resumé *Guest Star.* We think it's damaging to do this. It's not that you delude yourself, it's that you then skip the steps, or have no interest in the steps it takes to be an actor. It is not the industry that encourages the actor to put this on the resumé. Doing this is damaging because they are not a "guest" and they are certainly not a "star." Producers and directors don't care because it is of no interest to them whatsoever. This one line might make you money, make contacts, and get your foot in the door. These things are all necessary. However, it will become damaging if you feel this one line is the cornerstone of your acting career. It is like the individual who has fabulous headshots and looks like a star, but they just can't do anything. How often do you take a speech class, an Alexander class, a movement class, and a yoga class, go to the movies, watch a play, or workout in the gym? How often do you work on your body awareness, sensory awareness, imagination, improvisation, motor skills, nonverbal communication, and spatial awareness? Great actors do these things until the day they die. If you were really an actor, you would do these things. In terms of improvisation, Rob Kozlowski explains, "Sure, everyone can improvise. Everyone can paint, too, but that doesn't mean someone's going to buy their painting."[94] The most incredible thing about your creative instrument is that it is always hungry and constantly needs feeding.

Food for Thought

Acting exists because there will always be people, tall and short, of every calling, of every race, of every size, of every mentality, and of every background who have a passion for not only telling stories, but for creating characters. Acting is part of the human condition. If you find that is a condition of you, then you have a good chance of being an actor. If you are reading some of the exercises in this book, then it is very likely that part of your condition as a human is to be an actor. Our DNA gives us different conditions, and acting is one of the conditions that carries with it passion as many other fields do. As Kathryn Marie Bild explains, "One of the things that is beautiful about dramatic acting is that it is nondenominational in its elucidation of truth. It deals with the human condition shared by all men and women."[95] When discussing the term *dramatic,* Ron Marasco observes, "Actors are drawn to the dramatic. It's nothing to apologize about. In fact, it's an asset."[96] If you cannot stop thinking about acting, if it consumes your every thought, it is because it is part of your physical make up.

The Diagnosis

What you are achieving in this exercise is that you are clearing the palate and preparing the instrument. You are taking all forms of prejudgment and are rebirthing the instrument. You are taking the instrument back before it has opinion, before it has tradition, and before it has moral consequences. It allows you to clear yourself of all thought. This exercise is pre-work and pre-preparation. This makes it sound easy, yet it is not. It is a different exercise. It serves to prepare your body according to the shape and the coordination of your mind to your body. In this exercise you get to go backwards and go from talking to whispering to just a thought. If we started this exercise with a whisper, you would most likely find that you go into yourself and away from the world and the audience. Acting is never with the intent of being away from the audience in terms of your intent. You may find that you physically move away from an audience, but this is not what we are talking about here. Remember that you have to activate your audience's imagination, and you can't do this if you are not present.

In this exercise you have to be physically available and then your talent will be available. In order to access your talent you always want to go back to the first step. By eventually going back to the number one as a thought you are able to access this at the most primal level. If you are an Olympic athlete or a body builder, you have to warm up with a pre-event workout.

In this exercise we are stripping everything away. As we have already mentioned, many actors say, "If I could just have the right part, the right director, the right hair designer, the right costume, you would all be interested in me." It is going to be much more beneficial for you if you can interest directors and casting directors with only one thing: your imagination. When you can do this, the director or casting director will say, "I don't know what it is, but

---

94. Rob Kozlowski, *The Art of Chicago Improv* (New Hampshire: Heinemann, 2002), 174.
95. Kathryn Marie Bild, *Acting from a Spiritual Perspective* (New Hampshire: Smith and Kraus, 2002), 250.
96. Ron Marasco, *Notes to an Actor* (Chicago: Ivan. R Dee, 1997), 20.

there is something about him or her that intrigues me. Call him or her back." You got called back because you activated their emotion and imagination. Many actors are never comfortable with themselves and thus they never become comfortable with their characters. They fall into the trap of conformity. As Uta Hagen says, "We must overcome the notion that we must be regular. Be like one of us. Don't put on airs. Don't get so fancy. It robs you of the chance to be extraordinary and leads you to being mediocre."[97] Because acting is a lifestyle or way of being, you have to integrate it fully into your life, not as a part-time gesture. When you are working with these exercises, the only thing that is important is that they do something for you. The only importance it has to you is for you.

Food for Thought

I was told the story of a famous actor who was playing a part and was told by his doctor, "If you continue to play this part in this manner, you will do yourself physical and emotional damage. You must change the way you play it." I thought about that for a while and I said, "You don't have to change the way you play it, you just have to let it out." We learn acting things from everything. Don't you sometimes look at your friends and say, "If you don't let go of that you are going to explode?" Or don't you also say, "I almost exploded I was so angry." Well, you wouldn't explode, and your anger would be quite impressive if you let it flow through your body, but if you stop it at any place it will constrict who you are. Everything you do should make you freer and more malleable.

Food for thought

If you tell us in acting that this works, then we want to know what comes just before that, and then we want to know what comes before that, because if we can find these things out, then we know how to prepare. There is preparation for the actor, and then there is pre-preparation.

Final Thoughts

If you are out of breath or stressed, stop what you are doing, calm yourself down, and get your breath back. People tended to think for thousands of years that this was impractical, foolish, daydreaming, and poetic. Now we know that when you think a thought, it can actually change your pulse. Major hospitals around the world now recommend things such as meditation, biofeedback, right brain/left brain activity, and mirror neurons. These are now ways of proving things we used to think were figments of our imagination. They are not figments of our imagination, but rather physical things we can do. This exercise helps you balance the body, warm it up, and calm the body down. This exercise helps you to make any motion or any thought clearer. The mind and body are wondrous tools for the actor to discover and utilize. As William W. Hewitt says when talking about hypnosis, "Hypnosis is a technique that enables you to achieve this altered state of consciousness — the daydream state — deliberately and direct your attention to specific goals in order to achieve them."[98]

49. Air Bubble

Food for Thought

If your ability to understand love, fear, or anger has never been stretched to extremes, then you are not prepared to act anymore than someone playing the piano whose hand span couldn't reach an octave. As an actor you are going to have to stretch yourself in a multitude of ways. You will face numerous obstacles, and it is not the obstacle, but rather how you approach it that is going to make the difference. Bandler and Grinder explain, "Change the

---

97. Uta Hagen, *Respect for Acting* (New York: Macmillan Publishing Company, 1973), 31.
98. William W. Hewitt, *Hypnosis for Beginners* (Minnesota: Llewellyn Publications), xi.

frame in which a person perceives events in order to change the meaning. When the meaning changes, the person's responses and behaviors also change."[99] Each obstacle you face can be overcome, one step at a time.

Food for Thought

We want to be careful of the word *posture* because that is a result. What we are often moving towards is a better *use* of the body. Alexander himself discovered it was the use of the body that was of the utmost importance. If we can get a better use of the body, all things are possible in acting. You look at somebody and you say, "The use is bad, therefore nothing will come of it." Sometimes an individual will stand up straight to improve their posture, but unless they are engaging the necessary muscle groups, the body will find a way to go back to its incorrect form it has learned over a lifetime.

The Ingredients

Here is a little, simple exercise you can do because actors do tend to fidget with their hands, or tap their foot, or move their legs. What we would like you to do is put a little imaginary air bubble in the joint of your wrist where it bends. If your hands are moving, then you know exactly where your energy is being stopped – just before the fingers at the wrist joint. You go to the joint before your fingers and you put a bubble of air. When you think about putting a bubble of air in your wrist, you will usually find your hand becomes still. If you are tapping your fingers and somebody tells you to stop it, then you get rigid and numb. What you have done is stopped even more of a flow in your body. Now give that hand a slight and gentle stretch by clasping it with your free hand. If you find yourself tapping your fingers, you can think of your arm lengthening, particularly in this case, from your elbow to your fingertips, or from your shoulder to your fingertips, or from the center of your back through your shoulder, through your elbow, and through your wrist. You may find that your wrist was a little compressed and now it is lengthening.

Any time you find that you have unnecessary movement, put that little bubble there. You can do this with any part of your body. You do not physically have to move that body part, but imagine it lengthening and elongating through your imagination. Just notice you are tapping your foot and say, "I'm going to lengthen my ankle, and I'm going to lengthen it by putting air in the joint of my ankle." It will now become wider and less constricted and it will decompress.

We are often so compressed in life, but we use another term. We turn to one another and say, "Why are you so uptight?" The way not to get uptight is to do the opposite, and let everything that is going towards each other go away from each other. Let the arm lengthen, let the wrist lengthen, let the fingers lengthen, let the joints in the fingers lengthen, let the neck lengthen, put a bubble of air between every vertebrae, and put a bubble of air between every joint in the body. You are not only working with your body in this exercise, but you are also utilizing the opportunity to work with your imagination. Any opportunity an actor has to work with their imagination should be pounced upon.

Food for Thought

We think acting is the only art form you can work on one hundred percent of the time, if you choose to. You can walk down the street and focus on your breathing, you can sit on the bus and work on your posture, you can work on a character wherever you choose, and you can memorize lines lying down and whispering them practically in your sleep. There is not a moment of your existence in which you cannot work on your acting if you choose to. We want you to think about all the times you have told yourself that you couldn't work on your

---

99. Richard Brandler and John Grinder, *Reframing* (Utah: Real People Press, 1982), 1.

acting because you were not in a production or a class at that time. You can work on your instrument any time you like because it will follow you wherever you go. As Michael Caine tells us, "If you really want to become an actor, but only providing that acting doesn't interfere with your golf game, your political ambitions, and your sex life, you don't really want to become an actor. Not only is acting more than a part-time job, its more than a full-time job, it's a full-time obsession."[100]

Food for Thought

It would be foolish, almost criminal, if you said, "This is just a little theatre. It didn't cost us very much, and we are not even charging money. If I miss a show, it is not that big of a deal." It is criminal because people are depending on you. Your performance has to be so rich, so dense, and so complex that an audience could see the movie twenty times and still see something they didn't see the first time. Do you realize what this is like? Do you realize what a Herculean task this is? No matter what the location or setting, give everything you have because that is all you have. It sounds obvious because it is obvious. Do you do this in your own work?

The Diagnosis

This exercise is very good if you find that you have unnecessary movement that causes you to fidget. Creating space in these joints allows any unnecessary tensions to fade to nothingness. This in turn will stop the fidgeting and any unnecessary pull of focus. Remember that the only attention that you want to draw to yourself is the attention *you want* to draw to yourself. If it is distracting, it is distracting, and therefore unnecessary.

ACTOR: How will I know when it is distracting?

PAUL: The mistake you made there is that you just tried to get the golden answer. You will know. There is a famous story where an archery student is going on vacation and the instructor says, "Do not practice without me." When the student comes back from vacation, the instructor turns his back on the student and won't talk to him. The student begs for an audience and says, "Why won't you teach me?" The instructor says, "Because you practiced without me," and the student says, "How do you know that?" The instructor says, "Because you are doing it all wrong." What you tried to do was to jump to, "How can I get it right all the time?" The answer is you can't. The golden answer is in the doing, and making the discoveries yourself. Think of what you are doing as not taking something away, but adding something to yourself. Never do what a teacher asks you to at your expense. The other reason I ask you to put a bubble of air in your wrist, ankle, and knee is because there is something solid blocking a flow to the rest of your body. Once you put a bubble of air where it is needed, you are going to find you will immediately have a physiological response. Whenever you find your body with a twitch, you are trying to make the body longer, not stop yourself, which would be compressing or constricting the body. When you start getting nervous and tense, you will invariably start to constrict joints in your body. It's as if you pushed the arm into the elbow or the foot into the ankle, and now what we want to do is release and lengthen that at the joint.

Acting is by definition passion, and passion is by definition pressure. In the old days, a pressure cooker didn't have a release valve and occasionally they would put a little pressure valve on top of the cooker that would build up so much pressure that the top blew off. I have seen some actors who have built so much pressure up that instead of releasing it to go through the body, they just finally explode. It is not a pleasant thing to see and it doesn't do anything because it is a waste of the energy. There are some actors that actually think that this is a good thing, they actually try to do this, and they try to build this pressure

---

100. Michael Caine, Introduction.

until they explode. What they should be doing is building up pressure so that their body radiates. If you have a heater that is supposed to radiate heat throughout the house, if you constrict it until it's building up more pressure, it will eventually explode. Actors can have nervous breakdowns playing parts. If we find restrictions in the middle of a scene or any kind of work, we have to learn to address them as we see them.

GAVIN: One of the great things about acting is that you constantly have the opportunity to problem solve and make new discoveries.

Food for Thought

An actor must be able to channel anything. You have to play parts that cheat, steal, lie, are confused, are brilliant, etc. An actor must have strength and coordination to do anything. The more malleable your instrument, the more stretched, the greater potential you have to create.

Food for Thought

The biggest mistake actors make with a headshot is that their hair and makeup are perfect and the picture looks absolutely nothing like them. What we want it to look like is an attractive mug shot. Here's the deal: When you walk in the door, you have to look exactly like your picture. If you don't, they have every right to say you've misrepresented yourself. Anything that looks capable, our colleagues call talent. Anything that looks coy, our colleagues distrust, and when they distrust something they will say you are untalented. There are photographers that do wonderful glamour shots and there are photographers who take incredible wedding photos, but it does not mean they are the ideal choice for taking an actor's headshot.

Final Thoughts

There is an equation of thought, energy, and motion. We have to have thought before we can have energy, we have to have energy before we have motion. Motion is what the audience sees. They see the motion of our voice, which is the dialogue. They see the motion of our body, which is the physical action. If we could always count on the order of thought, energy, and motion, we would be home free. It always works unless something in the body stops or distracts the thought, the energy, or motion. We have to make sure that the pathway between the first thought and the motion that the audience sees is clear.

Through history we have had two ways of discovering things. One is the *eureka! thought*, the blinding thought that seems to come out of nowhere, telling us exactly what to do. The other is careful observation and hard work. A few people such as Ida Rolf, Moshe Feldenkrais, and Alexander, by long and careful observation as well as the fact that they were born or became geniuses, have come up with a technique that, for lack of any other term, is balancing and integrating the body. Because the body is balanced and integrated, we can go from thought, to energy, to motion with nothing slowing it down or stopping it. To an actor and an audience that is acting.

One of the things that seems to come up often is that there needs to be space in order for creativity to arrive. In this exercise the actor is given a simple way to create space by putting an air bubble wherever there might be some breakdown or tension. You can put an air bubble wherever you have too much fidgeting or movement. Never stop a movement in the body, for this will simply create more tension. By creating an air bubble you can create space and allow the tensions to dissipate. You can create space in your body and you create space in your life. If your days and your living conditions are always cluttered, then look into this. By creating space, you are forming a creative environment.

50. Elbow to the Knee

Food for Thought

I know a brilliant personal trainer who works with his clients in a way that, at first glance, appears very frustrating. Oftentimes people did not understand what he did. He fools the muscles all the time, so he never works on the same muscle exactly the same way because he will touch you and move you so he is constantly confusing the muscle. You are never using your instrument exactly the same way from one day to the next because each day brings new life experiences that slightly adjusts who you are. It is not possible for an actor to give exactly the same performance today that they gave yesterday, maybe something close or similar, but not quite the same.

Food for Thought

A famous quote, goes something like this, "Some books are to be tasted, others to be swallowed, and some few to be chewed and digested." Think about this in terms of the acting and performances you see. Very few of them are able to fit into the latter category, and yet this is what each actor we hope is striving towards.

The Ingredients

Always make things comfortable for yourself. I made the mistake of taking a yoga class where the instructor told us to feel the pain. I will ask you to be aware of your comfort. Some actors feel that if a director asks them to fall on concrete for thirty takes they should do it. You only have one body, so look after it. Don't forget that you are all that you have to offer. If you damage or abuse yourself, you will be of less value and have less longevity. It gives you confidence to actually learn to give yourself direction, to actually be on-set or stage and to actually direct yourself to do something – this is wonderful.

I want you to sit with crossed legs, it does not matter which leg crosses over which. I want you to switch legs at some point so that the other leg is on top. It is up to you to choose when this should happen. In a moment you are going to be giving yourself direction, and you know that the best director in the world for you is you. You are going to start by putting your hands gently over your ears so that your elbows are pointing out sideways. In a moment, you are going to start by leaning your right elbow towards your right knee. It does not matter if your elbow touches your knee or if you are less flexible and can only go part of the way down. You will simply be working another part of the spine however far you go, so it is not better to go further than you can.

Now you are going to take your elbows towards the same knee ten times. Then you are going to do ten with the left elbow towards the left knee. It is very important that, as you go through these actions, you say to yourself each and every time "elbow to the knee." With each of the ten repetitions you should have said this phrase to yourself ten times. I would now like you to work with opposites, so you are going to take the right elbow towards the left knee ten times and then the left elbow towards the right knee ten times. Now I want you to do ten in a circle motion by first leaning forward and circling towards the right knee, and then ten leaning forward with your pelvis and circling towards the left knee. Please remember to tell yourself "elbow to the knee" on every occasion.

There is no rush to finish this exercise, so work at your own pace and in your own time. Never feel that you have to play catch up with anyone. Sometimes an actor will rush through the dialogue of a scene. There could be thirty seconds of action before a word is ever uttered, and this could tell us a great deal about what is happening in the scene. As an actor, you should never feel rushed, and never rush to tell the story. We understand that the pacing of a thirty-minute television show, for instance, may appear to contradict this statement, but a story is still being told and every nuance lays bare.

Food for Thought

The reason you should study Feldenkrais, Alexander, Yoga, Tai Chi, etc., is that they are restructuring and making the body physically balanced. This gives the body its full potential for any kind of movement, and your best potential for response to a thought. These are outside of acting class, but they are adjacent to acting class. These fields do not specifically make you a better actor, but they do make you a better instrument to act with. Fields such as science and psychology have learned lessons from the discoveries of the actor, and acting in turn has learned lessons from fields outside the context of acting.

Food for Thought

Acting is, at times, an oxymoron and a contradiction in itself. We know on-stage or film in Moscow, New York, Cannes, Berlin, London, and Los Angeles there are great actors who are in terrible physical condition, yet they can perform Tony-winning shows on Broadway or Oscar-winning performances via London. Great performances have been given by actors who were alcoholics and drug addicts. It may seem that instead of giving you the answers, we are leading you deeper into the depths of confusion. On the contrary, your eyes are simply being opened to the realities of acting.

The Diagnosis

See if you notice any difference. Can you notice how your legs, hips, and health overall are changed? This is not just a stretch. What you have just done in this exercise works the sciatic nerve. This nerve is found when you push in to your glut muscle (buttocks) with your thumb right in the place where it concaves (dips) inwards. You will notice it is quite sensitive. It goes all the way down the leg to the heel. If you massage just below the ankle in the soft fleshy part, you will feel it releasing the sciatic nerve. It is a huge nerve, and it has a great influence. All actors who have trouble speaking should be aware that it comes from your posture. When you do this exercise you are going to speak better. To really grow as an actor you have to have the posture of an actor. Be aware of the results you are getting so you might notice, "I am speaking clearer this week than last week." Perhaps your audience doesn't know you have improved, but you will. The body is a totally integrated system in which one part affects another.

Food for Thought

The body tends toward health. As a complete organism and as a holistic instrument, our bodies tend towards health. It tends to heal itself. If it didn't, we'd all be dead. If you leave the body alone, and if you get out of its way, the body will heal itself emotionally, psychologically, and physically. There are many legal drugs readily available to us today. You want to be careful that these do not inhibit your acting or limit you in some way.

Food for Thought

A colleague of ours went to hear a talk given by a famous actor and he told us, "You know the most exciting thing was he looked, at any moment, like he might jump off the stage and kill somebody." In other words, they might look at you at any moment and say, "Pay attention!" If an actor is doing a performance for one person, then they should be doing it for all. Be an attentive audience member and you can mirror the actors on-stage or screen.

Final Thoughts

Here we are talking about big and little nerves. The sciatic nerve is the largest and thickest nerve in the human body. This exercise releases the sciatic nerve, which controls so much of the coordination of the body. Yet again, we are back to a simple exercise that ultimately results in a greater sensitivity and a greater ability of coordination. Actors often think that their emotions are blocked, when actually their nerves or their body is simply not warmed up enough and not functioning yet. This is another simple exercise in warming the body so that it can function and practice coordination. It is an actor's job to create a functional instrument in every sense. As Peter Egoscue says, "Muscles that were never intended to be involved in walking, throwing, bending motions, to name three basic functions, are called into action to replace dysfunctional muscles. This puts stress and wear on the musculoskeletal system that it was not designed to handle."[101] When you have an instrument that is functioning, your talent will be able to function.

51. Alexander Exercise

Food for Thought

Ultimately, you're the one who's going to have to pick your acting teachers. You're the one who's going to have to pick your voice coach, personal trainer, agent, hairdresser, Alexander instructor, and photographer. You are the one who is going to have to do all of this. If you get a good book that you can refer to as a manual, you can continue to go back to that book as a guide. We hope that this book will be a guide or a manual to you, because we do not want to give you a firm set of rules that you have to follow. If we did this, then you will always find experiences to contradict what is being said and this may lead to a good deal of confusion.

Food for Thought

The reason child actors are different is that there is nothing to fix at that age. It is not that we are saying something gets broken, not at all. As you get older something gets changed physically, and the use of your body becomes constricted. That's why we say "fix yourself then use yourself." Children learn to use their bodies more fully. As we get older, women are taught to keep their legs together, to walk, to stand, and use their bodies a certain way. Men are also taught physical and social rules. Not all young actors become senior actors. Some don't want to do it anymore or they physically lose the coordination of acting. They can't do it. Those who do continue often go back into training at their craft. Even the actor who is coordinated is not necessarily highly coordinated in all aspects of their life. This is why they continue to work on their instrument for all of their life.

The Ingredients

We are going to do an exercise that is formed from the most basic part of the Alexander Technique.[102] Alexander formed a technique based entirely on observations of his own body. Correct, Alexander technique cannot be done unless someone is touching you. If you are working with this exercise at home, you will not have an Alexander instructor with you, so you will be working with the spirit of the exercise, although technically speaking you are not doing the Alexander technique. The Alexander technique will usually take at least sixteen sessions before you start to have good use of your body. I recommend that each of you train in the Alexander technique. You will then go back periodically for the rest of your life so that the use of your body is monitored.

---

101. Pete Egoscue, *The Egoscue Method of Health Through Motion* (New York: Harper Collins, 1992), 25.
102. Paul Gleason is an accredited Alexander Technique Instructor.

The following exercise is a short and edited version of the work that Paul did with the actor that lasted one hour. You will not be doing the Alexander technique here, but work inspired by that technique.

PAUL: I want you to start by standing in front of the mirror and see if one arm hangs a little lower than the other. Don't make any adjustments to your body, just observe. Is there more space between your arm and your body on one side than the other? Do you think that one hip appears higher or lower than the other, or is it more forward than the other? Does one shoulder appear higher than the other? You can also do this by looking at your body standing sideways on the left and then the right. Just look at your body and see where there is symmetry and see where there is not. Now I want you to take a seat in this chair so that your back is not touching the back of the chair. *(ACTOR sits in a regular wooden chair. You may choose to have your chair facing a full-length mirror so that you are able to observe yourself.)* Now I want you to get up and then I want you to sit down. OK, now I want you to think these words, "Let the neck be free, to let the head go forward and up, to let the back lengthen and widen." I want you to repeat this to yourself throughout this exercise. You can also think of saying, "Forward and up." Think of your head going up a staircase, forward and up, forward and up, forward and up. Forward is where your nose is pointing, up is where your head is lifting. When I said that you pulled your chin in, most actors will look up towards the ceiling, and that is not accurate. Your head should stay on an even line.

ACTOR: I wasn't aware I did that.

PAUL: The problem in Alexander is perception. It is what you perceive your body to do as opposed to what it is actually doing. I want you to see what I see. When you think of the head, I want you to think about the top of the head as if you had a beanie on and the button would be over the back part of your head, just beyond your ears. *(PAUL puts his hands at the back of the ACTOR's scalp and below the chin.)* As I am touching you now, I want you to think of that button. Now relax your neck and move forward and up to standing. If you find that you are tilting your head back, you are actually getting shorter, not taller. *(ACTOR sits back down without resting against the back of the chair.)* Now I am coming around and putting my hand on your rib cage, can you feel that this is hard?

ACTOR: It feels tight.

PAUL: And what I would like is for it to be softer and freer. You may find that as you make these adjustments it feels a little uncomfortable to you, when in fact it is just unfamiliar to you. *(ACTOR continues to stand up and sit down with PAUL's guidance.)* I want you to stand up, sit down. Now if I was to put a string on the back of your head and allow it to taper down your back, you would notice as you got up it would go further down your back because as you get up you are tilting your head back. *(These observations are applicable to the actor working with PAUL. You may notice different things happening within your own body as you get up and sit down.)* You think you are bending your legs as you get up, but actually your legs cannot bend, they can fold. The legs are these wonderful things that lower and heighten the torso. As you stand up, your torso does not change. I want you to think of your heel going toward the ground, your head going up, and your torso unfolding. I want you to stand up now and I want you to inhibit that by saying to yourself, "I won't stand up." Now don't do what I said literally, I actually want you to stand up! I didn't say, "Don't stand up," I said you are going to say to yourself, "I won't stand up." If you say that, then all the muscles that are connected with saying that will come into play. If you say, "I'm going to stand up," then all the habits you have in standing up will come into play. *(Repeat this process sitting down.)* As you sit you should be saying, "I won't sit down," but instead you can say, "My head goes forward and up, my back is lengthening and widening." As you lower your torso your legs should fold. *(The exercise continues for a great deal longer.)*

GAVIN: Here we have given you a taste of what was done. Work this exercise by yourself and work it with a partner so you can observe their movements and habits they have formed.

Food for Thought

Acting is a physical thing. In acting, if we don't see it, it doesn't happen. Acting is not in the eye of the actor. Acting is in the eye of the beholder. It is in the eye of the actor in that the actor should see it before the audience does. The actor will respond in regards to the context of the situation, and in regards to the psychology, physiology, and sociology of the character.

Food for Thought

Take a fist and instantly squeeze it as hard as you can. Keep squeezing. Do you know what's happening? You're losing strength. The more you squeeze it, the more strength you lose. When you are in a show and an audience applauds you, in order for them to continue to applaud you, they have to continuously start over. For the most part, an audience does not begin applauding full of tension. They are generally relaxed and inspired. Between every single clap, they have to stop, relax, and go back to where they were.

PAUL: OK, now I want you to clap as fast as you can without stopping. Faster, faster, faster! Did you notice the tension building up?

ACTOR: I really felt it.

PAUL: When you really start getting fast you don't know how to relax in between those claps and you develop all this unnecessary tension. The secret is to continue to start over.

GAVIN: It is good to have tension in the body so you are able to recognize the difference when it is released.

The Diagnosis

The lessons from this exercise should not end here. You should be continuously working with them. It could not hurt you for the rest of your life to say, "Let the neck be free, to let the head go forward and up, to let the back lengthen and widen." If you forget, you can just say, "Head forward and up."

Alexander technique does not talk about psychology because it is not psychology or emotion. You may notice that when your head is free and your neck is free that the ribs slowly get softer and there may be somewhat of a release of anger. Although we are not allowed to say that it makes a happier person or that it gets rid of some of your anger, you may notice that it tends to do this. As the body becomes freer and more at ease, some of its tension begins to disappear. When a person is tense and in discomfort, one tends to find that their temper is shorter and they are somewhat more inclined to be unreasonable or angry. The reason that you would study with an Alexander teacher is so the work becomes muscle memory, and they will put you in that position often enough that your muscles will remember it.

In this exercise we talk about inhibiting your movement, and this is not used in a negative sense. It really means to redirect your energy, not to stop it. This exercise helps you to experience and understand yourself. In this exercise you are using your body, and you need to learn how to use your body as an actor. Many people hold tension and armor around themselves and their bodies, but you want to be able to strip all of this away so we can find you. Armoring is simply when you hold your body in such a position that it can't respond to a thought. Think about this: It means that an untrained actor is limiting the potential of their thoughts.

When we realize that imagination plays a large part of the actor's foundation, having as free a thought process as possible is crucial to the actor. This exercise gets us away from forming habits, and the old habits invariably become a form of armoring. They become a barrier between what we think and a muscle. The barrier is not on the outside, it is not on the inside, it is between two things. When you think something, the body should respond. Think about when a friend says, "I can tell when you are not happy because I can see it in your body." You cannot be one person for your friends, and one person for your acting career. As much as possible, you cannot have a barrier here. You have to be one person all of the time — yourself.

GAVIN: You can choose to exercise when you go to the gym, and you can also choose to exercise wherever you go. You can walk a little faster to your car or you can walk up the stairs instead of taking the elevator. In other words, you can integrate exercise into your life. Why be a part-time actor when you can be an actor wherever you go?

PAUL: When you watch a character and you say, "I really don't like that person" or "That character is so full of themselves," you may think that the actor is not particularly good. If you step back you will realize that they are probably the best actor because, through their acting, they have had the ability to affect you. The freer their instrument, the more potential they have to achieve this. How do you feel now?

ACTOR: I feel considerably different at this moment than when I came in here today.

PAUL: What else?

ACTOR: It is as if I have had a physiological response and gone over a plateau.

PAUL: You went beyond a plateau and you're still going.

ACTOR: The whole habit of the way I stand and move, as you said, has been inhibiting my thoughts and even after just a short experience I feel a shift.

PAUL: Thought comes before the energy, and when it starts working, there is nothing like it. The more you understand your body the better. When you give a fine performance it's not that you know how to do it, it's that when it kicks in, you know it's there. For these actors, acting becomes the best time, particularly when it's hard, dangerous, and challenging. This is the study of acting.

Food for Thought

When someone tells you in an acting class, "I want you to sit and think and relax. I want you to think of the same word over and over." That's not a bad exercise, but as soon as you stand up, everything stops working. You can't relax anymore. So that didn't teach you anything. What we should be teaching you is to know how to start over. The more you start over, the longer you will live. Each exercise has to be used in a manner that has practical implications for your acting that can be used again, and again, and again.

Food for Thought

The difference between when we think and what happens to a muscle is wide, and an actor shortens that muscle.

Final Thoughts

One of the greatest researchers on body techniques, balance, and function is Matthias Alexander. His work amounts to some of the most easily used, accessible, and understandable work on body technique used by actors that we have ever known and is taught at almost every major acting school in the world. What you need to know right now is that it has to do with the most efficient use of the body, which is the order in which the muscles are used and the combination in which the muscles are used.

Children used their bodies in a functional way, and it is only when we get older that we learned to use our bodies in a way that is not efficient. Alexander technique can, in a relatively short period of time, sort out the bad habits we have and put them in the most efficient order and best combination for our individual body. One reason the body stops doing things in the proper order and combination is because of emotional or societal things such as, "don't walk like that, don't sit like that." This causes our body to take on a form of armoring. Antonin Artaud said, when talking about human nature, "Society considers compliant people, those who never rebel, to be 'normal.'"[103] Just like Artaud, this exercise goes against the grain and what society perceives. In this exercise you are asked to say things like "I will not stand up," just before you stand up. As you say this, your body will respond by not doing the bad habit it has always done. Alexander teaches us to use the body in a more proper order and combination. There are good habits and bad habits. Once a habit is formed it can go unnoticed and act subconsciously on your behalf. The aim is to replace the bad habits with the good.

---

103. Gabriela Stoppelman, 142.

Chapter 11:
A State of Being

52. Being Present

Food for Thought

What really makes an actor is a combination of the experience and the confidence that what they are doing is what actors do. It is a difficult thing to know what acting is and having the confidence to know that what you are doing is what an actor does. An actor will progress the most by discovery. Acting is one complete evolution of discovery. The actor has made their instrument capable of physically doing what actors do.

Food for Thought

Who is the person who first recognizes an artist? Is it the teacher, the parent, the audience, or the friend? You! Without a doubt, actors discover themselves. They are not led into it by somebody. Every person who is a successful actor discovers it by themselves. Some actors quit high school. Some quit college and some have terrible fights with their parents. Actors always discover themselves. The actor has their own reasons for being an actor and perhaps they are selfish reasons. As Lajos Egri explains when telling a story of an individual, "Only those people die who are forgotten. I felt death is a small price to pay for immortality."[104]

The Ingredients

PAUL: Take a seat in the chair for me, please. I see that you are crossing your legs, which is the worst thing you can ever do in your life (unless it is part of your character) because it cuts down your circulation. I am going to ask you to uncross your legs. An actor prepares their body just as extensively as a martial artist does. When you are working for a casting director or a teacher train yourself to be an actor, and then be an actor twenty-four-seven. If you find yourself doing things that actors don't do, stop. This does not mean simply those who see themselves as actors. It refers to actors who walk and talk their acting. You must have a regimen that you do every single day, and you are doing it specifically because you are an actor. I want you now to take a little inventory of yourself. "What does my breathing feel like, what does my stomach feel like, what does my back feel like, how do my legs feel, etc.?" When you audition, if you take a quick inventory of yourself you will put yourself back into acting mode because you have trained yourself to do so. Again, I will ask you to just take stock of yourself at this precise moment. Now what I would like you to do is sit a little bit forward so that your back doesn't touch the back of the chair. Unless there is some profound reason for your back to be sunk against the back of the chair, your back should rarely be touching the back of the chair, especially in an audition situation. Just look at me for a moment. *(PAUL sits with his back off the back of the chair.)* I am auditioning and you are the casting director.

ACTOR: OK.

---

104. Lajos Egri, *The Art of Dramatic Writing* (New York: Simon & Schuster, 1960), x.

PAUL: What is the difference between this *(slouches)* and this *(back not touching the chair)*? Is there any difference at all? What I am doing is training you to look. Before you study acting you must be able to see things the way great actors see them. So what is the difference?

ACTOR: When you sit forward you seem more alert.

PAUL: OK, it is more alert, it's more prepared, and it's more ready to go in more directions. OK, now stand up, sit down. Now lean back against the chair, and get real nice and comfortable. Now stand up. It took more to stand up from that position than it did from the other position. You had to do more, and it wasn't efficient. Did you feel the difference?

ACTOR: It took a little more muscle.

PAUL: That little bit is called professional acting, and the smaller the bit, the better the actor. The most experienced, most brilliant actors use the least amount possible of physical activity. Their body is completely ready and prepared to turn any direction, to turn, jump, run, fall, sing, yell, and cry because the voice is also a muscle and their bodies are prepared to do anything.

GAVIN: When you hear the phrase *using the least amount of effort* you might assume this means the actor hardly moves. On the contrary, a brilliant actor doing a fight scene will appear to be using an enormous amount of energy, but the reality is they are using the economy of effort, because they have trained themselves to do so.

PAUL: If there is a time when you're asked to sit back in a chair for a scene or character, then you can still do so being uplifted so that you remain alert. I am talking to you about the difference between *relaxing* and *collapsing*.

Food for Thought

A famous actor and director was producing a movie and he knew who he wanted for the lead. To start with, he would call the actor on the phone, and then he would hang out with him and get to know him. There is a profound and wonderful lesson for the actor here. The reason that the director was hanging out with him was because he was saying, "I am going to be working with him for eight months, fifteen hours a day." And he was saying, "Is he going to last that long? Do I want to be around him for that long? If there is the tiniest little thing there, I won't use him. I'll look at someone else until I get what I want." Think about how this applies to you. You are not just being looked at as an actor, they are looking at you as a person. A director is thinking, "Do I want this person on my set? Do I want to be hanging around with them backstage?" There has to be a lot of compatibility behind the scenes as well as during the performance.

Food for Thought

At one time I taught a class in Ohio for aspiring actors and people from New York, London, and Los Angeles went to share their knowledge of acting. A young man started to perform and I thought "He's got a lot of wonderful passion. He's just never been able to use it." We rolled up newspapers and during the piece he started beating these newspapers. As opposed to going berserk, he just got better and better. He got more intelligent, better looking, stronger, more interesting to look at, and everybody watching him was just spellbound. Later, my great friend, who was a Broadway legend, said, "That's one of the most exciting things in theatre I have ever seen in my entire life!" The next day the entire town wanted to watch class! I have sat in a theatre in the sticks and seen some of the most wonderful acting.

The Diagnosis

This exercise is looking at how you use your body and your awareness of your body. All of your life you will be working with actors who mistake collapse for relax, but you will never be working with an experienced actor or a successful actor who confuses the difference between the two. Being collapsed is harder on your body and health. How you use your body determines how long you get to use it. Now we are talking not only about you having an acting career, but the longevity of your acting career.

PAUL: Somebody as young as you and with as much vitality as you is going to use their instrument more proficiently than you. That's why they are going to get the job. A casting director or director is simply going to say they are more talented than you. They might say, "She is not right for the part but she is talented. You know what, let's call her back anyway, because she is the only one today who had any talent at all!" What that means is that you are in control of at least one thing — talent. Look at famous old actors and famous young actors. They are never slumped or collapsed.

GAVIN: Just observing you from here you do look more professional, more ready.

PAUL: This exercise is so primary and so basic that an actor will automatically say, "Yes, I know exactly what you mean." If I asked them which one feels more comfortable, they will probably say collapsed because their body does not have the sensitivity of an actor yet.

ACTOR: At first I felt more constricted, but now I see that it is actually freeing. I feel so much more open and available now.

PAUL: Don't throw that one away ... you are what?

ACTOR: Available.

PAUL: Congratulations! I am pleased you came to that conclusion. We have taken many top professionals who already know how to get jobs and what we taught them was how to be more available. The more available you are the more potential you have for bigger roles.

Food for Thought

The reason child actors are different is that there is nothing to fix at that age. It is not that we are saying something gets broken, not at all. It's as you get older something gets changed physically, and the use of your body becomes constricted. That's what we mean when we say *fix yourself then use yourself.* Children learn to use their bodies more fully. As we get older, women are taught to keep their legs together, to walk, to stand, and use their bodies a certain way. Men are also taught physical and social rules. Not all young actors become senior actors. Some don't want to do it anymore or they physically lose the coordination of acting. They can't do it. Those that do continue often go back into training at their craft. Even the actor who is coordinated is not necessarily highly coordinated in all aspects of their life. This is why they continue to work on their instrument for all of their life.

Food for Thought

What we would like is for you to say, "How do I make myself good?" Your greatest teacher is yourself, not your ego. You have to look at acting through the right lens. You cannot see something that is not part of your perception. Let us say you were given a puzzle in which you were told there were five animals hidden. Chances are you look for them because somebody told you they were there. You say, "I can't see them," and the teacher says, "Well, trust me, they are there." Talent equals good, and good equals talent. You need to find a way to get to good instead of getting caught up in other insignificant distractions. Some actors give up before they get to good. They put in so much time, effort, energy, and money, yet they give up.

Final Thoughts

By definition, everything you are doing while you are reading this is in the present mode. Actors have a very different definition of the word *present.* To an actor, the word present means, "a heightened awareness of one's self." You have to remember that one of the difficulties in studying acting is the semantics. The way that actors use words is most often different than the way non-actors use words. Any acting teacher who is trying to get you to work in the present mode is merely saying that they want you to have a heightened awareness of what you're doing. Awareness can't happen if anything stops the flow of energy, circulation, and thoughts in your mind such as blockages because of emotions, what you've eaten that day, and muscular weaknesses. Build up an awareness of yourself and you will build up the potential and flexibility of self. You are building up the flexibility of your emotions, physicality of your intellect, and the flexibility of your imagination. We know that even actors have limited and, at times, inflexible imaginations. Think about the time that you have said, "I can't even imagine that." As you develop as an actor, you can begin to work in a creative state and live in a creative state.

53. Who You Are and Who You Are Not

Food for Thought

It's not necessarily what you don't understand, it's why you don't understand. If you have the right address and you walk down the wrong street you won't find the right address. That might frustrate you, but it's that simple. How do you get better? The teacher teaches you to walk better. Unfortunately, they are still sending you down the wrong street. If you keep doing this you are never going to get good. You have to walk down the right street with the right address. What is the price you are willing to pay for immortality?

Food for Thought

Great acting always feeds and nurtures us in some mysterious way. When we have been in the presence of great acting we can become overwhelmed. All forms of acting have the potential of teaching us something about ourselves. All performers are telling some kind of story that has the potential of changing a person's life, and if that's what you want to pursue, then there are some things that go along with it. You have an obligation to find people to train you in a serious, accurate manner. When you have found these people, you have to do something that many people may disagree with. You have to listen to them with blind faith. When you find great teachers, when there is no doubt in anyone's mind that they are great, then the only way to learn from them is in blind faith and not to question anything they are doing or asking you to do. The challenge is to find a great teacher who you can put your blind faith with. There may be a number of teachers from whom you should run away. The idea behind this book is not to specifically teach you acting, but to enhance your level of functioning so that you can make all the necessary decisions that you will need to make.

The Ingredients

Make a list of famous actors you admire most, you would most like to be thought similar to, or be like. Also make a list of movie roles they had that you think you would be perfect for. As you make your list do not worry about age, or looks, or color of skin because these are the actors whose *work* you admire the most. Now we want you to make another list, and this time you are going to put down all the actors who you would least like to be thought of, whose work you admire the least. Make a list of their movies or plays you definitely would not like to play in. Look at your first list and ask yourself if you would like to be thought of as one of these actors. Your answer should be yes. Look at your second list and ask yourself if you would like to be thought of as one of these actors, and your answer will most likely be no.

For the actors you would like to emulate, watch their work, see interviews with them, read about them, and get scripts of movies they have been in. If you can, get scripts of the people you didn't want to be thought of. See as much as you can about them, read about them, and watch their movies. Now your job is to do roles similar to those played by the actor you detest. This may even mean working a monologue or scene from one of their movies. You may not want to do this, which is precisely why you must. While we want you to stay clear of only playing roles that you would never be cast in, there is some advantage to working on a limited number of parts that you most likely will not be cast in order to strengthen and broaden your own abilities and range.

Food for Thought

If you do anything and you do it exclusively or for an extended period of time, people will recognize it. The reason that actors are recognizable is because all good actors have silent dialogue going all the time. If you ask an actor and he isn't aware he is doing it, that's like saying to an actor, "Do you know you're a good actor?" Well, they can't say no and yes. They know they're a good actor, but it is not something they think about, because they do it. You can't always get the answer you need from a skilled or highly experienced actor. They don't necessarily think about the questions you are asking. They just do it. Be careful because sometimes out of fun or obligation or whatever reason they will give you an answer that has absolutely nothing to do with what they really do. You will go away and say "I asked this great actor how they prepared a scene and they told me and it was not clear." We would say it is because they actually don't think about that anymore. They gave you an answer to be kind or entertaining or to get away from you. Their state of being is that of an actor.

Food for Thought

Intellect is the primitive part of us and response and inspiration are the magnificent parts. Judging and analyzing are the primitive parts of us, and we want to get beyond judging and analyzing. This is why great actors and actresses look like they are jumping without a net, because they don't do that. Starting is not preparing. Starting is beginning without preparation. If you appear less prepared, you look less studied and less tense. When an actor is truly prepared his performance appears less prepared.

The Diagnosis

You must understand that both these lists of actors are already successful. It is a weakness in the actor to rebuff these actors, because the actor must be willing to accept any role and any part. You are not famous for anything, so you have to go into the audition and be able to be anything they want you to be. You have just discovered one of the biggest weaknesses in your acting. As an actor, you must be at least able to attempt any part. You must be able to find the beauty in the roles and actors that you detest. If you will limit yourself in any way as an actor you will never reach your true potential. Not only will you not reach the level of those you admire most, you will also be a weak carbon copy of that person. In your acting training and career think about how much you have limited yourself. Now you can answer your own question and you have just proven how much you have limited yourself. The reason you do this exercise is that, for a period of your career, you are going to be hired because of what someone else thinks you can do, not what you think you can do.

If you got every part based on your opinion of yourself, you would get every part you went up for! Stop trying to be a carbon copy of someone else because we've already got them, and if we want to hire them we will. They want your unique personality, and as an actor you must have unlimited uniqueness. Acting is not about aptitude. Acting is about attitude. Aptitude is something someone thinks you might be good at, and acting is a decision or commitment you made by yourself. It is a way of being. If someone tells you, "You look like an actor," don't be offended by this, as it is a compliment. If they say you look like an actor, you say, "I want to look like an actor." All great performers have a great deal of intensity twenty-four hours a day. Even when you just see their back, there is an intensity that radiates from them.

While this is part of your job as an actor, looking like an actor does not necessarily make you an actor. As has been mentioned on many occasions, only continual hard work and dedication will accomplish this. An instructor I have met says there are those who like to talk about acting, but they procrastinate in regards to commitment. For example, only three percent of actors who say they will "do it later" actually return to their acting class. Commitment to the craft may become the biggest challenge of your life, as Gabriela Stoppelman explains in regards to Antonin Artaud, "At the end of this memorable event, the audience remained silent. They had been in the presence of a man who had been brutally beaten, but was not yet burnt out. From his pain and suffering, Artaud had extracted a vital force that paralyzed his audience."[105]

Food for Thought

We sometimes look at an actor and say, "They are not very smart, how could they be so stupid as to do that?" And yet, why is it that we can see performances by them that are very good? Some are alcoholics. Some are wayward husbands. Some don't know how to keep their bankbook. Yet they can act. The famous French actor Constant Coquelin has an excellent answer to this when he says, "The only intelligence indispensable to the actor is that which belongs to his art."[106] What he is saying is as long as you can do the work, then it's no one's business. He doesn't say you have to be smart; however, he says you have to be intelligent about your art. An actor does not have to be a politician, a scientist, or a great parent. Maybe we would like people to be these things, but why is it that there are actors who seem to fail in almost everything but acting? Read Coquelin's quote again and you will have your answer. Think about the pie exercise in A Way of Being. The actors put all of their energy into their acting and everything else has to take second place.

Food for Thought

We have often struggled with the question, "Does an actor have to be intelligent?" We wondered if more intelligent students of acting were more likely to succeed, and we realized there is no pattern whatsoever. Success is not a question of what is right or wrong, or what is moral or immoral. Success only has to do with how much you know about success, or how much you know about art. The actor that is likely to be more successful is the one who spends the vast majority of their time on their art and on their career. Some people say knowledge is power, but there are some very knowledgeable people with very little power. Other people say knowledge followed through with action equals power. We would say the second is a better fit for the actor.

Final Thoughts

This is an exercise that balances the strength of your body. If you work only one muscle, that muscle will strengthen only to a point and it will have a very limited potential. If you exercise a counter muscle, it will strengthen both muscles. The problem is, given the choice between two options, we always choose just one of them. An actor must not be limited by those choices. If you ask an actor what they like, they have to say, "Everything." The purpose in this exercise of choosing an actor you like and an actor you dislike is that one strengthens the other. You have to be able to show different sides, and if you are playing a villain, you still have to understand the saint of that character. You have to be aware of the yin and yang of your own personality and that of your character's.

---

105. Gabriela Stoppelman, 140.
106. Constant Coquelin, 906.

54. Inhibit

Food for Thought

There is never a time, professionally, when the director will say, "Why don't the two of you get together and work this out and then I'll look at it." It's not even in the time schedule. You learn it, they learn it, you meet, there are one or two rehearsals, and then you start filming. You don't need to know each other. In fact, this might be the first moment you actually meet.

ACTOR: It makes me feel that scene study class isn't really preparing you as a professional actor.

PAUL: Absolutely! Scene study classes are not acting classes, they are directorial classes.

GAVIN: We want you to be prepared, capable, and adaptable for a professional acting career.

Food for Thought

Acting has to be in your muscle memory. What we call *authentic* is what is in your muscle memory. When it's not in your muscle memory it can't be authentic. It is when it becomes automatic for you.

The Ingredients

Here is an exercise that will be very beneficial to you. What we would like you to do is, from time to time over the next week, when you are thinking about acting or doing something in acting, stop first. Perhaps you are reading a script, memorizing something, thinking about a vocal exercise, etc. Just before you begin we want you to stop and say to yourself, "I'm not going to do that." Let's say you are at an audition and the casting director says, "Why do you want to be an actor?" We want you to say to yourself, "I'm not going to answer that question." And then answer the question. You can also say to yourself, "I want to allow the impulse, and then as soon as I feel the impulse I will answer the question." What we want you to say to yourself is, "I'm going to stop doing anything, and I'm going to stop inhibiting. Whatever it is I do, or seem to be doing, I'm not going to do that." We want you to just give it up. The best way to give it up is to every now and then take a deep breath and sigh. Let's say you are feeling a little nervous or out of sorts in the middle of a conversation with a casting director. Pretend to drop something for a moment and say, "Excuse me," and in that moment regain your composure. Some actors fidget and embellish a great deal of unnecessary movement. This can be during a conversation with a director, casting director, or perhaps during a performance. The actor has to learn to let these unnecessary elements go. You are stopping yourself because you don't want that habit and you don't want to have insufficient knowledge. Do this exercise until it drives you mad, and then you should stop it. By this time it will be in your being and it will be part of you.

Food for Thought

I have seen actors in workshops where the teacher comes over and gives all the actors a hug. I got one and it was a great hug. I think it made the teacher's class very popular, but it has nothing to do with acting. I know many successful actors who never got that hug. At any given moment you want to be working with the maximum of your potential.

Food for Thought

I will never forget when I was in a class and an actor got up to work his scene. The teacher complimented him by saying, "His intensity was so great that his arm actually shook." I sat there and I didn't say anything, but I wanted to say, "Would you hold your other hand up and show it to the audience." His hands shook all the time. It made me angry. It was demoralizing because it wasn't acting, and yet that is what she saw. Acting is a subjective art.

The Diagnosis

We use the word *inhibit* incorrectly. We use it to mean to stop ourselves from doing something wonderful instead of doing something habitual. As you continue to work with this exercise it will make you appear much more powerful and even slightly intimidating to others. You are learning to let go of the impulse. It's never stopping and it's letting go. You have to let go of the habit and make room for the impulse. An instructor might ask you to do an exercise for an hour every day for the rest of your life, but it is of no benefit for you to agree to this. You should never say you are going to do an exercise for more than twenty, thirty, or forty seconds, because if you force yourself to do it, it will become a chore. If you are fighting yourself on it you won't be doing anything worth doing.

There is a great lesson in this exercise that you can do anytime and anywhere in that you must learn not to show any of your work. The reason we think great actors are not doing anything is simply because they do not show us their work. Great actors or great teachers learn by inhibiting. Take an extra moment to listen to what they say.

In this exercise you are asked every now and then to sigh. This huffing and puffing that we do sometimes when we are frustrated helps to let go of the frustration. We are not trying to show people that we are angry with them. We are trying *not* to show people that we are angry with them. Be careful when doing this exercise that you do not slip back into talking like a non-actor. You must always talk like an actor. Interestingly, it is easy to slip up because with this exercise you are doing so many new things.

This is another one of those exercises that you can do as often as you like, and when you get good at this exercise people will begin to remark. They won't say you look more like an actor, but they will say you look different. We want you to learn to use yourself rather than allow unnecessary habits to engulf you. You look much more grounded and more composed.

PAUL: Yes, you look like an entirely different person. What is great is the more you work this way, your instrument will eventually forget unnecessary habits because it won't remember them. It doesn't function that way any more. Tell me a little bit about what you have discovered after the exercise.

ACTOR: A loss of self.

PAUL: Let's call it a habit, because it's a discovery of self.

ACTOR: Physical relaxation of the body.

PAUL: Yes, some things are simple. We got there a long way around, but we got there. You are relaxed and not collapsed. Now you look like an actor. When you are like this I can talk more accurately with you. You are beginning to make discoveries of character.

GAVIN: With this actor we saw a gradual change in her from when she had arrived. It was a strikingly different actor who left from the one who had walked in. This is not because she had added things. It is because she was starting to take away the unnecessary things.

Food for Thought

You can't piggyback a famous movie star. It's like a roadie of a rock star who thinks because they hang out there they will be famous. Of course one in a million actors find their fame in this manner, but we don't like those odds. There is no profession we know of where people expect immediate gratification without putting in the time and effort. Yet there are a number of people who call themselves actors who expect all the fame and glory but refuse to do anything that might point them in this direction.

Food for Thought

Each day you have to ask yourself, "Am I having fun?" If you are not having fun, then why are you doing it? This does not mean every second of your life; however, this is what you should strive towards. Enjoy your life whether it is as an actor or anything else. Being an actor and all that entails is your choice.

Final Thoughts

The word *inhibits* means to stop you from doing something. All actors are bringing with them unnecessary habits. An actor wants to get back to the dexterity and freedom that a child has. Children use their muscles in a balanced way, and they respond spontaneously to the moment they are in. Inhibit gives you a chance to change and begin again. It allows us to stop a habit and return to our basic instinct, our basic imagination, our basic creativity, and our basic agility. As Picasso once said, "It takes us all of our lives to learn to be a child again." To inhibit is to say, "I won't do that, and I'll let my instincts tell me what to do instead." You inhibit one thing to replace it with something better. By stopping first, you are able to take away the predictability in your actions and thoughts.

55. Opposites

Food for Thought

The greatest part of any book on acting is whether or not it inspires you. The weakness of every book on acting ever written is that it's insufficient and inaccurate because there is no book on acting that can fabricate your circumstances. We suggest that you keep an acting journal because some of your greatest lessons will come from you.

Food for Thought

PAUL: You are going to ask me two questions. The first is, what do you do for a living? The second is, what do you do for a hobby?

ACTOR: What do you do for a living?

PAUL: I dig holes.

ACTOR: What do you do for a hobby?

ACTOR: I push people in the holes. I'm tricking you, and I don't mind telling you that because you have to understand function in order to be an actor.

GAVIN: The actor is always looking at what came before, and what preceded where your character is now.

The Ingredients

What we would like you to do for this exercise is to think of a character you have played or are presently working on. If this character is mainly serious, then we would ask you to do the opposite. We would ask you to do clowning exercises or cartwheels or anything that is fun and boisterous. If you are playing a comedic character, then we would ask you to create some very serious exercise and perhaps stay more still and stoic. In other words, we would like you to come up with exercises that are the opposite of the character you are working on. We want you to take your character and ask yourself what he or she wants. Perhaps they want to steal from someone, or love someone, or run from someone. We want you to play that scene, or monologue, or few words with the opposite intent. Instead of loving them, try to drive them away while you're playing the scene. Usually it is fairly easy to think of the opposite, but if you start to think of it, it will help you right from the get-go because first you're going to have to figure out what they want. Perhaps your character is in love with another character, but maybe they can find a different motivation such as simply wanting to get away from home and this is a way of escaping. This will strengthen the character. If the character wants to leave the room because they feel threatened, then you simply change the *want* and say something like, "I feel very comfortable being here." You could even do this with reading a script or play by yourself. Write down in the script all of your characters' wants and as you read it, put the opposites down and read the script again with all the opposites.

We would also like you to come up with physical things for your character as we discussed earlier. There are things you could do arbitrarily. For example, most characters probably would not do a cartwheel, so you can do a cartwheel. Most characters would not roll on the ground, so you can roll on the ground. Most characters would probably not take their pants or trousers off and put them on backwards, take their shoes off and put them on the opposite feet – that is exactly what we want you to do during the scene. Now it is not just the opposite, it is arbitrary in that it does not even make sense. It is arbitrarily something they would not do. Not only are you doing things the character wouldn't do, but also you are doing some things that perhaps you wouldn't do. For instance, if you have never done a cartwheel, then try one as best you can. The number of things you can do are infinite. You can do this as part of a warm-up for any scene if you choose to. Putting your character in new situations, different situations, and physical situations may tell you things about the character you had no idea were there. There is a lot of physical integration in this exercise that will lead to a real visceral response.

Food for Thought

There is a difference between those that people want to look at and at those that people want to listen to. When I was a little kid and went to the circus it was legal to have freak shows. Thankfully, it is illegal now. The only difference now is circuses no longer have freak shows and movies have them all the time. Movies won't hesitate to show you a man's head blown off. We have become so desensitized that shock value has become harder to attain. In tandem with special effects, it is the actor who is in demand to fill this vacuum.

Food for Thought

A friend of mine says a wonderful thing, "What I think about you is none of your business. And what you think about me is none of my business. And then we can get on to acting." Let's take all of these things away that cloud or confuse us.

The Diagnosis

When a muscle becomes weak, in order to strengthen that muscle you must not only strengthen that muscle you must strengthen the opposing muscle. If you are working out in the gym and working on just your upper body you will look disproportionate unless you also work on your legs. You must work the opposing muscles in order to have your muscles be at their optimum. Sometimes if you are ill it is because your body is out of balance, and by working opposing areas you can bring the body back.

This exercise called Opposites actually has a very profound use. This exercise is to stretch and strengthen your body in a balanced way. In this exercise you have to find what the character wants – this is of vital importance to the character. We have seen actors get deep into rehearsal and they still haven't found what the character wants. You always have to have a want. You can change the want at any given moment and that is called *imagination*.

One of the ideas behind this exercise is to strengthen you for a balanced performance. When you strengthen the opposite muscle you are working your body synergistically. When you work both muscles at the same time it will give you more than you are capable of. We have seen actors look at performances that they have done on film or stage and say, quite honestly and quite humbly, "I have no idea how I did that. I have no idea who that person is. I don't even know that person." This is because the sum total of their performance is greater than they can think of.

In this exercise you are asked to do things arbitrarily that your character would not do, such as a cartwheel. You are physically strengthening because, if you are good actor, whether you realize it consciously or not you will always want something. You will always be motivated in some way. Sometimes you don't even know it because at that moment it comes so naturally and so easily to you. In this exercise the actor goes from motivation to motivation to motivation, from wanting something, to wanting something, to wanting something. You may discover things about your character you do not like. You may have to step out of your comfort zone and put yourself in an unfamiliar place. It is not so much that you are taking risks, in actual fact you are creating them.

Food for Thought
As teachers we say, "If exercises work for you, pick them. If they don't, move on to ones that do." The only reason we say that is because we are not there to partner you in the exercise. The benefit of the exercise never comes until the exercise has been done on numerous occasions. What we mean is if you did an exercise every day for a year, you might realize the real importance of that exercise, and it would actually change you. If you did it for two years it would change you for the rest of your life. Be prepared to work on your instrument for the rest of your life.

Food for Thought
Exercises in any book explain things to you, reveal things to you, and can be inspiring to you. As a beginner they can build a foundation, when you are intermediate they are something you can always refer to, and when you are advanced you specifically know where to go to remind yourself. A good acting book will grow with you.

Final Thoughts
In order to have a strong body, the body has to develop muscles and opposing muscles as much as possible. If we don't use a muscle, we know that eventually that muscle will atrophy. It will get to the point where it is not usable. This is also true of our imagination and emotions. If you always start walking on the right foot, then the right foot is always prepared to start, and the left foot gets less and less prepared to start. In order to build a character, doing the opposite of what the character would do is not really doing the opposite. It is doing what the character would potentially also do in the given circumstances. Remember, characters we play are not only holding the mirror up to life, they are far more complex. If you have the ego of an actor and you have at one time or other done a really fine job of doing a part, can you really tell me that anything in your life or anybody else's life had the richness of that? Actors have to compress, and condense, and concentrate so much that the audience takes the performance home with them. Doing the opposite means not forgetting to use the whole body. Many of the things in this book may be unclear, and when you reach that place, go over that thought again, and again, and again. When you see a character with great pain and fear, it is only the case if that character is also capable of great joy. By practicing opposites you will be fuller, and you will have a wider spectrum. From a confused state you will be in a position to develop new ideas, new concepts, new thoughts, and to create your own.

56. Big Muscle, Little Muscle
Food for Thought
The actor has to eventually become his or her own teacher. They have to look everywhere for lessons in how to act, but not necessarily lessons in life. I have known many actors who were not necessarily wise in the way they lived their lives. Some were not very bright, some

were not very educated, but all of the great actors could become someone they are not. They were comfortable being someone they are not. You have to be able to look in front of a mirror and see somebody who you have never seen before. Sometimes actors appear to be strange or eccentric to others. This is because they allow nothing to get in the way of their creativity.

Food for Thought

There are two ways to study acting, but one is never done. One is to become an apprentice in a company so that every night, every day, you are seeing performances. And every day you are looking and saying, "What am I going to do when I do that part?" or, "I will be so much better in that part than they are." The other way is that you go to acting class and what actually happens is you don't go to acting class, you go to performance class or scene study class. We think this is enormously injurious and detrimental to the actor. Imagine being a student doctor in training and your first class is to perform an operation on a patient, wouldn't you want to have been to your anatomy, physiology, and pathology classes first? The industry is not at fault, it is the fault of ambitious people who have no respect for acting.

The Ingredients

What we would like you to do is take a scene, monologue, or any dialogue and we want you to *indicate,* because indicating is a kind of stretching. We want you to do anything that is indicating what you are saying, and we want you to do it without any inhibitions. When we say indicate we mean *do it huge.* If your character talks about burping, then burp, and hold nothing back. If your character is waving at someone, then wave at them for all you are worth. It is a question of indicating and also taking it to great physical extremes. We want you to look at how you can stretch, indicate, and overdo each and every word. You can stay on one word for as long as you like, indicating it in a variety of ways. Have fun with it without being inhibited and without allowing nerves to take over. In this exercise you can run, jump, hop, and do whatever you want. By not holding back you are working with your big muscles.

Food for Thought

Every minute of acting should feel good. It should feel good to die, it should feel good to get angry and throw the plate, and it should feel good to laugh. There should be no self-consciousness. Other things can happen too. Curtains go up at the wrong time, lights come on at the wrong time, mikes stop working, people cough, people forget their lines, and none of those things affects your ability. None of those things affect you if you are capable and prepared.

Food for Thought

Acting is ultimately experience. It is not taking a class or reading a book. It is experience on-stage, in front of a camera, in front of an audience — that's what acting is. As Richard Boleslavsky says, "Unfortunately it is acquired by long, hard work, at great expense of time and experience."[107] The more you understand about your craft the better. Michael Checkhov describes the experience of acting by saying, "It is evening, after a long day, much work and many impressions, experiences, actions and words you let your tired nerves rest."[108]

The Diagnosis

This exercise is called Big Muscle, Little Muscle because little children cannot thread a needle. They are learning to walk. It takes big muscles to be able to stand up and walk. Singing is little muscles, so why do you go to the gym to workout for singing? The reason is because you have to use big muscles to get to the little muscles and actors stop using them.

---

107. Richard Boleslavsky, *Acting* (New York: Theatre Art Books, 1949), 28.
108. Michael Chekhov, *To the Actor* (London: Routledge, 1953), 21.

An actor goes into a class and they are immediately trying to use small muscles. We are constantly trying to sugarcoat or put some kind of sugared coating on an actor who is not ready yet. We look at some actors and say, "They are not ready yet, so I am going to put some clothes on them so they look like an actor." That does not help the actor. It is not that an actor is not talented, it is that they need to know about acting, know what to do, and what not to do. In performance and in class we are often told not to indicate. A very respected teacher used to say an actor should never point (indicate). I saw a world famous actor pointing, and when I told her she said that was different. I now know what she meant was she was using it with intention as opposed to a mere gesture.

In this exercise you get up and use big muscles. When you have an emotional reaction in a performance you move muscle. It takes muscle to cry, laugh, sing, and frown. When you use muscle, that is what the study of acting is. The study of acting is not an intellectual pursuit. Acting is a very specific craft of its own.

Exercises such as these can have an enormously profound effect on your instrument, and that's what I believe the teaching of acting is. In terms of being specific, Larry Moss says, "Picking a specific intention is the same thing as a painter picking a specific shade or hue of a color to create a certain drama on the canvas."[109] Muscle, movement, and gestures could be considered external by their very nature and yet they can affect us internally. To say acting is internal or external can be dangerous because one continuously influences the other.

Food for Thought

In terms of your acting, you cannot share a lot with your non-actor friends because when they make fun of it or even when they laugh good-naturedly of it, they are diminishing its value. Everything you study in acting should have great value to you. If anybody inadvertently or lovingly diminishes the value of anything you are doing in terms of your acting, then you must find a way to separate yourself from them until you are not influenced by them. In order to put yourself in a creative state you need to live in a creative state.

Food for Thought

When actors study with great living teachers they say, "I am studying with Stanislavski, Uta Hagen, Lee Strasberg, Charles Jehlinger, Robert Edmond Jones, Sanford Meisner, etc." When they are dead you say, "I am studying the Stanislavski technique." In other words, we only call it a technique when they are dead. We cannot purely study a method. We can only study the manner in which they experimented because they were constantly changing their work. If you read a book by one of these teachers or took a course by someone other than them, there is no guarantee that you will understand what they were getting at. They would have to be there to tell you, "No, that's not exactly what I meant." A great teacher can diagnose your needs individually, specifically, and precisely at that moment. As Don Richardson says, "The modern American actor is taught mostly by amateur gurus who practice their own voodoo and call it Method."[110]

Final Thoughts

A big muscle needs to be strong because it is used constantly. It needs to be strong for what it does. What we know is that big muscles are called on to do large actions, to lift more, and to take more intensity. Small muscles are used for refinement. Do scenes with huge amounts of indicating, like crying ridiculously large or laughing ridiculously large. As you do that, smaller muscles will take over and you will refine it. Every exercise in this book should be something that makes your instrument move towards good. No exercise in this book should be directorial; therefore, when you do exercises you may not immediately see how it has

109. Larry Moss, *The Intent to Live* (New York: Bantam Books, 2006), 33.
110. Don Richardson, *Acting Without Agony* (Massachusetts: Allyn and Bacon, 1988), 4.

affected your acting. It's always fun when someone says, "That was so good, what have you done?" Tell them, "Thank you," and move on. An exercise that is directorial means that you have a good director, it does not necessarily make you a good actor.

Chapter 12:
Eureka!

57. Inside Out

Food for Thought

Creativity is a very singular thing. Painters paint alone. Composers compose alone. Dancers practice in class, but great dancers practice alone, and great actors prepare alone. Novice performers like the camaraderie of the group and the social aspects. You learn your lines by yourself. You do your research by yourself. It seems like it would be so much more fun to go to a class and be seen and watch others. Maybe it is fun, maybe it is entertaining, but it doesn't mean you are learning anything. If an actor tells you they have found the right way, they are a fool because there isn't a right *way,* there is a right *direction.* A right way means that you have reached some place and an actor never wants to reach some place, they just want to keep reaching. The discoveries and the eureka! moments are very personal to you, and can only be made by you. Our success as an actor will only happen in our lifetime. Actors by definition can only enjoy their success during their lifetime because that is where it happens. If it is on-stage it is only where it happens, and then after that it is only hearsay.

Food for Thought

A young, inexperienced actor has to live in a non-opinion state for a long time. And then one day they say, "Eureka! I now can have an opinion. I can have an opinion because I have sufficient knowledge." It may take years to get to this point, and then you are able to say to your teachers and peers, "I can disagree with you now, and I can say there is a different way. I can have an opinion now." You may not agree with this, and that is your prerogative. Think about how your family and friends who have never trained in acting, never performed in front of a live audience, love to give you advice on your performances and what you should do.

The Ingredients

We believe this exercise to be influenced by Carl Jung and dream analysis, although we are not going to ask you to analyze your dreams. It is also influenced by Fritz Pearls and Gestalt therapy, although we're not going to ask you to go into therapy. What you do is look at a scene you are working on. We want you to tell us about your character, but instead of telling us, we want you to choose an inanimate item in the room to tell us about the character. For instance, if you were playing a doctor, perhaps the stethoscope could tell us about the doctor.

ACTOR: Well, I've been working on this scene about this guy who works in Vegas, who is a musician, and he's going home and —

PAUL: *(Cuts ACTOR off.)* OK, that's all the information we need, because you want to find insight. You said he is a musician, so the obvious thing to talk to him is his instrument. So, what instrument does he play?

ACTOR: Drums.

PAUL: OK, now I want you to be the drums and tell me about him.

ACTOR: He hits me constantly, especially in one area, where I'm pretty much bruised, and that's the middle. He's constantly hitting me, and I think he hits me harder than the rest of the drums. I don't know if he has something in for me. I don't know what it is.

PAUL: When I'm teaching acting, I just say I love it, because when I work with the actor, you do something that never in my wildest imagination as a director could I ever get. You gave me, "He hits me constantly, and I'm bruised." Now instantly you got profound insight into the character. So let me ask you about the drummer, is that character bruised?

ACTOR: Oh yes, definitely.

PAUL: Does the bruising come from something that is constant and unrelenting?

ACTOR: Yes. In a sense, from his wife.

PAUL: It is quite profound the insights you can get on your characters in such a short space of time. All this information you got on your character came from your drums. How do you feel about what I just said? Do you feel it is all just hogwash?

ACTOR: No, I think it is very beneficial, and I am going to start using this stuff for working on my characters. It gives me imaginative details about my character that will manifest itself with other characters during the performance. It's going to affect the character that I am.

PAUL: I am guiding the actor here, but you can quite easily do this exercise on your own by asking yourself questions instead of having someone do it for you. While you are working this exercise there are likely to be some insights right from the beginning. You may even choose to record this exercise so that you are able to go back and listen to yourself and your exact wording. Let's say you were playing a prisoner. You could be the bars, or the lock, or plate of food describing this prisoner. For instance, if you were the bars you might end up saying, "I want to suffocate him." Not every piece of information that comes up will be useful or link to your character, but you will be surprised how much will.

GAVIN: What you are looking for in this exercise is what you can discover about your character through the eyes of the object chosen. If one object isn't working for you, switch to another object that is present in the room. When you are talking as the object, talk out loud even if you are by yourself. This will help you hear the object's thoughts out loud.

Food for Thought

Here is a great secret: You can turn anything you think or do while acting into an exercise and invent your own exercises. Almost all acting exercises have been developed after somebody saw something happen and they came from a eureka! moment. During the journey you will be the person who makes up the exercise that works best for you.

Food for Thought

I have sometimes said in acting class, "I'm going to draw an imaginary line here on the floor, and I want you to step over it." Do you know there are people who won't step over the line? If they won't, there is no chance of them being an actor. This may sound absurd and ridiculous, and so I want you to let it sink in and answer for yourself why they cannot be an actor unless they change their way of thinking. The biggest limitations facing an actor are often the ones put upon by themselves.

The Diagnosis

In this exercise you are being asked to take a step back so that you are able to make new discoveries about your character. One of the problems of studying acting is admitting that acting is fantasy and imagination that goes forever and ever. This exercise allows the actor to take a back door into getting profound insight into their character. This comes from your work as an actor, and it comes from your imagination, not ours. When we are working with you as directors, our job is to help you to stimulate your imagination, not our imagination.

When we are teaching a scene or directing we are not using our imaginations, we are using your imagination. We are not asking you to use this exercise because it is a good exercise, but because it stimulates your imagination. In this exercise we find out that our imaginations are far more accurate than our minds. The reason for this is that our imaginations are not inhibited by anything. Parents, environment, and society tell us not to use our imagination, but to conform. When you think about it, society is against everything we use in acting. This exercise shows you a way to always use your imagination.

Some casting directors will call this talent, but it is actually an understanding of how to *access* your talent. Our imaginations have become so suppressed that if we think in the terms that we are used to thinking, we cannot access our imaginations. We have to find a new way to think that is in no way threatened by society, or anything else for that matter. The wonderful thing about your imagination is that you can bypass all of this. While you may at times feel limited as an actor, your imagination is limitless. If we ask you what your character does in a certain situation, you are going to answer in the way society has taught you. This exercise allows you to answer how your imagination would like to. It is also possible to overanalyze a character, as Nikos Psacharopoulos says, "I wish you knew less about who these characters are. I wish the scene was not so accessible."[111] In this exercise you get to sneak up on the back door of your imagination.

Food for Thought

If we go back in history we find that actors have always been persecuted and looked down upon as immoral, illegal in some way, and a danger to society. Even to this day movies are graded and there seems to be more censorship on television and film than there is on-stage. Knowing the history of acting may not make you a good actor, but to have some knowledge on the history of your craft can only be a plus. As L. Du Garde Peach points out, "There is one name which anyone interested in the theatre ought to know and remember, the name of the first great dramatist of whom we know: Aeschlyus, born in the year 525 B.C. in Eleusis in a part of Greece then known in Attica."[112]

Food for Thought

Sometimes an actor will say, "I just want to be myself." The only problem is when you are yourself, you are so uninteresting. Of course just be yourself if yourself is the most fabulous and capable individual on this earth. The reason you work on your instrument, on yourself, is so that you can become the most highly functioning version of yourself. Then you can be yourself. When you become an actor you begin to rediscover yourself.

Final Thoughts

We've heard various actors, teachers, and directors say that they work from the inside out. In the past, it has been said that Americans tended to work from the inside out and the British from the outside in. Young children are often told, "You have quite an imagination there." An actor is also an athlete with an incredible imagination. If someone says to you, "You have an incredible imagination," they are talking about an imagination with big muscle. This is an exercise in using that muscle. This is an exercise in building an athletic imagination, an imagination far greater than any needed by the audience. By having an athlete's imagination you will stimulate whatever imagination you have. You are an athlete who is constantly in training in the most important race of your life.

---

111. Nikos Psacharopoulos, *Toward Mastery* (New Hampshire: Smith and Kraus, 1998), 64.
112. L. Du Garde Peach, *The Story of the Theatre* (Loughborough-England: Wills & Hepworth, 1970), 8.

58. Room Scan

Food for Thought

PAUL: Are you any better an actor now than when you first started acting?

ACTOR: Yes.

PAUL: Of course you are. Are you any better now than when you first started? It's not a trick question.

ACTOR: I hope so.

PAUL: I'm going to ask you, dear reader, a question and I'm going to presume the answer. You are better than when you started, are you good? No. There is no such thing as a person who is good who does not work. There's no such thing. You may be better than some, but that does not make you good.

GAVIN: There are many fine athletes but there are relatively few Olympic athletes.

Food for Thought

Actors get to do things that no one else on earth gets to do. Actors commit sins on-stage and screen so that you can see the consequences of that sin. You didn't in reality do what you did on-stage or screen, but your nervous system doesn't necessarily know that. Every thought, every breath, every movement, every utterance has a chemical response.

The Ingredients

This exercise is worked at a coffee shop. What we would like you to do for us now is scan the room for one minute. We want you to remember as much as you can with specific detail. We will then ask you to close your eyes, and then we're going to have you recollect everything you saw. We want you to do it in the order you saw it. For instance, if you see a picture first, recollect that picture first in as much specific detail as you possibly can.

PAUL: *(ACTOR looks around.)* Stop. Tell me what you recall. I am going to give you one minute to do this.

ACTOR: There is a painting of a guy standing on a green surface and he has a white coat on. I am not sure exactly what he is, he could be a cook. The guy below him has a beard and a computer and he is a sitting at a long table. The guy next to him is bald and the guy next to him has curly hair. They all have computers. There are four tables in that area there, and next to the chairs there is a big cabinet covering the whole wall. I didn't quite get what is in the cabinet.

PAUL: I'm going to stop you there. Open your eyes, have a good look around, see what you got out of what you commented on, and see what you missed.

ACTOR: I see the cabinet is full of coffee makers, but I didn't notice that. I didn't realize that guy had red hair.

PAUL: Keep going with the specifics. So you got the computers, did you notice that they were all Apple computers? Did you notice that computer has stickers all over it, including one of a skateboard?

ACTOR: I didn't notice it. I didn't even see that. I think I ended up going more for generalities.

PAUL: How did the time factor affect you in that you only had one minute to look around?

ACTOR: I think with more time I would have gone into more detail.

PAUL: Did your adrenalin pump, and were you focusing quickly to see as much as you could?

ACTOR: No, I didn't feel pressured.

GAVIN: This exercise was worked in a coffee shop, so your acting can be worked at any time and any place.

Food for Thought

Your thoughts are like surprises. When you get to the point in rehearsal that you carry the character with you day and night, make small changes in your daily routine and you will find that quite miraculously you will make new discoveries and have new insights to your work. Your thoughts are like surprises. As you change molecularly you will have new discoveries in yourself and in your character. As Lajos Egri says when quoting Henrik Ibsen, "When I am writing I must be alone; if I have eight characters of drama to do with I have society enough; they keep me busy; I must learn to know them. And this process of making their acquaintance is slow and painful."[113]

Food for Thought

Moving to an acting hub basically has to do with your search for excellence. If you are going to base your life on a search of excellence, then you have to go somewhere that you can accomplish that. There are a number of places, although they are not infinite. You can't do it by yourself on a desert island. First, you have to decide what you want. A search for excellence can be done in any place where major productions are happening. If you are in a place where you can only watch the pursuit of excellence and you can't do it yourself, then you should move to a place where you can search for excellence. Then you have to decide what you want to do with your life while you are searching for excellence. It doesn't matter which hub you go to because, as they used to say, all roads lead to Rome. Now all roads lead to success if you are on one of these roads. The question is not, "Where should I move?" or, "When should I move?" The question is: "Are you going to move?" The biggest percentages of people who go to those places only go to visit them. Whatever place you go to, be prepared to go there for a prolonged period of time. The worst thing that you can do in New York is if you go to an audition and say, "I just flew in from Los Angeles." You have already offended everybody there because they are saying, "This is where I live," and you're saying, "Here I am, you lucky people." And they are saying, "We want somebody who is solid here." When you are auditioning, if they don't think you are grounded to that place, if they think you are merely shopping, why would they give you a part? I have heard people in auditions say, "I have to decide whether I want to move here or not." What do you think they are going to say, "We'll wait for you?" When you move to a new city, in your mind you have to say, "I live in a new place, I don't live where I came from." Most actors come from a place where they have family, friends, comfort, and security, and the actor must be willing to leave those things behind and start fresh. This takes strength of character and a deep level of determination. Once you move to a new place you can once again begin to build a network or friends, comfort, and security. If you loathe the path you are on, you won't be on it for long.

The Diagnosis

In this exercise you were asked to come up with detail and to get very specific. If you remember a table, try to also remember what color it is, what is it made of, if there are patterns on it, and if it is clean or dirty. Generalities are the enemy of the actor in almost everything you do. You will never be playing a character that is twenty-something. Even if this is what the breakdown says, it is up to you to come up with a specific age. In this exercise you are given a limited amount of time. This might not seem relevant or even fair, because how is time a factor for the actor? An actor recalled that it was Kafka who said without limitations there is chaos. An actor is constantly under time constraints. If you are in an audition you may have a limited amount of time to work with the sides. In terms of time allocated for your audition, Rona Laurie says, "It is vital to keep to any stipulated time for the speeches."[114]

---

113. Lajos Egri, 32.
114. Rona Laurie, *Auditioning* (Great Britain: J. Garnet Miller Ltd., 1985), 64.

ACTOR: If you are filming, then you may be under pressure to get it right in a limited number of takes because of the filming schedule. When you hear that saying, "Time is money," they are not kidding. I was up for a new series last week and as I walked in they told me the scene had to move at a really fast pace and that the dialogue needed to be very quick. This wasn't the way I had pictured it at all, and yet this is what they wanted.

PAUL: In most professional auditions that you are going for you will initially receive about two or three minutes. The idea of working with a time element in this exercise may seem unimportant, yet your entire career you are faced with time constraints and expected to produce the goods. You are always adapting very, very quickly to the situation at hand.

GAVIN: We are working on acting in a coffee shop. Is there anything significant about this?

PAUL: The answer is yes. You could really do this exercise anywhere you wanted to such as in a doctor's waiting room, supermarket checkout line, on a train, anywhere. The benefit of any exercise is that it is much stretching, strengthening, and coordinating. It mentally allows him, forces him, or encourages him to use his imagination because the actor's greatest tool is his imagination.

GAVIN: Some actors believe that they can only work on their instrument in a class or in a workshop. Perhaps this is a self-created limitation.

Food for Thought

Here is an experiment you can do. As you are talking with a friend, absolutely stop talking in the middle of a sentence. You know what will happen? They will start talking, and they will not even know that you have not finished. The actor must know how to listen and how to react to his partner.

Food for Thought

There are many times when an actor needs to work alone. There are also times when it is wise to work with a partner. This can be in relation to a scene, rehearsing a play, an exercise, or whatever. You know body builders never get to be Mr. Olympia by themselves. You really do have to find other actors you can partner with. You can learn to grow, explore, and rebound ideas.

Final Thoughts

Too often actors will use generalities in terms of a character, a scene, and a part they are playing. Under these conditions their acting is at a disadvantage and their imagination is limited. By finding the detail and the specifics in everything they do, actors open up the stairwell of their imagination. The detail starts to bring the character alive for the actor, which in turn will bring it alive for the audience. If an actor cannot see, then how do we expect an audience to see? This exercise allows you to utilize your powers of observation and your ability to work with specifics. By working with these muscles, the actor is enabling them to grow stronger and become more accessible.

59. The Eureka! Moment

Food for Thought

I did a lecture with a colleague of mine to a group of actors. He was a famous actor, and after he gave a short performance I turned to the actors and I said, "What is the difference between all of you and John? It is very simple, it's your turn." Now what you need to consider is when it is your turn, are you going to take it?

Food for Thought

For my first show as a director I was privileged to work with some very well-known and respected actors. A mentor of mine said, "You don't know what your job is as a director."

I said, "Well, what is my job as director?" She said, "Get the curtain up and then to get it down. If your actors are any good, they'll do the rest of it." It wounded me so deeply. There is a way of guiding the actors. The director needs to have an overarching vision of what it is they are looking for. A teacher is to just teach acting and not to take care of their entire life. A director's job is to help the actors do what they do.

The Ingredients

What we would like you to do is think of a thought that relates to a specific situation. You can use an imaginary situation, or if you are up to it you can choose something from your own life such as "I'm in love with my boyfriend and he stopped returning my calls." What we would like you to do now is, using either hand, start to draw an imaginary circle in the air with your index finger in a clockwise direction. As you do this, say your sentence such as, "My mother doesn't like me acting." Keep going around in a continuous circle with your finger and, as you do, repeat your sentence adding another sentence each time. "My mother doesn't like me acting because there is no future in it. My mother doesn't like me acting because there is no future in it and she is worried. My mother doesn't like me acting because there is no future in it and she is worried I won't make a living later in life." If you go around that circle and you allow yourself to, it will jump off by itself and start another circle that doesn't seem to have any relationship to it. As one circle ends, another should begin in a continuous and seemingly endless fashion.

Here we go, "My mother doesn't like me acting because there is no future in it. My mother doesn't like me acting because there is no future in it and she is worried. My mother doesn't like me acting because there is no future in it and she is worried I won't make a living later in life. I wonder what I want to be later in life? I wonder what I want to be later in life, who I want to spend my life with? I wonder who I want to be later in life, who I want to spend my life with, will I enjoy my life?" Now you are on a completely different subject. It has jumped, so whenever you go round in a circle you will find that, if you go round it and encourage it, it will jump off into another circle.

As you jump off into another circle and another thought, it is important that you start to draw a circle with your finger in a completely new direction. To begin with, we ask that you start each sentence from the beginning and continue to add on until you jump to a new thought. For instance, "I wonder who I will spend the rest of my life with? I wonder who I will spend the rest of my life with, I want to find someone who I can really love." Later, you may find that you no longer have to start from the beginning each time, and that you just automatically go from thought to thought. You might start a circle with, "I wonder who I'll spend the rest of my life with? I want to find someone who I can really love. No, I want to find somebody who I could be with all of my life. I wonder what kind of house we would live in? You know what kind of house I'd like? A very modern house way out in the woods somewhere. That's what I always wanted to do, to walk out in the woods alone." Each one of these has jumped to a new circle. Sometimes it jumps very quickly, and sometimes it may take longer. Do not force it or preempt it, just allow it to happen and it will.

What is also quite exciting is that you will find that your thoughts do not necessarily follow any rhyme or reason. You might start off saying, "I want to be in love," and finish up by saying, "That's what a rock concert does." Look where you have gotten in just a few words. Practice this exercise on your own, as no one can particularly follow you and you don't want someone to follow you. Each circle you go to is as important as the circle that precedes it. You are practicing not staying with one circle. Remember that you are drawing your circles in the air and speaking your thoughts out loud simultaneously. In this respect, you are connecting the physical stimulus with the mental stimulus.

Food for Thought

Acting allows our lives to have infinite variety to experience every possible thing that we could. Most of all, acting gives us the opportunity to experience as much as we possibly can in our lives, and to know the consequences of that, such as knowing the consequences of being a thief, an addict, a cuckold, a fool, a liar, or a cheat. If you didn't have actors, then people would have to do all of these things and some do. Actors have to suffer the consequences of any role they play. If you are playing a murderer, your body goes through that and you have to suffer the consequences because the actor's nervous system does not know the difference between reality and acting, even though it will know it on some level. Your friends will live vicariously through you because they can only think about things your characters are experiencing.

Food for Thought

An actor learns to have two beings that coexists: one that watches this happen as an audience watches it, and the other that is experiencing it as it is happening. An actor thinks something causes certain vibrations in their body. This applies to artists of all types. Observations can be found in the works of those such as Coquelin. This is why it is beneficial to know the background of your craft so you can begin to connect the dots for yourself.

The Diagnosis

What this exercise does for you can be described in two ways: one is creative thinking and, very sadly, the other is attention deficit disorder. As we keep looking, we find out that acting exercises encourage us to do something that is part of our nature, and we are not encouraged or even accepted by society at large. We have already mentioned that this exercise enhances creative thinking, but it goes much further than that. What it does is it encourages you to exercise your ability of random thought. Random thought is what gave us the Pythagorean Theorem.

As the story goes, King Hiero had just commissioned a new crown made, but he was not convinced of the purity of the crown. He contacted Archimedes and said he wanted to know how to discover the purity of the crown without damaging it, but Archimedes had no answer. He went home deep in thought. Eventually, he went to take a bath. The tub was very full and when he attempted to sit down, water spilled everywhere. At this point he realized the now well-known facts of water displacement. It is said that in his excitement and euphoria to tell the king, he ran naked through the streets shouting "Eureka!" The word eureka actually means, "I have found it!" Now we use the term eureka! to describe a thought that bounces into our head and seems to come from nowhere. We need to practice having random thoughts and discoveries that seemingly come from nowhere. We cannot use wishful thinking to hope that we will get these thoughts. We can actually practice it. We warn you and remind you that an actor who is thinking in this way is called *making discoveries,* and someone who is not thinking this way is said to have *attention deficit disorder.*

What this exercise does is it makes you demand of yourself those things that are part of your nature. If you met a hundred famous inventors, we wonder how many of them could be said to have attention deficit disorder. One thing that is part of your nature is a discovery, and discovery happens because you are looking even when you do not know what you are looking for. Think about going to the beach and brushing away the sand day after day, and one day you brush away the sand and you find a diamond. You didn't know the diamond was there when you began. If you did, it is not a discovery. When you start a circle, each time you go to another circle you are practicing, "I've got it!" A eureka! moment.

In civilian life we are told to concentrate and stay on one subject, but because an actor must allow words of a script or a situation in a scene to go through his body, he wants to encourage these random thoughts to occur. Actors are able to do this when they allow and encourage their minds to wander. We think in civilian life you should not be thinking the thoughts or doing the things that an actor must do. We think a person who is not an actor – and we think actors would agree – should not do what an actor is doing in their everyday life, because they haven't practiced it, they don't understand it, it would confuse them, harm them, and be of no benefit to them.

Could you also say that this exercise aims to create and release inspiration? Inspiration and inhalation actually mean to take a breath, and come as a result of what you feed yourself. Eureka! comes from absolutely nowhere. If you read a script that you love over and over, and if you watch a performance that you love, you are inspired. If you want to know what inspiration is, it's that thing that happens when something strikes you so strongly that there's a quick intake of breath. The point of a eureka! moment exercise is that it takes absolutely no information, and that it just comes from seemingly nowhere. What is also amazing about a eureka! moment is that it is as accurate as any deductive reasoning you will have in your whole life. Thomas Edison had a eureka! moment when he invented the lightbulb after thousands of failed attempts. Your instrument has to be trained and open to the potential of these eureka! moments. A eureka! moment also comes from the ability to respond to the moment. We are taught to think before we speak, but this is not for the actor. A number of actors after great performances have said, "I have no idea how I did that." A eureka! moment exercise also encourages you to react, remember, cry, laugh, fear, and become angry. These are all responses to thought. There is nothing in acting that you do that cannot be practiced.

Food for Thought

PAUL: *(To the ACTOR after working on a scene)* You did something that you didn't intend and we saw something that we didn't expect. The purpose of technique is so that you can transcend yourself. That is why we call it creative. Otherwise it would be technical or mechanical. You know that you are practicing. You know that you are cooking, and you know that you are creating something when you do something that you did not intend. This can happen continuously and when you do something you did not intend, the audience sees something it did not expect. Why? Because your body language leads them a certain way, and when it changes and you didn't expect it to change, they don't expect it. As you are moving towards spontaneity you begin to move away from predictability.

Food for Thought

I have worked with many stars in movies. Not one of the stars I've worked with ever gave me the impression that they woke up one morning as a child and said, "I'm beautiful. Gee, I'm talented, I better be an actor and earn a lot of money." If you want to be an actor and are serious about it, then you should study it with great dignity, awe, and some fear. It should be the scariest thing you've ever done in your life. It should be the most fun thing you've ever done in your life. If acting is a part-time hobby for you, then keep it as a hobby. If it is a profession for you, then it will become a great part of your life.

Final Thoughts

Many times we've watched actors and, like Archimedes, we have seen their eureka! moment. It is just as exciting for the audience as it is for the actors doing it. When we ask how they did that, we usually get the answer from the teacher, the critic, and the director that it is their talent. In order for us to understand how the actor reached this point, we have to understand what they did before that happened. Archimedes was aware of everything that was going on around him. He coupled two things which were, "What are all the things transpiring around me, and what problem am I trying to solve?" When they happened together at one moment, that is called a eureka! moment. How in the world can we practice a eureka! moment? The answer to every good exercise is to keep it simple. People tend to get on one track and keep going around without finding the answer, so they give up. This exercise is a way of exercising the simplest parts of yourself. In this exercise you are giving your body a language that says, "After you have pursued something for a while, it is OK to go somewhere else to look for the answer." We are told all of our lives to concentrate and not think of too many things. There is nothing in our lives that we cannot practice that is in tandem with the body, the mind, and spirit. This exercise leads to random thoughts, and random thoughts open the gateway to our imagination.

60. The Memory Exercise

Food for Thought

When you are in a class don't force yourself to understand everything at that time. If you don't understand it, then do what you can to understand. Treat your body with enormous respect instead of beating it up for things. A mistake that actors make is that when they are in acting class, they want it to be about them. Every time your teacher talks to you, just periodically as they speak, add "in acting." If they say, "I don't like the way you're sitting," in your mind add "in acting." Or, "I don't like the way you are talking, in acting." The reason you do this is so you know it's not personal. Take criticism with a pinch of salt, not because it is not valid, but so that you are able to take more of it when it is needed.

Food for Thought

In order to be successful in acting you have to be single-minded and you have to have tunnel vision. It has to be all about you, and you have to be willing to be selfish if you want to compete. As an actor, you have to be a clean slate onto which anything can be written. You have to be a clear glass into which any kind of liquid, whether it is thick or thin, water or poison, can be poured. It takes a particular type of actor who can do this, and they tend to be those who struggle deeply in their own lives. This is not an encouragement for you to become an alcoholic, or a depressive, or drug dependent, but to realize that great actors often have great sensitivities not just in their acting, but also throughout their lives.

The Ingredients

What we would like you to do is close your eyes, put your feet shoulder width apart, and stand very still. If you can, face a mirror, but if not it will work just as well by standing in an open space and closing your eyes. What you have to think is, "I'm going to erase everything in my mind. I have no past, I have no memory." Look what a wonderful advantage you have by not having anything. Say to yourself, "I'm going to clear my mind so that I have no memory. I have no feeling of right or wrong, I have no feeling of what I could do, or should do, or what I want to do. I have no memory of anything." You have to erase all memory, joys, burdens, fears, and all the things you feel you lack or have accumulated until there is nothing. You have to practice having no memory.

In a minute you are going to open your eyes, but don't open them before you feel that you have cleared your memory, and you have no memory of anything that has ever transpired in your life before. When you do open your eyes you will be looking at the ground. Now, if you have really forgotten it all, open your eyes. As you do this, we want you to say to yourself, "I don't remember this body, I don't know how many fingers I have, I don't know how long my arms are, or how long my legs are." You can look around you body and say, "I don't recognize these shoes, I don't recognize these clothes at all." Raise your shoulders and drop them and say to yourself, "I don't remember how to lift my shoulders." Move your arms about saying, "I didn't know my arms could do this and were limited to this." You can also start to walk around the space and say, "How strange, I've never walked this way before. In fact, I don't know if I have ever walked at all before." Start smelling things and say, "I am not familiar with that smell. I don't remember this room or it ever being this quiet before." You may think there are no sounds, but as you move there is the sound of your feet or arms as they swing through the air and you say, "I don't remember hearing these things before." Move your tongue around, "What an interesting taste, I don't remember this taste in my mouth, I don't even know what this taste is." Think of your emotions and say, "I feel like laughing, I feel like crying. Why am I so angry, and what is anger?" Because you have never felt any of these things before, you are a clear instrument with no memory. It should give you a different feeling because there is nothing you remember about that person. You don't remember wearing those clothes. You don't remember having your hair that length. You don't remember that your eyes are that color. You have no memory. You have never seen that person before.

Do this exercise in two ways: sometimes by looking in the mirror and other times without being in front of the mirror. They will then be two very different exercises. As you look at an exercise like this you may become a little daunted by all of the things you are being asked to do. Please remember that these are examples of things you can think about and consider. As you work with each exercise it is up to you to have each exercise best fit your needs. As you work this exercise do not feel limited to where you utilize it. If you are at dinner with friends, look down for a moment and close your eyes for just a couple of beats and then look up at your friend and say to yourself, "I've never seen this person before." It's great fun and it allows you to realize you can work and adapt this exercise anywhere you want to.

ACTOR: Working this exercise gave me a slight feeling of apprehension and fear. As I looked at myself I said, "Who is this?"

PAUL: I like the words *apprehension* and *fear* because they are exciting. But apprehension is where we prepare and search our mind quickly to ask ourselves, "What am I going to do to handle the situation?" The reason we may feel afraid during this exercise is that if I am to be someone I have never been before, then I cannot rest on my laurels. I can't use any tricks I know as it is all immediate discovery.

GAVIN: If you read this exercise you will have an intellectual opinion. If you do it you will have a kinesthetic and visceral reaction.

Food for Thought

A coach gives you exercises, but you do those exercises by yourself. The best exercises in the world are the ones you can do on your own. Think about the rehearsal process in which you do the bulk of the work on your own time. This is what it means when the director asks you to come prepared.

Food for Thought

If you are not a person who likes to please people, you cannot be an actor.

The Diagnosis

When you look at that person to whom you have never seen before, that is where you must start when you are playing a part. This exercise is called The Memory Exercise and it's not how to memorize, it's how to forget. We make a big thing in our lives of memorizing lines, memorizing how to be, how to walk, who we should be, and what we know, but we don't take advantage of the fact that this is an exercise in forgetting and having no memory. It's a very good exercise to do before you read a new script or play. Just clear your mind and you will have no memory, you have forgotten everything you know, and everything you read in this play is news to you. Try watching a movie or going to a play and just before it begins say, "I have no memory." When you watch you don't say, "I've seen this type of thing before. I know someone like him. I know someone like her. I remember that emotion." Instead, you look and say, "I've never seen anything or anybody like that before. I've never heard anybody speak that way, and I've never seen anybody move that way," until you can begin to get a clear body. If you are creating a character, you can't create a character that's burdened with or covered by all sorts of things you remember. Think about it: Everything you remember has a value attached to it, whether a goodness, evil, pleasantness, or displeasure. If you clear your memory, then no thought that crosses your mind can have anything attached to it and you can start fresh. Only then will you begin to experience each day being somebody you are not. If you went to sleep in a pair of pajamas and during the night somebody unknown to you puts you in a full dress suit or a ballroom gown complete with shoes and you wake up in the morning, the first thing you will say is, "I don't remember feeling these clothes this way." And then you would look down and say, "Look at this, I have never seen these clothes before. How did it happen?" Then you get up and you look at the bed and say, "I have never been in this bed before." Only then when you go through this exercise or one similar to it will you get a feeling of what it is to create a character from a clean slate.

Because there is nothing about a character that you have ever seen or done before, you must learn to get to feel this as often as possible. Probably the worst thing an actor can ever say is, "I relate to this character. I know people like this. I have felt like this before." How can you create a character who has never been seen by anybody in the world? The performance must be fresh, spontaneous, and one that no one has ever seen. We have often gone to the theatre and said, "I have never seen anything like that before in my life." We have watched films and television and said exactly the same thing. Every day you want to experience unfamiliarity if you can do it. If nothing else, change the cover on top of your bed each day to something different and unfamiliar, or move the furniture around and bring something in you have never seen before so you can say, "I have no memory of that. What I'm doing starts now, and what I'm creating starts now." If you're in a play that plays time after time, night after night, or you are in a series where you play the same character, every time you play it say, "I've never seen this character before. I don't know this character, and every time I do it, it's somebody I am not." Wipe your memory clean before every performance. Your muscle memory will give you all the lines and the direction that you have been given.

I knew a famous ballerina who said, in an evening when they would do four or five very short ballets and she was in all of them, she would change her scent for each ballet. In other words, she would change the perfume for each ballet because if she was to be a different character, she didn't even want the smell of that character to be the same. She wanted to find the smell of that character, and very few of us think about how the character smells. If it becomes somebody you are, then that would become stale. The object is to become somebody you have never felt before. It is a difficult thing because there is no other time in life when you are asked to be somebody you have never been before. Everybody acts to a certain extent. Think about the person you are for your parents, friends, boyfriend or girlfriend, employer, and teacher. For each of these you create a slightly different version of you.

Food for Thought

Theatre of Consequence is something that, no matter how small, teaches us something about life. Sometimes it teaches us something we have never thought of. This can happen in all forms of acting. Don't think for a moment that I am saying that Theatre of Consequence is only serious theatre. I have seen it in high comedy and low comedy. Part of your training and growth is to understand the language and the vocabulary of acting. Acting has a vocabulary, and it does not necessarily apply for everything else in life. I have seen Theatre of Consequence in nightclubs, the circus, children's theatre, buskers in the street, in grand opera, and in the movies. Theatre of Consequence is not up to the material, it is up to the actor. It is not up to the production, the director, the designer. It's up to you. It is up to the individual actor. It is something that teaches you something about your life. In my estimation, it does this to every single person in the audience. If there are five hundred people in the audience, it manages to teach all of us something about ourselves. I saw a mime artist in the street who walked with people up some imaginary stairs and as he walked down the stairs with them, he became that person, he knew how to become the essence of that person. He got arrested because he had three hundred people in the street watching him, fixated on his every move. Acting has an incredible potential to reach people in an infinite number of ways. Acting does not have to take place on a set or stage, it can happen anywhere — it knows no boundaries.

Food for Thought

There is no great benefit to training as an actor if you are not using it as soon as possible. One famous actor commented on how there were so many people in a play he was working on that some nights he couldn't even get on the stage. But he went to the theatre every night, he thought about his character every night, and he was prepared every night. He was backstage with professional actors, directors, and producers. He heard their language, he watched their habits, he watched their motion, he watched them act, and he watched them prepare. We are talking about the integration between your training as an actor and your working as an actor.

Final Thoughts

The purpose of the exercise is to put actors in the position of where they have no baggage. When actors wake with no memory whatsoever, they have no baggage and no limitations. In this case, no memory is equal to no limitations, and it also means no restrictions. Now you can imagine anything and you can be anything. Being an actor is being all things to all people. People say they cannot be all things to all people, and yet there are actors who seem to be all things to all people. A newborn baby does not judge. It has not formed the ability to do so yet. We all love to watch a baby play partially because we are never quite sure what they are going to do next.

Chapter 13:
Creating a World

61. Begin Again

Food for Thought

See as much top theatre as you can. If you get the opportunity go to the West End of London and go to Broadway, you have to see as much fine theatre as you can. I once took a group of actors to London to see a very famous actor in a West End show and the actors came out and said, "I feel better about acting. I used to think that in London they knew how to act more than we did, and that's it! It wasn't a very good play at all." I said, "And that's why you have to see these plays in these cities because you have to see what it's all about." You cannot judge something until you know it.

Food for Thought

Some actors say, "Actors need a strong leader, director, or teacher." However, what are you going to do when there isn't one? If the industry is not going to change, what are you going to do about it? We have seen too many professional, fabulous shows where all the actors said, "There is no leader here, the director is doing nothing, and I hate my scene partner," and they are in the middle of a Broadway hit. If you want a leader in a company, start your own company. If you want a lead in a movie, produce your own movie. Ultimately, every actor has to become their own leader, their own instructor, and their own director.

The Ingredients

This is an exercise that singing coaches and vocal coaches have been using forever. For acting we want to make it an isolated exercise. This exercise is a very simple thing. It's kind of an abstract exercise, but after you do it you will get a sense of what it is to sustain a performance. Let's not call it a performance, let's call it a state of being. We want you to sing a note, it does not matter if it is pretty, it does not matter if you are a singer. What we want you to do is find a friendly vowel and just sustain that vowel. You can sing, "Aaaa," sustain it, and it will be, by definition, singing. It is not necessary that you become a singer, but it is necessary that you look everywhere and anywhere for exercises that help you be an actor. Here is the secret to this exercise: When you are doing your sustaining vowel, you have to think about the moment that you began. In order to sustain it you don't just do it and sustain it, you continue to begin again, over and over and over.

The first time we want you to begin and stop, begin and stop. So you go, "Aa, aa, aa, aa, aa." To begin with, you only sustain these sounds momentarily so that you know you have begun and stopped. Next, we want you to do the same thing again but even faster so that it almost sounds like a machine gun. Finally, we want you to put all of those segments together so that you know you are beginning and stopping in your mind, but the person listening to you doesn't hear it. You sustain the vowel, and in your mind you begin again, and again, and again, and again. In actual fact, you are now sustaining this one vowel for as long as you can, but in your mind you are starting over, again and again. Make sure you engage all the pieces of this exercise. It is very easy to go through the motions without really following through with each and every step.

Food for Thought

If we go back to even just the nineteenth century we will see that there were very few teachers of acting, as it wasn't thought of as something that was taught. It was taught in companies, so you would join a company knowing nothing and you would apprentice to the company. The other actors would give you clues and the lead actors would tell you what you must or must not do when you were on- or off-stage with them. The star system was very much in place. We used to kid when I was very young that the smaller the part, the more the makeup. When you read the wonderful books that have been written on acting, especially the ones that have been written by wonderful well-known actors and teachers, you only realize something important when you begin to see the similarities in the books. Notice what is being mentioned here is that great books are written by teachers and actors. There are many other books that will not and do not fit into this category at all. For example, why is the famous Russian different from the famous American different from the famous Frenchman different from the famous Englishman different from the famous Japanese, etc.? All countries have famous performers and teachers. When you find the sameness in them, then you have found something that can actually be used.

Food for Thought

Do you know what fishhooks are for women? They are little hooks that grip and have a string or elastic to connect them. Famous actresses would put them in their hair beneath their scalp. It was used for many years by actresses before the time of face-lifts. Older women grew their hair very long and pulled it into a knot and it gave them a do-it-yourself face-lift. What one person calls beauty another person will call talent. If this sounds ridiculous to you, then realize that some of these women were famous stars. They considered every possible angle that they believed influenced their talent.

Food for Thought

PAUL: What is the disadvantage of being you?

ACTOR: It's actually an advantage because of what I can bring.

PAUL: Good point. You bring in something that no one else in the world can bring because there is nothing like you. You can be your weakest link or your strongest asset. Are you interested in acting?

ACTOR: Yes, of course.

PAUL: I don't know, that's a fair question, isn't it? It is not said to tease you, or chide you, or embarrass you. Do you know how many people I've had in class who are not interested in studying acting or being in the industry? It might surprise you.

GAVIN: The greatest teachers in the world and the greatest productions will always have a certain number of actors that have little or no interest in acting. That just happens to be where they are in life.

The Diagnosis

In order to sustain energy, what the audience sees and what your own body believes needs to be consistent. In a performance there should be a level of energy that precedes the curtain going up, and it should remain through the entire show and a little bit before the curtain goes down. It's almost more difficult in film because it must precede the word "action" and continue beyond the word "cut." It's more exhausting on film because you have to stop and start this so many times. It's easier to do a four-hour play and sustain energy than it is to stop and start, and stop and start.

An actor must create a higher state of being. What is more important than the performance is your state of being. If we think of the performance, then we are what is called playing results, end gaming, or indicating. You have objectively thought of something and then you are objectively trying to do what you have thought of. There is never a part of creating an acting performance that should even use that process. In order to create a worthy performance you must be in a particular state of being that is not required for anything else. Acting has its own state of being. Not only are you in that state of being, but you must learn to sustain that state of being. If we tell you by exercise, by thought, by practice, by experience, or by observation, you should be able to get yourself in this state of being, arrive at this state of being, and then to stay there. The danger is that you one day say, "I think I'm in that state of being," and then you try to hook on to it. It's like trying to catch a butterfly. If we want to be poetic, it's like trying to catch a dream. The thought is there, but as soon as you reach for it, it's gone. Or you get tight or you get tension and that is the antithesis of acting. First we have to, by thought, relaxation, and exercises, get to a particular state of being. It takes a length of time and effort before you can be in that creative state, and it takes a little longer than that before you can actually recognize yourself in that state. Your teachers, your friends, and the audience will recognize that state before you do. It's fun, but it is also frustrating because they will say, "Yes, that's it!" and you say, "Oh, great!" You are so proud of yourself and you have no idea what you did. Then you try to do the same thing over and they say, "Why don't you have that anymore?" An older actor will say, "I don't think about those things anymore. When it happens it frustrates me because I now know it's great and I'm not sure why it's great."

We have already given you exercises that get you in that state of being, so make sure you utilize those. Eventually you will be able to say, "When I do this exercise not only do I recognize technical things that are happening to me, but that it's creating a state of being that is useful to me, that is pleasant to me, and that is exciting to me." You didn't get this state of being by dialing it up and you didn't get it off a computer. You got it by going through a series of steps. We begin a performance and then we start pushing, thinking that it is sustaining. It's not, and it stops what we're doing. Being in a state of being is such an important topic that great actors and great teachers have spent their entire lifetime questioning and searching for it.

Food for Thought

PAUL: What is the difference between going to a drama school and a university?

ACTOR: In college, you really get to understand where it all came from instead of just the craft.

PAUL: In my experience on Broadway, TV, and film, I have never heard a director or actor discuss history or style in any show in my life. No producer or director is ever going to think you are more serious about acting because you studied in college.

GAVIN: We are not saying you should not go to college. We are saying that it may not be a great advantage to you in regards to the industry. Remember that we are looking to connect the craft and the industry of acting.

Food for Thought

Over forty years ago Actors Equity did a survey of the colleges of the United States. Five thousand people a year were graduating with a degree in acting. At that time, there were only a few thousand members in Equity. The number of actors pursuing work will always heavily outweigh the number of professional jobs available. That is why your instrument must always be accessible and ready.

Final Thoughts

If you've ever in your life got it perfectly right the first time, then from that time on begin again until you get it right again and call that the first time. You are only as good as your last performance.

62. Begin Again Part 2

Food for Thought

A young actor on a movie set, a Broadway show, or a major television set will be treated the same as an adult actor. They are going to talk to you in the language they would use with any other actor, and they are going to express themselves in the way they would any other actor. There is not a special language for young actors. Therefore, it is necessary for young actors to learn to play their instrument in a professional way. Self-discipline and professionalism must be with you from the very beginning.

Food for Thought

Wouldn't it be fun if you had the time to go around the world and study with the best teachers from all over the world? Wouldn't it be fun to say, "Would you pay my room, board, and tuition so I can go study with them?" If there is a play you just have to see, an instructor you just have to study with, then do it. If you commit to it you will find the money somehow, but that opportunity may not arise again.

The Ingredients

This is a continuation of the Begin Again exercise. Please make sure you have worked with the first part before you move on to this part. We have split this exercise into two sections because there are a number of different elements to work with.

Snap your fingers together once. Now snap them three times in a row rather slowly. Now snap them at a faster pace. Now do it again and this time go as fast as you can comfortably. The faster you are, the better you are at it, and the more adept you are at it. Take a monologue or scene and start doing the monologue. Do three or four words, "The funny thing is," and stop, and then do the next three or four words, "I really liked her," and stop. Remember that each time you stop you are beginning again as if for the first time you have spoken. Don't make the stops at periods or commas. In fact, work against making the stops where they might happen grammatically and let them happen randomly. We want you to do a performance by yourself until you get so you can sustain it. Now that you have been given this work, make up your own examples. When you hear a singer, whether it be a rock singer or opera singer, what they are actually doing is beginning that note over and over and over in such small segments that they all seem to fit together.

Another step to this exercise is when you are working on a movie or play, never begin from the same place twice. If the director says, "Let's begin at the beginning of the play," that's fine, just go back a couple of thoughts before that. You can apply it exactly the same way if you have to do the same shot fifteen times. Or in your mind you can start from the end of the movie and meet them there, because if you start from the same place every time it will become stale.

GAVIN: The importance of the imagination comes up again, and again, and again. Never miss the opportunity to utilize and ignite your imagination.

PAUL: What I would like you to do now is continue to do your piece out loud and this time every three or four words I want you to say, "let." It is as if to say you are letting go, and starting over. You can continue.

ACTOR 1: A member of the book of the month *let* can you see yourself the wife of the emperor *let* even to get home in time *let.*

PAUL: You really want to prepare. There is a bell or something in you like Pavlov's dog, and what happens is we have to wait for you to do it. You have to give up. It is as if you have already made a decision, and actors want to get their bodies in a situation where they're not preempting any decisions. *(ACTOR continues with the scene.)* That was so much better. It had so much more texture, and all that stuff we call acting. I do not believe you could have intellectually made all of those decisions in such a short space of time. You were simply doing the exercise.

ACTOR 1: Immediately after starting again every few words it just felt fresher and more alive.

PAUL: Yes, it was different, and it was familiar and unfamiliar. Learn to enjoy unfamiliar.

ACTOR 2: I felt as if I was very focused on trying to do the right thing at first.

PAUL: Always remember to avoid doing the "lets" at periods. What I would like the two of you to do now is sit back to back and I am going to have you alternate doing your pieces.

ACTOR 1: This time it was Plantains, one hundred and six of them, *let.*

PAUL: Switch.

ACTOR 2: I didn't go to the moon, I went much further, *let* for time, *let* is the longest distance between two places.

PAUL: Switch.

ACTOR 1: I asked myself what is the purpose behind creating fruit, *let* that only exists out of reason.

PAUL: Switch.

ACTOR 2: Not long after that, *let* I was fired for writing a poem on the lid of a shoe box, *let.* *(ACTORS continue to work for the next fifteen minutes.)*

PAUL: How was that for you?

ACTOR 1: It's hard for me to explain.

PAUL: I love that, always love it when an actor can't explain and has the confidence to admit that. Remember, after the greatest performance he ever gave Olivier was angry and frustrated. His friend came backstage and said, "Why are you so frustrated? That was the greatest performance of your life!" And he said words to the effect of, "I know that, I just don't know how I did it!"

ACTOR 2: I loved having that other person who I could talk to.

PAUL: The actor has to continually learn to put themselves in that beginning state. What I would like you to do now is walk a few steps and then stop and start over, stop and start over. *(ACTORS start walking around the space.)* Good. Now I want you to continue walking without stopping, only this time every few steps you are stopping and starting over in your mind.

Food for Thought

The practical side of acting is that you have to accept anything: a soap opera, a commercial, fringe theatre, or whatever it may be. You have to take that opportunity to take care of yourself, your needs, and to practice. The shame and truth of it is what you can accomplish by pursuing an acting career or by wanting to become a great actor. The truth of it is that, to be a practical person, you should accept every possible thing. Get on-set and get on the boards. An old expression in theatre is that every time you appear on the stage, it's called, *walking the boards,* so everybody should walk the boards, and get on the set as often as possible. A great musician must practice every day, and part of the joy of being a great actor is the desire to practice every day. A great actor says, "I've got to find an audience to get in front of this evening." Then there is the joy of waking up the next day and repeating the process. We are not recommending you go out and work for a project where your gut tells you something is not quite right. There are people who are looking to take your money, or worse, whose ulterior motives have nothing to do with acting. A good actor is also intelligent and streetwise.

Food for Thought

There are those who are personalities or saleable commodities, but in all graciousness we cannot call them actors. You cannot be an actor unless you know what it looks like. If you are an actor, all roads lead to acting. Being seen as a saleable commodity and nothing else can lead to confusion and frustration for a number of actors.

The Diagnosis

Do you know what happens when you snap your fingers? Just before you begin to snap it the second time you relax. If you would sustain the amount of contraction and tension it takes to snap your fingers, you would tire ever so quickly. The only way you are able to snap consecutively is by snap, relax, snap, relax. You cannot snap your fingers and make it last. Just think about this: Do you realize that just before each snap you had to relax your hand? If you didn't, you could not continue for long, and that's the definition of a *sustained performance*. You can't clap your hands and make it last. When an audience applauds, they're doing one of the best acting exercises you could ever do. They clap once, twice, three times, and the longer they sustain it, the longer we call it your ovation. We sometimes say, "The applause lasted for two minutes," when in fact it only lasted as long as it took to clap your hands once. The applause started and stopped continuously for two minutes. That's all it lasted, then it was repeated, then it was repeated, and then it was repeated. We want to walk with you. We want to be there with you when you are in a sustained performance because it is so exciting. Acting is when words are coming from our mouths, our thoughts, our hearts, and our passion. As we have said, sustaining a performance is beginning again. When you do a performance and you know something wonderful is happening, you grab hold of it like the person applauding. This is why actors who are very experienced seem to go on forever. They don't hold your attention, they grab it continuously. An actor must go to great lengths to reach this level of performance to have the ability to begin again. It takes a lifetime of dedication.

Food for Thought

There are a lot of exercises that are similar because everybody came to the same conclusion. They came to these conclusions not because they were stealing from each other and not because they learned from each other, but because in Germany, France, Russia, and the United States we have similar exercises. That's just the nature of the beast and everyone who looked at acting closely recognized that. There are some exercises that are universal, no matter the language. It is possible to see a great performance in any country, in any city, in any town in the world, so great artists can exist anywhere.

Food for Thought

The Group Theatre, Moscow Art Theatre, Actor's Studio, as well as several other significant schools never charged anything, or if they did it was nominal for the participants. Isn't it significant that we tout these schools as being among the greatest schools in the history of acting? As Elia Kazan points out in regards to the formation of the Actor's Studio, "We want a common language so that I can direct actors instead of coach them. It's not a school. Actors can come and actors can go. It's a place to work and find this vocabulary."[115] A center that does not charge can say and do what it wants. It is not tied to a rigid set of rules where it has to constantly look for ways to pull actors in. It is able to pick and choose amongst the finest actors and most committed actors it can find. It is therefore in a position to experiment and build on any foundation it chooses at any point in time. If a project falls on its face, then so be it, because it is not charging the actors in the first place. A school that relies on income from its actors cannot afford for this to happen, and therefore may choose to play it safe and not take any unnecessary risks. We are not saying that actors should not be charged for training in their craft, but what is interesting is that when money becomes the primary motivator of the studio, theatre, or school, it is always the craft of acting that suffers the most.

Final Thoughts

The moment you start you have infinite possibilities. Once you have started and every second after that you have limited your choices. We have never liked the common usage of the term *choice* because it usually means we watch an actor decide on something. We've always thought the word choice should mean that it is exciting to see an actor each time they realize the infinite possibilities of a moment. Choice usually means that they have chosen one possibility. We don't want to see an actor ever choose one possibility. We want to see an actor realize the infinite possibilities of a moment. It's like seeing someone at an intersection and being excited when they decide which way to turn. Isn't it far more exciting to watch them struggle because they could go in any direction and they realize they have got all of these possibilities? Once they have made the choice, it is all over, and there is nothing more to see. You should always realize what you have done after you do it. If you decide on doing it, by the time you begin to do it, it's all over. The audience is interested in the search. You walk around the stage looking for diamonds, and we are so excited because we know you are going to find one because you are known for finding gems. The moment you find it, we are so excited we can't stand it. If you want to keep us in that state of excitement you have to throw it away quickly and start looking again. You didn't choose to find it, you chose to look for it. All moments are tiny components of other moments, and all actions are made up of these.

63. Sounds

Food for Thought

Here is a little story about American parents who decided to take a vacation to Italy with their son. As they get off the plane the boy says something in Italian to someone, and the parents say, "Isn't that cute! He picked up a couple of words on the plane." As they go to baggage he says a couple more words in Italian and they say, "Wow, he's a very quick learner." And then they get in a cab and, struggling with giving directions to the cab driver, realize that the little boy is able to tell the driver everything in Italian. Now the family begins to get a little perplexed and mystified. Then they get to the hotel and the little boy sees a little Italian boy, he goes over, and the two of them just start carrying on in Italian and having a great time. The parents now look at each other and say, "I am worried. There is something wrong with him!" The parents turn to the boy and say, "It's very nice that you can do that, but when we get home don't speak Italian anymore because people will think you are weird and won't understand." Young actors who find that they are different and have different interests face enormous pressures just to fit in with everyone else and give up their "idiotic" dreams. Think about your friends, your family, and all of the people you meet who encourage you to give up your dreams of becoming or staying an actor.

---

115. David Garfield, *The Actor's Studio* (New York: Macmillan Publishing Company, 1984), 54.

Food for Thought

We want you to read interviews with great actors in magazines, newspapers, and online. It is not what they say that is the most important part, it is that they remind you about acting. Take advantage of the vast amount of resources around you.

The Ingredients

Take a monologue or scene and simply put sounds into it wherever you feel they are appropriate. Instead of going through a script and looking for sounds such as *ah ha, mmmm, ooooh, shhhh, huh, hahaha,* you are going to add them in by yourself. First of all, do the monologue without adding the sounds. The second time, add the sounds in so it will go something like this, "Haha, so who's tying you down, mmmm? Just because your nurse mmmm puts you in a wheelchair, doesn't mean you have to sit in it, huh?"

ACTOR: You add the sounds anywhere you want?

PAUL: Yes, I'm adding the sounds anywhere I want. "The cab let me out in front of it yesterday, huh. Artificial arms ooooh, legs ahhhh hanging in the window ehhhh." Just have fun with it because those sounds are in your head.

Another piece you can do for this exercise is to write down as many different sounds as you can that you make. Make sure that you write them a little larger than usual and leave a gap between each one. Now take some scissors and cut out each sound, scrunch it up, and throw it on the floor. Pick them up in a random order and start your monologue and force yourself to make that sound somewhere in your monologue in the order that you have picked them up. Pretty soon you will find that it becomes logical.

Another part to this exerciseis to watch television (I say television because you can do this on your own without bothering other people) and start answering the actor talking with sounds. You will find it is very easy, and you will surprise yourself at the sounds that come out of you. Think about how often you reply to a person by simply using sounds.

Food for Thought

An acting class is not a performance class, it is a laboratory. In a laboratory you diagnose, treat, and investigate. You don't want to bring in friends and relatives into an acting class. It is not the place for the actor to be influenced and affected by an outsider.

Food for Thought

At one time I managed a famous actress who was playing opposite a famous actor and I negotiated a contract that said her name had to appear anywhere his name appeared concerning the show. You want to build a capable and efficient team in your corner.

The Diagnosis

We should remember that words are indications of sounds because notes on a score are indications of sounds. In music, the note doesn't tell you exactly the pitch or higher or lower. All is relative and it can change. If there are four quarter notes in a row there is no guarantee that each one will get exactly the same amount of time, even if by definition they should. Some actors can take any sound ever made or ever written down and make it interesting. But that's not the point. The writer didn't say you have to say that sound, it is just an indication. Is laughing hahaha, or is it hehehe? Why is it, then, that you feel the need to say verbatim sounds such as *huh* rather then letting something just come out of you? This exercise gets you used to making sounds. If someone asks you if you want to go out for a coffee you may reply, "Mmmmhmmmm," without uttering a coherent word and you are completely understood. Each person makes their own individual sounds. It is also interesting that as you add in these sounds you may find that they are strangely enough making great sense to you. These sounds seemed to give the dialogue a more natural slant because we do incorporate sounds all the time when we are talking or listening to others. What we do when we start acting is look at a word and forget all the potential sounds around them. We are surrounded by sounds, we answer as often with sounds as we do with words. An actor should be able to use sounds to develop a part as long as the sounds are not distracting. You may say, "I can't remember an actor ever making a sound," because it fits so much into the performance. Now when you go back and watch you will notice they do make sounds.

Food for Thought

A very well-known, seasoned actress was working on a famous series. The woman playing her mother was a very fine actress who had done a great deal of stage work and was very experienced. During the shoot, each time she would try something a little different. This show had a dozen or so writers. Finally, the seasoned actress went over and said, "I think what you are doing is wonderful. You are looking for new ways and new ideas, but I must tell you not to do this. If you got a laugh the first time, the director, the producer, the writers expect you to do it exactly the same every time. If you don't do that, they will change the line, fix it, and take the line away from you. They have very little time, and a very tight shooting schedule, and once they see what they like, they want it exactly the same way when they film it. If you don't do that, they will eventually cut more and more of your lines until eventually you have very little to do. In some cases they will simply cut your part out." This is all done in a matter of one or two days. Some of her lines were indeed cut, and then very quickly she took the advice of the seasoned actress. Your passion and love for the craft of acting can be meshed with your thorough understanding of the industry of acting.

Food for Thought

If you want to work in London, Hollywood, or New York, you have to go there! Famous movie stars may have come from Oregon, Texas, Cincinnati, Australia, or Spain, but the point is they got up and moved to these cities. The big thing is that you have to make the leap of faith. You may end up moving to one of these big cities because you find that you fit in there. As Augusten Burroughs explains, "Glittering in the distance of my mind, was New York City. It seemed to me that New York was the place where misfits could fit in."[116]

Final Thoughts

We don't know about all languages, but when a person makes sounds as you speak to them, they are signaling to you that they have your complete attention. It's amazing how many sounds we make and how many sounds we receive from others and we don't even acknowledge it. Next time you are out, observe how may different sounds you, the person you are with, the people sitting at the next table, and people walking beside you make. Observe how they communicate with these sounds. If you hear children playing, you will hear them squealing and making all kinds of sounds. They are not even talking to each other, and yet they are having a complete dialogue just in sounds. Again, we want to get back to that full-function of the body. Before we had language we communicated with sound. Language is an advance or a sophistication, and sophistication means artful deceit. In sounds we usually cannot lie. In words we can always lie. When a person makes a sound in response to what you are doing or in response to what they are observing, it's usually exactly what they mean and what they are feeling. When they make sounds as a response, it's really coming from their most primordial self. We are told as a child, "Stop making those sounds!" We wonder if we are taught that, will we ever tell anybody exactly what we are feeling? Antonin Artaud saw that words lead to a constriction of thoughts. He explains that, "Words carried with them fixed meanings. And meaning could not be fixed. To liberate meaning, you had to free thoughts from words."[117]

---

116. Augusten Burroughs, 316.
117. Gabriela Stoppelman, 13.

64. The Maybe Exercise

Food for Thought

A very famous silent movie director was the first one to cut pictures together. He took a lady tied to a railway track, then he cut to a train, and then he cut to a man on horseback. When he did it people saw no relationship between the pictures. In other words, there is a great deal in theatre and film we are taught to see. It is the technique of motion pictures, not acting. We know someone is acting when the audience doesn't have to be taught anything. It is the work of our predecessors that still influences the worlds of theatre and film today.

Food for Thought

Theatre was using movie techniques before movies were invented. When an actor on-stage really demands your specific attention, you don't see things out of the corner of your eye, which is a close-up. When there are fifteen people on-stage and we are only focused on two of them, that is called a two-shot. We sometimes make cuts on-stage when the main action is happening downstage left and in the meantime some people are leaving upstage right and you don't even see them leave the stage. There are those who believe there are only differences between theatre and film and yet the similarities are numerous.

The Ingredients

This is a very simple exercise on how to speak to yourself. When you are doing a scene or monologue, set aside time to be by yourself and say to yourself something like, "I'm going to walk this way and maybe I'll hop on one foot. I'm going to open the door here and maybe I'll close it." Play around with your scene using the word "maybe" as a precondition. Every time you use the word maybe it stretches your imagination because it gives you an infinite number of alternatives. If you say, "This character must do this," then you are not in search of anything, you are limiting yourself. If you say, "Maybe the character is doing this, I'd never thought of that," now you are open to anything. If you don't like the direction you have been given by the director, a very good way to get through that instead of fighting in your mind or fighting with them is to go off by yourself and don't look at it as if it was direction or as if they have told you what to do. Simply say to yourself, "Maybe they want me to do this." Granted, you know what they have asked you to do, but don't say that, say, "Maybe they want me to do this." You will find that it becomes an alternative action for you rather than their idea, and it now becomes your idea. The mind is as amazing as it is complex. Think about the person who is always saying, "I can't" compared to the individual who says, "anything is possible." Both create tangible realities in their own lives based on this.

Food for Thought

Acting is ultimately experience. It is not taking a class or reading a book. It is experience on-stage, in front of a camera, in front of an audience. That's what acting is. As Richard Boleslavsky says, "Unfortunately it is acquired by long, hard work, at great expense of time and experience."[118] The more you understand about your craft the better. Michael Checkhov describes the experience of acting by saying, "It is evening, after a long day, much work and many impressions, experiences, actions, and words, you let your tired nerves rest."[119]

Food for Thought

You may feel a camera technique class is the real thing, but it is not. It is a guarded situation and an opinionated situation. It has none of the pressures or immediate needs of the moment of a real film or television show. A professional actor is someone who is performing on-stage

118. Richard Boleslavsky, 28.
119. Michael Checkhov, 21.

or on-camera. A student actor is someone who is not performing on-stage or on-camera. Even if she is the best actor in the class and a scriptwriter comes and says, "That's wonderful. I want you for my next movie." Or the producer comes and says, "We want to build a series around you." Until that series is made or until that movie is made, you are a student actor.

So why go to class? You go to class to learn technique. A beginning actor will say, "Whenever you are ready." A professional actor will say, "I was ready years ago." When you do a scene in an acting class it should make you a better actor. It should not simply make the scene better. If the scene gets better and you didn't become a better actor, then you didn't learn anything. Every class should make you a better actor until you become a good actor. There is such a thing as a good acting class, there is such a thing as a professional student, and the professional student will never have an acting career as long as they are a professional student.

The Diagnosis

The way we talk to ourselves is influenced by the way we have been spoken to. The way we speak to ourselves is so terribly limiting. We have to find, at all stages of our career, a way to talk to ourselves that allows us the greatest freedom. In life, many people tell us what to do and we either do it because we want to, we admire them, or we're frightened by them. We don't do it just because it's an alternative. We do it for reasons such as, "I'll lose my job if I don't. They won't like me if I don't," and so on. There are many things we do without a sense of freedom, but rather with a sense of obligation. "Maybe" is not a hesitant phrase for an actor, it's a place from which you have unlimited choices. There has to be a sense of humor in acting. A great way to have a sense of humor is to say to yourself, when given direction, "Maybe I thought of that, maybe I wrote this script." The word maybe is of use because it is non-confrontational, and it also gives us infinite choices. We are working to be beyond the fears, the beliefs, the hopes, and the laws of any society. This is because we are going to have to play characters from all walks of life.

Food for Thought

Acting (creating a part) rests heavily on courage. Stay around people who strengthen your courage. Make a conscientious effort, even a plan, to avoid others who may weaken you as much as possible. Insight into the character is best when it is not self-conscious. Too much thought often confuses and weakens courage. Hamlet says, "Thus conscience (thought) doth make cowards of us all." Create your world around like-minded people. Negative influences could sabotage everything you have worked so hard to accomplish.

Food for Thought

Every great acting teacher was ultimately teaching the same thing. It's a foolish thing to try to pick the best technique without exploring all, because in their own way they all have the same goals. They were all trying to get the most effective thing between the audience and the actor. When Meyerhold was asked about his work in comparison with Stanislavski's he said, "Like the builders of a tunnel under the Alps: he is coming from one side, and I from the other, but somewhere in the middle, inevitably we must meet."[120] All great acting teachers are investigating acting, and each one has something to say or put on the table.

Final Thoughts

This is the simplest exercise of all the exercises in the book. When we are told to do something we equate independence and maturity with the ability to say, "No!" Every time we are told to do something a little voice in the back of our head says, "No, I want do that." If someone says, "Do you think maybe you could do me a favor?" Suddenly they've

---

120. David Allen, 102.

approached us and given us a choice. It is a very simple thing. Tell yourself that maybe you'll do it and maybe you'll do it. Tell yourself you must do it and chances are you won't. The word "maybe" creates opportunity, whereas the word "no" can only lead to an ending or a conclusion without a chance to reevaluate.

65. Inner Dialogue

Food for Thought

Actors have to stimulate themselves in every way of the world. We seem to think that the way an actor becomes a character is to immerse themselves in the character. That may be true, but I think it may be as far from the truth as we can possibly get. As Allan Rich explains in regards to Stanislavski, "Despite three books plus many essays and papers, he still considered his work incomplete at best."[121] The teacher is always searching, and the great actor is always searching.

Food for Thought

What does an actor do for a living? They compose a character, and it's a very difficult thing to do. Having a fully accessible instrument will increase your potential to do this.

The Ingredients

Inner dialogue or silent dialogue is when you are listening to someone and you are thinking very actively of all kinds of questions, answers, and comments. You are concentrating on what they are thinking and how they are feeling because of your character, because of the immediate situation, and how you feel because of what they are saying. What we would like you to do is say two or three lines out loud from a script of your choice. It is preferable that it is a character you will never play again in your life. Then we want you to do the lines again, but this time we would like you to paraphrase or improvise the lines. Then we would like you to do the lines for a third time, only this time say them in your own words as the character's inner monologue so they are not the actual lines. Say what the character is thinking. For instance, let us say the line is, "I always worry that people are not going to like me when I go to a party." Inner dialogue would be, "You know what, I'm lying. I never worry about it, I love to go to parties and I'm trying to get your attention and I'm trying to get you to like me and so there is this thing I do where I attempt to look really meek and humble." It is preferable that you say the inner dialogue in your head or silently. When you are speaking, you are also alternating between the words you are saying out loud and the inner dialogue you are saying silently. If you are alternating with a partner you can do the inner dialogue out loud if you prefer. The words you say out loud are those written by the playwright or screenwriter and the words you say silently are the words written by you. The inner dialogue is stimulated by the part, the character, and the play. In other words, you are not writing a separate play.

PAUL: What I want you to do is just read the first few lines of this dialogue.

ACTOR: Do you ever kind of get a sick feeling in the pit of your stomach when you dread things? Gee, I wouldn't want to miss a party for anything.

PAUL: Keep saying the character's inner dialogue out loud. *(The inner dialogue is done out loud because PAUL is working with the actor.)*

ACTOR: Sometimes I get a kind of sick feeling in my stomach and I feel kind of queasy and kind of nervous at parties.

PAUL: Did you think it would make people dislike you or make fun of you?

ACTOR: Yeah, I felt like perhaps I wasn't as good as them.

---

121. Allan Rich, *A Leap from the Method* (Indiana: Authorhouse, 2007), 52.

PAUL: Did you think that people would think you were foolish or crazy?

ACTOR: Yeah, I felt a little of that.

PAUL: Did you know you integrated some of the text in your inner dialogue?

ACTOR: I was not aware I was doing that ...

There are a lot of people for whom this exercise does not come easily, and yet this is a very important exercise for you to do. Earlier we asked you to choose a character that you would most likely never play again in your life. This is because a script can be very fragile, very delicate. As you work with this exercise, have two or three different scripts that you can work with in this fashion. These will become your practice scripts rather than ones you are working on for a part. Some other suggestions for this exercise are to use material from newspapers or comic books. A comic book would be very good because the material is very immediate, simple, and to the point. It is good to work with things that are not very dense or full of great discovery, but they are rather easy to work with.

This exercise highlights the fact that we all have inner dialogue going on inside of us most of the time, and so do your characters.

Food for Thought

We have worked with novice actors and said, "No, you must do this!" And we fought and they won. And when the very young beginning actor wins, we leave them alone. When they don't do anything we tell them to do and they are wonderful, we say, "Do it that way." Acting is a greater reality.

Food for Thought

If you get the opportunity to go to perform or study in other countries, then do so. Even if you had a great teacher in New York, they cannot give you England. They cannot give you that group of actors. If you get to do a Broadway show or a show in the West End of London, you will know what it feels like. Another actor may say, "I didn't want to do that!" When really what they are saying is, "I don't know, I never did it." When you take these opportunities you are able to say, "Oh, I see, that's what they are talking about. It's such a world, and I can see it, too." Take every opportunity you can, and create every opportunity you can.

The Diagnosis

It's fun to think that the screenwriter or playwright, whether by design or not, has allowed the actor to write a great deal of the inner dialogue because each actor writes different dialogue, and each actor comes up with a somewhat different performance. The difference in those performances is often called talent, whether it be greater or lesser. The actor writes this silent or inner dialogue, and they are two different things and they are often two of the same things. Silent dialogue is dialogue that crosses through your mind as you are listening or talking to someone. There are words in dialogue that cross your mind constantly. This is not necessarily the case for the non-actor. Think about when a teacher says, "Pay attention!" What they are doing is sensing that other things are crossing your mind and they are saying, "I don't want anything other than what I am saying to cross your mind." You practice not allowing anything to cross your mind. If you study meditation, you are taught that the perfect state of being is one of stillness where nothing crosses your mind. We are fans of meditation and that may be a perfect state of being, but then acting is not the perfect state of being.

In this exercise you will have all of this dialogue crossing your mind and it will create body language, activity, and an aura about you. You become more interesting for the audience to watch, and it is actually more interesting for you. It creates a constant involvement with you. Believe us when we say a great listener is one who has a great deal crossing their mind while you're talking to them. You know that a person is listening to you because you are reading the dialogue coming back to you through body language. Great actors often ask for a script long before the first rehearsal so that they can exhaust it. They know that when all of this dialogue is happening it makes their whole being more interesting and fuller.

The inner dialogue, or silent dialogue, is one of the most important things in acting. When you are thinking subtext it is either the words of the writer leading you or your own imagination leading you. It also exercises the ability to alternate between two things. Remember, we can only think of one thought at a time, but if we go between thoughts quite rapidly, it will appear as if we are thinking these thoughts at the same time. When we alternate between all of our different thoughts rapidly, that is what we call subtext. Subtext can also come by need. Suddenly the actor opposite you has forgotten his line. Suddenly the actor across from you has discovered something new about his character. They haven't changed their costume, they haven't changed the dialogue, the staging is the same, but they have done something so different than they've ever done that it startles you, it almost throws you. What has happened is that they have thought a new thought and you recognize that. It can startle you so much that it can happen that you forget your line. Your body and mind has to have the ability to alternate between thoughts so rapidly that when that happens, you are now able to select how to take care of it. This exercise gives you the stuff to work with and the technique to work with the stuff. It is not enough to just have the ingredients, you have to have the ability to put the ingredients together. You can integrate this exercise into your day-to-day life and do it anywhere at anytime.

Food for Thought

Some actors say, "I want to be an English actor because everybody knows that English actors know more about acting than Americans." Or, "I want to be like the American actors because everybody knows the Americans have more passion for acting." This is absolute hogwash! You mean Anthony Hopkins doesn't have passion? You mean that Meryl Streep is not as technical or as intellectual as any other actor in the world? We hear these things all the time and we simply choose to ignore them. Great actors come from all over the globe and their work has a global reach.

Food for Thought

The biggest mistake actors ever do in acting class is not learn how to act. They learn how to do everything else. They learn how take a picture, write a resumé, network, and learn who the top casting directors are, but they don't learn how to act! All these things are necessary alongside your acting, not instead of.

Final Thoughts

If you have trouble understanding the difference between the words the character is saying and the words they're thinking, then remember a time you were talking with someone and they said to you, "I hear what you are saying, but I don't believe you." Or think about when you have said to yourself, "I hear what they're saying, but it seems to me they're saying something else and I can't quite figure out what it is." The *what it is* is their inner dialogue. The *what it is* is the true thing they are saying. What's real is what you are thinking. It's more real than even what you know you are thinking. You're not always aware of your own reality. You have to guide the body to give that reality to an audience. People spend a good deal of time and money to be trained to stop thinking. Meditation is one example of this. What this tells us is that in all likelihood your character is constantly thinking their inner dialogue even if as the actor you have very few lines.

Chapter 14:
Mirror Neurons

66. Back to Back

Food for Thought

When you go to a party sometimes you are drawn to another person in the room because there is a tension between you. We should call it *attention* because you suddenly become aware of them, and they of you. You should be able to create this feeling with everybody, and great actors do.

Food for Thought

Walk behind someone in the street or in the mall and see if you can fall in line with their rhythm and their stride. See if you can adapt to what they are doing. If they become aware of you, move on.

The Ingredients

For this exercise we would like you to stand back to back with a partner. Push your back against each other and put your feet out a little bit so that you can support each other. What we want you to do is move towards the ground together so that you end up in a sitting position. Ideally, your butts are touching when you reach the ground. Once you have reached the ground we want you to get back up together.

ACTOR 1: Can I put my hands on the floor to push back up?

PAUL: You can put your hands on your knees for support. *(ACTORS make it to the floor.)* Let me have you two stand up, and this time I want you to say the thought process that is going on as you work. Say everything you are thinking, everything that can help you.

ACTOR 1: I am bending my knees a little more.

ACTOR 2: Shall I carry on down?

ACTOR 1: Can you slow down a bit because I'm going to fall.

ACTOR 2: OK.

ACTOR 1: My legs are burning a little.

ACTOR 2: I feel fine.

PAUL: The more you work this exercise the more you can refine it. Do the exercise again, and this time you cannot speak out loud, the talking is now done through your body language. If something is not working, pause for a moment and regroup.

GAVIN: You must take as much time as is needed.

Food for Thought

If you study with a very good acting teacher, we do not believe it is possible for them to teach you without diagnosing, prescribing, and adjusting to you. If you go to a class or school in which it is laid out what you do from day-to-day, moment-to-moment, if the moments that you meet are not adapted to the needs of that actor and that group of actors, then it is, by definition, a bad school. All it is doing is being a free clinic that gives aspirin for everything. Any exercise in this book or any other may be very different if a teacher worked with you because they would have to adapt it to you. Learning from experience can be just as good as learning with a teacher. It can be just as good – no better, no worse – and anybody that tells you that you can't is denying thousands of years of famous actors who never went to school. Acting schools, in terms of the history of acting, have only been around for a relatively short period of time. We have been in the presence of world famous actors who have said they never trained in any acting school or program. However, what stands out is the caliber of actors and directors they had the opportunity to work with throughout their careers. In other words, they were in acting school almost every day of their lives, they just called it by another name.

Food for Thought

Questions become vanity if they become, "How do I get attention? How do I get known from this person? What can I get from this person?" The hardest thing in the world is to ask a proper question.

The Diagnosis

In this exercise you are asked to stay as connected to your partner as possible, and that is one of the biggest things in acting. This is a diagnostic exercise. You have to know how to diagnose the situation for yourself and then use what is available to you. The director is not your teacher. They should encourage you to do what you do. Because of the close proximity to your partner, you are also learning to build up familiarity with intimacy. There always has to be a minute in acting class or rehearsal when you are diagnosing yourself. As you move towards the floor simultaneously you are doing billions of computations. Saying the thoughts out loud is more for training purposes, and once you get good at this exercise you shouldn't have to do this because you should automatically be making the necessary adjustments. The point is that when you are in a movie or a play you cannot say out loud that they need to adjust. You will have to find a way to get done what needs to be done.

PAUL: Tell us about how this exercise felt.

ACTOR 1: It felt really smooth and we landed well.

ACTOR 2: I actually didn't feel that stable. I thought I was going to fall.

PAUL: You may not get offended in any way by what she just said. If you do, which tends to happen, you have to say, "Let that pass." When he said, "It felt very stable," you can't say to yourself, "It didn't feel stable to me!" You have to say, "Let that pass." When you got up you took care of yourself, but you didn't make enough adjustments for her. And when you got up you did the best you could, but it burnt your legs. What we want to accomplish is a balance in this exercise where you take care of yourself and your partner. If you watch great actors, they won't work with somebody who won't take care of themselves. When you are right in the middle of the exercise, that is the fabulous stuff because you are learning about your own instrument and you are learning about what you know and what you don't know.

ACTOR 1: I found that you have to have give and take.

ACTOR 2: When you're not able to talk, the pausing really helps you to make the necessary adjustments.

GAVIN: What we don't know or don't understand we simply let pass.

Food for Thought

A colleague of mine was elected as deputy of the union. His job was to ask the questions that came from its members to the board. He did a very clever thing when he said, "I am going to write down your complaints and then we will address them one by one." So he had all the questions in front of him and read them out loud, one by one, to the members. As he would read them out they would say things like, "That's not a good question, that's a waste of time, and we know the answer to that." Out of one hundred questions they ended up with two. As you begin to ask a better form of a question you will save yourself a lot of time. You will be able to gear your energy into the direction it is needed the most.

Food for Thought

We hear actors all the time say, "She is playing against type." We say, "What are you talking about *against type?*" That's like saying you can't do Bach on a piano because it's against type. Bach was not written for piano. That is not against type, it is just a different instrument. You have to have the ability to evolve into any character. Evolution may take place over thousands of years, but for the actor it has to potentially be available in any given moment.

Final Thoughts

You have to take this exercise moment-by-moment in the same way you work a scene moment-by-moment. The better you get at acting the more parts of your body and mind will respond to the moment.

67. Connections

Food for Thought

If you didn't image yourself as an actor when you were very young, or if you can't remember imaging yourself as an actor, chances are you won't be an actor. You don't know why you want to be an actor, but you do know that you image it. I knew an actress who said, "I used to go into my bedroom as a child and watch the Tony Awards and cry because I wasn't there." She won a Tony. One has to ask oneself, "How obsessed with acting am I?"

Food for Thought

Actors get to do things that no one else on earth gets to do. Actors commit sins on-stage and screen so that you can see the consequences of that sin. You didn't in reality do what you did on-stage or screen, but your nervous system doesn't necessarily know that. Every thought, every breath, every movement, every utterance has a chemical response.

The Ingredients

For the following three exercises you are going to need a partner.

Part 1

What we would like you to do is to stand facing your partner and be palm to palm. Now slowly start moving your arms around simultaneously in different directions with your palms constantly touching. One of you should start as the leader and at some point you can switch. The next step would be to change the leader intuitively simply by using give and take. While it is your arms that are doing the majority of the movement, the rest of your body can be moving back and forth while you keep your feet on the same spot. It is OK to lift your heels off the ground if you like.

Part 2

Stand back to back with your partner and lean against each other with your backs touching. As you lean against each other try to stay in a comfortable, normal stance. Try not to adjust too much to the other person, but be yourself. Now one of you takes control by very, very slowly walking forwards, while the other partner will be moving backwards. Your backs should stay connected all the time, and there should be a certain tension between your bodies. Until you get the hang of it, walk only two or three steps together around the room in any direction. Later, see if you can go for a couple of minutes.

PAUL: *(Works with an actor.)* There is, at all times, a kind of give and take. Now you take control, now I'll take control. I can feel where your weight is. If you take your time you will actually find that you are moving with opposite feet from one another. This exercise is not an intellectual thing, just go with it. We obviously are not able to look at each other and this exercise is a difficult thing to do. It is easy to get off balance by being impatient with this exercise.

Part 3

Now we are going to have you do an exercise that is done with tango dancers. Turn and face your partner and lean in so that you are touching chest to chest. You can both allow your arms to rest by your sides. Each of you should also have your head leaning over your partners opposing shoulder. Now one of you is going to lead while the other one follows, always staying chest to chest and pushing against each other. You need to lean in more so that you are virtually off balance against one another.

GAVIN: In order to get the most out of these exercises you have to begin with give and take. Eventually there has to be a feeling of symmetry between the two of you.

ACTOR: I could feel myself losing contact.

PAUL: It is not the leaning but the tension between you that allows this exercise to work.

Food for Thought

One of the problems in acting is that actors will settle for simply being better. This may be out of frustration, desperation, hurt feelings, or pride. If they are told they are better, they go, "Wow!" If you are a good actor or a great actor and someone says to you, "That's better!" it would almost make you want to sock them. If you can't imagine saying this to a great actor, why would you say it to a student? It's a non-professional language. Can you imagine being a passenger on a plane and the pilot says, "I'm not very good at flying, but I'm getting better." Don't settle for this in your acting.

Food for Thought

Name one actor who's famous that doesn't think about what they look like. The young star who wears jeans half tucked in half tucked out and you're going to tell me he didn't put that together, that it was accidental? Your uniqueness is not *one* of your selling points, it *is* your selling point, because it is who you are without the façade.

The Diagnosis

In the back to back exercise the actors are asked not to adjust their bodies too much but to be themselves because otherwise they may become confused, limited, or resentful. In a performance, if you can really partner with another actor and make only little adjustments, then you can bring fully how much you have to the role. These exercises are not so much about concentration as they are about giving up concentration and thinking. If you can't think, then you have nothing left but to be right in that moment. These exercises give you a great deal more awareness of your own body, and they help you to access your own body for yourself. When you work the exercise chest to chest we have all kinds of social issues, physical issues, and sexual issues. This exercise is excellent in enabling you to break down barriers and inhibitions, which is imperative for you as an actor.

GAVIN: There will be times in your life when you will be working with another actor who refuses to or is incapable of working alongside you.

PAUL: That is not going to make or break your performance. Who are you doing this for?

ACTOR: Myself.

PAUL: No.

ACTOR: The audience.

PAUL: That's right. You are doing this with the audience. There is no great performer. There is no one who does not engage their audience. If it's not this, it's not acting. In these exercises your partner has to push against you, and we can call that push interest in what you are saying.

Food for Thought

Actors very often prepare very complicated back stories of details about the character. It never crosses their minds to prove one of those details. By proving the details the back story can be limitless and ever-changing.

Food for Thought

What does it mean to ask an actor, "What are you doing to pursue your acting career?" Johann Goethe puts it quite succinctly, "An actor's career develops in public, but his art develops only in private."[122] Some actors will get defensive and angry because you are asking a question that is very logical, obvious, simple, and to the point. Most actors know that they are not spending anywhere near enough time to pursue this goal, and so it embarrasses them. As David Mamet says, "Those of you with nothing to fall back on, you will find, are home."[123] It is not uncommon to hear terms like, "I'm taking a break. I'm waiting for my headshots first. I want to start by finding an agent." It is not only a form of procrastination, but it also allows the actor to feel good about what they are doing while in reality very little is getting accomplished.

Final Thoughts

Balance, by definition, is when there is an equal amount on either side or all around a center. When you are in balance you have the greatest potential. If you don't, you have stress or you have one side pulling against another. An actor has to find the balance during every performance in regards to their fellow actors. When there is a leader and a follower, or a follower and a leader, there is not balance. The only time there is balance between two actors is when the actors themselves, as well as the audience, cannot tell who is leading and who is following. We develop these simple exercises so that eventually the actors themselves, through their own sensitivity, cannot determine who is leading and who is following. It is at this point they can realize the potential of their own thoughts and their own creativity. Or as Camus said, "Don't follow, I may not want to lead. Don't lead, I may not want to follow. Walk beside me." In order to walk beside your fellow actor you have to be an actor.

68. Mirror Endowment

Food for Thought

We are all so busy in life that we don't get anything done, but we do get things done that we think we have to. We spend three times more time getting things done that we absolutely have to than we should. Then we don't get anything else done, especially in regards to our acting. Sometimes an actor will use everything else they have to do as an excuse as to why they don't have time to work on their acting or their career.

Food for Thought

Questions are not asked for the answers, they are asked to get you thinking. Sometimes we care about the answers, but just as often we don't care what you are thinking about. We just care that we got you thinking. There are results but before this are the steps that got you there.

---

122. Kathryn Marie Bild, *The Actor's Quotation Book,* (New Hampshire: Smith and Kraus, 2003), 7.
123. David Mamet, *True and False* (New York: Vintage Books, 1997), 36.

The Ingredients

Observed Exercise

PAUL: To start with, I would like you to tell me the name of an actress who you aspire to? *(A famous actress is mentioned here.)* Do you think she is versatile enough to do just about anything, capable of doing just about any role?

ACTOR: Yeah.

PAUL: I want you now to come up with an image of this famous actress just walking up and saying hello to you.

ACTOR: Got it.

PAUL: How are you getting that?

ACTOR: Through my imagination.

PAUL: Exactly, because you are imaging it. Imagination means to imagine, it does not mean to think up a good thought. I want you to close your eyes and get a picture of this actress. Try to do this with a clear slate without prejudging. *(ACTOR closes her eyes.)* OK, did you get a picture? Sometimes you may just get some kind of feeling about them.

ACTOR: I saw her acting out the roles of different characters.

PAUL: Good. Now I want you to close your eyes and repeat her name softly at a moderate pace, out loud, until I ask you to stop, all while keeping an image of her. *(ACTOR starts to repeat actress's name. About one minute passes.)* It got better as you went on because it got less complicated with your own thoughts. Now I want you to recite a monologue or a scene you know while keeping an image of this actress. You are not trying to be like her, but you have that image because science has taught us that when you have an image of anything, your mirror neuron will fire certain things that are not you. As Wikipedia says, "A mirror neuron is a promoter neuron which fires both when an animal acts and when the animal observes the same action performed by another animal."[124] If you are working a scene, just do your lines and not the other person's so that you can work this exercise alone. *(ACTOR performs her scene.)* Good. Here is the second part of the exercise. Can you think of an actress whose work you dislike?

ACTOR: I've got one.

PAUL: Now, get an image of this actor in your mind, their physicality, personality, what they are wearing, and where they are. Get specific.

ACTOR: I've got it.

PAUL: Now I would like you to walk to the door and back, and as you do this, I would like you to have an image of this actress whose work you don't like. I want to be very clear here in that I am not asking you to mimic their physicality or move like them. I want you to walk as you and simply have an image of them as you walk. *(ACTOR starts to walk.)* There is no need to pause at the door. Keep it moving and make it sprightly. Remember, don't try to be the actress; just be yourself. *(ACTOR comes back and sits down.)* Now I want you to get up, walk to the door, and walk back rather briskly while imagining the actress whose work you admire. *(ACTOR walks to the door and back.)* OK, when you sit back down, I want you to say the words of the scene and have an image of the actress whose work you admire. *(ACTOR starts scene and works the first half.)* OK, now I want you to do the rest of the piece, and this time have an image of the actress whose work you don't like. Remember, it is just an image, you are not trying to be her. *(ACTOR completes scene.)* I'll tell you what happened. I really saw you in both cases, and you didn't have an image of yourself. It took you a little while to get to this place, whether it was nervousness or being

---

124. Wikipedia, *Mirror Neuron.* http://en.wikipedia.org/wiki/Mirror_neuron.

self-conscious, and, by the way, you gave those up. The difference you should have had in each case was that you had a slightly different feeling, not that you made enormous discoveries.

ACTOR: I felt that especially when I was walking.

PAUL: Yes, it was apparent. Here is a golden rule: What you are learning is the difference between two things. You learn more about your feelings of both actors when you work with two images instead of one. In other words, you learned the difference between the two. You *taught* yourself the difference between the two.

GAVIN: In this regard, Robert Brustein says, "If your skin is too porous, you will not survive very well; acting does not care a fig about your feelings. If you develop too thick a protective crust, you will never be an artist."[125] We also use our mirror neurons to some degree when we build rapport with others. We often do this subconsciously, but we can also choose to do this consciously. Building rapport with others is of great benefit to the actor in audition situations and when working with other actors.

Food for Thought

Sometimes even great actors will throw up before filming or going on-stage, but they are not throwing up out of fear, they are throwing up out of excitement. There is a big difference. Throwing up out of fear paralyzes you and weakens you. Throwing up out of excitement is almost charming.

Food for Thought

The most important thing you can get from teachers who are no longer alive or teachers who are recognizably brilliant and destined to go down in history, you are not looking at what their exercises do, you are looking at their spirit. The spirit of all great teachers is the same. That's what makes them great teachers. It was the spirit that enabled them to create ever-changing exercises to solve ever-changing problems. If you preserve the spirit of great teachers you can continue to build on their discoveries, and continue to add new exercises as they would have if they had lived forever. What Stanislavski, Uta Hagen, Meisner, Meyerhold, Adler, Artaud, Strasberg, and others left us was not all they knew, but all they got to. They themselves would call it incomplete, so why do some people call it complete? Why do some actors limit themselves to an incomplete system? Exercises, like clothes, fit best when they are specifically tailored for one person. All great teachers are teaching not the technique but the needs of that particular actor. Great teachers also give exercises that are so general that the actor can tailor them to fit themselves. The more open and porous you are, the more you will be able to absorb from those around you.

The Diagnosis

If you do these exercises right, you now have an instrument that has the best possible chance of activating my interest and emotion. The most important part of the performance or audition is if you can activate our emotion and imagination. As a famous actor once said, "It is not important that the audience knows what you are thinking, it is only important that they think they know what you are thinking." What is important is that you do not become self-absorbed.

In this exercise you are asked to close your eyes and imagine a person. This is your pre-preparation. If you are at an audition you might turn away momentarily, close your eyes, and by the time you turn back, you are prepared and ready to begin. Instead of being the actor at the audition who says, "Can I have thirty seconds to prepare?" be the actor who says, "I was prepared before I got here."

---

125. Robert Brustein, 184.

What you have also discovered in this exercise is that when you have an image in your head, it changes the way you do something and the way you feel. By having two images you are able to discover the difference between the two, and this is what you learn. Provided you are prepared, this will add another facet to your work. This exercise is designed so that you can activate our emotions and interest. In this exercise you get to become familiar with an actor you dislike and an actor whose work you admire. In this exercise you get to imagine using your imagination. As Stanislavski says, "Physical bodily restraint, the taming of the anarchy of muscles, to reveal emotion in the strong places and think of nothing, to work out my own image which I was to copy and imitate."[126]

A girl I knew was doing a show at a very famous theatre. A woman came backstage and she said to my friend, "Could you tell me where the actress is who played Sally?" And my friend said, "I played Sally." And the lady said, "It couldn't have been you. She had blond hair. Were you wearing a wig?" She said, "No, I'm a brunette." The actress had imaged so clearly that the woman from the audience saw what the actress imagined, not who the actress was. This exercise shows you the power of the imagery and also to remind you that you only know the difference between two things. By working with two different actors you discovered the difference between the two. Discovering the difference between the two will give further depth to your character. We want to give you two different things and have you feel the difference. In acting there can't be a right way or a wrong way, just *a* way. If you were filming a movie yesterday and everyone said how wonderful you were and today you were filming and things were not quite right, what did you learn? You learned the difference between two things, between yesterday's performance and today's. We want you to know acting, to understand acting, not to know right and wrong. As you are going through these exercises you might think, "I want to adjust it slightly, I have a variation I would like to do." Go ahead. Remember, the exercises are for you, and you specifically. We want you to make this work your own way so that it is usable and of benefit to you. If you don't get the results, find another exercise and keep doing things until you get the results.

Food for Thought

You could be in the presence of the greatest acting teacher in the world every day for ten years and still not learn to act. Be in the presence of great actors as much as possible. Upon seeing one of the last performances by Eleonora Duse, John Gielgud commented that, "Her acting seemed very, very simple."[127] You could go to great performance after performance all of your life, never go to an acting class, and still learn as much about acting as you ever would in any class. These are strong statements and the question is not whether you believe they are true, but whether or not you believe in the possibility. When we already have preconceived ideas of what acting is and how to get there, we have closed ourselves off from possibilities and potential.

Food for Thought

For those searching for excellence, the search never ends, because no matter what they find, they're always in search of something. As Andre Van Gyseghem says, "If then, anything that you have read here prompts others to seek for further knowledge at firsthand, the main purpose of this book will have been achieved."[128] It is the purpose of this book to see you continue your search. We don't know how you can be a great artist if you don't live in this state. The reason a great artist is a great artist is because their process is to be in search. Every time they step on-set or stage they are in search. Every time they read a book they are

---

126. Constantin Stanislavski, *My Life in Art* (New York: Theatre Arts Book, 1952), 175.
127. John Gielgud, *An Actor and His Time* (New York: Applause, 1997), 17.
128. Andre Van Gyseghem, *Theatre in Soviet Russia* (London: Faber and Faber, 1943), 210.

in search. Every person in their life becomes part of their search. Everything they eat, wear, every place they go becomes part of their search. When you recognize the similarity between two things, you know that you are on the right road. Many people in life do jobs that they hate that have no meaning for them. This is highly unlikely to be true of great actors.

Final Thoughts

We know that a great deal of muscular function of the body is using muscles called flexors and extensors. We know that if we only exercise the flexors, we will eventually weaken the extensors. If you only aspire to what people have told you, you have done well in your career. If you only aspired to the actors you loved and admired and would like to be thought of, then you are only exercising half of your potential, half of your personality, and half of your imagination. While you can do this exercise with an actor you like and admire, you also want to do it with an actor whose work you don't like. Pick a scene that they have done, memorize it, and as best you can, copy them. In this way you are exercising both sides of your imagination, and you are exercising what you like and what you don't like. You are exercising your dreams of who you would like to be and the practicality of who you actually are. In this exercise do not give any thought to who you are, but who you would like to be and who you would not like to be. After doing this exercise you may find that your views have changed about the actors you chose. The reason for this is that when you have a balanced imagination, there is no part you can't or would refuse to play. When you have a balanced imagination, you are an actor. You may be cast in a role that you detest and another actor would die for. It is up to you to embrace the role and move forward.

69. Mirroring

Food for Thought

Remember, you always take bows at the end of your performance, but be careful when you take your bows — it might be the end of your career. I am not ready to take a bow for my career yet, and I probably will never be ready, because I don't want it to be over. How can acting still be interesting if it has all happened before? It can be interesting when the actor is in search of excellence. Great actors search better, they search more accurately, and they find more things than other actors. These are the people we want to hire because the producer and director recognize that actor. Great actors never stop searching, and they never stop asking questions. You may start your search on acting blindly, but there will come a point when you begin to see.

Food for Thought

Be careful if you think that you must find something different at any given moment. It can either be very dangerous or slightly amusing when an actor, director, screenwriter, playwright, or anyone connected with acting in any way says, "This has never been done before." This statement can be mildly musing, somewhat inspirational, or it can be somewhat dangerous. It stops your search for excellence. If you are doing something that has never been done before, it probably means that you have found what you were looking for. And if you have found what you are looking for, then it is all over. On the other hand, it is foolish to assume that in thousands of years of acting there is anything that any actor has done that hasn't been done before. We think one of the reasons someone says, "This has never been done before," is a matter of marketing, or they are saying, "I am better than anyone who preceded me," which is a total waste of time. Be careful of the teacher who tells you they have all of the answers. A good teacher never stops searching.

The Ingredients

PAUL: This is what you are going to do. You are going to read a few lines from this scene out loud, Actor 1, and you are going to listen to her, Actor 2. While you are listening you are mirroring to yourself, you are running it on your body. She is going to read it out loud, and then when it is your turn, you will read the same lines with your own interpretation. While that is happening, you are listening to him and you may say to yourself, "Yeah, I like the improvements and now I thought of something else." What you are doing is going back and forth mirroring each other.

ACTORS: OK.

ACTOR 1: Martha's lying, I want you to know that right now, Martha's lying. There are few things in this world that I am sure of. (Continues for another three lines.)

PAUL: OK, your turn. Now you listened to her. In your head you must have said, "This is how I think it should be done. I think she was going too fast, I think she should have paused here, and been more aggressive at this point." Now you are going to listen to him and do the same thing. Each time you are building on what the other person did.

ACTOR 2: Martha's lying, I want you to know that right now, Martha's lying. There are few things in this world that I am sure of. *(Continues for another three lines. The two ACTORS go back and forth with the scene three more rounds.)*

ACTOR 1: Martha's lying, I want you to know that right now.

PAUL: OK, now I want you to go back and forth with just that much.

ACTOR 1: Martha's lying! I want you to know that right now.

ACTOR 2: Martha's lying. I want you to know that right now. *(They go back and forth two more rounds.)*

PAUL: OK, what you are doing is listening non-judgmentally, and making the best of your worst habits. The worst habit an actor has is that they never listen to a fellow actor, they correct them. It's as if we are saying, "No, no, that's not what you meant, that's not how to say it, that's not what it means." You are doing the best of that by saying, "I kind of like that, that's a clever thing. She's doing it as if she is talking to her sister over there." As you continue your interpretation, the piece changes and grows.

ACTOR 2: It made me think that I've got a new interpretation, and I can go down this road now.

PAUL: The best part of this exercise is when you do not discuss it with the other actor until you have come to a completion.

GAVIN: An inexperienced actor will wait for their turn to speak rather than responding to what is being said. This exercise is an excellent way to have you actively listening to your fellow actor.

Food for Thought

Famous film directors and famous stage directors have said, "Cast the most talented person you can in the smallest role in the show." When it's the biggest part, the part is good, and therefore the actor can be good — they don't have to be great. When the part is not good, you need great actors in that part to balance your show. The stronger your technique, the more versatile you will be, and the more potential you will have to stay a working actor.

Food for Thought

It's a danger to think that people got work through various transgressions. There is a difference between getting a job and working in the industry. Getting a job is a onetime thing. Working in the industry is when you become a valuable commodity as an actor.

The Diagnosis

Many actors and directors don't understand each other because they think they are playing the same instrument. They think they are hearing the same things, but they are not. When you are watching really great actors and you try this exercise, there will be times when you will say, "I can't do better than that." Actors have to continuously be able to access their imagination. If your body is not stretched, strengthened, and coordinated, then it will not allow you to access your imagination to its true potential. This means you are limited by your body, not your imagination. If you are limited by your body people say, "She is not talented." This exercise encourages you to train your body to work in a non-judgmental way. It really works if you can get a partner you trust to work with. We have to tell you, you can't be an actor in a vacuum. You have to find a fellow actor who is a partner in crime. Acting is not acting until the person listening to you mirrors what you are doing. If you are watching a moving or harrowing scene, you should be so sensitive to what is happening that you almost have to leave. You may find it better to go see this type of movie on your own so that you don't have any social obligation when you see the film. You can go to a movie socially and you can go artistically.

ACTOR 1: I found that this exercise really frees me up a little bit. I feel like when I am listening I am getting out of thinking mode. It's a lot more empathetic, and the more we went back and forth the more it felt like something real as opposed to just saying words. I guess it's because I am picking up on the feelings that I'm getting from my partner. I found I was mirroring them or feeling them myself as opposed to saying words. I noticed that I was drawing on the feelings that you were giving me on your interpretation.

PAUL: Yes, by listening to your partner you began to experience it a different way yourself.

ACTOR 1: Right, exactly.

PAUL: You looked at it as a different experience.

GAVIN: You said that you felt freer. Can you expand on that?

ACTOR 1: I didn't feel like I was just saying words, I was drawing from the feelings I was getting from my partner and ingesting those myself. What came out of me the next time around, and the next time around felt a lot more ...

PAUL: Organic?

ACTOR 1: Yes.

PAUL: When you began, you knew you were being watched and you were self-conscious, and you felt you had an obligation and responsibility. When you simply took your turn you became freer because you didn't have a responsibility any more. Now, here is an interesting thing: When you read it the first time you were very self-conscious, and therefore mannered. You were sensing that you were being watched. When you started to work off your partner, it was simply your turn. When it was your turn you weren't thinking of us watching you. When you are acting in front of an audience, it is your turn. It is one thing to make the audience experience what you are doing, but for them to actually mirror you empathetically is a whole other idea. If your audience doesn't have a physical response to your acting, then you haven't reached far enough.

GAVIN: As your focus of attention shifts to the moment you are in, you have no time left over to be intimidated by an audience. Instead, you vibrate off them.

Food for Thought

Is a film the work of the actor, or the work of an editor and director? That is a dicey question. Actors have made many discoveries by asking questions and continuing to ask them.

Food for Thought

I used to take a group of actors into schools to give an example of what acting was as a technique, a profession, and an art form. By engaging the different elements that make up your acting you can develop all these areas simultaneously. I had a group of five actors, one became a famous director, one married the cop who held John Lennon as he died, and one became a famous actor. We asked the children a simple question, "What do actors use to paint?" They said, "Their bodies." We asked them, "What do they paint on?" They said, "Air and space." Then I said, "What do they measure with?" A young boy raised his hand and all the actors looked at me and looked at the boy because they didn't have a clear answer in their own mind. He said, "They measure with time." And he was absolutely right. He just overwhelmed me, and it was the most electrifying moment. We say that an actor must have good timing, and yet we have no idea what we are talking about. It's the time it takes to get from one word to another word.

Final Thoughts

Do you know that one of the main reasons people like to go to the theatre, movies, sports games, or circuses is because of mirror neurons? Simply put, when you watch somebody do something, say something, or wear something, the same neurons in your body fire as in their body and make you want to do that. When you watch a dancer do amazing things, your body is to some degree firing the neurons as though you are doing that. If you are saying famous lines from a script or play, your body is firing the neurons that cause you to say those things. If you think you know what an actor is thinking, then the neurons will form in your body. You strive as much as you can, not to listen to yourself, not to be aware of how you are speaking, and to let the audience be the recipient of that. Then you take it and use it, and put it in your thoughts. When you are watching it, your body begins to imitate not only the way you've done it, but also the way the person opposite you is doing it. Your body is saying, "Here is a more efficient way of doing it." You must know that many times people in the audience are saying, "I can do that better than the actor." Well, they couldn't because they don't have the tools to do it, but in their mind they believe they know how you could do it better. You are acting and reacting with your audience in a metaphorical sense and in a very real sense.

Chapter 15:
Intimacy and Confrontation

70. Limitless Possibilities

Food for Thought

If an acting teacher says, "Don't act," we would ask them, "Can you name one of the greatest actors you have ever known? What is it they do on-stage or film? What are they called?" They're called an actor, and what they are doing is called acting. How can we desecrate the word "acting"? We want to tell these teachers to be accurate in their terms, because if you tell an actor not to act, what are they going to do? It's like telling a violinist don't play the violin. If what you mean is don't have tension while you are acting, or your acting is external, then why not say this? The phrase, "Don't act" is dangerous to the actor because it is an oxymoron. On the one hand we tell actors to act, and on the other we tell them not to act. Teachers need to be careful how they use terms, because while they may know what they really mean, the actor may misinterpret this.

Food for Thought

Not every child is a child star. We cannot say that all child actors do it naturally as a child, because one in ten thousand does it. However, children do have an advantage, because children haven't yet been harmed by society. If they have eaten properly, been raised properly, and haven't been emotionally traumatized, then they are well-coordinated. If they have been raised in a healthy environment and are interested in performing, then they have the potential to create great performances. Living with or being around an animal is a great advantage in that it allows you to observe and engage in spontaneous action on an ongoing basis.

The Ingredients

When there are situations in your life where you feel uncomfortable, we want you to purposely follow through. This is not referring to dangerous situations, but things that make you uncomfortable that as an actor you have to get past. We also would like you to go into a quiet room by yourself and think about something that makes you uncomfortable, and then follow through with that action. You can also begin to take on roles, auditions, and scenes that you are uncomfortable with. Enable yourself to live outside your comfort zone.

Food for Thought

We've directed people we didn't like, and we've directed people who didn't like us. We put all that aside and we forgot about it. It has nothing to do with the work, and it's all about the work. Focus on what matters and let go of the rest.

Food for Thought

To see yourself as anything but an actor is to fit in with the crowd you are with. In this case, you are not being yourself, you are being the self of that group of people. When you are not causing eyebrows to rise or drawing attention, people will say you are being yourself. They will say, "You know what is so nice about you? You fit in and you are so much yourself." They think you are being yourself, but you are not. The self you are with them is the collective self of what they want you to be. You are what your instrument gives you or whatever you create.

The whole crux of this work is for you to learn to strip everything away that is unnecessary so that you can learn to be yourself. While this may sound simple, it is achieved only by dedication and constant work on your instrument. Being you is being without prejudice. It is being without opinion of right and wrong. It is being capable of being like a clear glass into which you can pour any color of water. The director or casting director wants to look at you and say, "You know what, we can pour any glass of water we want into this actor. Their instrument is so accessible." There are exercises to help you be yourself in this book and other books. If you have found the "right way" and limited your search to one *technique* or one idea, then you are limiting yourself. As Richard Bandler says, "Certainty is where people stop thinking and stop noticing. Anytime you feel absolutely certain of something, that's a sure sign you have missed something. It's sometimes convenient to deliberately ignore something for a while, but if you're absolutely certain, you'll probably miss it forever."[129]

The Diagnosis

There is not an actor in the world, unless they are very experienced, who can't say, "I'm uncomfortable doing this." Some actors don't like to yell or to cry on cue. An experienced actor who did something they were uncomfortable with but did it anyway found out one of two things: they were wrong and the director was right, or they were right and the director was wrong. They couldn't have found out either one of those things if they hadn't done it. If you are doing something that makes you feel uncomfortable, it is probably something you should address because you are an actor. Remember, as an actor you have to be able to portray the consequences of anything. Actors in a sense are a kind of warrior and have to be prepared for anything. If this exercise sounds a bit like the Cross the Line exercise or Breaking a Contract, or any other exercise, we have to remind you that when things appear to be the same, you have learned something. When things appear to be completely different, chances are you haven't learned anything. If you take a diamond and hold it up to the light, it's got facets. We are looking for all the facets that make up acting. An uncomfortable feeling reveals an undeveloped part of your talent. It points to a potential in you that has not yet been realized. What does an actor want more than to realize their own potential? These are things that we are most uncomfortable with that we cannot even think of in the presence of others. The actor must live in a world of limitless possibilities.

Food for Thought

A young actress had finished a play and was backstage when some people came back to see her, a little girl broke away from her parents, walked up to the actress, and said, "You must be a very good actor because I hated you." What a bright little girl! She understood that the person she was talking to was an actor. The actor had the confidence in herself to be somebody in the play who was not likeable.

Food for Thought

There's an expression in acting: *jumping without a net*. Well, we don't think it's wise to jump without a net, particularly if you are very high up, but we understand what the expression means. It means do something with the feeling that you are not prepared for the consequences of, and know that you will have to find a way to cope with that while you are doing it.

Final Thoughts

Let us look at the theory of the Four Es. When you are uncomfortable with something, use the four Es: examine, then embrace, then experience, and then eureka! If you are uncomfortable with something it is not saying, "beware," it is saying, "opportunity." When you are uncomfortable with something, the first thing you have to do is to witness and examine

---

129. Richard Bandler, *Using Your Brain for a Change* (Utah: Real People Press, 1985), 97.

it. The next thing you have to do is, while you are examining it, you should carefully embrace it. When you embrace it, you will begin to experience it. We have never met one actor who, after doing these things, didn't say, "I can't believe what I found out. I never would have done that!" They did it simply because they pursued something they were uncomfortable with. Sometimes it happens faster than you can say it and sometimes it takes a lifetime. What we know is that if you cease to pursue, you cease to discover.

71. Conversation with the Actor (Part 3)

Food for Thought

Gavin asked me what I thought of the idea of describing this book as an actor's companion. I responded that, in the United States, a companion refers to a person and not an object. Then I thought what a good thing it would be to have this book become something that hung around with you, that you carried around with you because you understood this book as you would understand a very close friend. This book would be somebody you could speak to as you could only speak to a very close friend. You want to be aware of the meeting place between the craft and the industry of acting.

Food for Thought

We really love when an actor is using and applying what they have learned. If you are not using it, then what is the good of it?

The Ingredients

Conversations with the actor are sometimes ten or fifteen pages of material. Because we did not think it practical to write a book of this length, each conversation has been cut significantly. Please bear this in mind as you read the following.

PAUL: What makes one actor better than another?

ACTOR: One actor explores the character and relates it to the audience in a natural way.

PAUL: Have some of your scene partners been better than others?

ACTOR: I don't judge other actors. I learn something from the other actor.

PAUL: Have you enjoyed working with one more than another?

ACTOR: *(Hesitates.)* Yes.

PAUL: OK, why do you hesitate admitting that?

ACTOR: Well, sometimes I connect more with one actor than another.

PAUL: All right, this is really important. It appears that you are not very willing to say that one actor is better than the other. Why are you not willing to give them a value judgment on the result of their craft?

ACTOR: For me, I feel I can learn from a bad or good actor.

PAUL: I don't agree with you at all. I'm going to continue to ask you the same question and you just react any way you want to. It appears to me that you are not willing to accept that there are good actors or bad actors. Why are you hesitant to give a value judgment on actors and the product they put out?

ACTOR: I feel like I don't want to judge them.

PAUL: Why are you not willing to judge an actor's worth?

ACTOR: I prefer to talk about the good parts.

PAUL: If you say you are willing to talk about good, then you are admitting that there must be something other than good. Why are you unwilling to judge actors or their technique, or the result, or anything about them?

ACTOR: That's a good question. *(Starts laughing.)*

PAUL: Why are you unwilling to judge an actor? *(This question is continually repeated throughout the session.)*

ACTOR: Who am I to judge them?

PAUL: Why are you unwilling to judge an actor?

ACTOR: Maybe I'm a spiritual person.

PAUL: Are you willing to judge a car as one being better than the other?

ACTOR: Sure, I feel it when I'm driving.

PAUL: Oh, you feel the car. I believe the thought that is crossing your mind at the moment is, "What more does he want?"

ACTOR: Yes, I don't know what else to say.

PAUL: Do you judge clothes? Do you say, "I like that dress. I don't like that dress."

ACTOR: I buy the one I like.

PAUL: Ah, then you are giving it a judgment. *(The conversation continues for another hour. Here are some of the other observations made.)* I'm going to tell you some things you said. You said, "I don't judge the other actor because who am I to judge? It's not polite, I don't want to hurt feelings, I'm not there to judge them, I'm a spiritual person, what else could I say? I'm not the other actor." About the car you said, "I use it, and I feel it." About the dress you said, "I try it on before I purchase it." I said why are you willing to judge a car? You said, "Because I use it." Well, you use your body, too. You should be judging. What's happening is you are restricting the use of yourself as an instrument. For you to work efficiently, you must be willing to judge the other actor. Two actors may work together and say to themselves, "I do not like you and I never will, but I really love what you do as an actor." You have to be willing to take these things on responsibly. Acting is a very hazardous thing.

GAVIN: During this discussion the actor had to confront her morals in terms of being an actor, because by separating one from the other her journey is being inhibited.

Food for Thought

PAUL: What are some of the challenges facing an actor in Hollywood?

ACTOR: One of them is to feel confident in yourself so that you are ready to compete for the roles and it also challenges you to create composure.

PAUL: Sometimes you walk in and there are twelve or thirteen people sitting around a table and it's challenging to keep your cool. Another challenge is that, once you have got the part, you have to be willing to show up on time, all the time, and to contribute to the project as much as possible. This sounds like a given, but there can be many long days, long hours, and a lot of waiting around. It is not all glitz and glamour that some people think. It's also a challenge to know your lines to such a degree to where you can't just forget them.

GAVIN: It is your responsibility to be prepared. There is a lot of work involved in being a good actor, so you have to ask yourself if this is what you really want, and if this is what you are prepared for.

Food for Thought

When I was very young I told a producer that I liked to talk to various artists of all types from all over the world. He asked me who I would like to meet, and I said Picasso. And he threw me entirely off by saying, "Well, what would you talk to him about?" If you had a chance to meet with your favorite actor, what would you ask them? Are you sure that you would be able to understand the answers they may give you? Do you believe your instrument is prepared enough to be able to converse on their level? I want to talk with these people because it changes me molecularly, it makes me more creative. All the great acting teachers like Stanislavski, Adler, Jehlinger, Uta Hagen, Strasberg, etc., sort out the greatest people they could find to learn from. Yes, as well as acting teachers, writers, painters, scientists, and people from all different persuasions.

The Diagnosis

PAUL: In this conversation I asked you the same question over and over, and you gave me a lot of information. You notice that I used a lot of repetition in this session. You have an urge to find something out, but you haven't found a way to ask a question to find it out yet. I kept going back to the same question because I was saying, "That is the answer and I do believe you don't like it." The pursuit of art is questions, not answers. The pursuit of art is asking more questions. The audience is always excited when they see you ask yourself a question, because when you ask yourself a good question you struggle with the answer. The longer you are in a production, the more questions you must ask yourself. I want to help you to think a different way. You are the other actor because, when you work with the other actor, you become one with the other actor. If you work on a series, or a play, or a movie, you become part of that entity. As an audience, we will judge these projects by saying, "I like the way all of these pieces fit together." This, by definition, is an ensemble, because whether you liked it or not they were in it together. In terms of the ensemble Lisa Wolford quotes Grotowski as saying, "In a recent essay Grotowski speculates on the disintegration of the stable ensemble structures within modern commercial theatre and on the negative implications this holds for the quality of the craft in performance work."[130] If you work with experienced, wonderful actors, it never crosses their mind to not be judgmental. If we get down to business, I would say you're not speaking loud enough — that's not good. You're not working with your fellow actor — that's not good. I think you are way off-base in what you're doing or not doing — that's not good. Please take note that whenever I am speaking to you, add "in acting." I am only talking about acting because your personal life is none of my business. If in your personal life you do things that stop the instrument from working, then your acting will be terribly limited.

ACTOR: I should always say something to the other actor?

PAUL: Good question. No, not necessarily, we don't know what we are going to do until the situation presents itself. If, however, you are unwilling to judge an actor, then you are abusing your own craft. We do not have to suffer to be good actors, but competent, good, responsible actors must judge all things around them. They must judge the room they're in, the set, the lights, the direction. You have to do it from the beginning and you have to get good at it. It's none of my business if you cop out, but it is my business to tell you what's the best function for you to be an actor, and if you're not functioning, then I have a right to say, "That is problematic." Judging is not giving me your opinion. Judging is knowing enough about something to make it good. An actor has the right to say, "Am I in class with good actors? Am I in class with a good teacher?" There are wonderful actors and teachers all around us. It is our responsibility to go in and judge those teachers and not be intimidated by them. Most actors do not ask this often enough. You may leave a class because you judge that it has a very good teacher who, for some reason, refuses to teach. When you say, "I like something. I don't like something," your next question should be, "Why do I like that? Why don't I like something?" Actors have a different language from everyone else, and I want you to embrace and get used to our language.

---

130. Lisa Wolford, *Grotowski's Objective Drama Research* (Jackson: University Press of Mississippi, 1996), 142.

GAVIN: Be willing to continually step out into the unknown, even if at first it feels somewhat uncomfortable. Many people spend their lives running around the same wheel like mice, but you must learn to get off the wheel and continually build new ones.

Food for Thought

When I had actors come work with me I used to tell them which hairdresser to go to. I would say, "You go in, you tell him I sent you, and sit down and he says, 'What do you want?' You say, 'Paul sent me.' And then you have nothing to say after that." Of course, they would protest and I would say, "What are you talking about? Don't you want somebody who is the best, and one of the most brilliant and artistic hairstylists in the world? You are going to tell him what you want? This is part of what will get you work!" They would laugh and go on blind faith. I never thought of it as a makeover, I thought of it as a step forward. A makeover is fixing something that is no good instead of shining something that is already good. An actor has to approach every aspect of their instrument. Looks and appearance may be only skin deep, but they also are part of you, and what sells you.

Food for Thought

PAUL: What is more important for the actor: learning the fundamentals and the basics of the craft, or how to deal with immediacy and inspiration and being in the moment?

ACTOR: I would say both of them are. One is not better than the other, because you need the fundamentals to get to the other stuff.

PAUL: What is acting?

ACTOR: It is a dance between two people.

PAUL: That, my dear, is as brilliant as any definition of acting you could ever say. When we act on-stage or screen, because of mirror neurons in the brain, if the audience is empathetic, the same neurons are fired in them. It is as if they are going through the process with you. We join actors in murdering people, in stealing, and in falling in love.

The purpose of this book is not to teach acting. The purpose is to show you how to study acting. Not simply for you to teach yourself, but to know *when* you are being taught, and *how* you are being taught. When you watch an actor in a movie or play you are being everything to them. You are being a partner to them, a recipient of it, but you are also being the cause of it. The better the actor the more we tend to say, "Well, they weren't doing anything." Why do we say that? "Because I was doing the same thing they were doing, and if I can do the same thing they were doing then they are not doing anything." Or we say, "Oh, if I can do what they're doing then I am much better than all of my friends. In fact, I'm a star." This leads to a lot of misunderstanding about acting. We are not giving you all of the answers. In some cases, we are leading you to more questions. As Dr. Wayne W. Dyer says when talking about his book *Your Erroneous Zones*, "This book has a lot of worms in its meaning, you will hear and perceive exactly what you want to hear based upon many of your values, beliefs, prejudices, and personal history."[131] This is also the case with this book. If you hear us talk about hard work, technique, and effort, and decide that it is not aimed at you personally, it is because you are hearing what you want to hear and not what you need to hear.

Final Thoughts

When we taste unfamiliar food our body is given the ability to say, "That is dangerous for me," or "That is good for me." We react immediately, and if we put something in our mouth that we think is dangerous, we spit it out immediately. That kind of sensitivity is to protect us, and we have to learn to use all of the functions of our body efficiently. When we are working

---

131. Dr. Wayne W. Dyer, *Your Erroneous Zones* (New York: Harper Collins Publishers, 1995), 2.

with another actor we have all kinds of concerns for what we are being paid for as well as what our responsibilities are to ourselves, the playwright or screenwriter, the director, and, of course, the audience. We have to make a technical assessment to say, "I like it. I don't like it." That is the immediate response that the body has. That's a natural response to draw it in, to swallow it, to crave more, or to spit it out and say, "Don't do that." We have done our homework and the other actors have done their homework, and we are working with preparation, release of reaction, impulse, and imagination. If we are clicking and cooking, then we have an obligation to put our bodies in such a state that it draws in what it knows by experience. It draws in what it's learning impulsively in that moment and it spits out everything else. It's a highly responsible thing to do. It is the most responsible thing an actor does is their judgment of their work. It's a very controversial and sensitive thing, but it is a very necessary thing, because it has to do with a good and bad performance. If your gut tells you something, then it is probably right. If you go for an audition and something feels a little off, or it doesn't appear quite professional, then pay attention to your gut. Better that you put your energy into where it is needed most.

72. Conversation with the Actor (Part 4)

Food for Thought

When I used to go to a play with friends, if it was a really good play, I would say at intermission, "Let's make a pact to not talk for half an hour after the play. We'll all go out and have coffee, but say nothing for half an hour." Because otherwise you get someone who, after a profound movie, says something like, "You wanna go to the beach tomorrow?" If I see an amazing movie or play it will put me in a more than ordinary moment of existence, a high-functioning state. Look for teachers who can put you in a high state of functioning and if you are brave enough, you might even see if you can live there. There is no need to rush to find a teacher who can help you reach a high-functioning state. Many teachers will let you audit their class so you can get a feel for how they teach. You wouldn't buy a new car without test-driving it first, so don't jump headfirst into a class where you don't know the teachers work or how they work.

Food for Thought

If a director asks you to do one thing, the producer another, the choreographer something else, and the first AD something totally different, you might say, "I cannot do four things at once!" What you can do is be in a state of high functioning. Then, miraculously the choreographer will say, "That is exactly what I wanted you to do," and the director will say, "Yes," and the AD will say, "Yes," and the costume woman will say, "You are the only actor who doesn't ruin my clothing." You become the actor whom everyone enjoys working with because you are able to take direction most effectively.

The Ingredients

You are about to read a brief, edited part of a conversation. An acting teacher or director may not always sound like your best friend. They are there to help you maximize your potential, and oftentimes that takes hard work and honesty.

PAUL: You are very intelligent. When I ask you questions you know the answers. You just haven't learned to connect the dots as an actor yet.

ACTOR: How do you know?

PAUL: I know from working with you. You don't speak an actor's language yet.

ACTOR: To work on acting can mean so many different things.

PAUL: No, it can't. Listen to this sentence: Speaking Italian can mean so many different things.

Studying acting can only mean studying acting. I want you to learn to speak the language of an actor because it's going to increase the accuracy of your time, and what you are going to get from your time. Don't be annoyed. I'm here because I love acting and I love the fact that you love acting. Other than that I don't know you. Tell me a little about you.

ACTOR: My name is different on my birth certificate. It's because my parents ran a graveyard and saw a name on a gravestone that they liked.

PAUL: What language are you thinking in at the moment?

ACTOR: I'm thinking in biographical language.

PAUL: No, but that was a good choice. You are not thinking in any language, you are thinking in impulses. That's what's so wonderful and mysterious about language. That's also why you can understand actors in other languages. Actors strengthen the impulse muscle, so they've got big impulse muscles. If you go see a play at the Comédie Française you will understand it, even if you don't speak French. You understand the impulses. I would like you to try to imagine what it would be like to only speak the language of an actor. Interestingly, you have tried to do that from instinct. You are thinking about the fact that you want to present yourself a certain way. That's not how to be an actor, but the impulse is wonderful. You are doing it the only way you know how to do it. When did you decide you wanted to be an actor?

ACTOR: When I had a sense of self. It was when I was very little.

PAUL: Really? You actually thought you wanted to be an actor?

ACTOR: I had a sense that I wanted to be everybody.

PAUL: Don't be poetic. Let's keep it in a technical sense that we can use. Tell me what images you had as an actress when you were young.

ACTOR: Sarah Bernhardt, my grandfather used to call me that all the time. He had a photo of her.

PAUL: She happened to have only one leg. She performed toward the end of her career with only one leg. Has anybody in your family ever been an actor?

ACTOR: No.

PAUL: Do you believe you will continue to book work as an actor?

ACTOR: Definitely!

PAUL: Good.

Food for Thought

There are some people who are in search of excellence. Anybody who becomes a recognized actor, not a saleable commodity, right from the beginning was in search of excellence. Everywhere in their career and in their training they are always in search of excellence. The danger can be that, as you begin, you don't know enough about your field. One does tend to recognize excellence even before they know what it is. The danger is when this actor goes to a class they have to be careful not to judge the director or teacher too quickly. A lot of very dramatic fights have happened between actors and directors who were both in search of excellence but didn't recognize the extent of excellence in the other person. As a great teacher once said, "Theatre is not about conflict, it is about agreement." The point we are making is if you are in search of excellence, the only way you can find it is if you are in agreement. If you are clenched some way, if you are frozen, then you stop the natural flow of things. If you are in search of excellence, then it is up to you to continue that search, it's up to you to prescribe your course to get there. It is not your exercises or the people you work with, but the course in which you do it because all along the way there will be a very few people who are also in search of excellence, and a very few people who are actually excellent themselves and a lot of people who aren't. Every so often ask yourself why you are an actor. Perhaps in the beginning it was because you loved the art and craft of acting. Perhaps now it is because you want more money or a big house. It is nice to have a big house and nice car, but if this has become your prime motivation, you may never find excellence as an actor.

Food for Thought

Actors often ask if they should have only one acting teacher. We say this is unlikely and not necessary because there are so many great teachers with so much to offer. However, if you find a great teacher you may find they have a magic door and that you become a different person when you walk through the door. You may love the person you become. You know if you are with a really good teacher because you are not going to become what they want you to be, you're going to become who you are. Be careful: If a teacher tries to make you in their image, get away from that teacher. If a teacher helps you discover your image, that's the person to work with. A teacher is not your teacher because they say they are, they are your teacher because you say they are. There will come a point where you will become your greatest teacher.

The Diagnosis

We cannot stress to you how important it is to speak the language of an actor. It's happened on many rehearsals on television, film, and stage that an actor has been annoyed with another actor who does not speak his language. An actress was working with a very famous actor who, at this point, was an older gentleman and he said, "Young actors don't know what they're doing!" and he proceeded to walk off the set. It was true, she was learning and she had the lead, but she was learning. We have talked about the importance of impulses. We can learn a language by learning to let our impulses come out a different way, and that's studying acting.

PAUL: *(To the ACTOR)* I told you not to speak in poetic language, and it wasn't because I wanted to be rude. There are people who get by with it, but that doesn't make it right. Be careful with the answers you give. Try to say what you want to say, the way you think a director or casting director wants to hear it. I asked you if you thought you will continue to book work because you will be surprised at the answers actors give. An actor said to me the other day, "There's so little work now!" I said, "There is more work now than there has ever been in the history of acting. If there's no work, it's because you can't book a job!" As a young actor I would say, "You know what, all I need is one job, so if there's only one I'll have it, thank you." It worked! The words "too slow" and "too fast" can be quite redundant at times, but if you have a supported voice and a released body, you will have much more flexibility and control of your voice. When I ask you questions I am not so much interested in the answer as am I in you hearing yourself talk. The lesson lies in you hearing your own answers. You have made some big changes. Do you have a sense of it?

ACTOR: Yes.

PAUL: OK, what is that going to mean to you?

ACTOR: I don't know.

PAUL: I don't either. You don't have to.

ACTOR: I had an impulse to answer you, and then I just let it go.

PAUL: You are learning to express yourself as an actor. You are not doing it out of need, you're doing it out of discovery.

GAVIN: You must believe that you are or will be a working actor or you would not be pursuing a career in acting in the first place.

Food for Thought

I once worked with an actress who said, "Last night and tomorrow night I will be waiting tables, and in between I have the lead in front of the Los Angeles Philharmonic at the Hollywood Bowl." She never figured out how she got there. She didn't think that she got it, and she honestly thought that it was an accident, like she won the lottery. She had no idea that I got her the job. I say this so that you understand that who you know can make a big difference in getting the job. Do not be afraid of nepotism because, like it or not, it exists and you have to be aware of this. Be aware of every possible angle that relates to your acting career. Not everything is related to your acting ability, and yet all of them have a part to play in the reality of you working. You may not like it, you may not agree with it, and yet you still have to embrace it. I've been to a lot of country clubs in my time, but most of the time I go in through the kitchen. I am never a member of the club; however, I'm in the club and I get to meet all the members.

Food for Thought

Sometimes when you audition for a part and they say you have to be over eighteen this is not because of a social or moral obligation in regards to the role. It just costs money to have schooling provided for you, etc., etc., and they don't want to have to deal with the hassle or the expense. There are some examples of actors under eighteen being cast in these roles by using the creativity of their imagination.

Final Thoughts

A person who speaks English rarely tells you why they speak English, how they speak English, or why they like to speak English. They never think about these things. They simply speak English. They think in impulses and they speak English. What I mean by that is the more you learn to act, and the more you think in the actor's language and impulses, the less you sit around and talk about acting. There are two kinds of people: those who talk about acting, and those who act. The people who talk about acting usually don't act, and the people who act usually don't talk about acting. It takes a great deal of courage and stamina to face rejection and disappointment day in and day out. It takes a certain individual to see their way through this.

73. Spontaneous Moves

Food for Thought

An actor once said that he would get very nervous before a performance, so he would pause for a moment. I suggested that he learn a new way of thinking about acting. Anything that inhibits the actor is not useful to the actor.

Food for Thought

Sometimes an individual will take a class simply to put it on their resumé. We do not believe that these individuals are actors, because if their thought pattern is to do that, then they don't have the basic gumption needed by an actor.

The Ingredients

What we would like you to do is divide your rehearsal space or stage into a grid of nine separate areas like the one you might play tick-tack-toe on. The grid should take up the whole area and you can do this in a number of ways. You can use a piece of chalk to draw your grid, you could use rope, you can put nine objects down such as a sock, or a hat, etc., so you know where each of the nine areas are. If you prefer, you can simply see the nine boxes in your imagination. What is important is that your nine boxes span and cover the entire space.

What we would like you to do in a moment is begin a scene or monologue, and somewhere during the scene, and for no reason at all, we would like you to go to one of the nine areas. By the time you have finished with the scene or monologue you have to have been in all nine boxes at least once.

Now we want you to pick a short scene that is a maximum of one minute in length. We are going to assume that you understand stage terminology such as upstage, downstage, upstage left, and so on. You can divide your grid in this fashion or in any way that works for you as long as you have all nine boxes covering the entire performance space. To begin this exercise you need to start somewhere in this grid facing the audience. Remember, you do not have to justify in any way why you are moving to each of these areas, but you must have been in all nine by the end.

PAUL: *(ACTOR performs the monologue moving to each box.)* I want you to continue, but have you used the three downstage boxes yet? I have seen you use the other six.

ACTOR: That's right, I forgot about those.

PAUL: OK, keep going. *(ACTOR finishes scene.)* Tell me what you felt about that.

ACTOR: It allowed me to throw out any preemptive blocking. It was tricky, but it was freeing. I had no idea where it was going in terms of movement and it made me see my scene partner in totally different places because as I moved around, so did she in my imagination.

PAUL: By doing it in this manner it changed the spacing of your scene partner as well. It took away your preconceptions. Another piece you can add to complete this exercise is to do the scene again with your original movement, only this time you have already done this exercise, and the subsequent performance will be full. Many good acting exercises don't have a chance to take a profound effect on the actor in the immediate sense. We are not looking to create a party trick. The results of this exercise may be realized in their entirety over time. We are preparing the instrument.

GAVIN: This exercise takes away your absolute certainties in the scene so that you can learn to begin again.

Food for Thought

A director may say, "Where are you today? You don't seem to be here, you are not giving me all of you." If you are not doing the work, it will probably frustrate you, embarrass you, and make you irritable. If you are doing the work, you will be happier than you can imagine. If you are an actor, you will be happy acting. It is certainly not a profession of suffering. There is not one accomplished actor we know who, no matter how crazy or troublesome they seem, does not have a good time when acting. If acting is not that for you, not only can you not be a creative actor, you cannot even be a pawn in someone else's game. Most people who act, when they make the decision to act, do not have anybody they can talk to about it. If you do talk to someone about it, they are most likely going to do two things. They won't understand what you are talking about, and they are going to try to talk you out of it. We have all heard the phrase, "Enjoy the journey." We nod in agreement as if to say we know exactly what this means. And yet for the actor it needs to be heeded in a very practical sense. If you do not enjoy your journey, it will most likely come to a premature end.

Food for Thought

We have heard an actor say words to the effect of, "under ideal circumstances, I am a good actor." And our question was, "What are you going to do when you are not working with ideal circumstances?" It is not acceptable to say that, if things go wrong, blame the director, the light or sound technicians, or the script. You are going to have to take full responsibility for every project you work on. What is suggested here may sound like a constraint, but it is actually very freeing for the actor. You choose to go or not go on an audition, you choose to work on or not work on a project, and you choose to sign or not sign with an agent. By taking full responsibility for all your actions and all of the outcomes you will become much more empowered. In terms of the word "action", David Ball suggests, "A play is a series of actions."[132]

The Diagnosis

We have been taught that center stage is not as nice a place to be as the corner of the stage, because center stage is taking too much attention. Some actors are not comfortable center stage. Some actors are only comfortable center stage, so is this an advantage or is it a limitation? Think about when you hear a friend say, "Oh yeah, they always have to be the center of attention." It is certainly not meant as a compliment, and so it can become ingrained in us. With this exercise you are able to become more familiar with your body on-stage and set. As you get to a set or the theatre, spend as much time familiarizing yourself with the space as you can. If possible, move around the space when no one else is around. Part of being an actor is being able to take direction, and this applies just as strongly for the film actor. You have to be able to take very specific direction for camera set-ups.

This exercise creates a kind of spontaneity. What an actor often ends up doing is directing and limiting themselves. They're saying, "I want to be here when I say that, I must be here for this." There is a similar exercise developed by Stanislavski. He built a round rehearsal room and he wouldn't tell anybody where front was. He would walk around the room and so the actors probably thought wherever he stood was front. He would change position so often that it didn't work. Finally, they gave up concerning themselves and moved towards spontaneous thinking. In acting you can think any thought, and it is amazing what thoughts we have trained ourselves not to think, "I must not think of having a hot fudge sundae. I must not think of money. I must not think about love." We have also trained ourselves not to do certain physical things, and this exercise allows you to develop freely and spontaneously. If you are working for film, then this exercise is excellent in preparing you to hit your marks. If you are not used to movement, you may appear clumsy and awkward as opposed to comfortable. On-set you are told, "Look this way, turn here, and move there." Quite often the person you are talking to is physically not there. You want to be able to move like a little kid who is able to move every which way with complete abandon and without judgment or fear. You may get confused because sometimes you have been asked in your acting to move with the least amount of effort; however, you cannot do this until you have learned how to move with your instrument fully. This is a very simple exercise, but don't underestimate the miracles that simple exercises bring about. Sometimes you yourself do not see the changes and yet a peer will say, "You are becoming a good actor." A casting director or director will turn to a colleague and say, "Last time I thought he wasn't particularly talented, but he is, isn't he?" In this exercise you are moving in all different directions so as not to limit yourself. You never want to limit yourself to one way of doing something.

Food for Thought

An acting school should not only be willing but also make it an absolute necessity to prepare its actors for the industry as part of their training. What is the use of having wonderfully trained actors who never work? It is sad that, over time, many of these actors begin to believe that their training now counts for nothing in the environment in which they are living. This is not the case, but they do need to learn to connect the dots between their technique and the industry of acting.

---

132. David Ball, *Backwards & Forwards* (Illinois: Southern Illinois University, 1983), 9.

Food for Thought

The wonderful thing about acting is you are doing a very dangerous thing in a very safe place. Nothing can happen to you because you are an actor. Nothing can happen to you when you take chances, because you are acting. You have this great security and safety because you are acting. In life you can't always reverse it and you can't always forget it. We are, in life, often burdened with past thoughts of embarrassment or sometimes of great winning. In acting, no matter where you are or what you do in a performance, when you get done that night you forget it all. This does not work for a civilian because they do not know how to be in that state. Why does it work for the actor? Because the actor is two people. They are the person creating who has no memory, who is capable of creating anything, who is particularly capable of experiencing anything, and forgetting everything. As an actor, you get to live out all of your fantasies, all of your fears, and there are no consequences for your actions.

Final Thoughts

When you first started reading the book we mentioned that we wanted things to be so primary that they would work for anyone and everyone. The most primary thing that makes acting work is for the actor to want something. Some people call that motivation or objective, but they forget that in order for an objective or a motivation or a want to work, the body has to be familiar with having gone to those places before. You can't have the objective to cry if you have never cried in your life. As far as simple things go, you may be uncomfortable moving too much because growing up you were told to, "Sit still!" We are dealing with three things: what your body wants to do while you are playing this character, what the character seems to want, and what the director wants. One of the simplest ways to be able to do what anybody wants is to train yourself to randomly move about the set or stage so that you have been everywhere possible the director might ask you to go. Think about when you audition for a play when you plant yourself in one place, you are not used to moving around and using all of the space available. You are preparing your body for many wants: yours, the character's, or the director's. Sometimes as you begin to move around the stage or set, your body becomes constricted and the movement forced. The random aspects of this exercise are aimed at reducing your preempted decisions.

74. Clean Slate

Food for Thought

Most private teaching, even with great teachers, is done as a source of income. The fact remains that when you get up to do that scene the teacher has probably seen it many times before. They have also seen more actors than you will ever see in your life. They not only know where the market is, they know where all the items in the market are. They can see the task to be done, and they can see all the tools it takes to do it. They can see all the ingredients that it takes to do it, and you can't. The problem is that they often forget that you can't see these things yet. It takes a considerable amount of time until you can see what they see. If you have a good teacher, you are given slowly one ingredient at a time. The challenge is that you forget where it is because you don't practice. Then you are given another ingredient and you repeat the same cycle. You then say to yourself, "I have certain skills now. I should be able to give a certain level of performance." You are absolutely right, but because these skills are not practiced, you are only able to come up with something very simple and rudimentary. A good teacher is becoming and influencing you so that they can then go away and you can do it.

What you are doing in any scene class is doing scenes that require enormous amounts of ingredients. It's the most difficult recipe in the world and you're trying to make it a boiled egg. You're trying to make it this one simple thing, but acting is not simple. When great actors get up to do performances they use ingredients and tools that belong to them. Just because you understand the result of what they created does not mean you can use their tools because they don't belong to you. You have to develop tools that belong to you. The experience that you bring to something belongs to you, not your teacher's experience. How do you think you can get up and do a scene that requires all of these things until you have acquired them? A great actor is exercising and refining everything they do. A beginning actor isn't exercising. They are learning how to do it. If you are signed up for a beginner's acting class and it is a scene study class, then this is an oxymoron. There is no such thing as a beginner's scene study class; however, as Paul has mentioned, teachers have to make a living and scene study happens to be a very popular class. It is up to you to know what you are ready for and what is going to serve you best in your acting. Some teachers will integrate acting exercises and scenes in one class, and perhaps this will be a better fit for you.

Food for Thought

It is more likely than not that those who love you the most will encourage you not to be an actor. One thing we never ask is what have those people done with their lives? We never say that. We never say, "Are you happy with your life? Did you peruse things in the right order? Have you been practical in your pursuit of a career? Did you always want to be a bank clerk?" The idea is to alleviate anything that is an unnecessary pressure or concern for you. Love your family, love your friends, and talk to them about everything except when it detracts from your acting. If you are frustrated with your life as an actor, then you might want to take heed of these words from Bradford Dillman, "No one ever held a pistol to your temple and demanded you be an actor."[133]

The Ingredients

What we would like you to do in this exercise is to stand alone in front of a mirror. Stand there with virtually nothing on or nothing at all and then describe yourself in only two words. You may find it difficult to describe yourself in only two words. You may want to say things like, "Aspiring actor of the year," or, "Elegant and classy lady," but you are only allowed two words to describe yourself. In this next part you may use as many words as is necessary. As you stand in front of the mirror say, "What am I?" Then say as many things as you can think of. The last thing you should say is, "Who am I?" Once you have completed this exercise, go to the Diagnosis section below to find the given answer to this exercise. There is no time limit in this exercise. Take a moment before you answer each question so you can give your most accurate answer.

Food for Thought

As an actor, you have to be healthy. Many times you could be on a movie set for a great deal of hours, and you have to have the stamina for that. You have to be healthy because enormous sums of money are at stake.

Food for Thought

Exercises in books are to warm up and to reveal more about the craft of acting. A great book on acting by a great teacher can never replace being there with that teacher. In a book they are writing about what they did in class, rehearsal, or performance. They are writing about what they demand of actors, they are writing about what they would do if they met you, but never forget it is about acting. They are not there to personally diagnose and

---

133. Bradford Dillman, *Are You Anybody?* (Santa Barbara: Fithian Press, 1997), 197.

prescribe for you. There are books that are inspiring and there are also books that ground you and give you such a firm understandable basis that you can always refer to them as a good manual. An acting book should be both practical and relevant to the actor.

The Diagnosis

There are only two possible answers to this exercise and they are: adult male and adult female. If you were standing facing the mirror with your arms to your sides and you were naked and you looked up, technically all you could say, is "Adult male," or "Adult female." This is all you can say because an actor is a clean slate. That adult male can play any part – man, woman, or child. That adult female can play any part – man, woman, or child. They must start with the most basic thing: adult male or adult female. The actor does this exercise because the actor has to be a clear slate. They have to think of themselves as the most simple, basic definition they can give of themselves. This means that when they begin a part they are not encumbered by anything. They are not encumbered by race, religion, age, gender, etc. If you take everything away you are still left with adult male or adult female because that is all you are going to see. We don't necessarily see a Russian woman or an Italian man, but we do see adult male or adult female.

You are trying to take yourself to the most primary use of your instrument. I am not saying the least of it that you have. I am saying the most primary definition of the instrument. At that point you can add attributes any way you want to and you can take them away. If you don't start from the most primary, then you are starting with an unnecessarily complicated instrument. You may say, "I have a master's degree in acting from Yale." You are going to have to give that up when you go on-stage or set. How often are you going to play a character with a Master's degree from Yale? If you are not playing that character, you must leave it at the door. "I am from London." This character is not from London, so you have to leave that at the door. Anything you can give up must be left at the door. What we are left with is adult male or adult female. That is a wonderful thing because it can strip away the prejudged prejudices against you. How often have you heard, "You can't play that part because you're too tall, you have the wrong accent, you're too thin, etc."? And yet everybody knows there are actors cast in parts in a way that we don't see them. When they go in to the interview they don't take any of these things in with them, they go in as a clear slate. They are so interesting and so exciting we see only the clear slate because that is all they show us. Directors and producers are then able to project their ideas and visions through a clear slate. To get your body clear you want to describe it, not reduce it, in the simplest of terms. As a famous teacher once said, "Acting is in the body." You were born as a clean slate, and if you start from this place you can add on the many layers that will make up each character.

Food for Thought

A good teacher is someone who sees more in you than you see in yourself. If they can see something in you that you do not yet see, then they will work on that. A good acting class is not a performance class. Rather, it teaches you to stretch, strengthen, and coordinate your body so it will respond immediately to your wishes and those of any director. Acting has to be as specific as brain surgery. You don't go to just anybody for brain surgery.

Food for Thought

A great director can see more than most directors. When they watch a play or movie they can see more potential, more meaning, and they can see more potential about how to get the meaning across to the audience.

Final Thoughts

Very often in history it has been very popular to say men and women are the opposite of each other. In recent times it has become more popular to say that men and women are so different from each other that they might as well come from two different planets. Therefore, if you begin to know who you are, don't define yourself by anybody other than yourself. We too often define ourselves as the opposite or the difference of something else, and a great artist knows that they are, that they are, that they are. I am, that I am, that I am. As you stand in front of the mirror say, "What am I?" Then say as many things as you can think of. The last thing you should say is, "Who am I?" It is the accummulation of all the things you have said before that. Learn to describe yourself in the most basic terms so you will always have a place from which to start.

75. Intimacy and Confrontation in Acting

The Ingredients

The following section comes from a Master's class titled Intimacy and Confrontation in Acting. Rather than give you an exercise, what follows is an edited version of the entire workshop. This session was geared more towards ensemble and partner work as you will observe. Twelve actors attended this session, many of whom had never met before.

PAUL: What does intimacy in acting mean to you?

ACTOR: I don't necessarily think that being nude or even being in close proximity to someone else has to mean intimacy.

PAUL: In other words, two people can be lovers and not be intimate.

ACTOR: Or they can be intimate and not touch.

PAUL: Exactly. I think intimacy is part of acting, I don't think you can do a scene without intimacy.

ACTOR: I think it's also about achieving the ability to be private in public.

PAUL: There is a famous actress who they always say can do very private things in very public places.

GAVIN: This discussion was a good deal longer and gave some clues as to the perceptions of these twelve individuals.

Part 1

We are going to start with a very simple exercise that is formed out of martial arts. What we would like you to do is stand facing your partner and be palm to palm. Now slowly start moving your arms around simultaneously in different directions with your palms constantly touching. One of you should start as the leader and at some point you can switch. The next step would be to change the leader intuitively simply by using give and take. While it is your arms that are doing the majority of the movement, the rest of your body can be moving back and forth while keeping your feet on the same spot. It is OK to lift your heels off the ground if you like. You are doing this exercise with a partner, and this is also what you should be doing with the audience. This exercise was immediately able to break down barriers amongst the actors.

Part 2

We hope you all have a monologue or a scene that you have done. If you don't, then use a poem or some other dialogue you have. Please go and find yourself a space somewhere in the room. We would like you now to walk around the room and do your monologue out loud. (ACTORS do their scenes at the same time.) OK, you can stop where you are. If I point at you I want you to start your monologue. Each actor, in turn, delivers two or three lines from their piece. Again, the actors are confronted with the idea of moving away from any barriers they may have put up. They begin their monologues in front of perfect strangers.

Part 3

Go and find a new partner now. I want you to do the hand exercise that we started with today. When you begin, both lead until you don't know who is leading. I want you to start doing your monologue while continuing the exercise. We hear twelve monologues simultaneously while continuing the exercise.

Part 4

I want you now to go and find a new partner. One of you is going to lie on your back and the other one will sit on the floor beside you. It is probably best if you take your shoes off for this exercise. The person sitting is the guide and the person on their back is the explorer. You do not have to have any knowledge of anatomy or physiology to take part in this exercise. You could do this exercise for the rest of your life and still be amazed at what joints can do. You are going to be amazed at what you discover. Check with your partner if they have any injuries you should be aware of. Be sure that if you are the guide, you are sitting in a comfortable position. If you are not, you will be projecting your tensions onto your partner. You are going to find out what joints in the body can do.

Start by picking up your partner's hand and ever so gently start bending a finger or two. Rotate the hand gently at the wrist and be amazed at how it moves. The person on the floor is simply experiencing what is happening. As you go through the body, be interested in what you discover. You can bend at the elbow, and you can cradle the whole arm. Once you have worked on one arm go and work on the other arm. Always put things back where you found them in a safe and comfortable fashion. At this point, the person lying on the floor should start their monologue. If you find that their leg is too heavy, then perhaps you can rest their leg on your leg to help you guide it. If something is too hard for you, don't do it. There is no race or rush, whatever you do is exactly what you are supposed to do. This is one of the most intimate exercises that you can do. Something miraculous happens to your body during this exercise. It releases your fear of intimacy. This exercise really brings the actors closer together and involves letting go on the part of the guide and the explorer.

Part 5

Everybody can sit up now by themselves. Turn to one side and lay in a fetal position. Just lay there for a few moments and be aware of your body. At this point I would like you all to stand up where you are and keep your eyes closed. I am going to move you into position and I want you to trust me to do so while you keep your eyes closed. (ACTORS line up, one behind each other, with their left arm outstretched onto the left shoulder of the actor in front of them. PAUL then leads the ACTORS in unison, still with their eyes closed into another room, into a different space.)

Part 6

Start your monologues once again. At this point, I want you to find a partner and, with your eyes closed, I want you to help each other to the floor very carefully. What you are going to do is start moving around the room on your hands and knees. You may bump into each other so move very slowly. If there is a traffic jam, just wait your turn.

Begin to crawl around now with your eyes closed. You can go in any direction you like. I want everybody to crawl towards the sound of my voice. (PAUL moves to different areas of the room.) I want everybody to crawl towards the sound of my voice. I want you to reach out and find a partner and you are going to help them get to their feet. I want you to enjoy helping them to get up, and I want you to enjoy being helped up. Now I want you to help each other back down to the ground. I am going to move you now into a very dense group so that you are as close together as can be.

(Once the ACTORS are all together, PAUL has them stand up as one. They are now tightly fitted together as if they are one organism.) You are now a monster that has one voice. The voice of the monster is actually a hum. (ACTORS begin to hum and automatically start to sway from side to side.) The voice of the monster begins to get louder, and louder, and louder. The voice of the monster begins to get softer, and softer, and softer. The voice now stops. You are now going to help each other get back down to the floor and you are going to give attention to the fact that you really like helping someone. I want you to start to crawl around on your hands and knees and as you do, I am going to guide you so that you end up standing with a partner.

This exercise is powerful to be a part of and it's just as impressive to watch. The actors really begin to move and hum as one.

Part 7

Take your partner's hand and hold it for a moment. I would now like you to reach out and put your hand on their face at the same time they touch your face. I would now like you to carefully begin to sculpt your partner's body using your hands. They are the clay and you are molding them. You are doing this without any talking. Put your arms down and take a couple of steps back. Now you are going to start to sculpt that person from muscle memory in midair. While you are sculpting that person, do your monologue. Help your partner down to the floor again. I want you to crawl around on the floor with your eyes half open until we are all sitting in a very large circle. (The ACTORS begin by exploring in very close proximity.)

Part 8

You are now going to say, "My name is ..." and then we are going to celebrate your name. We are going to say your name seven times, and each time we are going to get louder and louder and louder. Right after that you are going to begin your monologue. When you are done with your monologue, you say, "My name is..." and we celebrate your name again seven times.

ACTOR: My name is Gaye.

WHOLE GROUP: Gaye, Gaye, Gaye, Gaye, Gaye, Gaye, Gaye!

ACTOR: He told me that he wants a divorce. *(Completes monologue.)* My name is Gaye.

WHOLE GROUP: Gaye, Gaye, Gaye, Gaye, Gaye, Gaye, Gaye!

ACTOR 2: My name is Catherine.

WHOLE GROUP: Catherine, Catherine, Catherine, Catherine, Catherine, Catherine, Catherine!

ACTOR 2: As if you were somebody? *(Completes monologue.)* My name is Catherine.

WHOLE GROUP: Catherine, Catherine, Catherine, Catherine, Catherine, Catherine, Catherine!

ACTOR 3: My name is Ashley.

WHOLE GROUP: Ashley, Ashley, Ashley, Ashley, Ashley, Ashley, Ashley!

ACTOR 3: He said he really wasn't into me anymore. *(Completes monologue.)*

The same pattern is repeated with all twelve actors. The energy that is created around this exercise is quite amazing.

Part 9

The last part of the workshop was an exercise entitled "The Best Acting Lesson Ever." The exercise was created by Lloyd Richards, the former Dean of Yale School of Drama. It has not been included here. If you want to know more about this exercise, go online and you will find it just as we did.

Part 10

PAUL: Let's all come together now and sit in a circle. As you are sitting here now you are all very still. I couldn't direct you in these positions, and it is just wonderful. I want you to do your monologue one more time now and you can say it to yourself or you can say it to us. *(ACTORS say their monologues.)* I want to get your response to the work you have done today. You can talk about intimacy, your monologue, or whatever you want. Please talk to us.

ACTOR 1: I felt that my monologue took a different direction this evening.

PAUL: That's because it was good acting.

ACTOR 2: I felt relaxed and intimate. At the moment I feel fantastic.

PAUL: That feeling is acting.

ACTOR 3: I found the work effortless and much more generous.

PAUL: You did terrific work tonight.

ACTOR 4: I found less orchestration in my work.

PAUL: Good. Continue to do exercises that work on your instrument. I had a lot of fun watching your monologue.

ACTOR 4: I had a lot of fun having you watch my monologue. *(Group laughs.)* Seriously, I really did.

PAUL: You know I always know when an actor's done a good job. Because an actor, when they have done a good job, barely makes sense when they have finished. Good stuff tonight.

ACTOR 5: I find it very helpful doing the monologues in all the different places.

PAUL: If you exercise in this way you can break down barriers and gain intimacy much quicker.

ACTOR 6: It is nice to become what you are pretending to be.

PAUL: If you practice this way, then everything will come. You are exercising the body and all of its connections.

GAVIN: The actors arrived as individuals and left as friends.

In Closing

GAVIN: It is our desire not that you have all the answers, but that you are learning to ask a better question. It is our desire that you are learning to live in a creative state. As we have already mentioned, the best book on acting is your own personal journal, day-by-day-by-day on acting. At the end of the day, every actor must become their own teacher. While this is the end of the book, it is just a step on your journey. I will leave you with these words, "Goodnight, goodnight – a thousand times goodnight unto you all. So, if we be friends, give me your hands."[134]

PAUL: We enter this world crying with great intensity, perhaps our first expression of passion ... a passion for life. Actors spend the rest of their lives learning to conjure, create, and release that passion on cue and under any and all circumstances. My concept of acting is The Theatre of Consequences. Through our performances and our passions, show the audience the consequences of every possible scenario in life. The audience is then able to choose or avoid what they have seen and what you have made them experience through your passion, which was shaped by technique.

I would like to think that integrity, respect, morality, hard work, and even talent would be rewarded with great careers. And yet I have seen and worked with numerous actors who gave great performances that thrilled me and the audience and, in some cases, they had none of these virtues. But they showed up and they liked what they were doing. So there you have the secret of an acting career. First and foremost it is to show up for class, for rehearsals, for preparation, for daily work on self, to show up sometimes against overwhelming odds and negative comments. Society, families, communities, friends, and teachers often tell the actor, "Don't go there. It is too risky. It is not a real profession. You don't have the talent or the look." So you give up and the next person in line moves up to your place, your opportunities, and your career. It is hard not to give up. It is even harder to show up. Again, you must show up and you must like what you are doing. Notice I did not say "love what you are doing," for that is a form of passion. I would like to meet any and all of you who like acting. If you like acting and will always show up, I'm sure I will see you and your passion. Good luck, even though luck alone will never be quite enough.

Contacting the Authors

We want you to get the most out of this book. If you have a question about the work or simply want to pass on your discoveries, feel free to drop us a line.

We also offer visiting master classes. You may contact us with questions about teaching at your school.

Paul Gleason: www.acmt.org/ or pgg@acmt.org

Gavin Levy: www.gavinlevy.com or gavlevy@yahoo.com

---

134. Brian Burton, *Will Power* (Worcestershire: Hanbury Plays, 1995), 31.

About the Authors

Currently Artistic Producer/Director of the Paul G. Gleason Theatre in Hollywood, California, **Paul G. Gleason** has an extraordinary record of achievement in film, television, and theatre. He was fortunate enough to be involved in the golden age of Broadway and television and work alongside Judy Garland, Shirley Temple, Danny Kaye, Jack Benny, Yul Brynner, Jerry Lewis, Carol Burnett, Jackie Gleason, and Ed Sullivan. He also coached and directed Richard Chamberlain, Mary Tyler Moore, John Raitt, Constance Towers, Ed Asner, and Academy Award Winners George Chakiris and Shirley Jones. He also worked with Angelica Houston in her father's (John Houston) last film based on the James Joyce novel, *The Dead*.

Paul G. Gleason was on the selection committee for the United States' top artistic grant-giving agency, the National Endowment for the Arts, giving grants to some of the most recognized artists in the world. He was selected by the California Arts Council as artist-in-residence for the state of California.

He has run master's classes in theatre, opera, musical theatre, and dance at UCLA, USC, and International Artists Center: Tokyo, Japan, and London, England. Paul narrated *Peter and the Wolf* with the Los Angeles Philharmonic. He directed the first concert of Andrew Lloyd Webber's music at the Hollywood Bowl.

Paul G. Gleason is currently mentoring artists and is engaged in new and original works for film, television, and theatre. He has recently formed a partnership with the Stella Adler Studio of Acting. He is excited about the future.

Gavin Levy is currently running acting workshops in Austin, Texas. He instructed for a number of years at the American National Academy in Studio City, California. He also worked alongside Paul Gleason at the Paul G. Gleason Theatre on Hollywood Boulevard. He has led guest workshops at a number of organizations including the Creative Actors Alliance. He has also led master's classes including work with colleague Paul Gleason for the organization Women in Film. His first book, *112 Acting Games,* was published by Meriwether in 2005. Meriwether also published his second book, *Acting Games for Individual Performers.* His third book, *Reality Driven Monologues,* was released in 2008. His latest book, *Acting For Love & Money,* was co-authored with Paul Gleason.

Gavin Levy is a native Londoner who came to the United States in 1999. He received his ALAM from the London Academy of Music and Dramatic Arts and is also a graduate of the Academy of Live and Recorded Arts. From October 1992 through July 1995 he studied theatre at the world-renowned Academy of Live & Recorded Arts. ALRA recognized the need for a new kind of training, one that enabled students to grow into fully rounded professionals ready to meet the differing challenges of the stage, screen, and broadcast industries. Since that time, the ALRA has been training some of the best and brightest in the industry.

Gavin Levy became involved with Theatre in Education and in the Dragon Drama Theatre Company in London. He also wrote scripts for various workshops, directed plays, and was an instrumental force in after-show workshops that were designed to educate students. As an active member of the Dragon Drama Company, Levy continued to educate students with theatre by teaching them skills through acting and improvisation as well as organizing and coordinating acting workshops.

He has over twenty years of theatre experience, including acting, instructing, directing, and writing. Levy's desire is to share his knowledge in learning the craft of acting in ways that adapt to the needs of our modern culture and audience.

Order Form

Meriwether Publishing Ltd.
PO Box 7710
Colorado Springs, CO 80933-7710
Phone: 800-937-5297 Fax: 719-594-9916
Website: www.meriwether.com

Please send me the following books:

_____ **Acting for Love & Money #BK-B313**   **$19.95**
by Paul G. Gleason and Gavin Levy
Connecting the craft to the industry

_____ **275 Acting Games: Connected #BK-B314**   **$19.95**
by Gavin Levy
A comprehensive workbook of theatre games for developing acting skills

_____ **112 Acting Games #BK-B277**   **$17.95**
by Gavin Levy
A comprehensive workbook of theatre games

_____ **Acting Games for Individual Performers $17.95
#BK-B297**
by Gavin Levy
A comprehensive workbook of 110 acting exercises

_____ **Improv Ideas #BK-B283**   **$23.95**
by Justine Jones and Mary Ann Kelley
A book of games and lists

_____ **Acting for Life #BK-B281**   **$19.95**
by Jack Frakes
A textbook on acting

_____ **Lessons: The Craft of Acting #BK-B285 $19.95**
by Tom Isbell
Truthful human behavior on stage and screen

**These and other fine Meriwether Publishing books are available at
your local bookstore or direct from the publisher. Prices subject to
change without notice. Check our website or call for current prices.**

Name: _____ email: _____

Organization name: _____

Address: _____

City: _____ State: _____

Zip: _____ Phone: _____

❑ **Check enclosed**

❑ **Visa / MasterCard / Discover / Am. Express #** _____

                                                                              Expiration
Signature: _____ *date:*   _____ / _____
          (required for credit card orders)

Colorado residents: Please add 3% sales tax.
Shipping: Include $3.95 for the first book and 75¢ for each additional book ordered.

❑ *Please send me a copy of your complete catalog of books and plays.*

Order Form

Meriwether Publishing Ltd.
PO Box 7710
Colorado Springs, CO 80933-7710
Phone: 800-937-5297 Fax: 719-594-9916
Website: www.meriwether.com

Please send me the following books:

_____ **Acting for Love & Money #BK-B313**   **$19.95**
by Paul G. Gleason and Gavin Levy
Connecting the craft to the industry

_____ **275 Acting Games: Connected #BK-B314**   **$19.95**
by Gavin Levy
A comprehensive workbook of theatre games for developing acting skills

_____ **112 Acting Games #BK-B277**   **$17.95**
by Gavin Levy
A comprehensive workbook of theatre games

_____ **Acting Games for Individual Performers**   **$17.95**
#BK-B297
by Gavin Levy
A comprehensive workbook of 110 acting exercises

_____ **Improv Ideas #BK-B283**   **$23.95**
by Justine Jones and Mary Ann Kelley
A book of games and lists

_____ **Acting for Life #BK-B281**   **$19.95**
by Jack Frakes
A textbook on acting

_____ **Lessons: The Craft of Acting #BK-B285**   **$19.95**
by Tom Isbell
Truthful human behavior on stage and screen

These and other fine Meriwether Publishing books are available at your local bookstore or direct from the publisher. Prices subject to change without notice. Check our website or call for current prices.

Name: _____ email: _____

Organization name: _____

Address: _____

City: _____ State: _____

Zip: _____ Phone: _____

❑ **Check enclosed**

❑ **Visa / MasterCard / Discover / Am. Express #** _____

Signature: _____   *Expiration date:* _____ / _____
(required for credit card orders)

Colorado residents: Please add 3% sales tax.
Shipping: Include $3.95 for the first book and 75¢ for each additional book ordered.

❑ *Please send me a copy of your complete catalog of books and plays.*